CLARK GABLE

CLARK GABLE

A BIOGRAPHY

WARREN G. HARRIS

 THREE RIVERS PRESS • NEW YORK

Photograph on title page courtesy of Culver Pictures.

Library of Congress Cataloging-in-Publication Data

Harris, Warren G.

    Clark Gable: a biography / by Warren G. Harris.

      1. Gable, Clark, 1901–1960.   2. Motion picture actors and actresses—United
States—Biography. I. Title.

PN2287.G3 H25 2002

791.43'028'092—dc21   2001051660

ISBN 0-307-23714-1

Printed in the United States of America

DESIGN BY ELINA D. NUDELMAN

10 9 8 7 6 5 4 3 2 1

First Paperback Edition

FOR KYLE AND JACK,
WHO ARE ALWAYS IN MY HEART.
—UNCLE WIGGILY

CONTENTS

Clark Gable should not have been born at all. His mother, Adeline, or Addie as everybody called her, had been sickly for most of her life. Doctors warned her that bearing a child might kill her. It did, but she lingered on and managed to have ten months with her son before she died.

That somber episode began on February 1, 1901, in Cadiz, Ohio, a coal-mining town in that southeastern part of the state that borders on both West Virginia and Pennsylvania. Like most babies in those days, Clark was born at home. The Gables rented the upstairs apartment of a two-family clapboard house on Charleston Street. Instead of the usual midwife, Addie's frail health demanded attendance by a doctor. He charged a precious ten dollars and received volunteer help from a woman neighbor from downstairs.

The future "King of Hollywood" was born just ten days after the death of Queen Victoria and a month after the start of a new century. He was very much a child of the Victorian Era, a time of gaslight, horse-drawn buggies, and prudish conservatism. His mother garbed him in long white dresses and tried to train his abundant brunet hair to part in the middle.

His original name was probably William Clark Gable, but the usual authorities in such matters—including birth registrations and school records—contradict one another. The first name must have been in honor of his father, William Henry Gable, an oil prospector or "wildcatter" as they were described in those days. "Clark" was the maiden name of his maternal grandmother. In childhood he was almost always called "Clark," though some friends called him "Clarkie," "Billy," or "Gabe." His father confused things even more by always calling him "Kid" or "the Kid" when talking about him to others.

Will Gable and Addie Hershelman came originally from Meadville, in northwestern Pennsylvania. Both families were long established in that area and had German ancestry, with a bit of Irish mixed into the Hershelmans. The Gables, however, were Methodists, and the Hershelmans Roman Catholics. The latter were also a tribe of hardworking farmers who didn't approve of Will's religion *or* of his crazy pursuit of oil gushers. The newlyweds moved 120 miles away to Cadiz to escape the Hershelmans' opposition.

Will Gable's idol and role model was John D. Rockefeller, who started his Standard Oil empire in Ohio in 1870 and resided near Cleveland on a huge estate called Forrest Hill. Though Rockefeller and rivals had most of Ohio staked out by 1900, small speculators like Will Gable never gave up hope of discovering a payhole that could make them rich too. His sights were set on the booming oil fields around Scio, a village about twenty miles from Cadiz. Daily commuting was impractical, so for most of the week he lived in a tent with other workers. He headed home on Saturday afternoon and returned to the job very early on Monday morning. Such was the routine for many working people well into the new century.

Cadiz, as the seat of Harrison County and a thriving business center, satisfied Addie's need to be near doctors and emergency assistance. Records of her health problems are few and contradictory. She may have had epilepsy or some other disease of the central nervous system. Dr. Frank Campbell, who delivered her baby and continued to take care of them both, concluded from her symptoms that she had a progressive brain tumor. She suffered convulsions, and her behavior became increasingly psychotic. Campbell treated her with "cabinet steam baths," which were a popular cure-all in those days.

Whatever her illness may have been, it grew worse after the baby's birth. How that affected the sexual side of the Gable marriage can only be guessed at, but they were an odd-matched couple to begin with. Will Gable was tall and good-looking, with a reputation as a womanizer and a boozer. Addie was a plain, thickset country girl. Nearly thirty when she married, it may have been the first proposal she ever received.

The Gable baby weighed ten and a half pounds at birth and showed every sign of becoming a big bruiser like his father. His hands and feet were whoppers, and his ears stood out like cup handles. His large gray-green eyes and thick brows were obvious gifts from his mother. His father boasted that he was a "born blacksmith."

When the infant turned six months old, Addie persuaded a neighbor to take them to the nearest Catholic church for a christening. Since there wasn't one in Cadiz, they had to travel by horse and buggy to Dennison, twenty-five miles away. The priest berated Addie for delaying the ceremony so long, but that reproach was nothing compared to the tongue-lashing she received from her Methodist husband when he found out. Some of his anger may have been caused by the church certificate, which identified the anointed as Clark Gable rather than William Clark Gable.

In September came shocking news of President William McKinley's assassination, which placed "Rough Rider" Theodore Roosevelt in the White House. By that time Addie was so ill that Will had taken her and William Clark to the Hershelman farm in Meadville so that her family could take over nursing them. Addie died there on November 14, exactly 286 days after her son's birth.

According to one of the relatives who took care of her, Addie had become all but unmanageable: "In a fury, she once hurled Clark's bottle through a window. She went crazy, and then she died."

Only thirty-one years old, Addie Gable was buried in St. Peter's Catholic Cemetery near Meadville. The official death certificate cited a six-month case of epilepsy as the cause, even though epilepsy is not a killer disease. Crazy though such a diagnosis may seem, it is all we have to go by. Epilepsy is also not inherited, so whatever effect Addie's death had on her son was psychological rather than physical.

Many claims have been made that Clark Gable spent the rest of his life looking for a substitute mother. Whether his mind at the age of nine months was developed enough to be able to grieve or even to notice the disappearance of his mother is debatable, especially since a doting grandmother and an aunt were the dominant caretakers during Addie's final phase.

Will Gable left his son with the Hershelmans when he returned to Ohio after the funeral. No way could he take charge of the infant until he had made new living arrangements. Due to his fondness for the ladies, it seemed inevitable that he would marry again, but he apparently had no one specifically in mind. It took him well over a year to find her.

In the meantime "the Kid" was placed in the care of an uncle, Thomas Hershelman, and his wife, Elizabeth, who had no children of their own. Will gave them a hundred dollars as an advance against the baby's upkeep.

Clark's temporary guardians fell so in love with him that they wanted to adopt him. He adjusted easily to farm life. As soon as he could walk, he helped feed the chickens and gather eggs. He had a pet rabbit and chased squirrels in the woods. In later life he said that certain smells always made him homesick for the farm: tomato ketchup cooking, gingerbread baking, cocks crowing, crickets chirping.

In April 1903, two months after Clark's second birthday, Will Gable married thirty-three-year-old Jennie Dunlap of Hopedale, Ohio, an oil boomtown about seven miles northeast of Cadiz. They first met when Will rented a room in the Dunlap family's home on Church Street. Jennie ran a millinery shop and made many of the hats herself. Though not a beauty, she had great flair and was always stylishly dressed and coiffed.

Will Gable's second marriage was another odd coupling. What did a woman with such taste and talent see in a one-track-minded "oil monkey"? But Jennie's "career" proved to be only a substitute for what she really wanted from life: to be a wife and mother. Hopefully little Clark would be the start of a family that would eventually include children of her own.

The Gables decided to continue living in the Dunlap home until they could build their own house. Meanwhile Will placed a $150 deposit on two vacant lots on nearby Mill Street. Plans were drawn for a two-story, six-room house that he would construct himself, with help from Jennie's three brothers, who were coal miners. Needless to say, it became a part-time project as well as a lengthy one. It took five years to save the money for the house and another two years to build it.

When the time came for Will to retrieve his son from Pennsylvania, he encountered resistance from the Hershelmans, who'd made a sacred promise to Clark's mother that he'd be raised as a Catholic. Besides being a Methodist like Will, new wife Jennie also taught Sunday school! Will had to threaten legal action before the Hershelmans gave in. To keep peace in the family, he promised to send Clark for a long visit every summer.

"The best day of my life was the day I met my stepmother," he recalled many years later. "She was a wonderful woman, although I didn't realize it then. She was always looking out for what I needed. She must have loved me very much, because I was certainly not what you'd call well behaved. I was rather spoiled."

Some of the spoiling came from Jennie's brothers and sister. They'd all lived for years without a child in the household, then suddenly had one to lavish attention on. Clark never lacked for toys, but his favorite was a wooden stick pony. He tied it to the bedpost every night to make sure it didn't run away while he slept.

Clark grew up among attentive adults and became used to receiving rather than giving. In later years he always made it plain to those around him that he expected favoritism.

Although Jennie Gable longed to have children of her own, she never would, so she made Clark the center of her universe. She also may have been trying to compensate for Will Gable's neglect of his son, which was partly due to the demands of a job that kept him away from home for 90 percent of the time. But Will also had a stern nature: he wasn't the sort of father who could easily be a buddy to his son.

Friends and neighbors from Hopedale would later remember movie star Clark Gable as a very shy boy who always seemed to be smiling. "We all liked him," said Eunice Haverfield, "but he was not an unusual boy at all. Nobody expected him to go places in the world."

When he started first grade in the town's two-room schoolhouse, Clark loved the sing-alongs led by teacher Frances Thompson. Taller than the rest of the kids in the class, he also had the loudest voice, which landed him in the chorus for the Christmas entertainment. Stepmother Jennie could play the piano and started teaching him at home. She also sent him for brass instrument lessons when he expressed interest in joining Hopedale's town band.

Behind many a star has lurked a so-called stage mother, but it's doubtful that Jennie Gable had such dreams for Clark. For most Americans who lived outside metropolitan areas in the early 1900s, show business didn't exist, except in occasional visits from traveling circuses or tent shows that featured plays, vaudeville, and a new form of photography that actually moved when projected onto a screen. By encouraging

Clark's musical talent, Jennie was just trying to cultivate him, to save him from ending up a grimy wildcatter like his father.

Jennie also taught him personal cleanliness. She dressed him in the finest clothes she could buy and kept him immaculately groomed. All of his life he was well dressed, and as a female admirer once quipped, "He was so clean that you could eat off him."

At age eight he decided he wanted to become a doctor. But that dream vanished when he fell madly and forever in love with the newfangled invention known as the automobile. "If some rich man who owned a car that fascinated me had hired me as his chauffeur, I think I would have been happy for the rest of my life, driving it and keeping it in shape," he said many years later.

Automobiles also improved Clark's relationship with his father. When Will Gable bought a Ford roadster for $175, he was able to commute to work every day and spend more time with the family. Very mechanically inclined, he taught Clark how to strip down engines and to put them back together again. Cars and gabbing about them became their main bond over the years.

In 1910 Will Gable finally finished his house-building project on Mill Street, and the family moved in. Clark got one of the three upstairs bedrooms for his own and could also use the empty one for play space until a sibling came along. As homeowners, the Gables became more respected in the community. Will Gable now served as Sunday school superintendent of the Hopedale Methodist Church.

In March 1913, a month after Clark's twelfth birthday, the entire state of Ohio suffered some of the most devastating floods in its history, with 430 people killed and property damage of $250 million. Luckily for the Gables, the western part of the state was hardest hit, but for a solid week the rains poured down and threatened to wash away their three-year-old home.

Clark's Catholic mother probably would have disapproved, but he had just joined the Methodist youth group, the Epworth League. The Hopedale chapter met every Sunday evening and also held frequent "socials" such as dances, sleigh rides, taffy pulls, and berry pickings.

A belle named Marjorie Miller was Clark's first girlfriend, if not sweetheart. "The only time that I became angry at him was over a kissing game," she remembered. "Whenever we played post office, he always insisted on being postmaster, because then he didn't have to kiss me or anybody else."

The future superstud was a slow starter. "I was just an awkward, overgrown boy who never quite knew what to do with his feet. I liked girls but I was afraid of them. I used to envy the guys who could walk up to them and laugh and talk without blushing and stammering," he once recalled.

While school recessed that summer, Clark held his first job, driving a horse-drawn wagon and delivering sacks of flour for the local mill. The following summer he went into business for himself, supplying dehydrated coal miners with pails of cool well water. He earned as much as five dollars per day in charges and tips.

"The Kid was brought up to depend on himself," his father once recalled. "He was always pestering me to drive our car. I finally took him out into the country where the road was wide and there wasn't any traffic. I put him behind the wheel and slipped my arm around him to help him navigate, but there was no need. He shook loose of me and drove right off like he was born in the seat."

Though war broke out in Europe in that summer of 1914, Clark was hardly aware of it as he entered his last year of grade school. He was a fair student, good at subjects he liked such as spelling and grammar, but bored with arithmetic, history, and geography. He loved music and at thirteen was the only boy among the men in the Hopedale town band.

To improve his work in high school, his stepmother started tutoring him at home. Will Gable helped by ordering a veritable wall of books from mail-order catalogs, including a seventy-two-volume set of *The World's Greatest Literature,* William Shakespeare's complete works in thirteen volumes, and similarly sized collections of history, art, science, and Bible study.

Though his father later complained that "I never saw him open a single volume," Clark got hooked on Shakespeare and especially the sonnets, an interest that he tried to keep secret all his life because some might consider it "queer" and unmanly. But at home alone or in the company of those he trusted, he loved to read poetry aloud, to savor the words and meaning.

Will Gable, who belonged to the Freemasons and swore by its credos, wanted his son to be self-reliant and courageous. He taught him how to swim, fish, shoot, and hunt. "The Kid was a real he-boy and no sissy," his father recalled. But "to call him a sissy was the best way I could make him behave."

By his freshman year at Hopedale High School, Clark was almost as tall and strong as his father. He played on the baseball team, batting with such power that fellow players joked that one of his homers could kill a cow grazing in a nearby meadow.

His closest friend, Andy Means, whose father owned Hopedale's only hotel, later recalled that Clark was also a big talker. "He had the loudest voice of any guy in our neighborhood, and he knew how to use it. He never had one fistfight while he was growing up. If there would be an argument, and it looked like the other kid was going to belt him, he could always talk his way out of it," Means said.

Apart from church and school socials, Hopedale had little in the way of recreation for teenage Clark and his pals. They hung out at Jolly's Drug Store, went fishing in summer, and hunted raccoons in winter. Although there were no movie theaters in the vicinity, "flickers" were often shown in the town hall and even at school, but film was still a primitive medium.

In April 1917 the United States entered the European war, sending shock waves among families that might have to lose fathers and sons to battle. The Gables had nothing to worry about there, since Will was too old to serve and Clark too young. But Jennie thought it was a good time to make some changes. After fourteen years of marriage, it seemed unlikely that her family would grow any larger. For even longer than that Will had been working in the oil fields, chasing millions but never earning enough to accumulate any savings after the bills were paid.

She wanted Will to give up wildcatting, sell the Hopedale house, and buy a farm. It would be mainly for Clark's benefit. He could eventually take over the management and, if the farm was a success, be comfortably set for life. Certainly the chances were far better than finding untapped oil.

Will Gable had grown up on a farm, so he had plenty of experience and believed he could run one. He may have hated giving up his oil dreams, but Jennie was probably right in placing the family's welfare first. That summer moving became an even greater necessity as Will's creditors began to squeeze him.

Meanwhile sixteen-year-old Clark lost his virginity to a married Jezebel of the town. Hopedale buzzed with gossip about the affair between the handsome lad and the middle-aged woman, who had reportedly lured him into her house one afternoon when he happened to pass by on his way home from school. While Clark was the yielding partner in the seduction, the scandal could ruin him and his family. Jennie thought that he should be hauled away to a farm before his first taste of sex turned him into a tomcat.

As fast as they could, the Gables sold their house as well as Will's oil-rigging equipment, settled their debts, and bought a small farm near Ravenna, about sixty miles north of Hopedale. It was a very rural area, and unlike Hopedale it had no sense of community.

Clark became very unhappy at his new high school, which was five miles away and meant taking a bus packed with kids he didn't know and who behaved like country bumpkins. They razzed him about his natty clothes and his full-grown, manly appearance.

He also hated the new farm routine. Days spent in school were easier because he had fewer hours of manual labor. But as he later recalled, "I had to get up at four in the morning every day in the year, spring, summer, fall, and winter. I fed the hogs and other stock, plowed in the spring until every muscle ached, forked hay in the hot sun until I was sweating crops of calluses. I did what I was expected to do, but it takes a certain knack for farming in what was then the old-fashioned way. I just didn't have what it takes."

No doubt, after his sexual initiation, Clark was eager to get back to Hopedale and his lady friend. By Christmas 1917 he had talked his parents into letting him quit school to get a job with the Harmon Creek Coal Company in Hopedale. It was the end of his formal education.

Jennie arranged for Clark to stay with his Dunlap relatives. Again he earned five dollars per day delivering food and water to coal miners, and in the evenings he hung out with his pals at the Hopedale train station, the favorite congregating spot for male teens. He started chain-smoking cigarettes and drinking beer, wine, and liquor. He wanted to be known as Billy, which sounded ballsier than Clark. Cowboy outlaw "Billy the Kid" Bonney and movie star "Bronco Billy" Anderson were two of his idols.

Billy Gable started saving his money, and in anticipation of a future accumulation, he wrote to his father offering to buy his Ford roadster for its original price of $175. Cars were scarce while production was curtailed for the war, and Billy knew that his father would never sell for anything less. Will accepted the offer, hoping that by the time Billy saved the money, his rebellion would have passed and he would be eager to return to farm and school.

But Billy had other plans. Best friend Andy Means, four years older, had moved to Akron to work in a rubber factory. To fulfill wartime demands, the city's manufacturers were operating twenty-four hours a day. The military drain on manpower between the ages of eighteen and thirty had created so many vacancies that Billy's being hired was virtually guaranteed. He told his father he wanted to go to Akron to get a job.

Will Gable was furious because he really needed the Kid to help on the farm for the same reason: wartime shortage. But Jennie sided with Billy. She thought that he should be given a chance to try something that he really wanted to do.

"If it hadn't been for my stepmother, I'd probably be on a farm in Ohio," he would later recall. "I thought my father's opposition cruel. His stubbornness only increased mine."

But Will Gable stuck to his agreement and accepted $175 in cash from Billy for the Ford roadster. He hoped Billy would come home to visit, since Akron was less than twenty miles from Ravenna.

It was April 1918. In another seven months the world war would end with an armistice, but no one knew that at the time. Akron was a boom city, something that Billy had never experienced. Upwards of half of its 200,000 population often seemed to be crowding the streets at the same time. Blimps and surveillance balloons manufactured locally were always being tested in the skies overhead. The atmosphere reeked of molten rubber, the vapors from which also left a microscopic coating of soapstone (similar to volcanic ash) on everything.

Billy was quickly hired by Firestone Tire and Rubber. For lack of a high school diploma, he had to settle for the production line, molding treads on car and truck tires. Luckily for him, so many men were leaving for military service that he was promoted to a clerical job in timekeeping after three months.

The Akron phase of Clark Gable's life is impossible to describe with certainty. Both he and friends from that time, including Andy

Means, later told many contradictory stories. But he did work for a time at Firestone and, following that, for Miller Rubber.

By the time he arrived in Akron, the state of Ohio had voted itself "dry," prohibiting the sale and manufacture of alcoholic beverages. With so much spending money available, the world's rubber capital soon became a mecca for bootleggers, while some also dabbled in illegal gambling, prostitution, and drugs. Stories have circulated for decades that young Clark Gable worked for some of the Akron gangsters, though at nothing more criminal than delivering hooch or taking bets for bookies.

In Akron Billy Gable finally got bitten by the acting bug. It happened during his very first visit to a stage play, at the Akron Music Hall on Exchange Street. A resident stock company was performing *The Bird of Paradise,* a lurid melodrama by Richard Walton Tully that had been packing theaters since its first Broadway production in 1912.

Billy was dazzled. At seventeen he'd never seen anything as sexy as the title character, a Hawaiian princess dressed in a hula skirt, with only strands of pearls concealing her bosom. In the startling finale, after being rejected by her white American lover, she commits suicide by leaping into the crater of a bubbling volcano.

The performance of the stock company's lead actress, Pauline McLean, might not have equaled that of the play's original Broadway star, the great Laurette Taylor, but Billy Gable had no basis for comparison. "I clapped until my palms were sore," he would recall. "I'd never seen anything as wonderful in my life, which, I guess, had been pretty drab up until then."

Every chance he had, Billy hung around the Music Hall's stage door to watch the performers leave. Trailing them to their favored gathering places, he made a few friends. Soon he was working backstage as a volunteer "call boy": during performances he summoned the actors from their dressing rooms when it was nearly their time to go on. He also ran errands and swept the floors. Even though he received no pay, he was thrilled by the chance to learn about acting and stagecraft.

His eagerness was an automatic response, and he couldn't have done much rationalizing about it. He was simply a six-foot high school dropout who'd stumbled into an amazing new world and wanted to belong. When he'd attended movies (silent and monochrome in those days), he'd never felt any interest in becoming an actor. Perhaps he'd needed the stimulation of a live performance, of hearing words spoken, to realize what magic an actor could perform.

He was probably also entranced by the actors' lifestyle. In those days acting was one of the few professions where women were not only the equals of men but often enjoyed greater fame and success. The integration of the sexes, the unconventional working hours, and the exhibitionist streak in every actor made them a tribe of bohemians who made and lived by their own rules. They stood out from ordinary people. They had worshipers as well as censurers. The era's moral defenders considered them bums and degenerates.

For the time being Billy Gable had to settle for backstage volunteer work while he worked at his real job. If it was, as he later claimed, at a rubber factory, he would have earned $95 per month, or roughly $23 per week, half of which went to room and board. He spent the rest on clothes and such—he needed to look sharp when hanging out with his actor friends.

After the armistice of November 11, 1918, veterans started returning to reclaim their jobs in the factories. Jobs overall were fewer due to the cancellation of wartime contracts with the army and navy. Billy's friend Andy Means, who had a higher-paying job, was one of the first to be dismissed. He returned to Hopedale and became a farmer.

Also sacked, Billy remained in Akron, still hoping for a break from Ed Lilley, manager of the Music Hall's stock company. Finally, when a minor actor took sick, Lilley delegated Billy to replace him. The nature of the role is in dispute. Lilley later claimed that he hired Billy as a background extra in Shakespeare, with no spoken dialogue. But Clark Gable recalled it as a servant in a contemporary play: "I had one line, 'Your cab is here, madame.' I thought I'd die while I was waiting to go on. When I didn't fall on my face, I thought I was an actor. It was all over then, as far as my future was concerned. I never wanted to be anything else."

The year 1919 is a mostly unknown year in the life of Billy Gable. A postwar depression began. Factories were closing. Even bootleggers were feeling the pinch. Billy apparently remained in Akron and had a rough time, sometimes sleeping backstage at the Music Hall when he ran out of money.

In November he received word that his stepmother was seriously ill. Rushing home to Ravenna, he learned that Jennie had tuberculosis of the bowels and had only months to live. His father, now needing him on the farm more than ever, tried to dissuade him from returning to Akron, but without success.

Billy continued to visit Jennie frequently until she died on January 11, 1920. For the funeral he drove to Hopedale to bring her favorite minister to conduct the service. "I felt I had lost the greatest friend I ever had. She was very smart at figuring out what a kid without a mother needed," he would later remember.

Billy had now been nurtured by two mothers, the first for only ten months and the other for nearly seventeen years. Was that enough mothering for one man's lifetime, or would he need more?

Since Jennie had been the only person capable of keeping peace between father and son, their battles resumed after her death. Then Will Gable decided to sell the farm and to return to prospecting for oil. With the sale money he intended to move west. Big gushers were more likely to be found in Oklahoma or Texas than in rapidly depleting Ohio.

Without Jennie to act as referee, Billy was powerless against his father's fiery temper. Will was determined to bring Billy out west with him and "make a man" of his son. When he learned that "the Kid" wanted to be an actor and was associating with such vagabonds, he tried to prevent it by threatening legal action. In those days children were legally bound to their parents (or guardians) until age twenty-one. Billy still had two years to go. While it seemed unlikely that his father would go through with the threat, it was enough to cause Billy to yield to his father's will.

Billy also didn't want to risk losing the three-hundred-dollar trust fund that was due him when he reached his so-called majority. John J. Hershelman, Addie's father, had set it up when his grandson was born. Billy would be eligible to collect on his twenty-first birthday, in February 1922. If he and his father were still at war by that time, Billy feared that Will might try to attach the money.

Yet even these fears did not induce Billy to change his mind. After selling the farm, Will Gable left for Tulsa and stopped in Akron for one more try at persuading his son to accompany him. It failed, but Will swore that Billy would be hearing from him again as soon as he reached Oklahoma and found work.

By now it was the summer of 1920. Native Ohioan Warren G. Harding was campaigning for president of the United States and promising to end the business depression, which he blamed on incumbent Woodrow Wilson. Meanwhile Akron, like all industrial cities, had hordes of unemployed. People still lucky enough to have jobs were forced to accept pay cuts to keep the factories open.

Billy Gable held on for as long as he could. But was he a factory worker? Store clerk? Bookie? Pimp? All have been reported or rumored, but none is provable.

The widespread shortage of money also hurt the entertainment business. The Music Hall dismissed its resident stock company, which left to find a home in some other city. Billy lost his friends and what seemed his only chance of becoming an actor.

By September Billy was in such desperate straits that he tracked down his father and sent him a letter begging for help. Before Will Gable could even reply, Billy turned up at his front door in Big Heart, Oklahoma, eager to start work immediately.

Wildcatting for oil paid nothing until you struck some. Will Gable had always supported his prospecting by hiring himself out as a rigger and tool dresser. Over the years Billy had learned enough of the basics to qualify for an apprentice's job. More important than knowledge was strength and muscle, which six-foot-one Billy had in abundance.

"Dad got me a job as a student tool dresser at a dollar per hour," he would later remember. "The shifts were twelve hours on, twelve hours off. With a partner, I had to tend the seven-hundred-pound bit that drilled the hole in the ground. After someone else heated it to white heat, we stood on opposite sides of it and used sixteen-pound sledgehammers to sharpen the cutting edges. At the end of every shift, I also had to climb seventy or eighty feet to the top of the rickety wooden tower to oil the bearings of the crown block."

Billy worked seven days a week, for eight or nine weeks straight before he got a weekend off. Within months of such strenuous labor, he gained forty pounds and shot from 165 to 205. He was truly gigantic, but it was all meat and muscle, without fat or flab.

He was earning $84 a week at a time when the average salary in America was $24. But he despised the work, as well as Big Heart, a squalid settlement that contradicted its name. Merchants and food providers charged outrageous prices and got them because the oil workers had no place else to go.

Billy paid $25 a week to sleep in a huge communal tent. Rows and rows of cots were kept filled twenty-four hours a day as workers occupied them in shifts. Blankets and linens were provided. Fumigators came in once a week to spray for parasites.

After six months as a tool dresser, Billy told his father that he couldn't tolerate it anymore. Still stagestruck, he left for Tulsa, a boomtown with theaters and a night life. Without any acting credentials, he worked at whatever jobs he could find, first as a garage mechanic and then as a store clerk. He lasted only a few weeks at each due to the continuing economic depression.

Nearly broke, he returned to Big Heart and moved in with his father, who lived in a rented shanty that had a privy in the backyard. Will Gable thought Billy still needed toughening and found him a job in an oil refinery.

"It was a damned hot one," Clark Gable recalled. "I was part of an eight-man gang that cleaned out the sludge, which was almost like asphalt, from stills and storage tanks as soon as they were emptied. The interior temperature and oil fumes were so terrific that only one man would go in at a time, with a rope around his waist in case he passed out. Working with a pick and shovel, you could only tolerate it for about two minutes, so you were in and out every sixteen minutes throughout the twelve-hour shifts. I saw lots of men get a little hysterical. They started to laugh and had to be hauled out and sent home."

When 1922 rolled around, Billy started counting the days until liberation. The week before his twenty-first birthday on February 1, he told his father that he was leaving Big Heart and not returning. A violent argument ensued. The Gables swore to each other that they wouldn't meet again until heaven or hell. It would be more than a decade before they cooled off enough to reconsider.

BILLY HITS THE ROAD

On February 1, 1922, Billy Gable walked into the bank at Meadville, Pennsylvania, presented his credentials to the manager, and collected the three hundred dollars (plus interest) from Grandpa Hershelman's trust fund. It was hardly a fortune, but it was enough to buy two suits and an overcoat and still have some money to live on.

Although Billy was now legally an adult, his intellectual development seemed to have stopped when he quit high school in his second year. He was hardly an ignoramus, but he lacked initiative and foresight. He needed guidance and stimulation from others. When he didn't receive it, he just floated along with the tide wherever it carried him.

As a consequence, Billy Gable left few tracks during the first half of the 1920s. His activities from 1922 to 1924 are largely unknown except for his own subsequent recollections and those of a few people who claimed to have known him or worked with him.

This much of what we know is probably true. After collecting his inheritance, he returned briefly to Akron, where he connected with a traveling "tent show" that did one-night stands of plays and musical comedies in small towns and villages.

"I got the job only because they needed someone with muscles to do the heavy work," he later remembered. "I received ten dollars a week as a roustabout, stagehand, and caretaker of the horses that pulled the wagons. Whenever we arrived in a new place, we put on a parade to pull in the crowds. Since I'd played trombone in the high school band, they let me join in. I had to wear a clown costume and play real loud."

It was a period in show business when live forms of entertainment were still the most popular. Movies were coming up fast, but until they ended their silence, they lacked the excitement of a live performance. Every city in America had at least one live theater; in many there were enough to offer a choice among dramatic plays, vaudeville, and burlesque (pre-striptease). In addition, scores of circuses, rodeos, minstrel shows, and the like toured constantly. In sum total they created many thousands of jobs and were excellent training grounds for beginners who were willing to start at the bottom.

Live show business was divided into two categories. The "big time," with the highest salaries and ticket prices, included Broadway plays and their road companies; reserved-seat vaudeville shows with famous stars; and brand-name presentations like the Ringling Brothers–Barnum and Bailey Circus.

The other category was the "small time," which included theatrical stock companies, bargain-priced vaudeville shows without "name" headliners, and tent shows like the one that Billy Gable worked for. Such enterprises usually got stuck with performing in a town's worst theaters, or they had to rent the town hall or school auditorium. They preferred to perform under their own canvas where local safety laws permitted.

Clark Gable once said that he spent two years with the tent show, learning from the actors and eventually landing small parts in everything from Shakespeare to *Uncle Tom's Cabin*. Unfortunately, he never specified the name of the troupe, so it is impossible to track it down. But his recollections don't correlate with some known facts about a slightly later period. Most likely he spent no more than a few months with the tent show, then moved on.

But his explanation for why he moved on seems reasonable. The troupe got stranded in Butte, Montana, during a blizzard and was forced to cancel the rest of the tour. Billy had become friendly with a musician who had relatives about three hundred miles away in Oregon, so they stowed away on a freight train to get there. Unluckily, the relatives had moved. His friend decided to press on, but Billy was nearly broke and stayed behind to look for a job.

He found one in a lumber mill, unloading logs from delivery trucks. "Until I got my first paycheck," he recalled, "I couldn't afford gloves like the other guys wore. Lifting those logs was like grabbing hold of rough sandpaper. My hands were all cut and cracking open. I'd soak them in salt water and vinegar to toughen them. Alum too. When I finally bought some gloves, I found that I could work better without them because my hands had gotten so hard and leathery."

As soon as he'd saved enough money, Billy quit and left for Portland to find some easier work. He would later claim that he sold neckties at Meier and Frank's Department Store, but with his big, scarred hands, would anyone have trusted him with such delicate merchandise? More likely he did some heavy lifting in the stockroom. But in any case he became friendly with a salesman named Earle Larimore, who worked there temporarily while trying to become a professional actor and director.

A year older than Billy, Larimore was far better educated, a graduate of Oregon State University. He was also a nephew of the adored stage star Laura Hope Crews. Billy was doubly impressed when he discovered that Larimore belonged to one of the local theater groups, the Red Lantern Players. Larimore took Billy to some of their meetings and rehearsals but did not invite him to join the group.

"We all liked him," Larimore recalled, "but he was a big brute who looked like he might break the stage furniture if he sat on it. Probably due to undernourishment, he had a sallow complexion and decayed teeth. He tried to speak with his mouth closed to hide them. We thought he was only interested in becoming an actor because it was an easy way to meet girls."

By this time the twenty-one-year-old Billy Gable was far from a virgin. He confided to Larimore that his experience was limited to prostitutes and that he had too much respect for "nice" women to be a seducer. Thus he had had no serious romances. As he later recalled, "I never had time to fall in love. I was always trying to stay one jump ahead of the breadline. You can't have a sweetheart when all your effort is being put into getting a job or holding one."

But that changed as soon as he met an enchanting doe-eyed actress named Frances Doerfler, or Franz Dorfler as she wanted to be known professionally. A year older than Billy, she was the ingenue of the Red Lantern Players. When Earle Larimore introduced them, Billy reminded Franz of a lost Saint Bernard puppy who needed adopting. Whenever she had some spare time at the players' club, she coached him in rudiments like stage movement and reading lines.

In June 1922 Rex Jewell, managing director of a small-time stock company known as the Astoria Players, came to Portland to hire actors for its summer tour. Billy decided to audition when some of his Red Lantern friends did. With his employee discount at the store where he worked, he purchased a suit made by Brooks Brothers of New York, a white shirt with French cuffs, and links studded with his garnet birthstone.

His friends breezed through their auditions with Rex Jewell and were hired on the spot. Billy, however, made a clumsy spectacle of himself, blowing lines and not knowing what to do with his ugly, oversize hands. Many years later, Rex Jewell recalled: "I had not the slightest desire to add him to the company. He seemed to me to lack the slightest gift for the stage with nothing, absolutely nothing to offer then or in the future."

Afterward Billy broke down, telling his friends that he might as well commit suicide if he couldn't go with them on the tour. Earle Larimore intervened and pleaded with Jewell to hire Billy. At worst, he could earn his keep by helping with the heavy work. Jewell agreed.

Billy was overjoyed. He seemed as confident as Larimore when they quit their jobs at the department store. From now on it would be the actor's life for them.

Rex Jewell's wife, Rita Cordero, was the lead actress of the Astoria Players, which, during northern Oregon's severe winters, had its theatrical home in Astoria, a small city on the Pacific coast. But during the mild summers the troupe tried to perform in all the towns and villages between Portland and Astoria, traveling up the Columbia River on the paddlewheel ships that serviced the route. At each stop they got off to perform a one- or two-night stand. Sometimes they continued into the countryside by train or bus; they might be gone a week or more before returning to the river.

When the tour started, Billy and Franz Dorfler quickly became a couple, encouraged by Earle Larimore and his sweetheart, Peggy Martin, another alumnus of the Red Lantern Players. "Billy began to depend on me," Dorfler remembered. "He seemed insecure because of past hardships, financial troubles, and had to be reassured that he was liked. Once he confided to me that his mother had died of epilepsy, and he was afraid of having inherited the disease. But normally he was jovial and outgoing."

While they were rehearsing one day, Billy leaned over and kissed her. "I thought that a bit aggressive, because I'd been raised in a convent," Dorfler recalled. "I was shocked. I just sat there because I wasn't accustomed to it. But then I thought how wonderful this was. *I've met somebody who wants to be an actor, and so do I. Wouldn't this be fun?* So it didn't take me long to become terribly fond of him. Soon I couldn't bear to be away from him."

Rex Jewell refused to cast Billy in anything but bit parts until he proved that he could act. He was so clumsy onstage that audiences always laughed at him. Jewell kept threatening to fire him, but finally he didn't need to. Three weeks into the tour the box-office treasurer absconded with all the receipts. The Astoria Players tried to struggle on, but without cash reserves Jewell quickly went bust and closed down.

Actress Lucille Schumann's parents lived in Seaside, a resort town about twenty miles from Astoria, and she arranged for all the players to stay with them until new work could be found. Earle Larimore phoned agents in Portland and Seattle to try to get the group hired by another stock company.

The Schumanns' house was too small to accommodate everybody, so they took turns sleeping on the beach. Billy and Franz Dorfler rather enjoyed it. "We built a big fire and snuggled together in blankets against the bitter cold nights," she recalled.

The strandees were finally hired by another Astoria producer for an end-of-season river tour that would eventually land them back in Portland. Their salaries were even lower than before, and they traveled by milk delivery boats without passenger comforts. Rain or shine, everybody had to sleep on the open deck.

"It was early fall and not very pleasant," Dorfler said. "Billy wasn't very strong, despite his huge frame. The ill effects of the hand-to-mouth situation began to tell on him. With so little money we often had to choose between pie and soup for our meals. Some of our more desperate friends stole canned goods from stores and shared them with us."

Halfway through the tour Earle Larimore left for New York at the summons of his aunt, Laura Hope Crews, who'd arranged for him to join a prestigious stock company headed by actress Jessie Bonstelle. Billy offered to replace Larimore as the troupe's leading man, but he had to wait until two other actors quit the tour before he finally got the chance.

His performances may have been inept, but the troupe's manager couldn't really complain. "He paid me almost nothing," Clark Gable recalled. "And to be sure, I was worth every cent of it."

By this time Billy and Franz Dorfler had become engaged, though he couldn't afford to buy her a ring. "We were so happy that we were almost oblivious to the hardest conditions," she recalled. "Billy behaved much like a schoolboy in love for the first time. If I took a walk by myself, he wanted to know where I'd been. It felt strangely wonderful to be loved so passionately."

By the end of the tour, however, Billy had lost twenty pounds and was suffering from anemia and bronchitis. With no work in sight for either of them, Dorfler took him to recuperate at her family's farm in Silverton, Oregon. Since her parents had opposed her decision to become an actress, she wasn't expecting a warm welcome, but Billy won them over with his charm and friendliness.

"He was a glowing light, with his dimpled smile, infectious laughter, and desire to please," she said later. "It didn't take my parents long to accept the idea that we were going to be married. But they were a bit startled at his uninhibited manner of seizing me and kissing me wildly at any time, without warning, in anyone's company. He seemed unable to restrain himself."

Billy started addressing the Doerflers as "Mom" and "Dad." Back in Ohio he hadn't been able to stick it out more than six months as a farmer's son, but now he suddenly enjoyed working in the fields and milking the cows. Perhaps Franz made the difference. They picked berries, hiked in the woods, and made love in the haystacks.

Billy's unlucky experiences as an actor may have made him realize that being a farmer might not be so terrible if he had a loving wife and family surrounding him. He pressed Franz to marry him, but she kept putting him off. As much as she loved Billy, she still dreamed of an acting career. She didn't want to end up a farmer's wife; nor did she care to marry a penniless actor who couldn't even support himself.

When winter came, bringing with it a cutback in farm activity, Billy found a job in town at the Silver Falls Lumber Company. He earned $3.20 per day in the loading department, employed under the name of W. C. Gable, according to a pay receipt dated January 17, 1923.

Billy had only one set of work clothes, including a pair of riding breeches and boots that were part of a stage costume that Rex Jewell had given him in settlement for money owed him when the Astoria Players folded. The rough-and-tough mill workers, many of them immigrants from Sweden and Finland, were always making jokes about Billy's dudish outfit, but he was too proud to admit that he had nothing else to wear. His Brooks Brothers suit would have caused just as much comment.

The mill was seven miles from the Doerfler farm. Billy stayed at a boardinghouse in Silverton during the week and visited Franz on Sundays. His sweetheart, however, soon got depressed by the weeklong separations and by the pause in her acting career. She left for Portland to look for work.

"Billy didn't much like the idea," she recalled, "but it was just as easy for him to come see me in Portland as it was at the farm. We promised to write every day. Sometimes I would receive two or three letters that had been written the same day. They were filled with how lonely he was without me. And mine were filled with the same sentiments."

In the early spring of 1923, Billy quit his job at the lumber mill and moved to Portland. He lucked into a job in the classified advertising department at the daily newspaper, *The Oregonian*. While selling space for help-wanted ads, he learned of job opportunities before they got listed. For several weeks he collected his salary and waited for the right job to come along. He quit as soon as he found it with the Pacific Telephone and Telegraph Company as an apprentice lineman, climbing telephone poles and hanging wires. Since millions of American homes and businesses were still without telephones, it seemed a job with an unlimited future and opportunities for advancement.

Meanwhile his ongoing romance with Franz Dorfler hit a snag when a stock company hired her for a tour to Seattle and back. She wasn't happy about Billy's new telephone job, which seemed to be dampening his interest in becoming an actor. To give him something constructive to do while she was away, she persuaded him to take voice lessons with her friend and coach, Lawrence Woodfrin. It wasn't so much to turn Billy into a singer as to teach him vocal control and projection, which every professional actor needs to have.

By summer Billy had progressed enough to sing in a recital of

Woodfrin's students. Dorfler arranged time off from her tour to attend. "His voice wasn't outstanding, but enough to convince me that he could make it as an actor if he got the proper training and worked real hard," she recalled. "When I congratulated him afterward, he asked, 'Does that mean you'll marry me?' I wanted to say yes, but instead I told him to ask me again in six months."

Back on the road again, Dorfler learned that a new theater group was being started in Portland by Josephine Dillon, a onetime actress on the Broadway stage and now a respected teacher of the craft. Franz wrote to Billy and urged him to contact Dillon immediately. Unknowingly Franz had pushed the destruct button on their two-year love affair.

Billy Gable first met Josephine Dillon at the official opening of her studio in the rented house where she lived. About thirty people attended—young hopefuls who wanted to be actors, playwrights, or directors, mixed in with a few invited socialites who were potential financial "angels." Dillon asked for volunteers to join her in a reading of Royall Tyler's *The Contrast,* which was originally staged in 1787 and is regarded as the first American play by a native-born writer on an American subject.

Billy didn't participate, but he watched and listened intently as the reading progressed. Dillon kept stopping to talk about theater history and her own teaching methods. Billy was so impressed that he hung around afterward to congratulate her and to ask if he could stop by the next day after work to talk.

Within a short time Billy became Josephine Dillon's prize pupil and was also living with her. He'd just turned twenty-three, while she was on the verge of forty. Old enough to be his mother, she also looked it. Unlike most actresses of her age group, she didn't try to pass for younger with makeup tricks. Her gray hair and matronly appearance were probably deliberately cultivated, to earn her more respect as a teacher.

Born to an affluent Irish-American family of lawyers and artistic strivers, Dillon grew up in southern California and was one of the first females to attend Stanford University, from which she graduated in 1908. Her résumé as a drama coach claimed that she'd been a leading actress on Broadway and with stock companies, but those claims cannot be proven. She lived in New York for a time, and also in Paris. She'd never been married but had some close relationships with women and may have been bisexual if not lesbian.

Josephine Dillon may have had no sexual interest whatsoever in Billy Gable. Some people seek love only in its platonic sense, for companionship and/or for the satisfaction that comes from giving help. Dillon once said that she'd been waiting all her life for someone like him, whom she could guide and mold to perfection.

Some of Clark Gable's friends claim that he never slept with Dillon, that she never demanded it, and that he wasn't attracted enough to want to try. Cynics will believe otherwise.

Dillon transformed rough Billy Gable into suave William Gable. He was so undernourished that she sent him to a health farm for several weeks. She paid to have his teeth repaired, his hair restyled, and his eyebrows plucked. Plastic surgery was still too experimental to risk reducing his floppy ears.

She tried to make him forget all the phony acting tricks he'd picked up. She taught him total body control. Like many big men, he had a high-pitched voice that needed to be lowered if he wanted to qualify for virile roles. Fortunately, he'd had some musical training, so he made remarkable progress with Dillon's help.

"He sat at the piano for long periods daily, trying first of all for pitch and for accuracy of tone, and learning to listen," she recalled years later. "Then he would work the voice down, a half step at a time. The results of this work are noticeable in the amazing resonance behind his speech and in the firmness of the tones. He had picked up a conglomeration of vowels during his varied life, from Ohio to the Pacific Northwest, from farm and city, from laborers and hoboes."

When Dillon first met Gable, he had the furrowed, tight-set face of someone who'd struggled through life alone; it revealed nothing of his inner self. "All that had to be changed, but while working on his voice at the same time," she said. "It makes an actor less self-conscious to correct face with voice than to study facial expression alone. . . . As the muscles of his face relaxed in the assumption of correct speech habits, the forehead smoothed, the eyes opened, the lips began to be flexible, and a smile was born. I don't mean that he learned new things. I mean that his own best way of doing things was released and freed from the interference of wrong habits."

When Franz Dorfler returned to Portland from her stock company tour, she found only slight traces of Billy in the actor who now called himself William Gable. After considering his marriage proposal for several months, she'd decided to accept, but he told her, "I don't love you anymore. I never believed that this could happen to me. But I'm going to continue studying with Josephine Dillon for the next few years. Without her help I'll never get anywhere. Working with her has come to mean everything to me."

Dorfler was shattered. Several days later Billy phoned to apologize and to make a date. "When we met," she recalled, "he took me into his arms and said exactly what I wanted him to say. But somehow it was different. He seemed like a man carrying out an obligation. All his thrilling urgency was gone. Unable to endure it, I made some excuse to put the marriage off. He seemed relieved rather than disappointed. So I told him that under the circumstances it might be best to break off our engagement and leave things the way they were."

Franz found an acting job in Portland with the Forest Taylor Stock Company. Billy, still supporting himself by working for Pacific Telephone during the day, attended the evening classes at Dillon's studio and continued as her live-in companion.

In the spring of 1924 Dillon decided that William Gable was ready for public viewing. One way she earned money was to assemble short programs of dramatic readings for educational and social functions. For an afternoon gathering of the MacDowell Club for Women, Gable and another Dillon pupil, Alice Price Moore, performed Henri Murger's narrative poem, *The Ballad of Despair.*

Gable portrayed a poor, lovesick poet who pleads with an angel of death to end his suffering. With musical accompaniment by a female trio playing piano, violin, and cello, it must have been a tear-inducing treat, especially at the moment when the poet begins to worry about the fate of his pet dog after he's gone. He made such an impact that some of the club members started coming to Dillon's studio to watch him during the group training classes.

One night Gable and Dillon attended a performance of the stock company that employed Franz Dorfler. Afterward he introduced the two women. "Miss Dillon turned her nose up at me," Dorfler recalled. "I could tell she was in love with him. I didn't hate her, but she upstaged me that evening. And what was far worse, Billy did too. That was one lesson, upstaging, that he learned from her that he hadn't told me about."

By that summer Dillon had been based in Portland for over a year but was deeply in debt. Her devotion to William Gable may have been one reason. Other students felt neglected and quit. Portland didn't have enough stage work to support a year-round community of actors and such, so she finally decided to move on, taking her protégé with her.

Los Angeles seemed the only place to go. Besides being the capital of West Coast theatrical activity, it had become home to the motion picture industry. Between the two it offered unlimited employment opportunities.

Until she got resettled, Dillon decided that Billy should remain back in Portland. He'd quit his phone job, so she prevailed on Forest Taylor to give him a temporary berth in his stock company. That Franz Dorfler was a member of Taylor's troupe didn't worry Dillon. She knew that Billy would come running as soon as she whistled.

That took only two weeks, during which Billy worked with Dorfler onstage but seemed to be deliberately avoiding her otherwise. "Once or twice I accidentally ran into him backstage, and he looked through me like I wasn't there. I came close to telling him off, but instead I ran to my dressing room to stop from crying."

In the two plays in which he performed with Forest Taylor's company, he billed himself as W. C. Gable. Taylor might have been Dillon's friend, but he didn't trust her pupil's abilities and gave him only minor roles.

Appropriately made up, Gable played Chang Lee in the 1918 Broadway sizzler *East Is West* (heroine Ming Toy's forbidden love for an Occidental becomes acceptable when she turns out to be white!). In *Main Street,* based on Sinclair Lewis's esteemed novel about a small-town doctor and his wife, he portrayed a family friend.

Both plays were also currently making the rounds in movie versions: *East Is West* with Constance Talmadge, and *Main Street* with Monte Blue and Florence Vidor. But rather than diminishing the value of the plays to stock companies, such "filmizations" usually increased them. Lacking spoken dialogue and usually subject to stricter censorship than was live theater, the silent movie adaptations of plays were usually disappointments. Many people preferred to see the original work.

After his last performance in *Main Street,* Gable left Portland for Los Angeles. Swallowing her pride, Franz Dorfler decided to wish him luck. But when she went to his dressing room, he'd already packed his things and gone. It would be years before they met again. By then, Billy would be Clark Gable.

Josephine Dillon sent Billy fifty dollars toward the 950-mile trip south. An actor-friend with a car suggested that they drive down together, sharing expenses and taking turns behind the wheel. Billy accepted. As they were nearing Los Angeles, his companion lost control of the car, which skidded off the road and landed in a ditch. Except for some cuts and bruises, they were unhurt.

When Gable finally arrived at the hotel where Dillon was staying, he looked like he'd spent a week of combat duty in the trenches. After a much-needed shower and change of clothes, Dillon took him to supper at a cheap restaurant nearby. They talked until closing time, then returned to the hotel, where Dillon had booked him a separate room. Although they'd lived together in Portland, she thought that they should be more discreet now. Los Angeles had more than its share of snoops and gossips who could ruin reputations and careers.

By 1924 *Hollywood* had become a generic word for the American film industry, but an inaccurate one. The community of that name did have some movie studios, but there were just as many if not more in other areas of Los Angeles, including Lankershim, Burbank, Culver City, Beverly Hills/Westwood, and Edendale. The incorporated city of Hollywood had a bustling business district on Hollywood Boulevard and was also home to movie professionals, though not too many well-known names. Once they became established, they usually moved on to more posh and exclusive parts of Los Angeles.

Dillon rented a small bungalow in one of Hollywood's residential streets for twenty-four dollars per month. With furnishings borrowed from her family in Long Beach, she turned it into a professional studio, with living quarters at the rear and in the tiny attic. Advertising in trade papers, she started holding classes, but it would be some time before she attracted enough students to support herself, let alone W. C. Gable while he remained under her tutelage.

Since there was a very popular stage comedian and movie star named W. C. Fields, she advised Gable to drop the initials. However, Hollywood was already overflowing with Williams, so they settled on Clark after Dillon saw what she considered to be a good-luck omen on Hollywood Boulevard: crowds were always surging in and out of a bargain emporium called Clark's Dollar Store.

Until Dillon got established, Clark Gable supported himself by temping as a garage mechanic at gas stations and auto dealerships. It was dirty work, but it paid better than an office job. It also gave him a chance to indulge his love of cars as he learned the specifications of all the latest models.

Meanwhile Dillon used her college degree and stage experience to get a part-time job in the story department at Paramount–Famous Players–Lasky, the largest of the film studios that were actually located in Hollywood. Earning no more than a secretary, she read newly submitted scripts, then synopsized and evaluated them for executive distribution. She started making industry contacts who could send her students.

After several months of living separately, with Gable spending more than half his wages for hotel services, a merger became an economic necessity. He and Dillon were married in December 1924, eighteen months from their first meeting. He was pushing twenty-four. She gave her age as thirty-four, but she was actually forty-one.

One of Dillon's friends threw a party for the newlyweds. While Dillon stood chatting with guests in one room, she spotted her husband in the next, dancing with a beautifully dressed and bejeweled dowager. The woman's head rested on his shoulder as he whispered in her ear.

Dillon was furious but waited until they got home to explode. Gable just laughed: "The dame looked like she had lots of dough and connections. You can't blame me for playing up to her. She could be a help to both of us."

Gable and Dillon shared a bedroom that had been carved out of the bungalow's attic. Due to the slanted roof, it had only a small central space where he could stand without bumping his head on the ceiling. Whether there was one bed or two is unknown, as are details of their intimate relationship. Many years later Dillon would describe it as a marriage "in name only."

By the time they wed, Gable was ready to graduate from student to working actor. Whenever Dillon heard of an opportunity, whether in a stage play or a movie, she sent him to audition. Due to his lack of experience and credits, however, he usually couldn't get past the front desk.

Mainly by persistence he landed a few jobs as a movie extra. Exactly how many is unknown. The names of extras are never listed in movie credits unless the person performs something that stands out from the others. Identifying actors visually is usually impossible in silent films, since the vast majority of them no longer exist. They were left to disintegrate when the industry discovered sound and saw slight commercial reason to preserve an outmoded technology.

Gable always claimed that he made his debut as an extra in Ernst Lubitsch's *Forbidden Paradise;* it was one of the great films of its time and would be an impressive "first" credit for anyone involved. But just prior to that, he had played a bit part as star actress Alice Joyce's brother in *White Man,* directed by Louis Gasnier for B. P. Schulberg's independent company, Preferred Pictures.

Forbidden Paradise was the first dividend of Josephine's part-time job in Paramount's story department. As soon as she learned the starting date, she arranged for Gable to be hired as one of several hundred extras required for the crowd scenes. The sophisticated sex comedy about Catherine the Great was a showcase for the tempestuous European import Pola Negri, teamed with suave Adolphe Menjou and the super-handsome "Latin lover" Rod La Rocque. The studio spent $250,000 on indoor and exterior sets duplicating the magnificent Winter Palace in St. Petersburg.

Gable portrayed a soldier in the czarina's guard, but he never got a chance to actually meet Pola Negri. She'd become romantically involved with Rod La Rocque; between takes they usually relaxed together in her dressing bungalow.

Gable never again worked in one of the master director's films, but he learned the meaning of the so-called Lubitsch touch. In one crowd scene the czarina's finance minister, Adolphe Menjou, confronts a horde of revolutionaries. He reaches into his pocket, as if for a pistol, but draws out a checkbook, which effectively quells the uprising.

For his stint as an extra, Gable earned $7.50 per day, plus free lunches. Apart from the chance it offered to learn how movies were made, he hated it, since he was really just part of the background scenery. "They gave me a uniform to wear, a very hot uniform," he once recalled. "They also gave me a sword. Then they told me to stand in a certain place. And I stood. Is that acting? It was more like perspiring. I'd lost a couple of pounds by the time I finished."

Still, he continued to seek work even as an extra. With a Lubitsch credit, plus his ability to fill a military uniform to perfection, Gable passed the extras call for *The Merry Widow,* being directed by Erich von Stroheim for the new corporate entity Metro-Goldwyn-Mayer. The silver screen's silence necessitated a nonmusical version, but highlights of Franz Lehár's score would be played as background music when theaters ran the film.

Stroheim discarded most of the operetta's libretto and created a near sex romp for the two stars, John Gilbert and Mae Murray. Gilbert was then one of Hollywood's hottest stars and MGM's top male. Who could have known that one of the extras in *The Merry Widow* would replace him in not too many years?

The director was a possibly insane genius who thrived on being difficult with everybody. During the filming Stroheim's excesses drove MGM's "boy wonder" production chief, Irving Thalberg, to fire him, but when the two stars refused to work with another director, he reinstated him. Due to all the problems and delays, Gable got three more weeks of work than he'd expected. The twenty-six-year-old Thalberg, who had a history of cardiac problems, ended up with a heart attack and spent a month in the hospital.

After *The Merry Widow,* Gable did extra work in *The Pacemakers,* a series of two-reel comedies produced by F.B.O. Pictures, an important studio that eventually got folded into the sound era's RKO Radio Pictures. Gable also acted some bit roles in the twelve shorts, which were released at the rate of one every two weeks from March to September 1925. Most had wacky titles inspired by well-known plays and movies, such as *He Who Gets Rapped, Merton of the Goofies, The Covered Flagon, Three Bases East,* and *What Price Gloria?*

In between Gable's film jobs, Dillon kept sending him to audition for stage plays. One day she arranged a meeting with producer Louis

MacLoon and his director-wife, Lillian Albertson, who were casting minor nonspeaking parts for a West Coast tour of Shakespeare's *Romeo and Juliet*. Acting the title roles would be two of America's greatest stage stars, Jane Cowl and Rollo Peters. They had triumphed in the classic on Broadway in 1923 and had since teamed in hit productions of Maurice Maeterlinck's *Pelleas and Melisande* and Shakespeare's *Antony and Cleopatra*.

Jane Cowl, who at forty might have been stretching it a bit in portraying the teenage Juliet Capulet, was rehearsing onstage with the director when Gable arrived at the theater. Lillian Albertson spotted him walking down the center aisle toward them. "This big, awkward boy inquired for me," she recalled. "Jane and I were struck simultaneously by his height—which was one of the qualifications for the extras needed as soldiers. Jane said, 'He'll do. He looks like he has something.' I agreed. He was terribly thin, but he had a rugged combination of physique and personality that was arresting."

The twenty-four-year-old "boy" got the job, which paid thirty dollars a week for impersonating a spear-carrying guard. Legend has it that Jane Cowl had sexual designs on Gable and that he happily obliged her. Maybe—Cowl did insist on hiring Gable for the entire West Coast tour, which was almost unheard of for an extra. Extras were usually hired locally, city by city, to save paying for their travel and living expenses.

For Gable, the throaty-voiced Jane Cowl would have been quite a conquest. In a 1924 poll of drama critics, she was voted "the most beautiful woman on the American stage." Since her debut in 1912, she'd been the inspiration for a generation of stagestruck women. Besides Juliet, which she performed more times than any other American, she was most admired for *Smilin' Through,* a romantic tearjerker that she coauthored and that became one of the most popular and revived plays of the 1920s.

After the Los Angeles run of *Romeo and Juliet,* the tour continued to San Francisco, Portland, Seattle, and Vancouver. Gable's wife, of course, had her own work and stayed behind, their first separation since they married. But since Dillon had been an actress herself, she must have realized that that would often happen if he found steady employment in the theater.

Close friends of Jane Cowl (who died in 1950 at age sixty-three) doubted that she had an affair with Gable. They claimed that she was very happily married at the time to producer Adolph Klauber, a former drama editor and *New York Times* critic. Klauber had, in fact, resigned those posts by the time he fell in love with Cowl, deciding it would be a conflict of interest. Even more preposterous, according to Cowl's friends, is the story that during the tour she promoted Gable to the plum role of Mercutio. Her friends believed that Cowl was too great a star, and too aware of her glorious reputation, to risk ridicule by giving one of the most eloquent parts in Shakespeare to a novice.

Cowl returned to New York at the tour's end. Back in Los Angeles, Gable auditioned for the MacLoons' next road company, *What Price Glory?*, the 1914–18 War drama by Maxwell Anderson and Laurence Stallings that created a sensation on Broadway in 1924 with its profanity, brutality, and cynicism. Still playing to packed houses in New York, the play's rave reviews and publicity had made household names of the lead characters, Captain Flagg and Sergeant Quirt. The hard-bitten career soldiers are always feuding and chasing after the same French floozie, named Charmaine.

Gable auditioned for the supporting role of Private Kiper, an army roughneck. Director Lillian Albertson listened to his high-pitched voice and rejected him. "It wasn't quite heavy enough to match his general makeup. He looked the hardy, virile type, but he sounded like a pansy when he read the tough and salty dialogue," she recalled.

Gable must have rushed to the nearest phone booth. Albertson soon received a call from Josephine Dillon, who pleaded with her to reconsider. A former actress herself, Albertson had known Dillon for years and respected her. Dillon told her that if the two of them worked together with Gable, they should be able to train the voice down to an acceptable macho level. They succeeded, and he got the job.

What Price Glory? proved such a hit for the MacLoons that theater owners demanded a repeat tour several months later. One of the stars, Hale Hamilton, was unable to continue as Sergeant Quirt, so Lillian Anderson decided to give Gable a chance. The play's opening was too recent for newspaper critics to review it a second time. If Gable's performance wasn't as good as Hamilton's, there would be no negative reviews to dent attendance.

While waiting for the second tour to begin, Gable did some more work as a movie extra. During the filming of the *Pacemakers* comedy shorts, he became chummy with their director, Wesley Ruggles, who'd since moved on to B. P. Schulberg Productions and was about to start *The Plastic Age* with the up-and-coming jazz baby Clara Bow. Ruggles needed some muscular hunks to portray college athletes.

Gable hoped it would be the big break he'd been waiting for. One scene takes place in a locker room packed with young jocks in varying degrees of dress and undress: clad only in tennis shorts, Gable sits stretched out on a bench and mimes some wisecracking with the film's lead actors, Gilbert Roland and Donald Keith. But otherwise he wound up in the backgrounds.

Gable also did a bit in the independent Associated Exhibitors release *North Star*. The thriller provided a showcase for canine star Strongheart, the top challenger to box-office champion Rin Tin Tin. In a party scene Gable plays the piano while Strongheart, half-standing with his front paws on the bench, barks along. For the sensitive ear, it was one of the blessings of silent movies!

But *North Star* turned out to be Gable's last film for years. For the two tours of *What Price Glory?* he got fifteen weeks of work and was earning eighty-five dollars per by the end. Dillon thought that he should concentrate on the stage, get as much experience as he could, and prepare himself for an invasion of the ultimate beachhead—the Broadway big time.

Meanwhile the West Coast stage circuit was the next best thing. In Los Angeles there was always the chance that some studio scout or executive would attend a performance and spot something in Clark Gable that hadn't been evident in the movie extra. The same held true for other cities, though the spotters were more likely to be managers of resident stock companies who hired actors for entire seasons. The top companies paid good money and also offered more security; their actors were never out of work, going from one play to another for a considerable period of time (usually eight to ten months).

Stage acting also gave Gable more personal freedom, which was undoubtedly one of its appeals for him. He had less time to spend with his wife, not only when he was touring but even in Los Angeles. By necessity stage actors worked nights as well as two or three matinees per week. In between they rehearsed at the theater or went on auditions.

By this time Gable had gone about as far as he could with Josephine Dillon in terms of their teacher-pupil relationship. He'd learned the basics of acting and stage technique. It was now up to him to put them to use. She couldn't do much more than to help him to find work and to be his severest critic. When directors permitted her to attend rehearsals, she took copious notes and later drilled him on his deficiencies. On opening nights she always occupied a front-row seat. At intermissions she would rush to his dressing room with advice and suggestions.

Not surprisingly, Dillon's meddling, though well intended, caused Gable embarrassment. He became very sensitive about the seventeen-year age gap, which made him seem like an overgrown mama's boy. When they socialized, Dillon was very possessive and snubbed every woman who came near them. Observers wondered about the Gables' sexual relationship, if they even had one.

After *What Price Glory?* Gable stumbled into one of the longest personal friendships of his life, when the MacLoons hired him for a supporting part in a tour of Augustus Thomas's *The Copperhead* with its original Broadway star, Lionel Barrymore. The 1918 melodrama about an elderly Yankee accused of spying for the Confederacy in the Civil War had, in fact, made an overnight star of Barrymore, raising him to the elite level previously reached by his younger siblings, Ethel and John. As the senior of the three, Lionel had the most trouble finding suitable vehicles, so he often hit the road with *The Copperhead* during career lulls.

Barrymore also directed his plays, which threw fear into Gable. "Lionel wasn't too keen on me," he later confessed. "He considered me an unskilled amateur. He bawled me out during rehearsals like I'd never been bawled out before or since. On opening night I had an accident onstage and dropped my straw hat into what was supposed to be a deep well. Instead of leaving it there, I reached in and plucked it out. And the audience howled—right in the middle of a serious scene. I was surprised he didn't fire me right then and there."

Gable learned from the forty-seven-year-old star, especially from watching him in the play's final scene, which many critics who'd seen it regarded as one of the most memorable in American stage history. To answer his persecutors, Barrymore pulls out a letter that he's kept secret for many years and reads it aloud. Written by Abraham Lincoln, it not only exonerates him as a traitor but salutes him as a patriot. Barrymore exhibited such feeling and technical mastery that he always received standing ovations at the curtain calls (then a practice reserved for the extraordinary and not today's almost automatic response).

Although Lionel Barrymore had been acting in movies since the pioneer era of Biograph Studios and D. W. Griffith two-reelers, he preferred the stage and urged Gable to make it his career. When next they met, Gable would still be struggling toward that goal, and Barrymore would be a major screen star.

After *The Copperhead* Gable got more than he bargained for when he auditioned for a supporting role in *Madame X,* a phenomenally popular French play by Alexandre Bisson that made frequent West Coast tours. It was first staged on Broadway in 1918 with Dorothy Donnelly in the title role. But since 1920 it had become permanently identified with Pauline Frederick, who starred in a blockbuster movie version and later appropriated it for the stage when her screen career waned.

For her 1926 tour for the MacLoons, Frederick had the right to select the supporting cast. When Gable arrived to audition, he was wearing a gray suit that had started to yellow from too many dry cleanings. His reading of the role of the public prosecutor was no more than adequate, but he seemed earnest and in need of work, so she hired him. By the end of the tour, they were passionate lovers.

With a career divided between the stage and silent movies (the majority of them now "lost"), Pauline Frederick is almost forgotten today, but she was one of the most famous women of her time. Critic Harrison Fisher called her "the embodiment of intellectual beauty and physical perfection." She had hypnotic blue velvet eyes and long chestnut hair that she brushed back from her face to emphasize her wide forehead. Though she stood only five foot four, she had an aura of grandeur, with beautifully formed shoulders and perfect carriage. Many fans went expressly to watch her unique bow-taking. She bent low from the waist, as her hair swept down over the top of her head, then flew back into place as she straightened up and beamed at the audience.

Eighteen years older than Gable, Frederick had started as a chorus girl in Broadway musicals in 1902, but she quickly moved on to dramatic stardom, most notably in the 1913 biblical spectacle *Joseph and His*

Brethren. In 1915 she made her movie debut in Adolph Zukor's *The Eternal City,* which was such a hit that he signed her to a three-year $750,000 contract with his Famous Players company. During that span she made twenty-eight features and vied with Mary Pickford as the studio's top female. When her contract with Zukor came up for renewal, she became a bit greedy and accepted a more lucrative offer from Samuel Goldwyn's company. Unfortunately, all of her Goldwyn films except *Madame X* flopped. In 1923 she resumed her stage career, though she still made an occasional movie. Luckily, she'd invested wisely and could continue her lavish, bicoastal lifestyle, which included a mansion on Sunset Boulevard and a town house in New York City.

Besides inspiring countless imitations, *Madame X* has been staged and filmed umpteen times over the decades. The tearjerker centers on a so-called fallen woman whose husband disowns her and raises their young son to believe that she is dead. Years later the son, now a lawyer, has to defend the woman in a murder trial, unaware, of course, that she's his mother.

Gable played the role of the prosecuting attorney, wearing a fake beard for an older look. Since he didn't appear until the last act, he did double duty in the star's dressing room. "Miss Frederick is always complaining about her back. She likes me to rub it for her," he told a stage hand.

By the time she became involved with Gable, Frederick had been thrice married and divorced. She still carried a torch for husband number two, actor-playwright Willard Mack, but he was an incurable boozer and drug addict who'd almost taken her down the same path. No doubt her own philandering contributed to the divorces. She was a reputed nymphomaniac, though in those days they were more delicately described as "female Casanovas."

Frederick introduced Gable to the glamorous Hollywood lifestyle that he'd previously seen only in magazines. He'd never visited a star's home. He played on her tennis court and swam in her pool. They apparently spent much of their time in bed. "That woman acts like she never expected to see another man," Gable told a friend.

Gable and Pauline Frederick were involved for about two years, but not straight through. Whenever she did a West Coast tour, she found a role for him but never the lead. Though she may have found Gable a satisfactory lover, she still thought he had much to learn about acting, so she placed him where he could cause the fewest problems.

After *Madame X* he played the manager of a speakeasy in Sidney Howard's *Lucky Sam McCarver,* in which Frederick teamed with actor-director John Cromwell, the drama's original Broadway star. In Martin Brown's *The Lady,* Gable portrayed a bartender in the story of a widowed nightclub owner who tries to support a child and stay respectable at the same time.

In their private moments Gable called Frederick by her nickname, Polly. Whenever they ran into each other in later years, Gable would always drop to one knee and kiss her hand. Some of his gratitude may have been for Frederick's contributions to his ongoing attempts to salvage his rotting teeth. She allegedly paid the bills for some root canal work and gold inlays around prominent front teeth. To conceal the glint of the gold, Gable's dentist gave him a white enamel that he could paint on and reapply whenever it started to fade.

Gable's unattractive teeth were undoubtedly one of the reasons he'd never progressed beyond the ranks of background extra in movies. On the stage there were no close-ups except for the actors he worked with. Even people sitting in the front-row seats were unlikely to see a player's teeth unless they were watching through binoculars.

Gable's affair with Pauline Frederick quickly came to the attention of his wife. Dillon seemed remarkably tolerant, even continuing to do his laundry when he came home with bags of it after out-of-town tours. Gable's conscience eventually got the best of him, and he moved out. Dillon held on, guessing that he'd soon return. She was still shepherding his career, the only real manager that he had.

Gable checked into a cheap residential hotel that catered to touring stage actors and vaudevillians. By this time he'd become friends with two other struggling actors, Paul Fix and Stuart Erwin. "We used to bum around together," Fix remembered. "Clark had an old automobile that he was real proud of—an open-top Roamer. It was designed after the Rolls-Royce. He'd drive us out to Griffith Park, where they'd put in a public golf course. I owned a putter and Clark had an iron. We'd look around the roughs for stray balls, then play golf all day with the two clubs."

Since Roamers were manufactured by Duesenberg and were among the most expensive cars on the road, it's a mystery how Gable could afford to buy even a used one. But perhaps it was another instance of Pauline Frederick's generosity.

One of Gable's non-Frederick stage tours was in Edward Knoblock's *The Lullaby,* with pioneer film star Mabel Julienne Scott attempting a comeback in the leading role. Later filmed under the title of *The Sin of Madelon Claudet,* the tearjerker about an unwed mother was too close a copy of *Madame X* for Pauline Frederick to add it to her repertoire.

During the play's run in San Francisco, Gable had a reunion with his ex-fiancée, Franz Dorfler, after discovering that she'd opened a dance school in a building opposite the theater where he was working. He phoned to offer a free ticket and to make a supper date for after the show. Dorfler thought it might rekindle their romance, but he seemed mainly interested in her professional opinion.

"He asked me what I thought about his performance," she remembered. "I told him that he still seemed to lack polish, but that Miss Dillon had helped him enormously. He agreed but mentioned nothing about their marriage. He must have assumed that I knew about it."

After that Gable dated Dorfler whenever a tour brought him to San Francisco. "He always appeared glad to be with me," she said. "We'd kiss goodnight but didn't get more involved, even though he remained the love of my life. He still looked a bit underfed and haggard, but the dental work he had had done had improved his looks considerably. And he was slowly improving as an actor."

Drama critics finally started to take notice of Clark Gable in the spring of 1927, when he worked in the first West Coast road company of the recent Broadway hit *Chicago,* a bawdy courtroom satire about a gum-chewing mankiller named Roxie Hart. Author Maurine Watkins hated profanity, so she left many blanks in her script, leaving them to be filled in by the original director, George Abbott, in consultation with the actors.

Through the intervention of her husband, noted playwright Jack Kirkland, red-haired Nancy Carroll got the leading role (originated by Francine Larrimore) in the West Coast tour. The Kirklands had recently moved to Los Angeles so that Jack could write movie scripts. A showgirl in Broadway revues before quitting to have a baby, Carroll was raring to get back into action.

Thanks to the continuing support of producer-director Lillian Albertson MacLoon, whose devotion seemed almost as intense as Josephine Dillon's, Gable got a major supporting role. His character, Jake, is a cynical reporter covering Roxie's trial, in which she is accused of shooting her gangster-lover while he was buttoning his trousers after sex.

Nancy Carroll's performance as Roxie earned her a movie contract with Paramount Pictures, which quickly turned her into a star with the title role in the film of another Broadway smash, *Abie's Irish Rose*. Gable had no such luck, but he garnered some excellent reviews for his scrapbook.

Idwal Jones, drama critic for the *San Francisco Examiner,* raved that Gable gave "the only three-dimensional portrayal of a newspaperman that has ever been witnessed on the stage in San Francisco. He may not be a Henry Irving [a noted English Shakespearean actor who made many American tours], but his achievement is glory enough. His is the only stage reporter who manages to get the effect without looking like a crimp, pestering everybody with questions and plying pad and notebook with such frenzied *cacoethes scribendi* that he has to have his shoulder massaged after the act to evade writer's cramp."

During the San Francisco run at the Lurie Theater, a scout for a prominent stock company in Houston, Texas, saw one of Gable's performances and offered him a full season's contract, running from the autumn of 1927 through the spring of 1928. The salary was a guaranteed $150 weekly, with the roles changing as often as the plays—once a week.

At the same time Gable was also mulling an offer from a booking agency that handled tours of early movie stars who were fading in popularity but still had enough name value for the vaudeville circuits. If he accepted, he would act opposite Dorothy Dalton, one of the original sexpots known as vampires, in a twenty-minute dramatic sketch. Hopefully it would occupy the coveted next-to-closing spot on the customary eight-act vaudeville bills of the time.

If it had been up to Gable, he would have accepted the Dalton offer, which paid two hundred dollars per week and could wind up with a booking at the world-famous Palace Theater on Broadway. But Josephine Dillon was appalled. She thought it would be a total waste of more than three years of dramatic training. No doubt she also saw no positive influence in Dalton, who wasn't much of an actress and had a promiscuous reputation.

Dillon later confessed, "I thought my husband needed experience with a good stock company. I forced him to go to Texas by phoning Miss Dalton and lying to her that he'd signed with somebody else. I don't think Clark ever forgave me that."

The 1927–28 theatrical season was a peak time for stock companies in the United States, with 413 operating on the far-flung stages of all forty-eight states. According to Actors Equity, the average number of union members in each stock company was ten, so at least 4,130 actors were steadily employed in that sector of the stage industry alone. Thousands more were employed in Broadway productions and in traveling companies of current or recent Broadway attractions. Not to be confused with a road company, which traveled around to different theaters performing the same play all the time, a *stock* company was a resident group that put on a different play every week or sometimes a series of them in repertory.

Besides being a boon to actors, stock benefited writers because of its insatiable need for material. Many plays that flopped on Broadway got a second chance in stock companies and sometimes proved popular. Playwrights, including the most successful ones, often earned more from stock productions than from the original productions of their works.

Houston being rich in oil millionaires, bankers, and financiers, Clark Gable had landed in a city where much of its 165,000 population loved and supported the arts. Based at the 950-seat Palace Theater, the Laskin Brothers Stock Company was regarded as one of the finest in the southwestern United States. Managing director Gene Lewis strived for a blend of classics with more commercial dramas, comedies, and musicals. To compete against Houston's thirty-two movie theaters, admission prices were kept low, no higher than 75 cents at matinees and $1.10 at night.

When Gable first arrived, Gene Lewis restricted him to minor roles until he got adjusted to the acoustics of the theater, which had two balconies and were a challenge to his vocal cords. Newspaper critics took some swipes at his first efforts, but by the time of Gable's first leading role, as the abused husband of a domineering bitch in George Kelly's Pulitzer prize-winner *Craig's Wife,* he made a strong impression.

"In appearance he is admirably cast. His voice, which in times past has been too high-pitched and strained in moments of tenseness, was held in well-bred restraint, and with the exception of a few lapses did not fall into the unpleasant harshness that has sometimes marred his readings. He has a charming stage personality," said the critic for the *Houston Press.*

In another Pulitzer prize-winning drama, Eugene O'Neill's *Anna Christie,* Gable played the Irish seaman who loves her but is unaware of her past as a prostitute. In the title role company tragedian Eveta Nudsen won standing ovations at every performance. Gable had to be content with a rave opening-night review that said, "He took the spotlight early in the play and, through the character's ready wit and wisdom, kept the audience in an uproar from the opening scene to the final curtain."

Proving his versatility, Gable sang and danced in *The Gingham Girl,* a "musical comedy of sweetness" with a score by Albert von Tilzer and Neville Fleeson. Portraying a country bumpkin adrift in the big city, Gable stole the show with his snappy wisecracks and outrageous costume. He wore a loud black-and-white-checked suit that was deliberately designed to be several sizes too small for him.

In *The Noose,* written by Pauline Frederick's ex-husband Willard Mack, Gable played a murderous gangster. In Leon Gordon's *White Cargo,* a sex sizzler that was one of the most performed plays in the history of the American theater, he became the umpteenth jungle plantation owner to be seduced by the gorgeous half-caste known as Tondeleyo. In *Is Zat So?* he played a punch-drunk boxer who teams up with his equally dim-witted manager to work as servants in a Fifth Avenue mansion.

As his wife had predicted, stock gave Gable the acting experience that he still needed and also helped him become more disciplined. Besides acting ten performances per week, he attended daily rehearsals of the next play on his agenda. He had to store two roles in his memory at the same time and make sure that he didn't mix them up when he went onstage.

On Monday nights, usually the least attended performance of the week, the Palace Theater held autograph parties in honor of one or another of the stock company actors. Everyone purchasing a ticket that night received a signed photograph of the honoree. By the time Gable's first turn came around, he'd acquired so many fans that the theater ran out of photos and had to dole out rain checks. For the rest of the season, Mondays were exclusively "Clark Gable Nights," with females composing about 75 percent of the audiences.

They could sometimes be heard swooning during romances like Michael Arlen's *The Green Hat* and especially Guy Bolton's *The Dark Angel,* which was Gable's greatest success in Houston. As Hilary Trent, a British flying ace in the 1914–18 War, he captured the accent and manner perfectly. In the second act he also had some challenging moments after Trent is permanently blinded in combat. On first reunion with an adoring wife who hasn't been informed, he tries pretending that he can still see.

Gable's association with the Laskin Company turned him into the matinee idol of Houston, partly because of his stage performances and partly by sheer luck. Except for stars who passed through town briefly with a road company or vaudeville unit, Houston had few resident celebrities beyond the Palace stock company and "voices" working for the local radio station. Every season the female populace seemed to get hooked on one particular Laskin actor or another until he inevitably moved on to greener pastures than Houston could provide.

Conceivably a matinee idol could be an actress, but the term was applied only to men, which is probably why it rankles modern feminists. It dates back to an era when the majority of women were homemakers who had more leisure time than men and who liked to go out during the day to a play or movie. Matinee audiences, especially midweek when men were at their jobs and children were in school, tended to be about 90 percent female, so producers and theater owners used them to measure an actor's popularity. When an actor proved that he could draw large crowds of women, he was considered a matinee idol. Rightly or wrongly, this practice was based on the assumption that women were interested in only one thing—men. So *matinee idol* also came to signify an actor with exceptional sex appeal. To have that, he usually had to be handsome, romantic, and not a boy, but not too blemished by age either.

Clark Gable, who turned twenty-seven in the midst of his Houston contract, had all the "idol" qualifications. Teenage girls started hanging around the stage door to spy on him. Women's clubs feted him at luncheons. An amateur theater group persuaded him to direct a production of *Marry Me,* which suggests some wishful thinking by some of the members.

One of Gable's most ardent fans was forty-four-year-old Maria Langham, a wealthy divorcée with three children. How they first met is unknown, but it may have happened even before his arrival in Houston. Langham was a frequent traveler to the West Coast, where she had many friends in Los Angeles and San Francisco. She could have seen Gable in some plays and fallen for him, but that is only speculation. Legend also has it that Langham pulled strings to get Gable to Houston, that she invested money in the Laskin stock company to make sure that he got lead roles, and that she expected stud service in return. Only the latter has some truth to it.

Known to her intimates as Ria, she was born in Kentucky as Maria Franklin, allegedly to a penniless family. At age seventeen, in the year of Clark Gable's birth, she married William Prentiss, an Illinois businessman, with whom she lived for four years and had a son. When they divorced, she took the boy to Houston, where they stayed with relatives while she held day jobs and attended night school to learn bookkeeping. She eventually became manager of a jewelry store, which in a wealthy city like Houston was an ideal place to meet "sugar daddies." She discarded a flock of suitors before marrying building contractor Alfred Lucas, a widower twenty-two years her senior. They produced a daughter and son before Lucas died in 1922 at age sixty. Except for bequests to the two grown children of his first marriage, Ria inherited the Lucas fortune, which was believed in the millions. For more than thirty years, he had supplied most of the bricks and other materials that were needed for Houston's building projects.

In 1925 Ria Lucas married the socially prominent Denzil Langham, but they divorced two years later, citing incompatibility as the cause. She emerged with her inherited fortune intact, plus an additional bundle in the divorce settlement.

What attracted Gable to Ria Langham, apart from her money, is impossible to know. But if he was seeking a mother substitute, she qualified on most counts. She did, however, seem a mismatch for such a giant, standing only five foot two and starting to show signs of middle-age spread. She had a doll-like face with expressive eyes and a porcelain complexion. Probably a beauty in her youth, she now looked matronly, no matter how hard she tried to hide it with expensive clothes, modish hairdos, and makeup tricks.

The affair was conducted very privately. Langham had her social position and three children to consider. If she and Gable were seen together in public at all, it was during chance encounters at social gatherings or at a country club where both often played golf with their friends.

Actor cronies who lived in a cheap hotel for theatricals wondered how Gable could afford a furnished apartment in one of Houston's best buildings. They noticed a rapid improvement in his personal wardrobe—his faded suits were replaced by new ones from the city's best tailors. He bought the latest Ford sports roadster and had it painted and trimmed to his own specifications.

Ria Langham seemed to have taken over where Josephine Dillon left off in the transformation of Clark Gable. Dillon's raw material was now being polished into a gentleman.

His wife, however, was still very much in the picture. She made several trips to Houston to catch his performances. After seeing his exceptional work as the blinded aviator in *The Dark Angel*, she decided that he'd reached Broadway standards and that they should move to New York at the end of his Houston contract.

Gable was thrilled by the prospect, but not by the thought of living with Dillon again, which would be a financial necessity while they got settled. He and Ria Langham had already done some pillow talk about his future. She was prepared to move to New York and be his "sponsor," provided that they married as soon as he could obtain a divorce.

Dillon exploded when Gable revealed this plan. No way would she divorce him now that her promise to make him a star seemed so near fulfillment. She left Houston in a rage. Returning to Los Angeles, she gave her students two weeks' notice and proceeded to shut down her studio. She then entrained to New York to investigate the new 1928–29 theatrical season that would be starting in September.

Meanwhile Gable took the attitude that if Josephine Dillon was so determined to find him work, he certainly wasn't going to stop her. She knew quite a few Broadway agents, producers, and directors. She also persuaded Gable's former employers, Louis MacLoon and Lillian Albertson, to send letters and telegrams to their many contacts.

In the summer of 1928 the whole stage industry, including what *Variety* called "legit" and "vaude," was anticipating fallout from the new medium of sound movies. But not enough "talkies" had been released to cause any significant drop in attendance for live presentations.

The first talkie feature, *The Jazz Singer,* released in October 1927, was a bit of a tease, containing as it did background music and sound effects but only one brief scene with spoken dialogue. Not until July 1928 did the first 100 percent talkie come along: *Lights of New York.* So far a mere 6 percent of America's 20,500 movie theaters had been wired for sound, the majority of them in cosmopolitan areas. Most rural residents had yet to hear what all the excitement was about.

The ten-month Broadway stage season that ended in May 1928 had seen a total of 264 productions, including 183 straight plays, 53 musicals, and 28 revivals. It was an all-time-high activity record that has never been surpassed. Josephine Dillon's chances of finding work for her husband couldn't have been better. The 1928–29 season promised to be equally productive: more than two hundred projects were on the drawing boards when she arrived from California.

Ironically, Earle Larimore, Gable's ex-cohort from Portland, had recently become a star as one of the four leads in Eugene O'Neill's *Strange Interlude,* the nine-act marathon that had just won a Pulitzer Prize. That gave Dillon an incentive to find something equally prestigious for her husband who, to her mind at least, could act rings around Larimore.

She found it sooner than expected in *Machinal,* an avant-garde drama being readied for a September opening. After Gable finished with the Houston stock company, he had lingered on to be with Ria Langham, but when Dillon summoned him by telephone, he grabbed the first train east. By the time he arrived in New York, she'd persuaded agent Chamberlain Brown to represent him. An audition had been arranged with the play's producer-director.

Arthur Hopkins was one of the theater's most respected impresarios, known as "the Sphinx of Broadway" because he spoke little but always concisely. From his office above the Plymouth Theater, where he staged many of his productions, he had been responsible for such notable plays as *Anna Christie, What Price Glory?, Burlesque, The Hairy Ape,* and John Barrymore's legendary *Hamlet.*

Gable couldn't have landed in better hands for his Broadway debut. Hopkins always encouraged newcomers and gave such currently popular stage actors as Humphrey Bogart, Spencer Tracy, Edward G. Robinson, and Barbara Stanwyck their starts. He'd also just hired a gangling red-head named Katharine Hepburn for a minor role in another of his upcoming plays, *These Days.*

Hopkins liked Gable immediately and hired him to play one of the top supporting roles in *Machinal,* a stark drama written by Sophie Treadwell, a leading feminist of the time. The two-act, ten-scene play was loosely based on the sensational murder trial of Ruth Snyder and her lover, Judd Gray. After both were found guilty of killing Snyder's husband, they were executed at Sing Sing in January 1928. While Snyder was being electrocuted, a reporter with a hidden camera snapped a photograph that, when published on tabloid front pages the next day, horrified the nation.

Sophie Treadwell borrowed elements from the case for her play, but she wrote a different story that focused on the woman and blamed machine-dominated society for corrupting and destroying her. She used terse, staccato dialogue and gave all the characters only generic names like "The Woman" and "The Young Man." Her suggestions for gloomy, impressionistic sets were carried out by the great designer Robert Edmond Jones, another of Arthur Hopkins's many discoveries.

The producer-director had selected twenty-four-year-old Zita Johann, a protégée of Alfred Lunt and Lynn Fontanne, for the leading role. When Hopkins told her that he'd signed Clark Gable to play the lover who drives her to murder, she was disappointed because she'd been expecting an established name. Hopkins admitted that Gable was a "Woolworth Romeo" whom he hired cheap for a bottom-line two hundred dollars per week, but he predicted that he'd go the distance.

Gable's contract specified that if he proved unsatisfactory, he could be fired after five days of rehearsals.

After a brief tryout at the Shubert Theater in New Haven, Connecticut, *Machinal* opened in New York at the Plymouth on September 7, 1928. Gable later described his jitters: "I panicked, but dear old

Hopkins told me to forget the house was full of people and to play it the way we rehearsed it. He was quiet and relaxed, said he'd be sitting in the back of the auditorium where he always did. I felt better, but I was anxious just the same. I'd heard how the New York critics could make or break an actor. I wanted to see exactly what they would do to me."

He had no reason to complain the next day. "Clark Gable played the casual, good-humored lover without a hackneyed gesture," said *The New York Times*. "He's young, vigorous and brutally masculine," said the *Morning Telegraph*. However, critics were more excited by Zita Johann and by Sophie Treadwell's writing, which the *Herald-Tribune* described as "stunningly effective."

Zita Johann, who'd been skeptical about Gable's ability when she first met him, recalled years later that "he was very good in the part. He gave me complete support. He didn't have ups and downs. He knew his lines and didn't make mistakes." She once barged into his dressing room and found him sitting in front of the mirror, covering up his gold dental inlays with white paint.

Born in Hungary, Johann had come to New York at age seven with her family and had done enough acting in high school plays to qualify for an apprenticeship with the Theater Guild, where she caught the attention of the Lunts. She wasn't beautiful, but she had charismatic eyes, a seductive voice, and a good figure. Gable tried to get friendly, not knowing that she was already involved with actor-writer John Houseman, whom she eventually married.

"Clark was an actor with impact, but he had none for me personally," Johann said. "We were on good terms. I liked him. Sometimes he walked me home, but to the door only. I didn't even go out to supper with him. But he was genial, affable, lovable. Perhaps *bemused* would be the best word for him. He was bemused."

Josephine Dillon, who'd worked so long and diligently to plant her husband on the Broadway stage, missed his opening night. She tried crashing one of his rehearsals but was ordered to leave by a Hopkins flunky. Gable exploded. "He phoned me to keep out out of his life, said he was through with me," Dillon remembered. "I told him that I was going back to California and that he'd better become the best actor he could, because he could never be a man."

His wife's departure coincided with the arrival from Houston of

Ria Langham, who rented an apartment on the Upper East Side and enrolled her two oldest children in suburban boarding schools. The youngest would live with her and attend a private day school.

Langham almost missed seeing Gable in *Machinal,* which lasted only ninety-three performances. Despite excellent reviews, the play was apparently too grim and offbeat for the average playgoer. Arthur Hopkins was forced to close it at the end of November to avoid the box-office doldrums that always set in between the Thanksgiving and Christmas holidays.

Gable's excellent reviews helped agent Chamberlain Brown to quickly land him another job, but it turned out so disastrous that Gable tried to wipe it from his credits, and it has never been reported until now. The play was *House Unguarded,* a murder mystery that strived to be different by giving three accounts of the same killing before the truth is revealed in the final act. Actor-director Lester Lonergan, a longtime matinee idol now getting on in years, had the lead. As the commander of a military base in the Panama Canal Zone, his character also happens to be the murder victim.

Gable played a naval lieutenant who is having an affair with the commander's considerably younger wife. Dressed throughout in a snazzy white uniform, Gable had plenty of opportunities to upstage Lester Lonergan, who was, after all, the star. In his dual capacity as director, Lonergan gave Gable a hard time during rehearsals and kept threatening to fire him from the $250-per-week assignment.

In the custom of those times, *House Unguarded* was booked for a short break-in tour prior to its Broadway opening. The first stop was a three-day stand at the New Rochelle Theater in that Westchester city, beginning December 13, 1928. On the last night Lonergan dismissed Gable for incompetence and replaced him with John Marston, another actor in the cast. The play finally arrived on Broadway on January 15, 1929, at the Little Theater, but it received bland reviews and lasted only five weeks.

Gable lost only about $1,750 in potential salary, but the blow to his ego was considerable. The Broadway stage industry was so small and self-contained that gossip always spread quickly. The firing might not have been his fault, but it could still raise doubts about his talent among casting agents and producers.

The year 1929 would be nearly half over before Gable found further employment. Meanwhile Ria Langham took care of his financial needs. For the sake of appearances, he stayed at a residential hotel in the theater district, but he spent most of his time at Langham's apartment on East Eighty-first Street, off Park Avenue.

They wanted to marry, but his wife, of course, was an impediment. Langham asked her own attorney to help Gable get one of those quickie Mexican divorces that were then popular in wealthy circles. After all the necessary documents were obtained, Gable traveled to Los Angeles by train to coax Dillon into signing her portions.

Not surprisingly, she refused. Gable's round trip, in deluxe compartments on the Twentieth Century Limited and Santa Fe Chief, was a waste of Langham's money.

Dillon later claimed that she had withheld her signature only because of her mistrust of the Mexican legal system. After Gable returned to New York, she realized that no reconciliation was possible and decided to file for divorce her way, under California law. Charging desertion, she was granted an interlocutory decree, which meant that neither Dillon nor Gable was free to marry again until the divorce became final one year later.

Ria Langham was furious, but her liaison with Gable endured. Under her guidance he'd developed into a suave New Yorker and displayed no traces of his hobo past. He had a closet full of Brooks Brothers suits and formal wear. On social evenings he always wore a tuxedo or tails. He favored derby hats and carried a cane.

His mistress introduced him to the best restaurants and the smartest nightclubs. She took him to social register parties and on weekend visits to her friends' estates in Connecticut and Long Island. Through absorption he learned etiquette, how to make polite conversation, and the secret of a very dry martini.

He continued to make the audition rounds. He read for the lead in *Conflict*, a drama about a much-decorated 1914–18 War hero who uses his fame to buy a rich wife and social position. But the director preferred Spencer Tracy and hired him instead.

Conflict, which lasted only fifty-two performances, did not turn Tracy into a star, and it probably would not have done so for Gable either. But Tracy's performance earned him a contract for another play, the one that would make him famous, *The Last Mile.*

Meanwhile agent Chamberlain Brown persuaded George M. Cohan, the "President, King, and Emperor of Broadway," to audition Gable for his next production. Now fifty years old and a professional since infancy, Cohan was an actor-singer-dancer-director-writer-composer-producer who'd practically invented American show business and was personified by his most famous song, "Yankee Doodle Dandy." His next play would be *Gambling,* his first attempt at a murder mystery, which he would produce and direct but not appear in.

Gambling was so different from Cohan's previous works that he opted for a spring tryout in Philadelphia, prior to a Labor Day weekend opening on Broadway. The stage industry's traditional summer pause (few theaters had air conditioning in those days) gave him ample time to make any improvements that seemed necessary.

That might be the reason Cohan hired Gable for the leading role, figuring that he could be easily replaced if he wasn't satisfactory. But Gable seemed to fit the part of a casino owner who relies on his gambler's luck to solve a brutal murder.

Gambling opened at the Garrick Theater in Philadelphia on May 13, 1929. Rather brazenly, for the duration of the play's two-week run, Gable and Ria Langham shared a suite at the Warwick Hotel. They were registered as "Mr. and Mrs. Clark Gable," apparently counting on the fact that he wasn't famous enough for anyone to challenge the lie.

Neither Gable nor *Gambling* received good reviews. More than one critic suggested that Cohan should have acted the leading role himself, which is perhaps exactly what the director-playwright wanted to hear.

On closing night Cohan fired Gable and then rewrote the script, making the gambler middle-aged and adding some humorous and poignant touches that Cohan fans always expected. When *Gambling* finally had its Broadway opening at the Fulton Theater on August 26, it proved a big hit for Cohan the actor, if not the author. Critics disliked the play but raved about Cohan's performance. He toured in it for years and in 1935 starred in a movie version.

In the meantime Clark Gable recovered from the disappointment and won the leading role in *Hawk Island,* a three-act melodrama by Howard Irving Young, author of a modest 1926 hit entitled *Not Herbert.* Gable portrayed a prankster playboy who throws a party on his island estate and fakes a murder to enliven the festivities. Needless to say, a murder really is committed, and Gable has to solve it.

Hawk Island opened at the Longacre Theater on September 16, 1929, just a bit more than one year after Gable made his debut (and only Broadway appearance so far) in *Machinal*. If critics remembered him at all, they didn't mention it in their reviews. Bide Dudley wrote that "Mr. Gable seemed to be hoarse last night. Nevertheless, he proved himself a likable actor." Stephen Rathburn noted that "Clark Gable was a well-mannered, likable host whom nobody could possibly have believed capable of committing a murder."

Readers of Gable's capsule biography in the program were informed that "in addition to acting, he is qualifying to become a licensed aeroplane pilot, an exceptional accomplishment for one following so exciting a career as that of the stage." In whose fertile imagination that originated is unknown.

While *Gambling* was playing to packed houses two blocks away, *Hawk Island* sank into oblivion after twenty-four performances. As luck would have it, three weeks later, Wall Street stock prices started crashing. In a matter of days thousands of investors were wiped out, and billions of dollars in capital were lost. Although no one knew it at the time, a decade of economic depression had begun. By the end of 1929 six million people would be unemployed in the United States alone. The world total would be incalculable.

Despite his career setbacks Gable was better fixed than most struggling actors, thanks to his liaison with Ria Langham. Only she and her closest advisers knew exactly how much she was worth, but friends believed it was at least a million dollars, most of it in rock-solid investments like Houston real estate and oil refineries.

After his experience with George M. Cohan, Gable should have become wary of Broadway's living legends, but a chance to audition for God himself, David Belasco, was too good to resist. Gable didn't expect to be hired, but his agent's asking fee of three hundred dollars per week may have been the deciding factor. For a leading role, Belasco couldn't have found anyone cheaper.

Now seventy-six years old, the master innovator was mounting his three hundred and seventy-third production. *Blind Window* was a showcase for the latest of a series of young protégées who were known in stage circles as "Belasco's little nuns." Though their names are virtually forgotten today, they were some of the finest actresses of their time, including Mrs. Leslie Carter, Lenore Ulric, Blanche Bates, and Frances Starr.

The current "nun," Beth Merrill, a blonde with mesmerizing slate-colored eyes, was already a star when Belasco became obsessed with her and signed her to a five-year contract. *Blind Window* would be their third collaboration and the first since Belasco's recovery from a 1927 auto crash that nearly killed him.

Gable had landed in strange territory, not even counting the play itself, which was an English translation of a Hungarian drama by Elemer Boross. Belasco was attracted by its murky atmosphere. The action took place entirely within the confines of a European prison, which allowed him to demonstrate his genius for lighting and special effects.

Laughable though the plot may seem today, Gable and Merrill played two prisoners who meet accidentally while he's trying to escape. Both are due to be executed for their crimes, but they fall in love and get the warden's permission to be married in the prison chapel. When Merrill turns out to be pregnant, she pleads for a stay of execution until after the baby's birth.

Unfortunately *Blind Window* was yet another of Gable's plays that never reached Broadway. The three-acter required a cast of twenty-two, plus extras for prison guards and inmates. With all the scenery and Belasco's fondness for special effects and offstage musical accompaniment, the maestro ran out of money during the tryout tour in December 1929.

Blind Window did five days at Ford's Theater, Baltimore, and then a full week at the Broad Street Theater, Philadelphia, before shuttering on December 14. Newspaper reviews, or what passed for them in those days, seemed written under the supervision of Belasco and/or his press agent. Belasco and Beth Merrill received most of the praise doled out. Gable was lucky to get mentioned in the cast listings. Presumably his performance satisfied. No critics panned him, and several gave blanket commendations to the entire cast.

Back in New York again, Gable celebrated the year-end holidays with Ria Langham and her three children. He was becoming more and more discouraged. In a few months he would turn twenty-nine. For a young actor striving to become a star, thirty seemed an end to the rainbow. If you hadn't made it by then, you became a supporting actor or you moved on to some other type of work.

While he was waiting for another job offer, Gable usually visited Chamberlain Brown's agency every morning, then partook of a liquid lunch at one of several speakeasies in the Times Square area where actors and other stage professionals congregated. For thirty-five cents he could get a shot of illegal liquor: the real stuff, imported from abroad and not distilled locally in somebody's bathtub.

Gable had been frequenting such watering holes since his stagestruck youth in Akron. Heavy drinking had become as much a daily habit for him as chain-smoking cigarettes. In those days both were "in" things to do. Few people worried or even knew about the possible health dangers.

Many of Gable's drinking cronies were in awe of his ability to consume great quantities of booze without getting drunk or losing control of himself. He became acquainted with other barflies like Humphrey Bogart, Spencer Tracy, and James Cagney. They too were all fledglings waiting for their ships to come in. They gossiped and exchanged job tips but rarely saw each other outside the drinking spots.

At the beginning of 1930 the stage industry was being clobbered by the economic depression and the simultaneous phase-out of silent movies. Talkies had taken away the last competitive edge that plays and vaudeville had over movies. Because of the expense involved in putting on a live production, admission prices needed to be much higher than for movies. But an exhibitor rented cans of film and needed to employ only a projectionist and house staff. Even in the best of times a ticket to a live event was a luxury item for many people and purchased sparingly. Movies, however, were a nickel-and-dime form of entertainment that everybody could afford.

Since many plays planned for the remainder of the 1929–30 Broadway season were being canceled, Gable had to endure two months of unemployment before Chamberlain Brown finally succeeded in placing him with producer A. H. Woods, a legendary Broadway character who called everybody "sweetheart." Specializing in lurid melodramas and sex romps like *Getting Gertie's Garter,* he often had twenty or twenty-five shows running simultaneously on Broadway and the road. He was known in the business as a plunger, meaning that failure never discouraged him. If a play flopped, he started rehearsals for a new one the next day.

He was obviously the kind of ally that Gable needed. Although Woods was tottering on bankruptcy due to his ownership of four heavily mortgaged theaters in New York and Chicago, he still had enough resources to fund *Love, Honor and Betray,* with stage and screen favorite Alice Brady as the star. For one of the main supporting roles, Gable received four hundred dollars per week, which Chamberlain Brown claimed he was now worth after getting three hundred for *Blind Window.*

The deal was a double ego-booster for Gable because of his acceptance by the play's director—none other than Lester Lonergan, who'd fired him from *House Unguarded* during the New Rochelle tryout. This time Lonergan was only directing the play and not acting in it as well. There was no way that Gable could upstage or steal scenes from him, which may be the reason why he decided to give him another chance.

Love, Honor and Betray was an English translation of André-Paul Antoine's recent Paris success, *L'Ennemie,* a sophisticated comedy that today would be categorized as "black." The story begins in a Paris cemetery, where two men who loved the same woman are buried in adjacent plots. First one ghost, then the other, arises from the earth and tells how the woman drove him to his grave. The woman, of course, also appears as the experiences are dramatized. In the final act the ghost of the woman's most recent lover comes to the cemetery and tells his story while waiting for his funeral cortege to arrive.

Robert Williams and newcomer George Brent portrayed the other lovers. Gable had the good luck of being the last to appear. The final act of a play is usually the one that audiences—critics included—remember the most after the performance is over.

Not since Jane Cowl and Pauline Frederick had Gable worked with one of the great divas, but thirty-seven-year-old Alice Brady was less regal and more down-to-earth. The daughter of eminent producer William A. Brady and dancer Rose Marie Rene, she had showbiz in her veins, spoke the foul language of stagehands, and was a playgirl who often overdid the fun. Her boozing lost her the lead in Eugene O'Neill's *Strange Interlude,* where she was replaced at the last minute by Lynn Fontanne.

Whether Gable or Alice Brady initiated it, an affair erupted between them during the rehearsals for *Love, Honor and Betray*. It may have been just the natural result of the hottest love scene that Gable had ever been required to act out, taking place in what was supposed to be Brady's boudoir. With Brady in a filmy negligée and Gable wearing a silk lounging robe, he maneuvers her onto a couch, then sweeps her into his arms and proceeds to devour her with kisses.

An unexpected complication in rehearsing the scene was Gable's mustache, or rather his lack of one. He'd always maintained a clean-shaven look, but director Lonergan claimed that if Gable wanted to be believable as a French gigolo, he needed to have some tactile hair on his upper lip. They experimented with several fakes before settling on a wide but ultrathin design.

Unfortunately for Gable, Alice Brady was a prankster. Whenever they rehearsed a kiss, she found some way to make the mustache fall off or go askew. Gable was forced to grow one of his own, but he eventually shaved it off at the end of the run.

The affair heated up in the course of the two-week tryout tour. During the Hartford and Atlantic City engagements, Gable and Brady had adjoining hotel rooms, but he never slept in his, according to other members of the company. No hotel was required for the final stop on the tour, which was just across the bridge from Manhattan at Brooklyn's Flatbush Theater.

Strange though it may seem today, new plays were often tried out in Brooklyn, at admission prices well below those that would be charged on Broadway. Producers saved the expense of lodging and transporting the company. If the play generated favorable word of mouth, people who missed it in Brooklyn would go to New York to see it at the higher price.

Returning to Gotham, *Love, Honor and Betray* opened March 12, 1930, at the Eltinge Theater, one of ten playhouses on West Forty-second Street that would not survive the Depression and would be converted for use by movies or burlesque shows. As first-nighters arrived in tuxedos and evening gowns, peddlers of apples and matchbooks were fighting one another for space on the sidewalk.

Dripping in jewels, Ria Langham was escorted to the opening performance by a group of friends. No doubt she squirmed in her seat when Gable and Brady acted their big love scene. In the next day's *Telegram*, critic Robert Garland wrote that "Mr. Clark Gable wins the kissing prize. He busses Miss Brady with vim, vigor and vitality. Few, if any, such Kraft-Ebbing busses have been displayed in public before on a local stage. He should be commended for his skill at such psychopathic endeavors."

Broadway seemed to have a new idol, yet the production and its star received mostly negative reviews. "Miss Brady does not enhance her reputation greatly," said Stewart Beach of *Theater* magazine. "I found almost nothing in the play to persuade me that it was anything but tedious, heavy, somewhat bewildered. . . . One does not know during most of the love scenes whether they should be considered as satire or farce or more serious business."

A. H. Woods posted a closing notice for March 22, but then an upsurge in the sale of matinee tickets caused him to reconsider. Women were congregating at the stage door after performances to get Gable's autograph. It was a good omen, but it also needed advertising support, and Woods didn't have the money. He kept open as long as he could but finally pulled the plug on April 19 after a total of forty-five performances.

The closing also put an end to Gable's affair with Alice Brady. They no longer had an excuse to be together, and he was already committed to Ria Langham. In fact, Gable and Langham may have been married by this time. They were certainly posing at it. He had moved into her New York apartment, which was now listed in the building's lobby directory as the residence of Mr. and Mrs. Clark Gable. The couple would later claim that they were secretly married on March 31, 1930, which would have been during the run of *Love, Honor and Betray*. If they were, they neglected to register it. No record has ever been found.

The play's closing left Gable up the proverbial creek without a paddle. The Broadway season would end in May. Everything still due to open had been cast. Shows were opening and closing so fast that it was unlikely there would be much call for replacement actors. Gable's only hope for immediate work was in a road company or summer stock.

Through a mix-up at Chamberlain Brown's agency, Gable lost a chance to make a screen test for Mary Pickford's independent production company. One of her Broadway scouts had seen Gable in *Love,*

Honor and Betray and had suggested him for the romantic lead in Pickford's next starring vehicle, *Secrets*.

Chamberlain Brown's Hollywood representative, Maurice Revnes, was delegated to supply Pickford with some photographs of Gable. But when Revnes checked his files, he found only some not-too-flattering headshots that were taken two years before for *Machinal*. Rather than show them to Pickford, he cabled New York to rush something more glamorous.

Unfortunately in those days the fastest coast-to-coast delivery service was by propeller-driven airplane, which took a minimum of three days, depending on weather conditions. By the time the new Gable photos arrived, a rival agent had moved in and sold Pickford on his client, Kenneth MacKenna. Perhaps it was good luck for Gable rather than bad. Halfway through filming *Secrets,* Pickford became dissatisfied with MacKenna and decided to junk the whole project. Two years later she revived it with Leslie Howard as her costar. It was a box-office flop and became the last film of Mary Pickford's legendary career.

Chamberlain Brown finally came through with another Broadway assignment for Gable, but for the fall season. A. H. Woods had hired Laurence Stallings, coauthor of *What Price Glory?,* to write an adaptation of Ernest Hemingway's *A Farewell to Arms* for a September premiere. Woods intended Gable for one of the major roles, possibly even the lead, but he wanted to wait until the script was completed before he did the casting. He gave Gable a tentative contract for five hundred dollars per week, which was the next step up from the four hundred that he paid him for *Love, Honor and Betray.* As part of the agreement, Gable was prohibited from taking any interim work that would prevent him from being available when Woods needed him.

A temporary job filled the void. One of the few box-office hits of Broadway's current season was John Wexley's *The Last Mile,* which made an overnight star of Spencer Tracy in the role of "Killer" Mears, the leader of a group of death-row inmates trying to escape from prison. Producer Herman Shumlin leased the West Coast production rights to Gable's friends and former employers, Louis MacLoon and Lillian Albertson. The latter immediately thought of Gable for "Killer" Mears, but Chamberlain Brown drove a hard bargain. He demanded five hundred dollars per week for Gable for the monthlong tour, which was more than the Depression-strapped MacLoons could afford to pay.

Gable was caught in the middle. While eager to do the play, he felt obligated to Chamberlain Brown, who'd worked long and hard to raise him to the five-hundred-dollar level. Ria Langham (or Ria Gable, as she might have been by now) came up with a solution that satisfied everyone. She contributed $2,500 toward the funding of the MacLoon production of *The Last Mile,* which was the equivalent of Gable's salary for four weeks plus another of rehearsals.

Before leaving for California in May, Gable went several times to the Harris Theater to study Spencer Tracy's performances. On each visit he came away awed, his confidence shaken. Tracy had the ability to mesmerize an audience without indulging in showy theatrics. The role of the monstrous "Killer" could easily cause laughter rather than chills if the player pushed too far.

While directing the rehearsals in Los Angeles, Lillian Albertson encouraged Gable to be himself and to avoid trying to copy Tracy's interpretation. By the time *The Last Mile* opened at the Belasco Theater on June 7, she had succeeded.

Edwin Schallert, then the drama critic for the *Los Angeles Times,* later recalled that "I must have seen every one of Gable's previous plays in Los Angeles, yet I had trouble remembering them. His work had not been outstanding. But in the role of the convict sentenced to walking that 'last mile' to the electric chair, Gable literally knocked everyone in the audience between the eyes with the fierce, bloodthirsty, vindictive and blasphemous way he tore the part open."

At the final curtain on opening night, Gable received a thunderous ovation. He beckoned to Lillian Albertson in the wings to come out onstage to share it with him. When he returned to his dressing room, people were lined up to congratulate him. Among them was movie director Mervyn LeRoy, who later recalled the encounter.

"I was getting ready to make *Little Caesar* for Warner Bros. Gable seemed perfect for a major supporting character named Joe Massara. Clark was very handsome and all man—the type who never went unnoticed. He also had a certain magnetism—a quality that I never would be able to comprehend completely. I asked him if I could talk to him. He was very cordial and polite and listened patiently to what I had to say.

When I asked him if he was interested, he answered quickly, 'I certainly am.' I told him that I would first have to make a screen test to show to Jack Warner and Darryl Zanuck. We arranged a date," LeRoy said.

The character Joe is the protégé of a power-hungry gangster and inadvertently causes his downfall. "I directed the test myself and was very impressed," LeRoy said. "As soon as it came back from the lab, I called Zanuck and Warner and said I had a surprise for them. They came to the projection room, and I ran the film. When the lights came back on, Jack Warner screamed at me, 'Why did you throw away five hundred dollars of our money on a test for that big ape? Didn't you see those big ears when you talked to him? And those big feet and hands, not to mention that ugly face of his?' Of course, Gable went on to be the biggest star in the world. Many times I would pester Jack Warner with the question 'How would you like to have him now, or just his ears?' "

The role went to the more perfectly formed Douglas Fairbanks, Jr., who up to then had been coasting along on the fame of his father and the publicity of his own recent marriage to Joan Crawford. *Little Caesar* finally made Junior Fairbanks a star in his own right, though he was more than a bit overshadowed by Edward G. Robinson in the title role.

The Last Mile ran three weeks in Los Angeles and then did a week at the Geary Theater in San Francisco, where Gable received more rave reviews. "Gable had all the fearsome litheness of a caged panther. His every movement was a menace. He made the killer a character to be remembered," said Lloyd S. Thompson of the *Examiner.*

Unfortunately the tour ended in calamity when producer Louis MacLoon disappeared, taking with him all of the box-office receipts. Everybody guessed it was due to longtime marital problems with Lillian Albertson. She eventually divorced him on grounds of desertion.

Since Gable had a wealthy wife, the loss of a week's pay didn't cause him hardship, but the other actors in the cast weren't that lucky. Jobs were so scarce that when they signed up for *The Last Mile,* they had waived their rights to Actors Equity protection. Normally a producer had to post a bond with the union so that the actors would get paid in the event of any wrongdoing.

Happily, before the tour left Los Angeles, MacLoon had provided all the cast members with round-trip train tickets to San Francisco. At least no one got stranded there.

Back in Los Angeles again at the end of June, Gable still had two months to kill before his Broadway commitment for *A Farewell to Arms*. He decided to stick around to meet with some of the agents who'd been badgering him since he opened in *The Last Mile*. Since his contract with Chamberlain Brown covered stage work only, he could have separate representation for movies.

Before Gable had time to talk to other agents, a very aggressive Minna Wallis took over. New to the talent-peddling business, she was determined to land some clients with star potential, and Clark Gable seemed to have "it" in capital letters. While he was working in San Francisco, she'd taken the liberty of setting up an audition for him for a $750-per-week job in a western at Pathé Pictures. How could he refuse?

The movie was *The Painted Desert,* a contemporary western in which cowboy-miners battle over tungsten, the rare element used in electric lamp filaments. Legend has it that when Minna Wallis took her new client to meet director Howard Higgin, she did all the talking, neglecting to mention that Gable didn't know how to ride a horse and had never even been near one. After he got the job, she allegedly sent him to a riding school in Griffith Park, where a retired, one-eyed stuntman put him through a crash course in four weeks.

The legend is far from true. Gable learned to ride as an Ohio farm boy, and during his stock period in Houston he went riding on the city's public bridle paths nearly every day. But he did spend some time with the old duffer in Griffith Park, learning how to protect himself against production accidents: in falling off a horse or in a fistfight with another cowboy character, he could easily scar his face, break some bones, or worse.

Clark Gable had to start somewhere, but *The Painted Desert* didn't get him much more than his first screen credit and some experience before the cameras. It was one of the last productions of the once-eminent Pathé Pictures, which, together with its crowing rooster trademark, was in the process of being folded into its new owner, RKO Radio Pictures. The film's three stars, William Boyd, Helen Twelvetrees, and William Farnum, were all Pathé contractees destined for dismissals, though Boyd later became more popular than ever as Hopalong Cassidy in low-budget movies and on television.

Gable played a villainous brute who fancies Boyd's sweetheart and also tries to bankrupt the hero by dynamiting his tungsten mine. Like 99.9 percent of all movies then, the cinematography was in black and white, so moviegoers had to imagine the hues of the painted desert. But the outdoor scenes were shot in the real thing—a region in north-central Arizona famous for its multicolored rock surfaces.

While Gable was away working on location, Minna Wallis did more negotiating. Making her job easier were some exceptional business connections. Her brother, Hal Wallis, was a top production executive at the consolidated Warner Bros.–First National Pictures. Minna herself had once worked there as an assistant to Jack Warner and Darryl Zanuck, who still were her close friends. In those days a woman had almost no chance of becoming a studio executive, so Minna finally quit to learn the talent agency business from two more of her friends, partners Myron Selznick and Leland Hayward. After her apprenticeship, Minna borrowed ten thousand dollars from them and started an agency in partnership with the already well-established Ruth Collier. Minna seemed to have all the bases covered. Her closest friend was Norma Shearer, the actress-wife of MGM's production chief, Irving Thalberg.

By the time Gable finished *The Painted Desert*, Wallis had three more jobs for him, one at MGM and the others at Warner–First National. A major obstacle, however, was Gable's Broadway commitment for *A Farewell to Arms*. Chamberlain Brown had just cabled him to return to New York immediately to start rehearsals. A. H. Woods had signed Elissa Landi, a rising British-European star, and the highly regarded Glenn Anders for the leads. Rouben Mamoulian would direct. It promised to be a very prestigious production. Gable would have a choice supporting role as Anders's friend and romantic rival.

Gable mulled it over and decided that he wanted to stay in Hollywood. He was furious at Woods for casting the lead actor without first giving him a chance to read for the part. And now that he'd gotten his feet wet in movies, he realized that he had a much better chance of becoming successful there than in New York. If the play flopped, which was more than likely due to the increasingly gloomy economic climate, he'd have to go back to making the audition rounds and waiting hopefully for the phone to ring.

Gable's refusal landed Chamberlain Brown in deep trouble with A. H. Woods, who filed a complaint with Actors Equity. The producer demanded that a fine of five thousand dollars be levied against agent Brown and client Gable for breaching the contract. Until the case was settled, Woods also wanted Equity to suspend Gable's membership so that he couldn't get work.

Woods soon dropped the charges. As before, Gable's wife may have spread some money around. In any case, *A Farewell to Arms* opened without Gable at the National Theater on September 22 and lasted all of twenty-four performances. Had he been in it, the run would have tied with *Hawk Island* as the shortest of his Broadway jobs. (The longest was his first, *Machinal,* which survived for ninety-three performances.)

During the summer Ria Gable gave up her New York apartment and moved to Los Angeles, bringing two of her children along and leaving the third and oldest in boarding school in Connecticut. The new Gable residence was in the Ravenswood Apartments, a sprawling art deco building on the eastern edge of Hollywood near the ultraexclusive area known as Hancock Park.

Since the children would be attending local schools in the fall, Ria rented two apartments so that their comings and goings would be less disruptive. Teenage Jana Lucas and her eleven-year-old brother, Alfred, shared the smaller of the two apartments. Ria and Gable, of course, occupied the larger, which had west-facing windows with fabulous sunset views.

Whatever the legality of his relationship with their mother, Gable tried to be a real father to her two kids, at least when the spirit moved him. Jana Lucas, whom he always called "Sister," later remembered that "Clark could charm everyone, regardless of age or station in life. And for a person who had not had any more education than he had, he was very smart. He could listen to your conversation and the next day repeat exactly what you had said."

Actor-friend Paul Fix, who'd recently worked onstage with Gable in *The Last Mile,* was baffled by his "arrangement" with Ria. "I don't think they were married," Fix recalled. "He was furious when Ria followed him west. Callous though it may sound, I think that Clark decided that he really didn't need her anymore. His career was looking up. He had new people around him who were better equipped to help him. Ria's wealth was no longer a factor. He wanted to dump her. But a decent streak in Clark made him feel that he owed Ria something for all that she'd done for him. So he stayed with her and tried to keep her happy."

Ria quickly became jealous of Minna Wallis, who was now *the* woman in Gable's life. Wallis spent so much time with Gable that Ria suspected them of having an affair. Perhaps they were, though Wallis had other reasons to dominate Gable's time. Always very busy socially, she took him as her escort to dinners, parties, and premieres to make sure that he met the VIPs of the industry. It was a faster, more direct route to employment than through auditions for minor functionaries in casting departments.

Wallis also introduced Gable to a master dentist. His upper front teeth with the gold inlays were extracted and replaced with a partial plate. The denture caused a slight bulge of his upper lip, but not enough to be noticeable.

As soon as he finished *The Painted Desert,* Gable started the next job that Minna Wallis had lined up for him. The role in MGM's *The Easiest Way* wasn't big enough for Gable to receive billing in the opening credits. His name did appear in the cast list at the end of the film, but in last place.

Considered a shocker when first produced for the stage by David Belasco in 1909, Eugene Walter's *The Easiest Way* was by now a cliché. A poor working girl takes the easiest way out by becoming a rich man's mistress and eventually ends up a streetwalker. The story was already considered old hat in 1917 when it was filmed with Clara Kimball Young. But Irving Thalberg dragged it out of mothballs in order to test the box-office strength of Constance Bennett, a freelance star whom he was considering for a long-term MGM contract.

Adolphe Menjou portrayed Bennett's sugar daddy. MGM's rising romantic star, Robert Montgomery, played a playboy-journalist who falls in love with Bennett and then dumps her when he discovers that she's a kept woman. Bennett has a "good" sister (enacted by Anita Page) who takes the straight path to happiness by marrying her childhood sweetheart, helping him to become a success, and winding up with a child and a cozy house in the suburbs.

Gable portrayed the good sister's lover-husband, who starts out as a delivery man—truck driver for a commercial laundry and works hard to become his own boss by the end of the film. He appears in only scattered scenes, mainly to register disapproval of Bennett's transgressions and to warn her of the consequences. In the finale, taking place on a snowy Christmas Eve, Gable spots Bennett wandering the streets, takes pity on her, and brings her home with him for a tear-filled reconciliation with her sister and young nephew.

One of the few advantages to being a supporting movie actor was (and still is) that you usually don't have to stick around for the whole length of production. You do your few scenes, often in one or two days, and then can go straight on to another job. In Hollywood's heyday, when the major studios were each producing forty to fifty films annually, a supporting actor could work in two different movies in the same week or even in the same day.

As soon as he finished his bit at MGM, Gable played two villainous parts in *The Finger Points* and *Night Nurse*. Ironically, his employer, Warner Bros.–First National, had rejected him for *Little Caesar,* but this time the roles weren't important enough for his oversize ears to cause concern. The two films were so-called programmers that theaters often ran at the bottom of double bills.

In *The Finger Points,* the latest in a gangster cycle that Warners had started with *Little Caesar* and *The Public Enemy,* Gable played a vicious killer in the Edward G. Robinson–James Cagney mold. But again it was a subordinate part in a showcase for the studio's longtime star from silent days, Richard Barthelmess, who portrayed a corrupt newspaper reporter with secret ties to the underworld.

In *Night Nurse* Gable played the chauffeur for a wealthy household where Barbara Stanwyck (a recent addition to the Warner contract roster) is nurse/companion to a widowed dipsomaniac and her two children. Ben Lyon, another star of the silent era, played Stanwyck's bootlegger-lover. Together they stop Gable and another servant from carrying out a horrific scheme whereby Gable would marry his rich employer, then murder her *and* the two children, and inherit everything.

Director William Wellman encouraged Gable to play the loathsome monster with all stops out. In the scene where Stanwyck discovers his plans, Gable had to slap her face and warn her not to tell. Wellman showed him how to do it without bruising Stanwyck, but Gable got carried away and handled her so brutally that she finally begged him to stop before she landed in the hospital.

By the time Gable completed his two Warner assignments, MGM had edited *The Easiest Way* and was getting ready to test public reaction with a sneak preview at the Alexander Theater in suburban Glendale. Irving Thalberg was being pressured by Constance Bennett's agent, Myron Selznick, who had RKO primed to give her a long-term contract if MGM wasn't interested.

The screening on November 12, 1930, went well, but not for Constance Bennett. Comment cards filled in by the capacity audience of two thousand rated her a six out of a possible ten. Thalberg and his boss, Louis B. Mayer, decided that Bennett had little to offer MGM that it didn't already have in contractees like Greta Garbo, Joan Crawford, Marion Davies, and of course Norma Shearer Thalberg. To RKO Miss Bennett went.

But Thalberg was impressed that night by the unbilled actor in the cast. "The audience sat bolt upright whenever Gable appeared. He projected a tangible magic," studio executive Samuel Marx recalled. "In the lobby afterward, women were going up to ushers and asking 'Who's that handsome laundryman?' "

Rumor has it that Minna Wallis stacked the audience in Gable's favor that night, which, if true, wouldn't have been the first or last time such a trick was pulled. In any case she went to her friend Thalberg's office the next morning and sold him on signing Gable to a contract. It wasn't a high-paying one, but a first step toward it.

The deal was for one year at $650 per week. At the end of it, MGM could drop Gable or give him a longer-term contract with an escalating pay scale that started at $1,000 per week. During the trial period MGM was risking only $26,000 on Gable. Studio calendar years were counted as forty weeks, during which the contractee got paid whether he worked or not. If that seems crazy, consider that most films in those days were produced in a month or less, and that no star made more than five a year and usually fewer. So for about half of the forty weeks they were idle except for being on call for publicity interviews and such.

Clark Gable happened to be in the right place at the right time. While MGM had an abundance of female stars, it was running short of males, especially in the romantic category. John Gilbert and Ramon Novarro, who were hugely popular during the silent era, were showing their age and also had speaking voices that didn't match their heroic images. William Haines, another carryover from silents, was a light-weight comic type. And the gravel-voiced, leather-faced Wallace Beery was no love match for any of the MGM queens except the aging and bulky Marie Dressler.

With Minna Wallis egging him on, Thalberg decided that Gable could be MGM's next big star. At a meeting with his production executives and members of the story department, Thalberg told them that he wanted to cast Gable in standout roles with all the MGM sex symbols. "We'll want scripts for him right away opposite Norma and Greta. At least one with each of them, maybe two with Joan," Thalberg said. "He should be in a couple of he-man vehicles too. Strong action stuff. I'd like to see him do eight pictures this year so that the public gets to know his face."

Gable was summoned to a meeting with MGM's publicity manager, Howard Strickling, who would be responsible for creating his image. As Strickling later recalled, "He was the biggest man I ever saw. His hands, feet, head, and, of course, his ears, were tremendous. He was the biggest guy I ever knew, and I would say one of the most powerful. One of his great fears, I learned as I got to know him, was that he might hurt somebody. Physically. He never did. He always knew he had this tremendous strength, but he never used it.

"What a hell of a man," Strickling continued. "There was nothing effeminate about him. Nothing actorish. He came in, sat down in a chair, and right away you could see he knew how to handle people. When Gable gave an interview, he would know more about you than you would know about him. If you walked in and started talking to him, before you knew it you were talking about yourself and liking it. From the very first time he talked to me, he was interested in me."

A former newspaper office boy, Strickling had been a movie publicist since 1919 and had worked with many of the great stars since then, including Rudolph Valentino, John Gilbert, Mae Murray, John Barrymore, Lillian Gish, and Lon Chaney. As an image-maker, his greatest achievement up to now was turning a Broadway chorine named Lucille Le Sueur into Joan Crawford. But Clark Gable would be his masterpiece.

"With Gable there was only one way to go," Strickling recalled. "He was the personification of the old American expression 'he-man,' so all we had to do was build on that." Strickling and his staff combed through

Gable's past and wrote a press biography that vaguely resembled the truth, saying that he'd been a hardworking farm boy, an oil wildcatter, a lumberjack, a garage mechanic, and a telephone lineman.

Gable's interest in cars became the nucleus for his image as a rugged, outdoorsy type who loved to go hunting and fishing. Since he'd dabbled in those things in his youth, experts were hired to help him become a crack shot and master flycaster. Gilbert Adrian, the studio's chief fashion designer, advised Gable on how to dress in casual sports clothes, riding breeches, and turtleneck sweaters.

"Clark liked the image and fit into it," Strickling said. "He was willing to be molded. He wanted to be a star. He wanted to be a success."

MGM also sent him for new dentures. The makeup department restyled his hair, parting it on the left and stressing a natural cowlick that had a tendency to break loose and dangle over his right eye. His brutish eyebrows, reminiscent of boxers Jack Dempsey and Max Schmeling, were shaped and plucked to more debonair proportions. The studio gym helped him to develop broader shoulders and a narrower waistline.

Still photographers Clarence Bull and George Hurrell idealized him in their portrait galleries. "Gable had something extremely rare," Hurrell recalled. "He looked good from any angle. Most people have a good side and bad side, best from one angle only. Gable could be photographed under any lighting conditions, [from] any camera angle. He was the least self-conscious person in front of the camera."

Gable's one-year contract with MGM became effective December 4, 1930. In keeping with Thalberg's plan, his first assignment was in the Joan Crawford vehicle *Dance, Fools, Dance,* directed by Harry Beaumont (maker of *The Broadway Melody,* MGM's first Oscar winner in the best picture category). Since the 1928 *Our Dancing Daughters,* which Beaumont also directed, Crawford had been the studio's number-one box-office draw, though critics tended to rate her behind Garbo and Shearer in acting ability.

Lester Vail, another MGM hopeful with Broadway stage experience, had already been cast as the romantic lead in *Dance, Fools, Dance,* which found Crawford as a spoiled rich girl who's forced to get a job when her bankrupted father commits suicide. Coming into the project at the last minute, Gable got the villain's role, which Thalberg ordered rewritten to give him some steamy scenes with Crawford.

Gable played a bootlegger and mob leader who's responsible for at least a dozen murders before the film ends. Crawford, by now employed as a newspaper reporter, gets herself hired as an entertainer in Gable's nightclub and becomes cozy with him to learn his secrets. One too many is that her alcoholic brother, also left penniless by their father's death, has joined Gable's gang.

The filming caused the first tremors of what later became an intimate relationship. "There was a scene where Clark grabbed me and threatened to kill my brother. His nearness had such impact, my knees buckled. If he hadn't held me by both shoulders, I'd have dropped," Joan Crawford recalled. "It was like an electrical charge between us. We both felt it."

Before "it" had a chance to progress, however, both actors moved on to other movies. Gable's next showcasing was in what Thalberg prescribed as "strong action stuff"—a Wallace Beery gangster thriller, *The Secret Six*. A favorite in silent films since 1913, the forty-four-year-old Beery had become a major star in talkies thanks to his unique gravelly voice and his ability to use it for comic or fright effect. In *The Secret Six* he portrayed a vicious gangster whose long list of slayings has earned him the nickname "Slaughterhouse."

Gable shared featured billing with another of the studio's candidates for stardom, twenty-six-year-old John Mack Brown. Unknown to either actor, Thalberg was putting them to a test. Prior to Gable's arrival at MGM, the ex–college football star had been getting the same kind of rugged he-man promotion. But did the studio need two such types? Gable seemed to have the edge. Brown, who'd entered films in the last year of silents, when voices didn't matter, had a languid southern drawl that detracted from a macho image.

Gable and Brown played newspaper reporters who infiltrate Wallace Beery's gang to get evidence that will land the villains in the gas chamber. Also in the supporting cast was platinum blond starlet Jean Harlow, as Beery's gun moll. Under personal contract to independent producer Howard Hughes, who'd introduced her to the screen in *Hell's Angels,* Harlow had been loaned to MGM for the one film only.

In *The Secret Six* Harlow falls in love with Gable and spills the beans about Beery's heinous crimes. In the few days that they worked together, Gable became chummy with Harlow and her constant companion Marino Bello, her stepfather and business manager. During production breaks the trio usually sat together gabbing and playing cards. It was a brief beginning to a complex friendship.

After *The Secret Six* Thalberg decided to risk casting Gable with his most precious jewel, Mrs. Thalberg, in *A Free Soul*, helmed by MGM's top director, Clarence Brown. Gable's old friend Lionel Barrymore would be Norma Shearer's costar, with Leslie Howard featured as the romantic lead.

The melodramatic shocker introduced Gable to another woman who would be a major force in his career—Adela Rogers St. Johns, a pioneer female journalist, screenwriter, and author of the best-selling novel on which the film was based. Prior to casting Gable, Thalberg had intended the role for John Gilbert. To make sure that Gable was acceptable to St. Johns, Thalberg sent him to meet her at her beachfront house in Malibu.

When Gable arrived, St. Johns was dressed in turquoise silk lounging pajamas. She fixed drinks for them using gin that she manufactured in her home distillery. What happened immediately after cocktails is known only to them, but St. Johns, then thirty-six years old, became Gable's lifelong friend, confidante, adviser, and press propagandist.

One of Hollywood's most famous—and unprovable—rumors claimed that they even had a child together. When once questioned about the possibility, St. Johns answered, "What woman would deny Clark Gable was the father of her child?"

Needless to say, Gable got the role of wicked Ace Wilfong in *A Free Soul*, which blended fact with fiction by using the author's father, legendary criminal lawyer Earl Rogers, as the model for one of the lead characters. The alcohol-addicted Stephen Ashe, played by Lionel Barrymore in what turned out to be an Oscar-winning performance, agrees to sober up and to stop drinking forever if his rebellious daughter ends her intense affair with the gambler-mobster.

Casting Norma Shearer as Jan Ashe was Irving Thalberg's latest attempt to bolster her screen image as an ultrasophisticated, oversexed woman of the world. In dramas Shearer anguished over her sins; in comedies she laughed them away. *A Free Soul* had an added incestuous element that was never developed. But the daughter is obviously more in love with her father than with any of her suitors, who only provide the sex that she can't have with Daddy.

Before production started, Lionel Barrymore warned Gable to be cautious of their coworker, who preferred to be called "Miss Shearer" by subordinates and had been behaving even more like the queen of MGM since recently giving birth to an heir apparent, Irving Junior. On the first day that Barrymore saw Gable and Shearer working together, they were rehearsing a romantic embrace. When Gable spotted Barrymore, he relaxed his grip on Shearer and gave him the high sign that all was well.

No doubt Gable and Shearer immediately noticed their physical imperfections: his oversize ears and her partial cross-eyedness. Shearer used sheer willpower to control her problem, but Gable's was more difficult to manage. Today a skilled plastic surgeon could easily perform an ear reduction, but in 1930 such operations took place only in science fiction.

Director Clarence Brown, however, asked the makeup department to work some magic. "They pinned Gable's ears against his head with fish skin," publicist Larry Barbier recalled. "He went along with it for a couple of days. Then suddenly he ripped off the tape and said that they had to film him the way he looked or he was going back to work in the theater. I guess he considered it a compromise, going Hollywood, pretending to be something he wasn't. He was too natural a guy to try to fool anybody."

Despite many rumors, Gable never had his ears "fixed." His "flops," as he used to call them, were easily made less conspicuous by letting his hair grow fuller at the sides. Cameramen tried to avoid photographing him head-on, with both ears showing. In a side view, or with his face turned slightly to the left or right, only one ear showed, and its extension from the head was less obvious. For over-the-shoulder shots, where the backs of the ears showed, they were darkened with pancake makeup to diffuse the lights.

Gable had only scattered scenes in *A Free Soul,* but he was its driving force. His sexual power over Shearer finally causes her fiancé, Leslie Howard, to kill him. When Shearer realizes how many lives she's destroyed by lusting after Gable, she persuades her father, Barrymore, to defend Howard in court. While addressing the jury, Barrymore gets so carried away by emotion that he drops dead from a heart attack.

As the "free soul" of the title, Shearer goes wild in Gable's company. In their first moment alone, she's unable to resist his kisses. "A new kind of man, a new kind of world," she moans. In a later scene she lies back languorously on a couch, stretches out her arms to Gable, and brazenly purrs, "Come on, put them around me." He treats her like a wolf devouring a lamb. He's all over her, biting her on the lips and nibbling at her ears.

When Irving Thalberg saw the early rushes (the unedited footage of a prior day's filming), his belief in Gable's star potential was confirmed. But he also realized that Gable would end up stealing the movie from Mrs. Thalberg. To prevent that from happening, he instructed Clarence Brown to add a brief moment where Gable all but wallops Shearer in the face. Thalberg theorized that audiences would be so appalled that Shearer would win all their sympathy.

Lionel Barrymore, who watched the scene being shot, said later that Gable "was like a lean and hungry Jack Dempsey. His opponent was a lot prettier and more delicate than most. But he delivered a bona-fide sockeroo that rocked Norma almost off her feet."

By the time he finished *A Free Soul,* Gable had become acclimated to MGM and its hierarchy. The studio covered 172 acres in Culver City, a small middle-class community about six miles southwest of Hollywood. For Gable, going to work there was reminiscent of going to work at the rubber factories in Akron: once inside its Greco-Roman main gate, he was stuck there for the day. About 99 percent of all production took place in MGM's thirty soundstages or on outdoor sets built on 128 acres of backlot. Films were completed at the rate of one per week, but shooting overlapped, and five or six were usually being made at the same time. The daily workforce, including actors, technicians, and office staff, was about four thousand. With extras employed for crowd scenes, it could often be twice that.

Metro-Goldwyn-Mayer was a subsidiary of Loew's, Inc., a publicly owned company which had headquarters in New York and was founded in 1910 by Marcus Loew, an owner of penny arcades and nickelodeons. After building a large circuit of movie and vaudeville theaters, Loew needed a steady supply of films and in 1920 expanded into production by acquiring Metro Pictures. In 1924, after acquiring Goldwyn Pictures (by then minus cofounder Samuel Goldwyn) and a production company bearing the name of owner Louis B. Mayer, Loew merged the three studios into one, with Mayer as its chief executive. When fifty-seven-year-old Marcus Loew died from heart disease in 1927, his longtime associate, forty-six-year-old Nicholas M. Schenck, became head of Loew's, Inc., with Mayer continuing in charge of MGM.

So far Gable had had only slight contact with the forty-six-year-old Mayer, who relied on Irving Thalberg to oversee production while he kept the studio humming according to policies set by Nicholas Schenck at New York headquarters. MGM supplied about 60 percent of all the movies shown at Loew's-owned theaters, which numbered about 175. It was hardly the largest circuit, but Loew's dominated the heavily populated northeastern United States and was also represented in major cities nationwide. MGM films, of course, were also rented to non-Loew's theaters, which numbered about twenty thousand in the United States and at least that many more in the rest of the world. Those were the days before multiplexing; no movie theater had more than one screen.

Gable's boss, if that's the right word, was thirty-two-year-old Irving Thalberg, who ran production with help from a staff of supervisors that included Paul Bern, Harry Rapf, Hunt Stromberg, Bernard Hyman, and Albert Lewin. Reporting to them was the studio's large roster of directors who were under exclusive contracts: Clarence Brown, Jack Conway, Victor Fleming, Harry Beaumont, Fred Niblo, Robert Z. Leonard, Sidney Franklin, Sam Wood, George Hill, King Vidor, W. S. Van Dyke, and George Fitzmaurice, among others.

MGM films tended to be manufactured like cars on an assembly line: part by part. If one piece didn't work, it could easily be replaced. Gable learned that lesson when he was rushed into *Complete Surrender,* a melodrama that Joan Crawford made immediately after working with him in *Dance, Fools, Dance.*

John Mack Brown, MGM's other he-man candidate, had been teamed with Crawford in *Complete Surrender,* but Brown's clumsy romancing in the love scenes provoked gales of laughter at a theater preview. Thalberg decided to replace him, which was easily accomplished by disposing of Brown's scenes and reshooting them with Gable. Since it was a Crawford-dominated vehicle, Brown's scenes totaled about one third of the film.

Gable took over the role of a Salvation Army officer who saves Crawford from degrading herself in an affair with a traveling salesman. The ludicrous story may have been part of the reason previewers roared, but director Harry Beaumont took advantage of the natural chemistry between Gable and Crawford and made it seem more believable.

MGM also gave the film a new title, *Laughing Sinners,* which would prove prophetic in the budding personal relationship between Gable and Crawford.

By the early spring of 1931, Gable's first batch of films had been released. Though he starred in none and had only minor roles, he was starting to be recognized by trade press critics and fan magazine editors. "Newcomer Gable shines briefly," said *Motion Picture Herald* of his bit in *The Easiest Way. Variety* described his gangster in *Dance, Fools, Dance* as "a vivid and authentic bit of acting." *Film Daily*'s review of *The Finger Points* said that "Gable again scores with his fine voice and magnetic personality."

Thalberg took notice and gave Gable his first starring vehicle, *Sporting Blood,* which would also test his drawing power at the box office. Gable was on his own, without one of MGM's queens to lure crowds. His leading lady, twenty-two-year-old Madge Evans, had been one of the first child stars of the silent era, but moviegoers lost interest after she reached the gawky age of twelve. Ironically, in her adorable phase, Evans had played daughter roles to two of Gable's ex-flames, Pauline Frederick and Alice Brady.

British-born Charles Brabin, who'd been directing films since 1910 and was the husband of retired sex siren Theda Bara, guided Gable through *Sporting Blood.* The central character was a racehorse named Tommy Boy. In yet another role as a gambler, Gable wins the thoroughbred in a bet and goes on to enter him in the Kentucky Derby. Of course Tommy Boy wins, despite some illegal attempts by Gable's gambler rivals to prevent it.

While Thalberg and staff were making plans for Gable's next project, a major crisis erupted in the Gable household. What caused it can only be guessed at, but Ria decided to complain to Louis B. Mayer. She got no further than Mayer's confidential secretary, Ida Koverman, who had long experience with outraged spouses and insisted on taking her instead to PR chief Howard Strickling.

In the meeting with Strickling, Ria broke down in tears, claiming that she'd been living with Gable for years, with the understanding that they'd get married when his divorce from Josephine Dillon became final. But since then, Ria claimed, success had warped his mind; he not only refused to marry her but also wanted to dump her. She told Strickling that if Gable didn't marry her immediately, she'd "make a stink to high heaven" by phoning every columnist and reporter in town.

Strickling calmed her and urged her to do nothing until he'd had a chance to discuss the matter with his superiors. After Ria left, he reported everything to Irving Thalberg, who phoned Gable's agent, Minna Wallis, and ordered her to bring him to his office as soon as possible.

When Gable and Wallis arrived, Thalberg waved Gable's contract in the air and quoted from the "moral turpitude" clause, which stipulated that the agreement could be canceled if he engaged in sexual and/or criminal misconduct. His living openly with a woman who wasn't his wife clearly breached that rule. If Ria carried out her threat, the industry's self-appointed moral guardian, Will Hays, would be compelled to order Gable's dismissal. It would be the end of his movie career. No other studio would dare hire him.

Gable didn't hesitate for a moment in deciding what to do. Thalberg asked Howard Strickling to handle the wedding arrangements.

Before the marriage took place, Strickling had to figure out an explanation that would satisfy the press, which had been led to believe that the Gables were already husband and wife. A story was concocted that when the couple married, they forgot to wait for his interlocutory divorce decree from Josephine Dillon to become final. In the eyes of California law, Gable hadn't been a single man at the time, so he and Ria were simply taking their vows again to remedy the mistake.

The wedding was set for June 19 at the courthouse in Santa Ana, a small city about eighty miles southeast of Los Angeles in Orange County. The prospective groom filed for a license in the name of William C. Gable, but the ruse failed. A crowd of reporters and photographers was waiting outside when the couple arrived that morning.

After the private ten-minute ceremony in a judge's chambers, the newlyweds emerged and were immediately surrounded by reporters shouting delicate questions. They wanted to know about Ria's wealth, her previous marriages and three children, and her role in furthering Gable's career. Howard Strickling and another studio publicist tried to keep order, but Ria collapsed in tears and pleaded to be left alone.

Gable put an arm around her, guided her to their car, and drove off. There was no honeymoon.

6

THE GREAT GOD GABLE

Ria Langham got her wish. She was finally Mrs. Clark Gable, but in name only. For the sake of appearances, the couple continued living under the same roof, but separately. They moved from the Ravenswood Apartments to a rented mansion on San Ysidro Drive in Beverly Hills, not far from the legendary Pickfair. The forty-two-room residence of Mary Pickford and Douglas Fairbanks was home for another sham marriage, with Fairbanks by now retired, absent most of the time, exploring remote parts of the world and chasing women.

In their new residence, each of the Gables had their own bedroom suite, at opposite ends of a long corridor. When he was working, which nowadays was most of the time, Gable needed to be at MGM by seven in the morning. Whatever life he shared with his wife was in the evenings, when they did the expected married-couple things like entertaining friends at home or going out to parties, movie premieres, and nightclubs. Though Ria wanted more, she settled for the satisfactions that came with being the wife of a public idol. She became famous in her own right and was envied by other women. No one needed to know that Gable gave her neither love nor sex.

Ria was at least gaining more from being Mrs. Gable than Josephine Dillon had before her. In fact, the marriage so enraged Dillon that she resorted to a bit of blackmail. In August she sent a letter to L. B. Mayer, describing Gable as an ungrateful chiseler who'd used her to become a star and then deserted her. She claimed that Gable left her in such desperate straits that unless MGM could arrange some financial assistance, she would be forced to write the story of their relationship and auction it off to one of the major newspaper syndicates or magazines.

Dillon's letter brought fast results. After investigating her complaints, Mayer set up a fund for Dillon out of Gable's wages. He ordered the payroll department to deduct two hundred dollars every month and to send it to Dillon by check until further notice.

Mayer's meddling into his private life quickly alienated Gable, who despised the mogul and tried to have as little contact with him as possible. Mayer, whose efforts to play father to his stars were not always welcome, realized that and placed Gable in the charge of studio vice president Edward J. Mannix. The tough Irish-American from Hoboken, New Jersey, had once been a security bouncer at Palisades Amusement Park, whose owner-brothers, Nicholas and Joseph Schenck, took Mannix with them when they linked up with Marcus Loew in Loew's, Inc. Mannix was later dispatched to Hollywood as the studio's troubleshooter. He did all the delicate dirty work, supervised MGM's private police force, and had powerful friends in government and the underworld. A boozer, gambler, sports enthusiast, and womanizer, he was a perfect match for Gable, and they became lifelong friends. Whenever Gable had any kind of a problem, at MGM or personally, he could always rely on Eddie Mannix to help solve it.

If MGM's efforts to protect Gable from scandal seemed excessive for an actor who'd yet to earn the rank of star, by the summer of 1931 the press had pegged him as Hollywood's most promising male newcomer since the transition to talkies in 1929. His biggest boost came from *A Free Soul,* which had millions of moviegoers buzzing about his brutal treatment of Norma Shearer. Fan mail, then considered an accurate barometer of popularity, poured into the studio by the sackload.

Screenland magazine dubbed him "a lumberjack in evening clothes, the answer to ten million maidens' prayers, a big kid playing with fireworks." William R. Wilkerson, editor-publisher of *The Hollywood Reporter,* wrote, "A star in the making has been made, one that, to our reckoning, will outdraw every other star pictures has developed. Never have we seen audiences work themselves into such enthusiasm as when Clark Gable walks on the screen."

Thalberg decided that Gable was finally ready to be matched with the Divine Garbo. Publicity claimed that Garbo "demanded" him, as if she had sexual designs on him, but at the time she was actually involved in a lesbian affair with artist-writer Mercedes De Acosta. It simply made smart box-office sense to cast Gable with Garbo. None of her three sound movies to date had been as passionately charged as her silents with John Gilbert, whose alleged vocal deficiences, as well as personal problems with L. B. Mayer, had landed him at the top of MGM's black-list for the duration of his contract.

Susan Lenox: Her Fall and Rise was based on the 1917 best seller by David Graham Phillips, who ended up being shot to death by a reader outraged by its depiction of women as whores. Twenty-two writers under contract to MGM's story department contributed to the script, which had farm girl Garbo sleeping her way all the way to the top of the social ladder and then falling into the gutter. With all hope gone, she takes a boat to South America to search for Gable, a construction engineer whom she once loved but discarded for a wealthier man.

The film concluded with a reconciliation scene that became a camp classic. Garbo moans that "We are two cripples clinging to each other for salvation." Gable stares at her and sneers, "You have a very queer view of things."

Four years younger than Gable, Garbo was almost as tall and broad-shouldered as he was. Director Robert Z. Leonard had to choreograph their romantic clinches so that they didn't look like wrestlers. It was hardly one of those proverbial matches made in heaven. Garbo couldn't warm up to Gable. When she kept delaying production by suddenly taking days off to tryst with Mercedes De Acosta, he got disgusted.

Due to Garbo's absenteeism, *Susan Lenox* took forty-nine days to shoot, the longest of any of Gable's films so far. It was also the most expensive, costing $580,000. When released later that year, it earned $1.5 million in rentals worldwide, leaving MGM with a profit of $364,000 after the costs of prints and advertising were deducted. Such were the rewards in an era when the average price of a movie ticket was twenty-one cents.

When Gable finished *Susan Lenox,* Thalberg considered casting him in a follow-up to *Trader Horn,* an African jungle thriller that was MGM's biggest hit since the Depression started. Thalberg had purchased the rights to Edgar Rice Burroughs's *Tarzan of the Apes* and intended to film it on the studio's backlot. For authenticity, leftover footage shot in Africa for *Trader Horn* would be blended in.

Tarzan seemed a perfect fit for MGM's new he-man star—until he stripped down and put on swim trunks for a camera test. Now thirty years old, Gable still had a muscular physique, but it was not one that could win more than a booby prize in a bodybuilding contest. The role finally went to twenty-seven-year-old Olympic swimming champion Johnny Weissmuller, who also flunked a screen test but got hired after he agreed to undergo plastic surgery on his overlarge nose.

Losing the role may have been a lucky break for Gable. *Tarzan* was such a success that MGM started a series of sequels with Weissmuller but never permitted him to act any other character for the entire ten years that he spent under contract to the studio.

Gable, however, moved on to his third pairing with Joan Crawford, for the first time in a role that was equal in size and importance to hers. Scripted by weepy romance specialist Lenore Coffee, *Possessed* blended politics with sex. Gable played a wealthy New York lawyer with gubernatorial ambitions, Crawford his recent bride, an uneducated, ex–factory worker from the slums. Until she can learn the social graces and become an asset to his career, the marriage must be kept secret. Needless to say, Gable's political enemies find out and start a smear campaign to stop him from running for office.

Possessed finally ignited a full-fledged affair between Gable and Crawford. Director Clarence Brown was partly responsible. "He sensed the volcanic attraction between his stars and used that for all it was worth," Crawford remembered. "In the picture Clark and I were supposed to be madly in love. When the scenes ended, the emotion didn't."

Adela Rogers St. Johns later described it as "the affair that nearly burned Hollywood down." At stake were the careers of Gable and Crawford, both married to others, and the exalted reputation of their employer, MGM. It was a time when Hollywood was under heavy bombardment by lawmakers and religious pressure groups over the sexual content of movies, as well as the loose morality of stars and others in the industry who were said to be setting bad examples for the public.

Currently in its second year, Crawford's marriage to Douglas Fairbanks, Jr., had been wracked by career jealousies and their inabilities to resist extramarital temptations. But they stayed together for the sake of their image as Hollywood's most idyllic couple. The high divorce rate of movie stars was a favorite platform of moral crusaders.

Her marriage to Fairbanks had elevated Crawford to royal status as daughter-in-law to "the King and Queen of Hollywood" (with allowances made for the fact that Mary Pickford was Junior's stepmother). It was an amazing career-advancing accomplishment for the former Broadway chorus dancer, who earned her ticket to Hollywood by playing cozy with Harry Rapf, a large-nosed MGM executive also known as "the Anteater." Her next conquest was another of Thalberg's production supervisors, dwarfish Paul Bern, who had molded her into a star.

Ironically, Crawford had a striking facial resemblance to Pauline Frederick, who'd recently played her mother in *This Modern Age*. How Gable reacted to that casting is unknown, but the likeness may have been one of Crawford's attractions for him. But she was also beautiful, sexually aggressive, and one of the most desired women in the world. Gable fell hard. Like all of her intimates, he called her "Billie," a childhood nickname that she favored over "Joan," which MGM had pinned on her as part of the makeover of Lucille Le Sueur (pronounced "Le Sewer" by some of her enemies).

Gable and Crawford conducted the affair as guardedly as possible, mostly during working hours. They arrived at the studio earlier than required and stayed later. Their trysting place was Crawford's plushly furnished dressing room, which was actually a small trailer with wheels. Doug Junior had given it to her as a wedding present and was still paying for it on an installment plan.

Once or twice a week Gable and Crawford lunched together in the studio commissary, but anything more public than that would have raised suspicions. If the day's filming ended earlier than scheduled, they drove separately to a motel in Playa del Rey and spent the balance of the afternoon in bed.

Rather brazenly, they also double-dated, dragging their spouses along to movie premieres and nightclubs. One night a friend discovered Gable and Crawford necking behind the bandstand at the Cocoanut Grove while Ria and Fairbanks were sitting out front at a ringside table.

In a community with the third-largest press corps in the nation—about four hundred reporters and columnists representing publications all over the world—the affair didn't remain secret very long. The lovers may have been too reckless. Rumor had it that Crawford got pregnant and had an abortion.

In any case Louis B. Mayer became outraged and threatened to cancel both their contracts if the affair didn't end immediately. It did, or at least for a while. When two people are that passionately involved, new outbreaks can always be expected.

To save them from temptation, Mayer removed Gable from what was intended to be his next film with Crawford, *Letty Lynton*. Robert Montgomery took over the role, while Gable landed in another teaming with Wallace Beery and their *Secret Six* director, George Hill.

Hell Divers was a rip-off of *What Price Glory?*, with Gable and Beery as navy air force pilots who are friendly rivals and constantly feuding over service duties and dames. The story was in the he-man action category, and Gable's romantic interludes were limited to a few moments with a hard-to-get redhead played by Dorothy Jordan.

MGM rarely made films beyond its studio walls, but *Hell Divers* was an exception: the sea and aerial scenes were photographed with the cooperation of the navy at a base near San Diego. Gable underwent several days of training with the pilots who would double for him and Beery in the film. Gable needed to know the rudiments so that he looked convincing in close-ups where he was supposed to be behind the controls. Beery, an aviation fanatic who'd been flying his own planes for years, insisted on doing all but the most dangerous of his scenes without a double.

Hell Divers started Gable's career-long identification with aviation. He played pilots more often than any other type of occupation. For a he-man it was the noblest profession. Charles Lindbergh had soloed the Atlantic just four years earlier. The vast majority of people had never been up in a plane. Flying was daring, heroic, the mode of the future.

By the finish of *Hell Divers*, Gable was nearing the end of his one-year MGM contract. Thalberg's plan to match him with all the studio divas had been accomplished except for Marie Dressler and Marion Davies. The story department had yet to find a suitable vehicle for Gable and the sixty-two-year-old Dressler, so Davies got him next.

The thirtyish ex–Ziegfeld showgirl was unique among the MGM queens because of her liaison with William Randolph Hearst, America's richest and most influential press baron. Through a company called Cosmopolitan Pictures (named after one of his magazines), Hearst produced several films a year for MGM release, some but not all of them Marion Davies vehicles.

The association was one of MGM's most treasured. Although the majority of Davies's films were box-office flops, it was really Hearst who lost the money. MGM, however, gained preferential treatment for *all* its movies in Hearst newspapers and magazines, as well as the distribution rights to the extremely popular Hearst Metrotone News. In those pre-TV times, many people flocked to movie theaters *just* to see the newsreels.

For all the power that she represented, Marion Davies was a fun-loving, generous "broad" with peroxided hair and a tendency to stutter. Everybody became her friend, including Gable as soon as they started working together in *Polly of the Circus.*

Based on Margaret Mayo's Broadway hit of 1907, the romantic drama was well known to Gable, who'd acted one of the minor roles during his ill-fated summer tour with the Astoria Players back in 1922. It was gently amusing hokum about a trapeze artist who marries a small-town minister, much to the disapproval of a congregation that considers her a showbiz trollop.

Davies had been making Hearst-financed films since 1918, but not until 1929 did he have enough trust in his paramour to end a ban on kissing scenes with her leading men. Davies once confided to a friend, "Mr. Hearst is past his peak in the boudoir," so she often had little flings when her costars seemed interested. (In cases like the gay William Haines and Nils Asther, they weren't.)

Gable took the bait, but their trysting place was far larger than Joan Crawford's dressing trailer. It was a fourteen-room Mediterranean-style villa that Hearst had built for Davies in 1926 on a corner plot smack against the walls of MGM. A side door gave direct access to the studio.

During the filming of *Polly of the Circus,* Gable's one-year contract came up for review. MGM had the option of not renewing it or giving him a new contract at better terms. His present salary was $650 per week. Thalberg had promised agent Minna Wallis that a new contract would start at $1,000 per week and have escalators for periodic raises.

But in view of Gable's increasing popularity, Minna Wallis thought that he deserved to be paid more, beginning at $1,500 per week. Still furious over the Gable-Crawford affair, Louis B. Mayer said that Gable should really be tossed to the wolves, but he would agree to $1,250 per week and not a cent more.

Gable had become intimate enough with Marion Davies to seek her help. He told her that he thought he was worth $2,000 per week, and she agreed. She phoned Hearst and told him to apply pressure on Mayer and Thalberg. The result was a two-year contract that made Gable happy, though the weekly take-home pay would be $1,500 per week, with another $500 per week put into a trust fund similar to a pension.

Gable was forever grateful to Marion Davies. Though their dalliance was brief, Davies adored him and made him part of her inner circle of friends. He received an open invitation to stay at the fabled Hearst Castle at San Simeon, midway between Los Angeles and San Francisco. Nearer home, he was also always invited to the parties and masquerade balls that Davies threw at her 118-room Ocean House on the beach at Santa Monica.

Gable's new MGM contract became effective on January 22, 1932, ten days before his thirty-first birthday. The previous year, 1931, had been extremely lucky for him, but it was also the one in which the Depression had finally caught up with the movie industry. Even with many theaters reducing ticket prices to a dime or less, average weekly attendance in the United States plummeted from 110 million to 75 million. Warner Bros., Fox, and RKO suffered multimillion-dollar losses. Paramount was verging on bankruptcy.

Loew's, Inc., owner of MGM, was an exception, though it showed a profit of only $12 million, three million less than in 1930. The company's success was attributed to better-quality movies, shrewd management, and minimal ownership of theaters. (Paramount had ten times as many, most of them heavily mortgaged.)

MGM's strong point was summed up in its slogan: "More stars than there are in heaven." In 1932 Thalberg and Mayer added the long-established John Barrymore and the promising Jean Harlow and Myrna Loy to the firmament.

The studio purchased Harlow's contract from Howard Hughes for $60,000 and signed her to an escalating seven-year deal that started at $1,250 per week. Paul Bern, the production supervisor who had "created" Joan Crawford, took charge of molding Harlow, starting off with

Red-Headed Woman. Specially designed for her by staff scriptwriter Anita Loos, the film immediately established a permanent screen image for Harlow as a warm-hearted, wise-cracking slut (subsequently, usually with the platinum-blond bleach that she preferred).

By the time she joined the MGM roster, Gable's relationship with Harlow had developed into something rare and beyond sex. After meeting during the filming of *The Secret Six*, they were briefly lovers, but as Gable got drawn into her domestic life, they became more like devoted siblings. It was impossible to know Harlow without getting involved with the domineering Mama Jean and stepfather Marino Bello. The trio had been together since Harlow was fourteen. Bello had both women under his thrall. The possibility of sexual abuse, physical as well as psychological, hung over the house that they shared on Clubview Drive in Westwood.

Gable visited frequently, but often just to play cards and booze with Marino Bello, who fast became a close buddy. Swarthily handsome and a snazzy dresser, the mustachioed Bello spoke with a slight Italian accent and had Mafia connections. He was chummy with mobsters like Longy Zwillman and Johnny Rosselli, but that was a side of him that Gable knew little about.

What Gable did know was that Bello had friends who ran gambling dens and high-priced whorehouses. Bello introduced Gable to all that and often accompanied him there. Bello also liked hunting and fishing, so they spent lots of time together—probably more time than Gable spent with his wife.

The marriage of convenience had turned chillier since Ria's discovery of Gable's affair with Joan Crawford. Ria was furious. Gable hadn't slept with her for years, but she still loved him and felt betrayed. She wanted to punish him, and the best way to do that seemed to be through his checkbook.

Though Gable now earned two thousand dollars per week, Ria was still paying most of the household bills from her own assets. After five years of togetherness, she told him that it was about time that he took over as provider. He gagged but gave in. He really had no choice except to propose a divorce, which would cost him more because Ria was entitled to 50 percent of everything under California's community property law.

Realizing also that she'd never get any of her own money back, Ria started spending Gable's lavishly, redecorating the house, hiring more servants, and buying clothes and jewels. Gable ranted and raved, forever accusing her of trying to replace Marion Davies as Hollywood's most prodigious spender.

With his new contract Gable became a full-fledged MGM star. He would no longer play secondary roles as villains or "the other man." And never again in any one year would he make eight films, as he did in 1931.

By February 1932 all of those films had been released. Surprisingly, the most successful was *Hell Divers,* in which he teamed with Wallace Beery, followed closely by *Possessed* with Crawford, *Susan Lenox* with Garbo, and *A Free Soul* with Shearer.

With additional help from MGM's publicity machine, Gable had started a new vogue for the he-man hero, whose fists and sarcastic wise-cracks were his sole weapons. He was proving to be one of the few stars who appealed both to men, who admired his mastery of the female, and to women, who, in those days at least, expected or wanted to be mastered.

It was also Gable's good luck that Hollywood needed new romantic idols. Except for Rudolph Valentino, who died in 1926, all the silent kings had been dethroned by the transition to sound. Even those with stage-trained voices, such as John Barrymore and Douglas Fairbanks, had grown ridiculous with middle age and their over-the-top histrionics.

Less classically handsome than his silent predecessors, Gable had a vibrant masculinity that, combined with his imperious voice and stac-cato diction, made him the first "immortal" created by the marriage of cinema and sound recording. Moviegoers had never experienced anyone quite like him before, so the very novelty was initially one of his greatest appeals.

His close chum Adela Rogers St. Johns, the most influential jour-nalist covering Hollywood, paid him the ultimate compliment, dubbing him "the Great God Gable" in an article for *Liberty* magazine. "A year ago not a soul in Hollywood had ever heard his name. Today he ranks ahead of every established favorite," she wrote. "The public has made a star. The motion picture industry is still gasping for breath. But Clark is the same man both on and off the screen, which is true of few stars. He has the same smile. The same animal magnetism. The same charm which no psychologist has ever explained, but which probably got Eve in the Garden of Eden when she first saw Adam."

The reason for Gable's popularity, she claimed, "is very simple. He is a man. They seem to be sorta scarce these days. And we are not nearly so complex nor so civilized as we like to pretend."

His first assignment under the new MGM contract was another teaming with Norma Shearer, in what promised to be one of the most unusual movies ever produced by a Hollywood studio. As a showcase for his wife, Thalberg had purchased the rights to Eugene O'Neill's 1928 Pulitzer Prize–winning drama, *Strange Interlude*.

Delving into the "strange interlude" that every woman goes through between sexual awakening and menopause, the play introduced O'Neill's invention of "interior monologue." The characters spoke both their conscious and unconscious thoughts, thus revealing themselves more completely than ordinary dialogue permits. The device revolutionized modern drama in the same way that James Joyce's stream of consciousness narrative revolutionized fiction.

Adding to the complexity of O'Neill's technique was his neurotic heroine, Nina Leeds. Her possessiveness and insatiable sexual appetite compel her to seek self-fulfillment through simultaneous attachments to three men who are for her, respectively, father image, husband, and lover.

Due to the superabundance of dialogue, *Strange Interlude* filled nine acts and required five hours to perform, making it about two and a half times longer than the average play. For the original Broadway production, there was only one performance daily, starting at 5:15 P.M. At 7:15 the curtain came down for an intermission of an hour and a quarter to enable the audience and the company to dine and refresh themselves before the start of the play's final three hours.

Due to its style, length, and sexual content, *Strange Interlude* seemed next to impossible to film, but Norma Shearer lusted to play the central role, in which her idol, Lynn Fontanne, had triumphed on Broadway. Thalberg assigned the adaptation to staff scriptwriter Bess Meredyth, who had helped to condense Lew Wallace's long-winded novel *Ben-Hur* into what became MGM's highest grosser to date.

Director Robert Z. Leonard, whose career dated back to 1916 and covered every genre of moviemaking, decided that O'Neill's device of the interior monologue was too unrealistic for the general public. With cinematographer William Daniels, Leonard developed an alternative method in which the scene "froze" while the actor's inner thoughts were heard on the soundtrack but were not actually spoken, as they were on the stage. But stopping the action too many times would test the audience's patience, so the device was used very sparingly and not in every scene.

Gable played Nina's longtime lover, who fathers a son who is passed off as her husband's. When the boy grows up and becomes engaged, the overly possessive Nina tries to prevent the marriage by informing his fiancée that insanity runs in his father's family. To undo the lie, Gable confesses to being the real father, which wreaks more havoc before everything comes together in a semioptimistic ending.

The story covered thirty years, and makeup artists turned Gable and Shearer white-haired and wrinkled for the concluding scenes. As Gable aged in the film, he also went from clean-shaven to mustachioed. It marked his first screen appearance with shrubbery (fake in this case), but only because the role required it.

While filming *Strange Interlude,* Gable was one of the first to learn that Jean Harlow had accepted a marriage proposal from Paul Bern, the production supervisor who'd been her mentor since she joined MGM. Gable's informant, Marino Bello, had no explanation except that his stepdaughter had flipped her lid and didn't know what she was doing.

But Harlow and forty-five-year-old Bern had been keeping company for several months. He escorted her to movie premieres, and she frequently visited him at his house in Benedict Canyon. "Paul explains things and lets me know I've got a brain," she later told a friend. "He's different and doesn't talk fuck, fuck, fuck all the time."

A private wedding ceremony was held at Bern's home on the evening of July 2, 1932. The next afternoon Gable and his wife were among those invited to an outdoor reception on the patio beside the swimming pool. When Harlow started to cut the wedding cake, the first two slices went to Norma and Irving Thalberg. Amidst all the gaiety there was nothing to suggest a tragedy to come.

As luck would have it, Gable became the first costar of the new Mrs. Paul Bern. Thalberg had been planning to team her with John Gilbert in *Red Dust*. But Gilbert's continuing descent into alcoholism made him a bad risk; under a contract negotiated in the silent era, when he was MGM's number-one star, Gilbert was entitled to $250,000 per picture. So Thalberg picked Gable to replace him.

With the shift from Gilbert to Gable, production supervisor Hunt

Stromberg ordered writer John Lee Mahin to revise the script. "The original intention of the movie was to use Harlow to restore Gilbert's fading image," Mahin recalled. "Gilbert had a high, squeaky voice, and was too thin from drinking and everything else, and nervous because he was unsure of himself. Gable, however, was like a raging bull. We had to rethink the whole concept and get rid of the director, Jacques Feyder, a sweet, delicate Frenchman who was one of Garbo's favorites."

As a 1928 play by Wilson Collison (coauthor of *Up in Mabel's Room* and *Getting Gertie's Garter*), *Red Dust* lasted just one week on Broadway but had a moderate success in stock due to its lust-suggesting title and lurid content. The Indochinese jungle locale enabled MGM to use backlot sets built for *Tarzan, the Ape Man,* which kept the total production cost of *Red Dust* to a moderate $408,000.

Collison's original story remained, but it was heated to a sizzle for Gable and Harlow. The manager of a rubber plantation falls in love with a prostitute while hiding her from the police. Just as they're settling into a meaningful relationship, he also becomes involved with the sex-starved wife of his chief engineer.

Gable made a friend for life in the replacement director, Victor Fleming, who'd only recently joined MGM but had a distinguished career, including a long association with his best buddy, Douglas Fairbanks. A "man's man," Fleming also raced cars and motorcycles, flew planes, and was a master mechanic, big game hunter, and female chaser (including Clara Bow and Norma Shearer before she married Thalberg). He made a perfect mesh with Gable, who was eighteen years younger and grew to respect him like a father.

Fleming and scriptwriter Mahin were the first to recognize that Gable was at his best when he played the foil. "When I wrote for him," Mahin recalled, "I gave Harlow the wisecracks because he was funniest when he reacted. And he'd say, 'Jeez, John, those lines are not particularly funny.' I'd tell him, 'But your expression when we cut to you—that's the funny thing. The audience doesn't really start to laugh—doesn't really get it—until that big kisser of yours comes on and you're terribly uncomfortable or sore.' Clark accepted that."

Gable's romantic scenes with Harlow and "the other woman," Mary Astor, were tremendously sexy without being graphic. "We did it with inferences," Mahin remembered. "Let people use their minds; let

them work. Harlow had a scene where she's taking a bath in a rain bar-
rel. Gable stands there looking at her, but you don't see more than her
bare shoulders. But you can tell what's going on in his mind."

Gable had a unique way of looking at women. "It wasn't a leer, it
was a pleasant look," Mahin said. "His eyes were open and frank, like a
child's. There wasn't any filth in them. Gable was frankly admiring. A
woman never feels bad when she's told that she's got a lovely body, and
that's what his eyes said."

Throughout *Red Dust* Harlow wore clinging, low-cut dresses, and
as was her personal preference, she was without undergarments. Gable
got turned on whenever they did love scenes, some of which may have
resumed in Harlow's dressing room after Fleming shouted "Cut." Gossip
swept the studio that they were having an affair, but it was more likely
a series of spontaneous combustions that had no ongoing emotional
complications.

Red Dust was filmed during the late summer of 1932, a time when
soundstages lacked air conditioning and all studios observed a six-day
work week. Comforts were minimal due to the simulation of Indochina
and its intolerable humidity. Everything dripped and stank like a real
jungle. Moths and other nonstinging insects were always being let loose
for realism.

Gable's only extended break came when Hollywood shut down for
Labor Day, September 5, which gave him Sunday and Monday off. On
Saturday night, he and Harlow's stepfather, Marino Bello, drove to Long
Beach, where they boarded a chartered yacht and sailed for Catalina
Island to do some marlin fishing. Bello had also arranged for two prosti-
tutes to keep them company.

Meanwhile, back on the mainland, Hollywood's greatest unsolved
mystery was in the making. At eleven-thirty on Labor Day morning,
police were summoned to the home of Mr. and Mrs. Paul Bern in Benedict Canyon. When they arrived and entered Bern's bedroom, they found
his naked body sprawled on the floor, his brains blown out, and a
revolver clutched in one hand. In the absence of Jean Harlow Bern, the
welcoming committee included Louis B. Mayer, Irving Thalberg, Eddie
Mannix, Howard Strickling, assorted other MGM executives, and the
house's staff of servants.

What really happened prior to the arrival of the police may never be known, but the sequence of events *after* Bern died seems to be this: Someone, either Harlow or a servant, panicked and phoned MGM's security chief, Whitey Hendry, for help. Hendry sent an SOS to Mayer, Thalberg, and others, all of whom arrived at the house within minutes of each other. The first order of business was to remove Harlow from the house. If Bern had been murdered, his wife would be the prime suspect. Howard Strickling drove Harlow to her mother's house and then returned to help Mayer and the others to prepare for the arrival of the police.

Gable and Marino Bello knew nothing until that afternoon, when they returned to Long Beach from their fishing expedition. Passing a newspaper stand, they spotted late editions with HARLOW'S HUSBAND DEAD in black headlines. While racing back to Los Angeles in Gable's car, they decided to separate when they reached the city limits. Bello took a taxi from there. He didn't know what to expect when he got home. But pulling up with Clark Gable would only implicate him if there were reporters and photographers waiting outside.

The official verdict on Paul Bern's death was suicide, based largely on a cryptic note that he allegedly wrote and left on the mantelpiece.

Dearest Dear,

Unfortunately, this is the only way to make good the frightful wrong I have done you and to wipe out my frightful humiliation.

Paul

P.S. You understand that last night was only a comedy.

The police autopsy revealed that Bern had the sexual development of a preadolescent, with tiny genitals that would have made it difficult, if not impossible, for him to engage in "normal" intercourse. The report was kept secret at the time, but it got dredged up several decades later by Harlow biographers seeking an explanation for the mysterious suicide note. According to the 1964 *Harlow* by Irving Shulman, Bern was a sadomasochist who treated his wife brutally from the wedding night onward. Supposedly the postscript "comedy" consisted of Bern strapping on a huge dildo and attempting to rape her.

If true, that might have given Harlow more reason to murder Bern than for him to commit suicide. It does seem now that Bern was murdered, but if not by Harlow, by whom? During the district attorney's inquest, another suspect was considered—Dorothy Millette, a New York stage actress who long before had lived with Bern as his common-law wife.

A case was presented that Millette, who had a history of mental illness, visited Bern on Sunday night and killed him during an argument. But while police were trying to locate Millette for questioning, *her* body was found floating in the Sacramento River, about a hundred miles from San Francisco. Investigators theorized that a guilty conscience drove her to commit suicide by jumping off a steamship-ferry.

Had MGM's executives not tampered with the evidence from the outset, the mystery of Bern's death might have been solvable. But nothing can be taken for granted, including the alleged suicide note, which may have been forged and/or planted.

It was the first great scandal in MGM's history, and L. B. Mayer ordered it squelched as quickly as possible. It stayed in the headlines for a few days, but Mayer pressured William Randolph Hearst and other publisher friends to go easy. Mayer's main concern was the upcoming presidential election. A devout Republican, he was one of the leaders of the California campaign for incumbent Herbert Hoover. He needed to keep the studio's reputation immaculate.

The Bern-Harlow marriage had lasted sixty-five days. The twenty-one-year-old widow was given temporary leave from *Red Dust* for the private funeral and a period of mourning. Meanwhile Gable continued working without Harlow, shooting scenes with Mary Astor, Gene Raymond, Donald Crisp, and others in the supporting cast.

Harlow returned on September 12, one week after Bern's death. Looking a bit puffy-eyed, she refused to do close-ups but made a few long shots with Gable and then left for the day. "That little lady has more guts than any *man* in Hollywood," Gable told a reporter who was visiting the set.

Harlow sailed through the rest of *Red Dust*, enabling production to finish on its originally scheduled forty-fourth day. To capitalize on all the publicity, New York headquarters ordered a rush distribution, which would mean postponing the release of *Strange Interlude*. It didn't make box-office sense to have two Gable films competing against each other. It also gave Thalberg more time for repair work on his wife's latest effort, which had been bombing in test previews due to the confusing interior monologue technique.

The reversal of release dates helped both movies. *Red Dust* was a smash hit and also caused a censorship furor with its steamy sex. MGM took advantage of it by advertising *Strange Interlude* as a similar sizzler and enjoyed another success. In fact, *Strange Interlude* had world film rentals of $1.24 million, slightly ahead of the $1.22 million for *Red Dust*. The latter, however, earned a greater profit for MGM because its production costs were $200,000 less than those for *Strange Interlude*.

After completing *Red Dust,* Gable received his first lesson in the frequent industry practice known as a loan-out. Buried in the boilerplate of every star's contract was a clause stating that their services could be loaned to another studio, where they would be entitled to the same salary and coddling that they received at their home lot. In a loophole that favored the studios, the loaner could charge the borrower more than the star's contract rate and keep the difference for themselves.

Some loan-outs were also swaps, where stars were traded when a studio was unable to cast a role from its own roster. At MGM Marion Davies was getting ready to make a musical entitled *Going Hollywood* and would consider only one leading man—Bing Crosby, America's number-one crooner and a prized Paramount star.

As MGM's hottest property of the moment, Gable was swapped for Crosby. Paramount offered Gable a choice of several scripts, but the only one that appealed to him was *No Man of Her Own*. The melodrama had been scheduled for direction by his friend Wesley Ruggles, with whom he had worked during his days as an extra.

Miriam Hopkins, Paramount's most temperamental star, was selected to team with Gable. But true to form, she demanded another assignment upon learning that *he* would receive top billing in the credits and advertising. She was replaced by Carole Lombard.

7

Eight years before he was swapped to Paramount, Gable had worked there as an extra in Lubitsch's *Forbidden Paradise,* but no "welcome back" banners greeted him when he arrived to start *No Man of Her Own.* As he drove through the main gate on Marathon Street, he realized how small the studio was in comparison to MGM. Packed into several square blocks in central Hollywood, it was mostly soundstages, with a small backlot that bordered on Hollywood Cemetery.

Paramount-Publix Corporation's combined studio, distribution, and theater divisions were running $18 million in the red. In another few months the company would declare bankruptcy, but Gable's temporary employment there shielded him from all that. Working at Paramount wasn't much different from working at MGM, except that it spared him the longer commute to Culver City.

Gable already had a nodding acquaintance with twenty-four-year-old Carole Lombard. Their travels on the Hollywood social circuit had often intersected but only for idle chitchat, usually in the company of their spouses. Lombard's husband, debonair William Powell, was a much more important star than she and also sixteen years her senior. By coincidence, she had married Powell in the same month of 1931 that Gable had wed (or rewed) his considerably older wife.

Lombard, however, was deeply in love with *her* spouse and was trying hard to make the marriage a success. Rumors were already flying about the age difference and career rivalries. Gable stood no chance of becoming anything more than Lombard's friend, although there is no evidence that he even desired that. He just wanted to make the movie and return to MGM, where he felt more at home.

Their first encounter at Paramount found Lombard in a foul mood. She had just returned to the studio from a two-picture loan-out to Columbia Pictures, and she gave Gable a blistering account of the dirty dealing that went on. Paramount charged Columbia $1,500 per week while she worked there, but she received only her customary $1,000 per week while Paramount pocketed $500 for itself. Her rantings were punctuated with some of the most obscene words that Gable had ever heard from a woman. He laughed, but he wasn't sure that he approved.

Scripted by Maurine Watkins (author of *Chicago*) and Milton Gropper, *No Man of Her Own* had originally been intended for Paramount's contract star, George Raft. But Gable easily fit the role of a crooked New York gambler who, while hiding out in a small upstate town, falls in love with the local librarian. On the flip of a coin, they decide to get married, though she's unaware of his illegal occupation. Taking her back to Manhattan with him, he keeps his activities secret by pretending to be a Wall Street broker. But while he's away on what he claims is an urgent business trip to South America, she discovers that he's really serving ninety days in jail.

Gable and Lombard proved an acting team worth repeating in what turned out to be their only movie together. "I was damned impressed by their work, especially in the romantic first half of the picture, which had a lot of comedy crammed in," director Wesley Ruggles recalled. "Clark was a damn sight better light comedian than he ever got credit for being. Yet I thought Carole was the revelation. Her work didn't *look* like acting, it was so damn natural, so fresh."

Dorothy Mackaill, who portrayed Gable's discarded mistress in the movie, remembered a flare-up between Gable and Lombard on the set. "Election Day was approaching, and Clark came in wearing a Hoover button. Carole ripped it off his lapel and told him to shove it up L. B. Mayer's ass. All the MGM employees had been more or less ordered to vote for Hoover. Carole warned Clark that if Roosevelt didn't win, the Depression would get worse, the studios would close, and we'd all be living in the streets with the hoboes."

How Gable finally voted is unknown. But on November 1 Franklin Delano Roosevelt was elected the thirty-second president, carrying forty-two of what were then forty-eight United States.

At the final-day wrap party, Lombard gave Gable something to remember her by: a ten-pound smoked ham with his photograph pasted on the packaging. If it was a gibe at his acting ability, he didn't seem to mind as he took her into his arms and gave her a farewell kiss.

Three weeks later Gable was back in harness at MGM, teamed for the first time with its most atypical star, thirty-two-year-old Helen Hayes. A queen of the Broadway stage, Hayes had just won the Oscar for Best Actress of 1931–32 for her screen debut in MGM's *The Sin of Madelon Claudet*. (In those days the qualifying period ran from August through the next July, with awards presented in November.) Since making that film, MGM had loaned Hayes to Samuel Goldwyn to costar with Ronald Colman in *Arrowsmith* and to Paramount for *A Farewell to Arms* with Gary Cooper.

Irving Thalberg believed that Hayes could be a radiant emotional diva in the tradition of Lillian Gish (who was still alive and kicking at thirty-four but was considered finished because of her identification with the early silent era). Hayes wasn't much younger, but she was still a new face to moviegoers who'd never seen her on the stage.

Hayes had an inferiority complex about her plain beauty and believed that she wasn't glamorous enough to be a movie star. But she went along with it to please her husband, journalist-playwright Charles MacArthur, who'd become one of Hollywood's highest-paid scriptwriters and wanted to settle there.

For Hayes's second MGM film, Thalberg ordered a remake of one of Lillian Gish's greatest, *The White Sister*, made in 1923 with Henry King as director. It was a risky choice because the Gish version was only nine years old and had been rereleased in 1928 with recorded background music and sound effects. Exquisitely photographed on location in Italy, it was a classic of silent cinema and had launched its leading man, Ronald Colman, into orbit as one of the screen's romantic gods.

Gable, needless to say, would be filling Colman's boots—and military uniform—in what was actually a remake of a remake. (Preceding Gish's version was one made in 1915 with Viola Allen and Richard Travers.) Almost forgotten today, *The White Sister* was a phenomenon of its time, starting out as a novel by F. Marion Crawford, a prolific American writer who spent most of his life in Italy. Published in 1901, *The White Sister* became an immediate best seller. In 1905 Walter Hackett adapted it into a play that ran for two years on Broadway and the road, after which it became a perpetual favorite of stock companies.

Gable played Giovanni Severa, a pilot in the Italian Air Force. While marching in a parade on a religious holiday, he accidentally meets a convent-raised aristocrat, Angela Chiaromonte, who has sneaked out to watch the festivities. They fall in love, much to the opposition of her father, who has a wealthy fiancé selected for her. The two lovers finally run away and live together until he's called to active duty in the 1914–18 War.

Two years pass without news of Giovanni, but finally comes word of his death in combat. Unable to face life without him, Angela enters a convent to become a nun in the White Sisterhood (the color of their habits). Meanwhile instead of being dead, Giovanni has been held captive all this time in an Austrian prison camp. Driven by his passion for Angela, he finally escapes, steals an Austrian plane, and flies back to Italy to find her.

Get out your handkerchiefs. By the time Giovanni locates Angela, she has taken her final vows. Only by special dispensation of the pope can she be released from them. Giovanni begs her to try, but during their long separation she has become more enamored of God and Christianity. Giovanni is heartbroken and leaves. Minutes later he is mortally wounded in a bombing raid. Sister Angela is summoned to his hospital bed, where he dies in her arms, finally reconciled to her decision.

Donald Ogden Stewart, another celebrated New York writer (and Algonquin Round Table wit) who'd succumbed to the golden lures of MGM's script department, did the screenplay. He updated the action to the 1914–18 War to further Gable's identification with aviation. Earlier versions, like the original novel, were set in the 1880s. In those days, of course, there were no planes. Ground army officer Giovanni drowned in a flood caused by an eruption of Mount Vesuvius!

Gable's new director-friend Victor Fleming was again on board for *The White Sister*. With Donald Ogden Stewart prodding him, he tried to restrain the two stars from overacting: the melodrama had so many contrivances that it could provoke laughter instead of tears if not deftly handled.

Due to Gable's stage training, Hayes loved working with him. "I'd just done a film with Gary Cooper, a beautiful and talented man, but not an actor in the traditional sense. He'd never been on a stage in his life, so you had to be patient with him and do things over and over until he got it right," Hayes recalled. "But Clark was a real pro. It's a pity that he never returned to the theater. He would have been wonderful, but Hollywood spoiled him. It was an easier way to earn a living. Once a performance is down on film, you don't have to repeat it night after night, month after month, sometimes year after year."

The White Sister was nearly completed by the time of MGM's annual Christmas party. Although the nation's newly elected president had promised a quick end to Prohibition, the studio's workforce wouldn't have to wait. Several truckloads of illegal liquor, beer, and wine were delivered, courtesy of Louis B. Mayer's close friend Frank Orsatti, a Mafia-connected bootlegger and a recent convert to talent agenting.

Before the party began, five hundred baskets filled with turkeys and other holiday goodies were distributed free to the public at the studio's main entrance on Washington Boulevard. Paid for by William Randolph Hearst, they were doled out by Gable and Marion Davies, dressed in their minister and clown costumes from *Polly of the Circus*. The baskets were intended for the destitute, but they were snatched up so quickly that it was impossible to tell how many fakers might have been in the crowd.

The studio's largest soundstage was converted into a restaurant so that all the employees could enjoy their gift of a turkey dinner at a single sitting. During dessert L. B. Mayer mounted a rostrum and predicted rosy times ahead: "There is nothing in this business which good pictures cannot cure. They will do well under any political administration. Naturally, if the economic state of the country improves, our industry will have less to worry about. But first, of all considerations, comes the product. If we continue to turn out the hits, which we can do with all of us working together, the Depression will soon be ancient history."

After his speech Mayer walked around the tables to shake hands and then left the studio. His departure marked the start of the real party, which turned into a bacchanal that spread to all the soundstages, office buildings, and outdoor sets on the backlot. Stag movies were shown nonstop in the projection rooms. In the publicity photo gallery, anyone could have their picture taken, provided that they first stripped naked.

Stars and laborers, executives and secretaries shared drinks and paraded the streets. People were making love on the tops of desks as well as underneath them.

Gable was such a magnet that his face and ears were covered with lipstick marks. When last seen that evening, he was headed for his dressing bungalow, accompanied by two starlets.

Irving Thalberg, whose doctors had restricted him to one cocktail or glass of wine per day, lost count, becoming so drunk that Norma Shearer rushed him home in their chauffeured Rolls-Royce. Several hours later Thalberg suffered a heart attack. He was confined to bed, with doctors and nurses in attendance around the clock. MGM announced to the press that he had influenza and would be working from home until he recovered.

Thalberg's health was the main topic of conversation at L. B. Mayer's annual New Year's Day party at his Spanish-style mansion on the Santa Monica beachfront. Attendance at the buffet brunch was more or less obligatory for all of MGM's stars, directors, and top executives.

Gable brought his wife *and* Jean Harlow, who'd been married and widowed since Mayer's 1932 gathering. Afterward the trio stopped off at the Thalberg residence, which was just down the road. Norma Shearer turned them away at the door, claiming that her husband was still too ill to receive visitors.

Several days later Mayer announced that he was taking charge of production until further notice. One of his first and easiest decisions was to approve Thalberg's already-hatched plan to get Harlow working again, in another teaming with Gable. Anita Loos came up with the original idea for the script, which she cowrote with Howard Emmett Rogers.

Hold Your Man was a hard-boiled comedy-drama that stuck to the formula of *Red Dust* but made Gable as shady a character as Harlow's tough girl. A slick con artist, he uses her as a sexual pawn to blackmail married men. When he accidentally kills one of their victims, he vanishes and leaves Harlow to take the rap. While serving time in jail, she turns out to be pregnant with Gable's child. As soon as he finds out, a guilty conscience compels him to set things right. With help from an expert lawyer, he gets off with a short prison term. On release day he finds Harlow and their baby son waiting for him.

Sam Wood, another one of MGM's contract directors who had been grinding them out since the early silent era, filmed *Hold Your Man* in eighteen days, at a cost of $266,000 ($142,000 *less* than *Red Dust!*). The film was Harlow's third in a row with cinematographer Harold Rosson, who'd become her close friend and confidant since Paul Bern's death.

By February Irving Thalberg's health had improved enough that doctors prescribed a rest cure for him at Bad Neuheim in Germany. Norma Shearer and a retinue of medical professionals would accompany him on the trip, which was expected to take three months. Travel was largely by ship, from Los Angeles to New York via the Panama Canal, and then a transfer to a transatlantic liner.

In Thalberg's absence Mayer began to reorganize production, turning supervisors into producers who each ran a unit responsible for a specified number of films per year. He offered one of the units to his son-in-law, David O. Selznick, who currently headed production for RKO Radio but was eager to leave the bankrupt company. Selznick accepted, on condition that he report only to Mayer and not also to Thalberg when the latter returned from Europe.

Upon arriving at MGM, Selznick requested Gable for his first project, *Dinner at Eight,* which would have an all-star cast similar to the one that Thalberg had assembled for the studio's recent blockbuster, *Grand Hotel.* But the only role in *Dinner at Eight* that suited Gable was a secondary one of a Park Avenue doctor. Mayer thought it would be a waste of Gable, and Selznick had to settle for Edmund Lowe. But Jean Harlow landed in the mix, along with Marie Dressler, Wallace Beery, John and Lionel Barrymore, Jean Hersholt, Lee Tracy, Billie Burke, and Madge Evans.

Ironically, the production shake-up at MGM coincided with southern California's first major earthquake, which struck Long Beach on March 10 and killed 115 people. It was hardly as devastating as the one that hit Japan just eight days earlier and killed 2,990, but at 6.2 on the Richter scale it was powerful enough to jolt Los Angeles, forty miles to the north. At the movie studios there was pandemonium as electricity went off, soundstage floors buckled, and workers fled through the gates in panic.

Gable, who was at home that day, later recalled: "Suddenly the whole house started to shake like hell. I looked out the window and palm trees were bent double. I just stood there and then this big sofa shot out from the wall. I was scared and got out of there quick."

Three days later Gable experienced a different kind of shock. Mayer summoned stars, writers, directors, and department heads to a meeting and announced that every employee earning fifty dollars per week or more would receive 50 percent less for the next eight weeks. It was an industrywide decision in keeping with President Roosevelt's temporary closure of the nation's banks as the first step toward ending the economic depression.

Gable's next paycheck shrank from $2,000 to $1,000. Along with many others, he was furious because MGM and its parent company, Loew's, were not only solvent but had reported a 1932 net profit of $9.3 million. In response to many such grumblings, Mayer canceled the pay cut after six weeks.

By that time Gable, together with his wife and two stepchildren, had moved from Beverly Hills farther west to Brentwood. The area was more secluded and too far from Hollywood for most autograph hunters and sight-seeing buses. The new house, another rental, was a two-story white Colonial set back from the road behind trees and shrubbery.

A new addition to the household was Gable's father, who'd drifted into town with a caravan of dustbowl refugees from Oklahoma and had turned up at MGM's front gate one morning asking for his son, the movie star. Gable, working in *Hold Your Man* at the time, got summoned to identify him and was shocked by his appearance. Though only in his early sixties, Will Gable had shrunk from malnutrition and looked a grizzled eighty. His clothes were ragged, and he smelled as if he hadn't bathed in weeks.

Gable didn't know what to do, so he led Will to his dressing bungalow and phoned Howard Strickling for help. They decided that Gable should take his father home with him as soon as they could clean him up, send him to the studio barbershop, and outfit him with some new clothes from the wardrobe department.

The two Gables had been separated for eleven years. If it had been the son's choice, the estrangement would have continued. But for the sake of appearances, he had to take over his father's care and try to develop a cordial relationship.

Will's arrival delighted Ria Gable. "Mother had a great sense of family," her daughter Jana Lucas recalled. "She thought that Clark's father should be welcomed and have a place in her home. They built another bath and gave him my younger brother's room. Then they turned the sewing room into a bedroom for my brother, and he shared a bath with me. Grandpa Gable wasn't a bit well when he came to live with us. He gained weight and looked fine. He was sweet; we all liked him. I don't think Clark thought about it much one way or the other. I don't think he had much closeness there. But he accepted it."

By now Gable and Ria had been legally married for going on two years but living together for five. She seemed content with her name-only status. To protect Gable's romantic he-man image and to spare his unmarried female fans disillusionment, MGM's publicity department tried to hide his domestic situation with a much older wife and two teenage stepchildren. The public never knew that he was even going through the motions of being a husband and father. He tolerated Ria's fondness for throwing dinner parties for the Hollywood elite. He adored his stepson, Alfred Lucas, whom he took to sports events, fishing, and swimming. He screened all of stepdaughter Jana's beaux and eventually stood in for her deceased father at her wedding to a young doctor.

Gable was still involved with Joan Crawford but not as intensely as before L. B. Mayer ordered them to stop. Crawford had tried reconciling with Douglas Fairbanks, Jr., but when he finally discovered her philandering, he decided to sue for divorce.

Mutual friends told Fairbanks that Crawford and Gable had been having "an intense and fully requited love affair for almost two years," he recalled in his autobiography. "To record that I was surprised must prove one of this book's greatest understatements. . . . But Clark was such a nice guy that even in my private distress I couldn't blame him. Had our positions been reversed, I wasn't sure I wouldn't have been equally deceitful."

Fairbanks had, in fact, also been unfaithful with a string of "singularly attractive women," but that didn't stop him from condemning Crawford. When he threatened to name Gable as corespondent in the divorce, she rushed to L. B. Mayer to confess everything and to plead for help in averting a scandal that could destroy all three careers.

It seemed like a replay of an earlier crisis. But Mayer had warned Gable and Crawford then of the consequences if they disobeyed him. MGM now had no choice but to terminate their contracts if Fairbanks cited their affair in his divorce action.

But Mayer also had an obligation to Loew's-MGM. If he dismissed two of its most valuable stars during that time of economic chaos, the stockholders might be outraged and demand his replacement.

Instead, Mayer had a meeting with Crawford's husband and ruffled his male ego. Mayer told Fairbanks that he'd look like a "schmuck" if he blamed Gable for the breakup of his marriage. The public would assume that "Junior" wasn't man enough to keep Joan Crawford sexually satisfied.

Fairbanks agreed to take the gentleman's way out—that is, to let his wife divorce him. Such was the customary legal procedure in those days, when women were considered "the weaker sex." The wife could simply claim incompatibility, and no sordid secrets had to be exposed.

Crawford retained the expert Jerry Giesler to represent her in court. On May 13, 1933, she received her freedom. The marriage had lasted nearly four years, or about three years and eleven months longer than Hollywood gossipmongers had predicted.

Meanwhile Gable's supposedly happy marriage continued, so any public romance with the suddenly single Crawford was still too risky. But the affair was far from over, though subject to changes in the weather. Both had roving eyes and low resistance to temptation.

"Clark was the least selective lover in the hemisphere," MGM casting executive Billy Grady recalled. "He'd screw anything—a girl didn't have to be pretty or even clean."

Myrna Loy, one of the few MGM contract stars who'd yet to work with Gable, remembered that "he was always on the make at the studio, after everyone, snapping garters left and right."

Gable and Loy first met at one of the monthly dances held by the Mayfair Club, a social group that all the Hollywood stars and VIPs belonged to. Gable came with Ria and agent Minna Wallis, who was one of Loy's best friends and who introduced them. When the band started playing "Dancing in the Dark," Gable invited Loy for a whirl around the floor.

"He acted like a perfect gentleman—attentive, but not aggressive," Loy recalled. "He was vibrant and warm, a marvelous dancer. It was divine."

When the crowd started to leave, the Gables offered to share their limousine with Loy and Wallis. After Wallis was dropped off at her home, Loy found herself sharing the backseat with Gable and Ria. "He started edging toward me—with his wife sitting there right beside him. Of course, he was probably loaded by that time. We all were, to a certain extent."

When they reached Loy's house, Gable insisted on escorting her to the front door. "As I turned to unlock it, he bent down and gave me a 'monkey bite,' which left a scar on my neck for days. I turned around and gave him a shove, sending him backward two or three steps off the porch and into the hedge. As he stumbled back, I remember he laughed a little, which infuriated me all the more. It was just the idea of his wife sitting out in the car. I'd had quite a few beaus, but this was different. This was not right. I wanted no part of it."

When Loy next saw Gable at the studio, he walked right past her with his nose in the air. Soon after that they were cast in the same movie, but not to act together. Their scenes were filmed separately, and they were never on call at the same time.

Night Flight, based on the highly acclaimed novel by French aviator-writer Antoine de Saint-Exupéry, was Gable's first assignment with David O. Selznick's new production unit. Selznick intended a high-adventure tale of airmail pilots in the Andes, with spectacular flying scenes that would outdo such classics as *Wings* and *Hell's Angels.*

But that plan didn't mesh with Saint-Exupéry's book, which was short on plot and crammed with poetic and philosophical musings. To turn it into a vehicle for Gable, Selznick hired John Monk Saunders, a 1914–18 War hero pilot who had scripted *Wings* and similar epics, to devise an exciting story to blend together with whatever could be salvaged from the novel.

Oliver H. P. Garrett, a favorite scriptwriter of Selznick's and a specialist in patchwork, did the final draft, which still disappointed the producer and caused him to make more changes. In the end he turned *Night Flight* into an episodic *Grand Hotel* of the skyways, with Gable topping an all-star cast that also included Helen Hayes, John and Lionel Barrymore, Myrna Loy, and Robert Montgomery.

The White Sister had been a bigger grosser than any of Gable's teamings with Crawford, Garbo, Shearer, or Harlow, so for *Night Flight* Selznick insisted on a rematch with Helen Hayes, even though it was something of a cheat. Except for an early scene establishing them as a married couple, Gable spends the whole movie in the air, while Hayes sits at home, gazing fondly at his photograph and praying that he'll return safely.

The film centers on a South American airline managed by John Barrymore, a strict disciplinarian who forces his pilots to fly under the most dangerous conditions, including night flights over the snow-capped mountains of Patagonia. After several narrow escapes, Gable dies in a crash while flying urgently needed serum to typhoid-infested Rio de Janeiro.

During production Gable did most of his flying on the ground, sitting in a replica of an open cockpit, with the sky projected on a screen behind him. But director Clarence Brown also took him to Denver for location scenes that used the Rocky Mountains as stand-ins for the Andes.

In one scene Gable's character made a parachute jump that had to start at an altitude of 25,000 feet in order to give the camera crew enough time to film the chute opening and floating down. Dressed in Gable's pilot outfit with helmet and goggles, stuntman Ivan Unger was taken up in the plane. When he reached 20,000 feet, he collapsed from lack of oxygen and had to be rushed to a hospital. Clarence Brown jokingly asked Gable to take over, but there was no chance of that, and the shot never got made. Back at MGM the special effects department tried faking the scene with miniatures and rear projection, but the result looked far from the real thing.

David Selznick, who was delighted to get Gable for *Night Flight* after being denied him for *Dinner at Eight,* said at the time: "He has that God-given thing: a theatrical personality, the ability to communicate with an audience, which all the training in the world can't give you. Experience helps, but without that other quality there is no such thing as the star personality. The public caught it in Gable the first time he walked on the screen."

Gable, however, was unimpressed by Selznick. The producer was such a perfectionist that the filming ran over schedule for a full three weeks. Gable had to cancel a fishing-and-recreation trip he had planned with Marino Bello. He began to worry that Selznick might eventually replace Thalberg as head of production and cause chaos: Selznick couldn't make up his mind and kept changing it. Gable, for his part, liked order and discipline.

Gable was hardly overjoyed when Mayer assigned him to Selznick's next project, *Dancing Lady*. Thalberg had intended the backstage melodrama for Joan Crawford, but Selznick wanted to replace her with Jean Harlow, who'd just done wonderful work for him in *Dinner at Eight*.

When Crawford found out, she confronted Selznick, who told her, "I don't know if you can play the part. She's a bit of a hooker. I think it's more Jean's style." Crawford bristled and said, "Listen, David, I could be a better hooker than Harlow any day of the year." Both started laughing, and Crawford was reinstated.

Gable hadn't worked with Crawford in the eighteen months since Mayer broke up the acting team as punishment for their misconduct during the production of *Possessed*. Mayer still disapproved of their personal relationship, but Crawford's box-office ratings had plummeted. Her last two films, a heavy melodrama with Gary Cooper entitled *Today We Live* and a remake of *Rain* in the famous role of Sadie Thompson, were bombs. Hitching her to Gable's ever-increasing popularity seemed a quick way to restore her popularity.

Based on a novel by James Warner Bellah, *Dancing Lady* was the sort of rags-to-riches saga that MGM usually turned out in two or three weeks. But Gable got queasy when Selznick decided to expand it into a semimusical with spectacular production numbers and guest appearances by Fred Astaire, Nelson Eddy, and Ted Healy's Three Stooges.

Selznick hired Richard Rodgers and Lorenz Hart to write the songs. He wasn't much impressed by their first attempt, "That's the Rhythm of the Day," but kept it and then fired them. Burton Lane and Harold Adamson took over. Among their contributions was "Everything I Have Is Yours," which became one of the biggest hits of the 1930s.

Scriptwriters Allen Rivkin and P. J. Wolfson were ordered to use the recent Warner Bros. blockbuster *42nd Street* as their model. Gable played Patch Gallagher, a hot-tempered stage director who turns a crass burlesque dancer into a Broadway star. He found that he had nothing in common with the role, in which he was supposed to be choreographing dance routines, telling composers how to write songs, and selecting sets and costumes. From his viewpoint, the character went nowhere and was just a foil for Joan Crawford.

As filming progressed, Gable became increasingly unhappy with Crawford. For the role of her millionaire admirer, she had demanded Franchot Tone, with whom she had worked previously in *Today We Live*. They had became intimately acquainted. Gable, who'd hoped to spend some quality time with Crawford in her dressing trailer, found himself locked out. A romantic triangle developed that was more impassioned than the one that Gable, Crawford, and Tone formed in the movie.

Prior to starting work, Gable joined some friends on a hunting trip to Jackson Hole, Wyoming. After his return on June 11 he was supposed to report to the studio the next day, but during the night he awakened with a high fever. In a panic he phoned Howard Strickling, who immediately summoned MGM's medical consultant, Dr. Edward B. Jones.

The diagnosis was grim. Pyorrhea had developed in Gable's always-troublesome teeth and gums. The infection was rapidly spreading through his system and threatened to kill him. Dr. Jones rushed him to a private hospital for treatment.

After several days on drugs, Gable rallied. Oral surgeon George Hollenbach, Jr., then took charge and, in one lengthy operation, extracted almost all of Gable's teeth. Two weeks later, when the gums were starting to heal, impressions were made for a set of false teeth.

Meanwhile Selznick and director Robert Z. Leonard were "shooting around" Gable, trying to finish all the scenes in which he didn't appear and saving his for last. Joan Crawford and Franchot Tone fell more deeply in love. Helping them was an intimate swimming pool scene that required them to master the technique of kissing underwater.

On July 30 Gable was feeling secure enough about his new teeth to come in for two hours to film a short scene with Crawford and Fred Astaire. Making his screen debut, Astaire had already shot his one dance number with Crawford so that he would be able to start his new long-term contract with RKO Radio the next week.

The one-day return proved too much for Gable. "He was so weak, perspiration broke out on his face. I never felt so sorry for anyone," Crawford recalled.

That night Gable developed another high fever and landed back in the hospital. His previous infection had apparently reached his gallbladder, which became inflamed and had to be removed. Doctors said it would be at least a month before he'd be strong enough to work.

Selznick wanted to replace Gable with Robert Montgomery, but L. B. Mayer wouldn't agree. MGM's season contracts with exhibitors had promised a Gable-Crawford starrer for Christmas, and the studio had to deliver. By August 25 Selznick had shot everything else he needed for *Dancing Lady*, so production was suspended until Gable could return for his scenes.

Since he first missed work on June 12, Gable's paychecks had also been suspended. He'd lost nearly $22,000 in wages, which pained him more than some of his health problems. He got so angry that he ignored doctors' orders and returned on August 29, only to collapse after a half-day's work. He went home and stayed in bed for a week.

Feeling fully recuperated, he finally returned on September 8, the thirteenth day of the longest production shutdown in MGM's history. Everybody applauded when Gable walked onto the set. Work went smoothly from then on. He finished his last scene—the fade-out clinch with Crawford—on October 20. Due mainly to the delays caused by Gable's health, the production cost $923,000, or $150,000 over budget.

Within four days Selznick assembled a rough cut for a sneak preview to gauge public reaction. The screening at the Fox Wilshire Theater in Beverly Hills was well received except for numerous comment cards expressing shock over Gable's haggard looks in the close-ups that were made right after he returned from his sickbed. Selznick decided to call him back for several days of retakes, which gave Gable more cause to dislike the producer, even though it was for his own benefit.

Due to his absences—and no doubt also to insecurity over his new dentures—Gable neglected Joan Crawford during the sixty-five-day shooting schedule, but Franchot Tone kept her busy. By the end of filming, Crawford and Tone were so passionately involved that they took off together for a New York vacation, boldly sharing a bedroom suite on the Santa Fe Chief–Twentieth Century Limited rail connection.

Gable was furious and became angrier still when informed that *his* next trip would be a loan-out to one of Hollywood's "poverty row" studios for a comedy about overnight bus service.

8

A Hollywood legend claims that Louis B. Mayer loaned Clark Gable to minor-league Columbia Pictures as punishment for the problems he caused during *Dancing Lady,* but that's not true. Between his illnesses and his suspended salary, Gable had been "punished" enough. It was simply a business deal that benefited both studios. MGM had no project of its own ready for Gable, and it also earned $500 per week by charging Columbia $2,500 instead of the $2,000 that he received at home.

Undercapitalized Columbia couldn't afford a large contract roster like MGM, so president Harry Cohn was always borrowing stars for the "A" releases that he produced to upgrade the studio's image as a factory for cheap programmers and short subjects. While borrowing Gable for *Night Bus,* Cohn also took MGM's John Barrymore for *Twentieth Century.* From Paramount he obtained Claudette Colbert for Gable's costar and Carole Lombard for Barrymore's.

To Gable personally, going to work at Columbia probably *seemed* like punishment after the posh comforts of MGM. He remembered the small studio in drab central Hollywood from his struggling actor days. He used to frequent the nearby intersection of Gower Street and Sunset Boulevard, known as "Gower Gulch" because shoestring producers came there daily to hire extras and bit players for westerns.

According to Frank Capra, who would be his director for the four weeks of the Columbia loan-out, Gable had to fortify himself with booze before he could face reporting to the studio. When Gable arrived for a script conference, he called him "Mishter" Capra and said, "I've always wanted to visit Siberia, but why does it smell so bad? And why ain't you wearing a parka?"

Infuriated, Capra said, "Mr. Gable, you and I are supposed to make a picture together. Shall I tell you the story, or would you rather read the script yourself?"

"Buddy, I don't give a shit what you do with it," Gable replied.

Capra saw that Gable was too intoxicated to reason with, so he simply handed him the script and escorted him to the door. As he left, Gable started singing the old saloon favorite "My Gal Sal."

Once he'd sobered up and read *Night Bus,* Gable decided that it wasn't any worse than some of his MGM scripts. Ironically, the original short story by Samuel Hopkins Adams had once been optioned by MGM after it was first published in Hearst's *Cosmopolitan* magazine, but when the studio decided to pass, Harry Cohn purchased it for five thousand dollars for Capra and scriptwriter-partner Robert Riskin.

Due to a recent flurry of bus movies, including MGM's *Fugitive Lovers* and Universal's *Cross Country Cruise,* Cohn ordered Capra and Riskin to find a more provocative title. The *It* in *It Happened One Night* could really stand for almost anything, although the neuter pronoun had been widely used as a euphemism for sex since the Middle Ages.

Retaining only the shell of the original short story, Robert Riskin wrote a script that started or at least perfected the genre known as screwball comedy. A hot-tempered newspaper reporter, just fired for impertinence while on assignment in Miami, heads back to New York by bus to find a new job. Sitting next to him and traveling incognito is the runaway, spoiled-bitch daughter of a millionaire. Daddy has posted a ten-thousand-dollar reward for her return, so it's not long before the reporter recognizes her and realizes his good luck. Besides collecting the reward money, he can also write a juicy story about her and sell it to the highest bidder. To make sure that others don't recognize her, he persuades her to leave the bus and to travel the rest of the way to New York by hitchhiking on the back roads.

Much of the script was left open to suit the improvisational style of Frank Capra, who had learned the ropes by creating visual gags for Hal Roach and Mack Sennett slapstick two-reelers and who had done his first feature directing with the silent comedy star Harry Langdon. Since joining Columbia in 1928, Capra had directed nineteen comedies and/or dramas. From his first collaboration with writer Riskin on *The Miracle*

Woman in 1931, his films had become increasingly laced with social comment that championed the ordinary citizen and moral goodness.

Gable had met Claudette Colbert during his Broadway period; she was an established stage star by the time of his debut in *Machinal*. He also knew that she was a lesbian in a sham marriage with gay actor-director Norman Foster, so he never tried to make a pass or to entice her into the temporary dressing suite that Columbia gave him.

"Clark had a ball making the film," Frank Capra remembered. "He was playing himself, and maybe for the only time in his career. That clowning, boyish, roguish he-man *was* Gable. He was shy, but a lot of fun with people he knew. He was very sensitive about those goddamned ears, but he made jokes about them. After a shot, he'd ask, 'What'd they get— an ear?' He didn't look like anyone else. It was not only physical. He had mannerisms that were all his own: ways of standing, smoking, and a great flair for clothes. Whatever came natural to him, I let him do it."

"Gable, I believe, idolized Capra," said the director's longtime sound mixer, Edward Bernds. "Gable's initial hostility was gone by the time we started, which was with a night scene at the Greyhound bus depot in downtown Los Angeles. Gable very quickly became friendly with the crew. I think he found that with Capra, picture making could be fun."

The story builds to a scene where Gable and Colbert must share overnight accommodation in a one-room tourist cabin. Colbert's actual reluctance to undress in front of the cameras gave Capra the idea for the "Walls of Jericho," a blanket hung from the ceiling to divide her bed from Gable's. While undressing behind the blanket, she drapes some of her clothes and undies on it, which turned out sexier than if she'd actually revealed herself.

As Gable strips down in the same scene, he removes his shirt and has nothing underneath. In real life he never wore undershirts, so he didn't want to be bothered with one for the film. Capra went along with it.

During the filming of the "Jericho" scene, Gable and Capra pulled a prank on Colbert. The director called her over to Gable's side of the curtain with "We've got a slight problem here. Clark wants to know what can be done about it." When she came around, Colbert found Gable under the bedcovers, smirking, with a large bulge rising from his crotch area. He'd taken a prop kitchen utensil and positioned it under the blanket.

"Awww!" Colbert laughed. "You guys!"

In his handling of Gable, Capra erased the dividing line between hero and comic. He gave Gable routines that were usually reserved for slapstick comedians. Gable teaches Colbert how to dunk a doughnut and also how to thumb a ride. She does him one better by sticking out a shapely gam and getting a passing car to stop immediately. The audience could laugh at the hero as well as admire him.

The thirty-six-day filming ended just before Christmas and cost $325,000. "Clark and I left wondering how the movie would be received," Claudette Colbert recalled. "It was right in the middle of the Depression. People needed fantasy, they needed splendor and glamour, and Hollywood gave it to them. And here *we* were, looking a little seedy and riding on our bus."

During 1933 Gable had made five films. *The White Sister* and *Hold Your Man* were hits. *Night Flight* disappointed but still earned a profit of $175,000. *Dancing Lady,* just being released as he finished *It Happened One Night,* proved a blockbuster. It was Gable's biggest grosser so far and also succeeded in its mission to restore Joan Crawford's popularity.

Right after his loan-out to Columbia, Gable returned to MGM for *Men in White,* based on a current Broadway smash (and soon-to-be Pultizer prize-winner). It marked the first time that the studio purchased a property expressly for Gable, a sure sign that he was no longer considered just a gigolo for its female stars.

Sidney Kingsley's *Men in White* had been hailed as the ultimate in social message drama. Set in a large metropolitan hospital, it exposed the inadequate training of interns and had stark depictions of operating room procedures. The first commercial success of the radical Group Theater, it was directed by Lee Strasberg and acted by an ensemble that included such future luminaries as Morris Carnovsky, Luther Adler, Clifford Odets, Elia Kazan, and Sanford Meisner.

Monta Bell, a longtime MGM director who'd been promoted to running a production unit, took over *Men in White* and assigned it to a partisan of the Group Theater. Polish-born contract director Richard Boleslawski had worked with the Moscow Art Theater under Konstantin

Stanislavsky, with Max Reinhardt in Berlin, and with the American Laboratory Theater in New York. Brought to MGM in 1931 by Thalberg, Boleslawski proved his mastery over actors with *Rasputin and the Empress,* which was the first and only teaming of all three Barrymore siblings—Ethel, John, and Lionel—on screen or stage.

With scriptwriter Waldemar Young, Boleslawski kept the core of *Men in White* but eliminated some of the subplots and toned down the realism to satisfy the Hollywood industry's new self-enforced censorship code. With most of the focus on Gable's character, it might have been more accurately titled *Man in White,* but it was still strong stuff and more daring than any of his previous films.

The play and movie started a minor industry in hospital doctor dramas that continues to this day on television, so the basic story now seems hackneyed instead of shocking. A brilliant intern and protégé of a noted surgeon is torn between going to graduate school to become a specialist and marrying his wealthy fiancée and starting a general practice on Park Avenue. While wracked with indecision, he becomes sexually involved with a student nurse, who gets pregnant. After a secret abortion that nearly kills her, she lands back as a patient in the very hospital where they work. The intern and his surgeon-mentor try to save her in an emergency operation, but too late. But there's still room for a happy ending. The shattered intern's fiancée not only forgives him but also supports his decision to continue his medical studies.

Men in White gave Gable his first chance to work with Myrna Loy, who played the fiancée. Due to that real encounter when he nibbled at her neck and she pushed him off the porch into a hedge, Loy trembled over the assignment. "Oh, wow, this is going to be something. I'm in deep trouble," she later recalled telling herself.

But Loy didn't reckon on the actress who portrayed the nurse— Elizabeth Allan. "Clark developed a pretty serious thing with Elizabeth. Every morning he greeted her with coffee and cakes. The crew always put out goodies, so Clark would load up and walk right past me like I wasn't there. That was his way of punishing me. We managed to be convincing lovers on camera, which wasn't easy while he virtually ignored me the rest of the time. He just wasn't taking no for an answer," Loy remembered.

Twenty-five-year-old Elizabeth Allan was a recent Hollywood

import from Great Britain, where she first attracted notice in stage plays and the internationally released Leslie Howard movie *Service for Ladies.* With her light brown hair, deeply set green eyes, patrician nose, and delicate complexion, she was once described as "pure English beauty at its best."

Add to that a curvaceous figure and a seductive speaking voice acquired at the Old Vic training school, and it becomes plain why Gable fell instantly in love with her. Before the filming of *Men in White* was even over, he insisted that MGM sign Allan to a long-term contract. That Gable had a wife in Hollywood and Allan a husband back in London didn't stop an affair from developing.

Men in White took only eighteen days to film and cost $213,000, including the $25,000 spent for the screen rights to the original play!

Without giving Gable time to rest, MGM sent him on a cross-country publicity tour that coincided with his thirty-third birthday. He was not in a mood to celebrate. For the sake of appearances, he had to take his wife along, share hotel suites with her, and pretend that they were happily married.

Simultaneously Columbia Pictures was getting ready to launch *It Happened One Night,* so publicists from both studios infected the nation with Gable Fever. In every city that he visited, female fans found out where he was staying and followed him around like wolf packs whenever he went out.

It all reached epidemic proportions in New York, where *It Happened One Night* premiered on Washington's Birthday (then a national holiday) at Radio City Music Hall, together with a stage show featuring the theater's resident orchestra and corps of entertainers. The first day's receipts set a house record and press reviews were generally favorable. But attendance plummeted on the third day, when Gable started a week of personal appearances only a block and a half away from Rockefeller Center, at the Capitol Theater on Broadway.

It was one of the most bizarre examples of the cutthroat competition that went on in the movie business during the Depression. MGM literally turned Gable into a vaudeville performer at the request of its affiliate, Loew's Theaters, which ran the 5,500-seat Capitol and had tough sledding against both the 6,200-seat Music Hall and the 5,900-seat Roxy, not to mention the 3,700-seat Paramount and 3,300-seat State in

Times Square. Incredible though it might seem today, all five of those palaces showed a feature movie with a stage show, with a combined total of 24,600 seats that had to be kept filled as much as possible.

Gable was drafted into stage service to compensate for the weakness of the Capitol's screen attraction, an MGM suspenser with Robert Montgomery entitled *The Mystery of Mr. X*. The film's leading lady just happened to be Elizabeth Allan. To keep Gable happy, MGM dispatched her to New York to do press and radio interviews. While she stayed at the Waldorf-Astoria, the same hotel where Gable and his wife were staying, the lovers managed to squeeze some private meetings into their hectic schedules.

Gable worked harder than he had in years during his stint at the Capitol. MGM spared no expense in preparing an act for him that included a re-creation of the major scene from *Dancing Lady* where he tussles with Joan Crawford while rehearsing a production number with her and a group of chorines. Stage actress Ruth Matteson was hired to play Crawford's role, with the dancers drawn from the Capitol's resident Chester Hale Girls.

The scene, with a rendition of "Everything I Have Is Yours" added, took about fifteen minutes to perform, but Gable also had to be emcee of the entire one-hour stage show. He gave a welcoming speech and introduced each supporting act, which included singer Charles Carlile, a comedy trio, a dance team, and several others.

Admission prices were 25 cents from ten A.M. until one P.M., 50 cents until five P.M., and 75 cents until closing time. Since the Capitol operated on a continuous basis, Gable was required to do five stage shows per day, or every ninety minutes, allowing time for the movie to unreel. When the ticket windows opened on the morning of the first day, the waiting line extended completely around the theater, from Broadway to Eighth Avenue and back. By the last performance, thousands were turned away, so a sixth stage show was added for the remainder of the run.

To give Gable time to rest, performances were scheduled so that he started his first show at noon and the last at eleven-forty-five. Due to the enormous crowds always waiting outside the theater, MGM arranged a police escort from the Waldorf-Astoria to the stage door to help him get through. Once inside he never left the theater until the end of the last show at nearly one in the morning. During the breaks he relaxed and entertained friends in the baronial nine-room apartment that was the on-site residence of Major Edward Bowes, the Capitol's managing director and founder of radio's legendary *Amateur Hour.*

For all his sweat during the one-week stand of forty-one performances, Gable received nothing more than his MGM contract pay of $2,000 (about $49 per show!). But it was a tremendous boost to his ego. In three years of working in playhouses near the Capitol, he'd never been in a hit or even seen his name in lights. He hadn't been able to draw people *into* theaters, but now many refused to leave. Needless to say, most of them were female, and they stayed all day, whooping and swooning whenever Gable opened his mouth. The younger and more agile tried to climb up onto the stage and had to be ushered back to their seats.

The competition with Gable's Capitol appearances resulted in *It Happened One Night* lasting only one week at Radio City Music Hall, which replaced it with *David Harum* (starring Will Rogers) and a whole new stage show. It should be noted that since the Music Hall started showing movies in January 1933, only one, RKO's *Little Women,* had done enough business to be held over for a second week, so the failure of *It Happened One Night* to do so was no disgrace.

Happily for Columbia and Frank Capra (who got 10 percent of net profits), *It Happened One Night* became a smash hit, although not immediately. Openings in other major cities were also disappointing. But enthusiastic word of mouth from moviegoers who did go to see it began to spread, and theaters suddenly had to extend the run or arrange a return engagement.

"Everybody began to talk about it—'Let's go see that Gable picture again and take so-and-so with us this time.' The *people* discovered that picture," Capra recalled. Domestic film rentals were about $1.1 million, which was a huge amount for a small studio like Columbia that owned no theaters and had to charge exhibitors low rates in order to obtain bookings.

Gable's impact on the public was immense. Men grew brasher and perhaps *too* macho for some women. "Who do you think you are? Clark Gable?" became an overnight catchphrase.

Gable's apparent disdain for undershirts in the "Walls of Jericho" scene caused retail sales of the item to plunge by 75 percent. Conversely, several things that Gable did wear in the film became male fashion fads: a single-breasted jacket in the Norfolk style of English tailoring, a V-neck sweater, a felt fedora with a snap brim that could be turned up or down, and a trenchcoat.

Since some of those were too pricey for the average Depression Joe, Gable's most copied accessory was his pencil-thin mustache. Every adult male was free to grow one, and they seemed to do so by the millions.

Up to now Gable's mustache had been an on-and-off adornment, depending on the characters he played. After making *It Happened One Night,* he shaved it off for the young intern in *Men in White.* He'd also gone without in *Hold Your Man* and *No Man of Her Own.* In private life he favored one because it suited his large expanse of face and drew attention away from his big ears.

The public response to *It Happened One Night* made him decide to keep it permanently, or at least as ceaselessly as an actor can. A mustache may not be acceptable for some types of roles, but it did suit his next film at MGM, which had already started production by the time he returned from his promotional tour. *Manhattan Melodrama* was Gable's first stint with director Woodbridge Strong Van Dyke II, who signed his work as W. S. Van Dyke and had the studio nickname "One-Take Woody." A veteran of silent westerns, which he often shot two at a time by overlapping actors and sets, Van Dyke knew every time-saving trick of assembly-line production and rarely worked in sequence with the script. Scenes were shot randomly and finally put together in the right order during the editing process.

Manhattan Melodrama had an episodic structure that required Gable's presence for only twelve of the twenty-four-day shooting schedule. Van Dyke did him a favor by making the scenes all in one block. Gable wanted to spend as little time as possible around David Selznick, again his producer-in-charge. Selznick now enjoyed equal status with Irving Thalberg, whose continuing frail health had forced him to step down from overall production chief to head of his own unit.

Based on a story idea by Arthur Caesar, *Manhattan Melodrama* was pure fiction spun from one of history's worst maritime disasters, the 1904 fire aboard the excursion boat S.S. *General Slocum,* in which 1,021 picnickers from the Lower East Side immigrant community perished. Among those left orphaned are three boys who help each other to survive the hard life of the ghetto. Jim Wade grows up to be a lawyer, Joe Patrick a priest, and Blackie Gallagher a big-time gambler.

The priest fades into the background as a conflict develops between Jim, a candidate for district attorney, and Blackie, by now a murderous prince of gangland. Caught in the middle is Blackie's moll, Eleanor. Through a chance encounter with Jim, she falls in love with him and they eventually marry. When Jim's political enemies threaten to use his wife's shady past in a mudslinging campaign, Eleanor asks Blackie for help. During a scuffle with one of the blackmailers, Blackie kills him. As district attorney, Jim must prosecute his childhood friend and gets him sentenced to death. The conviction helps Jim to win the gubernatorial election, but on the day of the execution Eleanor confesses that it was for his sake that Blackie committed the murder. Jim rushes to the prison to commute the death sentence, but Blackie won't permit his friend to betray his principles. He walks bravely to the electric chair with Father Joe, the third ex-ghetto boy, as his spiritual escort.

Manhattan Melodrama was another of MGM's joint efforts with Hearst's Cosmopolitan Pictures and further proof that not all were Marion Davies vehicles. Selznick picked Myrna Loy for the female lead and pulled a switch on Gable's recent roles by casting him on the wrong side of the law as Blackie Gallagher. Character actor Leo Carrillo got the featured part of Father Joe.

Except for Gable and Robert Montgomery, whom Selznick considered too bland for the role of Jim Wade, MGM's contract roster had no major male stars to choose from except John Gilbert and Ramon Novarro, tarnished holdovers from the silent era. Selznick turned to the open market and hired William Powell, who'd recently been released from a six-thousand-dollar-per-week contract at financially strapped Warner Bros.

Since Powell just happened to be a client of Myron Selznick, David's agent-brother, Gable suspected the move was a plot to bring the actor to MGM permanently and to give him choice roles that might otherwise have been his own. Powell did end up with a long-term MGM contract, but Gable's fears were groundless. Nine years his senior, Powell was too mature-looking and also too much the debonair farceur to qualify for the rugged he-man roles that were Gable's specialty.

Gable found Powell easy to work with, and they became studio chums if not close friends. Powell was a moody intellectual and tended to be a loner, or so Carole Lombard complained when she divorced him in 1933 after twenty-eight months of marriage.

Manhattan Melodrama introduced Gable to a thirteen-year-old freelancer named Mickey Rooney, who portrayed him as a youth in the first part of the movie. Needless to say, they never shared a scene, but Rooney landed an MGM contract on the strength of his performance and picked Gable as a role model in his own climb to stardom. Unfortunately, Rooney eventually stopped growing at five foot one, so any physical resemblance to the adult Clark Gable would be only in his imagination.

By the time Gable finished *Manhattan Melodrama,* he was finally starting to soften in his attitude toward Myrna Loy, or at least in front of the cameras. "Clark suffered so much from the macho thing that love scenes were difficult for him," she recalled. "He kept very reserved, afraid to be sensitive because it was against his masculine image. I had to play it a bit rough with him, to bring him out."

When released that summer, *Manhattan Melodrama* made front-page headlines as the movie that lured murderous bank robber John Dillinger to his death outside the Biograph Theater in a Chicago neighborhood. FBI agents who'd been tipped off to his attendance gunned him down as he left the theater with his female betrayer, who wore a red dress as a code signal. News reports claimed that Dillinger was such a Clark Gable fan that he would never miss one of his movies, even at the risk of his life. Perhaps. Subsequent investigations hinted that Dillinger set the whole thing up and that a henchman really died in his place. The case was never officially closed, and it remains a mystery.

In the spring of 1934 Gable acquired a new stepmother who already happened to be his aunt. Will Gable married Edna Gable, the widow of his brother, Frank. The wedding cost Clark Gable a bundle, but it at least got his father off his neck to some degree. At the urging of Ria Gable, he bought Will a bungalow in North Hollywood for $3,500 and also agreed to pay him a living allowance of $500 per month.

Though his son was now one of the most famous men in the world and was earning $2,000 per week, Will Gable still considered acting a sissy's profession and kept nagging him, "Kid, why don't you get out of that silly business and do a man's work?" To please his father, Gable finally acceded to his longtime wish that he join the Freemasons. To become a member of the secret fraternal order, a man must first be nominated by someone within. Will Gable had been a Mason for many years, and since moving in with his son, he'd been affiliated with the Beverly Hills lodge.

After serving his apprenticeship, Clark Gable became a Master Mason and eventually also joined the auxiliary charitable order known to outsiders as the Shriners. Many U.S. presidents and other world leaders have been Masons, whose ideals include "kindness in the home, honesty in business, courtesy in society, fairness in work, and understanding and concern for the unfortunate."

According to some of Gable's friends, he took his vows very seriously, even when it came to casual sex. He would not go to bed with any woman whose husband, father, or brother happened to be a Mason. How he learned that is unknown, but perhaps he asked before indulging.

Following *Manhattan Melodrama,* Gable moved on to a rematch with Joan Crawford for two back-to-back projects, the first a romantic melodrama for Hunt Stromberg's production unit and the second a screwball comedy with Bernard Hyman as producer.

After the smash hit of *Dancing Lady,* Crawford's next movie, *Sadie McKee,* had flopped, which exhibitors blamed on her coactors, Gene Raymond and her real-life swain Franchot Tone. Both were second-string stars and apparently lacking in box-office strength, so to save Crawford's popularity from slipping back to its pre–*Dancing Lady* low point, MGM's sales force demanded more teamings with Gable.

In the seven months since they made *Dancing Lady,* Gable had become seriously involved with Elizabeth Allan, who was currently working at MGM for David Selznick's unit in *David Copperfield.* Crawford, meanwhile, had started living with Franchot Tone, at least part of the time. He'd rented a house near hers that he used as a retreat whenever they had one of their frequent squabbles. Like Gable, Tone loved to booze and to chase women, but he did so more recklessly and to the detriment of his career. Crawford had threatened several times to leave him, especially after discovering a secret that could ruin him if it ever got out. Tone had an illegitimate child who was being raised by its mother, a Broadway stage star, and her unsuspecting actor-husband.

In the three years since they first worked together in *Dance, Fools, Dance,* Gable and Crawford had developed into the sort of friends who sleep with each other now and then just for pleasure. During their latest collaborations, "We grabbed every chance to be alone," Crawford remembered.

Directed by Clarence Brown, *Chained* was the weightier of the two vehicles, with Gable as a wealthy rancher and Crawford as the mistress of an older and much richer business tycoon (played by the suave character star Otto Kruger). While waiting for Kruger to get a divorce from his grasping wife, Crawford falls in love with Gable, but drops him out of loyalty to her sugar daddy, whom she marries as soon as he becomes free. Gable is heartbroken and decides to confront the new groom, who gallantly offers to "unchain" Crawford when he realizes how much the two young people love each other.

"One-Take Woody" Van Dyke, who'd just made *The Thin Man* in eighteen days, took over the direction of the next Gable-Crawford package, *Forsaking All Others*. Staff writer Joseph L. Mankiewicz did the script, which was based on a 1933 play that returned Tallulah Bankhead to the Broadway stage after ten years as the darling of London's West End. Unfortunately for Bankhead, who had invested forty thousand dollars of her own money in the production, it flopped. But MGM had already purchased the screen rights and proceeded to film it, though with some drastic changes to the plot.

Mankiewicz borrowed some of the elements of *It Happened One Night,* expanding the romance into a triangle between Gable, Crawford, and another of MGM's top stars, Robert Montgomery. Crawford played a spoiled socialite (is there any other kind?) who has been stringing Gable and Montgomery along since they were all kids together. Without realizing it, she has always loved Gable more, but she winds up engaged to marry Montgomery, who strands her at the altar by eloping with his longtime mistress. Gable moves in to fill the void, but when Montgomery's marriage turns into a quick divorce, Crawford forgives him and another wedding is scheduled. Not too surprisingly, Crawford finally comes to her senses and dumps Montgomery when she learns that the disgusted Gable is about to sail for Europe and may never return.

The movie was the liveliest of the Gable-Crawford collaborations so far, with a supporting cast of comic actors including Billie Burke, Charles Butterworth, Ted Healy, Arthur Treacher, and Rosalind Russell (a recent addition to MGM's contract roster). There were slapstick moments of Gable teaching Crawford how to split logs with an ax, and of Montgomery and Crawford falling off a tandem bicycle into a pigsty. In the fade-out scene in a ship's cabin, Crawford thrusts a hairbrush at Gable and playfully offers herself for the hard spanking that he once said she deserved.

With two Gable-Crawford movies in the can, MGM had enough to satisfy its needs for a year, so the team was temporarily dissolved. Crawford left for a long vacation with Franchot Tone, while Gable took a deep breath and started his fifth film of 1934—*After Office Hours,* directed by Robert Z. Leonard for Bernard Hyman's production unit.

In July, one of MGM's box-office treasures, Marie Dressler, had died of cancer at age sixty-five. As a seriocomic actress, she was irreplaceable, and she left a void in the studio contract roster that had to be filled with more stars. One of the first to be signed was Constance Bennett, who through the manipulations of her longtime agent, Myron Selznick, got a three-year contract at $150,000 per picture. Included was the right to choose her leading men, and being no dope, she wanted Gable for *After Office Hours.*

The movie brought Gable full circle with Bennett, who had been the star of his first MGM movie four years before. For his bit role in *The Easiest Way,* he was listed at the very bottom of the cast list, but in *After Office Hours* they shared star billing above the title, with Gable's name coming first.

The script by Joseph Mankiewicz's older brother Herman (future author of *Citizen Kane*) was a blend of screwball comedy and murder mystery, with Gable as a newspaper editor and Bennett as yet another spoiled heiress—this one trying to become a reporter. Gable fires her for taking a job away from someone less fortunate, but he soon realizes that he needs Bennett and her social connections to substantiate a possibly libelous story about the death of a millionaire's wife.

During production, Gable learned that his next assignment would be a loan-out, to a new company that didn't even own a studio. He threw a fit, but there were worse aggravations ahead.

Secretly Louis B. Mayer and his Loew's boss, Nicholas Schenck, had become major financial backers of 20th Century Pictures, an independent company formed by Joseph Schenck, Nicholas's older brother, and Darryl Zanuck, who resigned as production chief at Warner Bros. to run the new enterprise. Since Joseph Schenck was also board chairman of United Artists, which intended to distribute 20th Century's product, some of the arrangements were in violation of federal laws restricting monopolistic practices.

As part of the deal, which included the employment of Mayer's son-in-law William Goetz as a vice president of 20th Century, Mayer promised to loan the company whatever MGM stars and other talent it needed until it became self-sufficient. For the first 20th Century effort, *The Bowery,* MGM supplied Wallace Beery, who then ranked ahead of Gable as a box-office draw, and child star Jackie Cooper.

Gable's turn came with *The Call of the Wild,* based on Jack London's famous novel about prospecting for gold in the Klondike region of the Yukon territory in northwestern Canada. The lead actress would be Loretta Young, whom Zanuck pried loose from Warner Bros. and made 20th Century's first contract star. Director William Wellman insisted on location filming but found exactly what he needed within the continental United States in northern Washington. The snowbound country surrounding two-miles-high Mount Baker could have fooled Jack London if he'd still been living.

Scriptwriters Gene Fowler and Leonard Praskins took a major liberty with London's novel, which had a sled dog named Buck as the main character and showed how he coped with man and nature. Buck remained very much in the story, but the focus was on a romance between prospector Gable and the married Loretta Young, who are thrown together when her husband disappears during an expedition to find a lost gold mine.

Before production began, Gable had to spend two weeks rehearsing with Buck, a 225-pound mongrel Saint Bernard with huge soulful eyes. The dog's trainer taught Gable how to control him and make him do stunts on command. Buck became so devoted to Gable that when it came time to film a crucial scene in the movie, he wouldn't budge from the actor's side.

"I finally sent for a female dog in heat," director William Wellman recalled. "We let Buck sniff her, and then I took her with me to the other side of the set while Gable restrained Buck. When I gave him the signal, he released Buck, who raced toward the camera like greased lightning. Was he disappointed! We took the bitch away before he could have his way with her. Gable hated himself for doing it. He said, 'I feel like I've just double-crossed my best friend.' "

Gable first met twenty-one-year-old Loretta Young during the costume fittings in Hollywood. As rugged as most of the clothes were in the movie, Young's fur coats and parkas were specially designed for her by Omar Kiam, a protégé of MGM's Gilbert Adrian.

Though Gable was still involved with Elizabeth Allan, he responded immediately to Young's ravishing beauty—her doelike gray eyes, full lips, and sculpted cheekbones. By the time they were ensconced at Mount Baker Lodge, the home-away-from-home for the entire cast and crew during the Washington filming, an affair had erupted.

Young had just ended an intense relationship of more than a year with Spencer Tracy, which had started while they worked together at Columbia Pictures in A Man's Castle. They finally separated when Tracy refused to get a divorce so that they could marry. Though a devout Catholic, Young seemed to love by her own rules. At seventeen she had eloped with actor Grant Withers, lived with him for a year, and then gotten a divorce, using as her moral justification the fact that he was a non-Catholic.

If Young had any marriage notions about Gable, she had as much chance of that happening as of striking gold on the summit of Mount Baker. Conveniently separated from his wife for the duration of the arctic weather shoot, he was interested only in playing house.

William Wellman hoped to finish *The Call of the Wild* in six weeks, but blizzard conditions forced him to spend a full two months. Snowplows worked around the clock trying to keep the roads clear between the hotel and the locations. The company included more than a hundred actors and technicians. Food often ran low and had to be flown in from Seattle, with planes dropping the parcels on parachutes. Below-zero temperatures froze the lubrication in the cameras and made them inoperable.

Gable divided his spare time between attending to Loretta Young and carousing with his pals. Jack Oakie, who portrayed his trusty sidekick in the movie, remembered, "We were an almost all-male group, so we met every night to play cards and to get plastered. Weather permitting, Clark would requisition a car and take a bunch of us to Bellingham, where we had our choice of several cathouses."

Gable's behavior enraged William Wellman, who later recalled, "He wasn't tending to the business of making pictures. He was paying too much attention to monkey business. I called him on it, lost my easy-to-lose temper, and did it in front of the company, a bad mistake. I almost punched him, but his face saved him. I needed that handsome mug for the picture, but I could have turned it into mincemeat."

Wellman's reaction may have been spiked with jealousy. While working with Loretta Young on three previous movies, he'd been intimately involved with her. Wellman could have been expecting a replay, but Gable got there first.

The affair continued when *The Call of the Wild* finished production in early February 1935. Young went straight to work at Paramount in Cecil B. DeMille's *The Crusades,* while Gable received some surprise news. He'd been nominated for an Oscar for Best Actor of 1934 for *It Happened One Night.* The movie was also nominated for best picture, actress, director, and screenplay, which made it a contender in all of the top five categories.

The 1934 Academy Awards were the first to cover a traditional January–December calendar. In prior years the period of eligibility ran from August through the next July. The very first Academy Awards were dated 1927–28. The 1934 awards would be the seventh set presented.

The categories were fewer than in later decades. There were no awards for supporting performances, or for costume design, makeup, or special effects.

There was also no fixed number of nominees within the categories. Gable's opposition for best actor consisted only of William Powell for *The Thin Man* and Frank Morgan for *The Affairs of Cellini*. But for best picture, *It Happened One Night* had *eleven* competitors: *The Barretts of Wimpole Street, Cleopatra, Flirtation Walk, The Gay Divorcée, Here Comes the Navy, The House of Rothschild, Imitation of Life, One Night of Love, The Thin Man, Viva Villa!,* and *The White Parade.*

Bizarrely, ballots for the 1934 awards had a write-in option that permitted voters to pick whomever or whatever they preferred in any category. It was the result of a protest from Bette Davis, who questioned the Academy's integrity when she didn't get nominated in the 1932–33 batch for her critically acclaimed performance in *Of Human Bondage.* Many others in the industry supported Davis, so the Academy's board of governors adopted the write-in to soothe wounded egos.

The big night was February 27, 1935, a time when the ceremony was a semiprivate industry gala, with some press invited but no radio coverage (let alone TV, which was still in the experimental stages). The awards were always handed out as the climax to a formal-dress banquet and dance at one of the grand hotels, this time at the Biltmore in downtown Los Angeles.

Gable would have preferred to take Elizabeth Allan, but no way could he escort anyone but his wife. Ria treated herself to a new evening gown and spent the better part of that day getting beautified at Max Factor's salon. With Gable in white tie and tails, the couple looked resplendent as they arrived in a group with the Irving Thalbergs and the Charles MacArthurs (Helen Hayes).

The revered humorist Irvin S. Cobb emceed the ceremony and handed out all the awards. The first-ever Oscar for best song went to "The Continental" from *The Gay Divorcée*. When the writing awards came around, Robert Riskin won for *It Happened One Night* (best screenplay based on material from another medium). Another Gable movie, *Manhattan Melodrama*, won Arthur Caesar an Oscar in the category of best original story.

Frank Capra, nominated for best director against Victor Schertzinger *(One Night of Love)* and W. S. Van Dyke *(The Thin Man)*, won for *It Happened One Night*. Recuperating from a recent and nearly fatal attack of appendicitis, Capra was too weak and too overcome by emotion to give anything but a murmur of thanks.

Gable's turn came next. He had a hunch that William Powell would win for *The Thin Man,* but when he heard his own name announced, he marched to the podium and smilingly accepted the Oscar from Irvin Cobb. "I honestly never expected to win one of these," Gable told the audience. "There are too many good actors in this business. But I feel as happy as a kid and a little foolish they picked me."

As he walked back to his table, he was heard muttering to himself, "It's not going to swell my head. I'm still going to wear the same size hat."

Gable's costar, Claudette Colbert, up against Norma Shearer for *The Barretts of Wimpole Street* and Grace Moore for *One Night of Love,* won the Oscar for best actress. Bette Davis's write-in campaign had obviously failed. Colbert, who'd never expected to win, was at that very moment at nearby Union Station about to entrain for New York. Someone remembered and phoned the station to stop her so that she could accept the award. A car with a police motorcycle escort was dispatched to pick her up.

While waiting for Colbert to arrive, Irvin Cobb presented the grand prize of best picture, which, to no surprise, went to *It Happened One Night.* It was the first time in Oscar history (and the last for forty-one years) that one movie won all five of the awards that were considered the most important: best picture, director, screenplay, actor, and actress. It was a fantastic coup for Columbia Pictures, which could no longer be tabbed as a "poverty row" studio.

Claudette Colbert turned up just as Irvin Cobb was getting ready to present a special honorary Oscar to six-year-old Shirley Temple, who'd stayed up three hours past her bedtime to accept it. Cobb pressed Temple into service and stood her on a chair so that she could hand the Oscar to Colbert, who left immediately to board the train that was being held for her at Union Station.

Before the banquet switched into a party for the victors, Cobb gave Shirley Temple her miniature Oscar. Though supposedly honoring "her outstanding contribution to screen entertainment during 1934," it really recognized her box-office strength. Temple's seven releases in that

Depression-wracked year packed theaters and earned big profits for the studios that made them.

Among the many congratulating Gable that night was Phil Berg, who, with partner Bert Allenberg, ran one of Hollywood's most powerful talent agencies. One of Berg's ways of gaining new clients was to inflate what he already knew about them. "I heard that Minna got you three grand a week on your last contract," Berg told Gable. "I think you proved tonight that you're worth more, and I can get it for you."

Gable happened to be earning only two thousand per week, so he was very impressed by Berg's numbers. "So what are you waiting for?" he answered.

A year younger than Gable, Berg was a brash ex–New Yorker notorious for stealing clients from rivals. In Gable's case he had to contend with Minna Wallis, who'd been representing him since *The Painted Desert* in 1930. According to Berg, he paid Wallis and her agency partner, Ruth Collier, $25,000 for Gable's contract.

Minna Wallis, however, later denied it. "Money never entered into it. Clark and I talked it over thoroughly. Berg-Allenberg was a bigger organization that could do things that I couldn't. If Clark stayed with me, he would have been unhappy no matter what I did."

Gable and Wallis remained lifelong friends. "It was a relationship that is difficult to explain," she recalled. "I adored him, just adored him. He was sweet and wonderful to me always."

It should be noted that the "contract" obtained by Berg was one that gave the Berg-Allenberg Agency the right to represent Gable and to collect 10 percent of his earnings from whatever deals it made for him. Gable's employment contract with MGM, of course, was something separate and apart.

Using Gable's Oscar win for ammunition, Berg got him a new seven-year contract at $4,000 per week for the first three years, $4,500 per week for the next two years, and $5,000 per week for the last two. In each calendar year of forty weeks, MGM could use Gable for a maximum of three films. If the studio wanted him to do more than three in those forty weeks, he would receive an additional $25,000 per picture.

The deal immediately increased Gable's weekly salary from $2,000 to $4,000 and also made him a paper millionaire. By the end of the seven years (in 1941), he would have earned a minimum of $1.24 million.

Gable had now reached the Hollywood pinnacle. No star in history had ever risen so fast or with such impact. Of course, it was a simpler time when no other entertainment medium—not even radio—had the star-creating power that movies did. He was also a beneficiary of the Depression era, which needed new heroes and role models. He was handsome, magnetic, and aggressive. On-screen at least he pushed people around, including women, but he always got what he wanted and without being evil or detestable.

Gable's first assignment under the new MGM contract marked a reunion with Irving Thalberg, who'd been without need of his services since stepping down as production chief to head his own unit. Of six films that Thalberg had produced since then, the most notable were *The Barretts of Wimpole Street,* with Norma Shearer, Fredric March, and Charles Laughton, and Ernst Lubitsch's *The Merry Widow,* with Maurice Chevalier and Jeanette MacDonald.

Thalberg requisitioned Gable for *China Seas,* which would be the producer's return to the all-star-cast format that he had introduced at MGM with *Grand Hotel.* The melodrama was sort of a nautical facsimile of that and *Shanghai Express,* with the latter's scriptwriter, Jules Furthman, concocting the story.

Furthman envisioned Gable playing a ship's captain who marries a beautiful Chinese heiress and has a child with her. Thalberg decided that it would never be approved by the administrators of the industry's new Production Code, which included miscegenation on its list of forbidden subjects, so he ordered a rewrite to conform with Gable's usual type of slam-bang romance. Furthman came up with the character of Dolly Portland, aka China Doll, a well-traveled courtesan similar to the Shanghai Lily that he created for Marlene Dietrich in *Shanghai Express.*

Thalberg gave the role to Jean Harlow, who hadn't been teamed with Gable for nearly two years for lack of a suitable script. Wallace Beery, her costar in *Dinner at Eight,* was also added to the name-heavy cast, along with Lewis Stone, Rosalind Russell, C. Aubrey Smith, and humorist Robert Benchley.

China Seas finds skipper Gable trying to save his cargo/passenger liner from fiendish Malaysian pirates who are intent on stealing a fortune in gold bullion that's being transported from Hong Kong to Singapore in the ship's safe. As Gable's discarded floozy, Harlow books herself on the voyage in hopes of reconciling, but she hasn't reckoned on competition from Rosalind Russell, a rich widow in the midst of an around-the-world tour. To make Gable jealous, Harlow becomes cozy with passenger Wallace Beery, a wealthy trader who turns out to be the leader of the pirates.

China Seas was Gable's most action-packed movie so far, with $500,000 spent on special effects for spectacular scenes of sea battles, a typhoon, and the final bombing of the pirates' ship. Director Tay Garnett, a freelancer who'd proved himself a master of shipboard drama with the 1932 *One Way Passage,* injected some rowdy humor into the tussles between Gable and Harlow. Her expectedly revealing costumes by Gilbert Adrian included a sheer satin evening gown that fitted so tightly across her abdomen that her pubic hair had to be shaved to avoid an outline.

In real life Gable was still very chummy with Harlow. Since their last teaming in *Hold Your Man,* she'd not only married the considerably older cinematographer Harold Rosson but also dumped him after only eight months. Though not yet divorced, Harlow had recently found the makings of husband number four in William Powell. While working together in *Reckless,* they had fallen madly in love and were now talking about getting married as soon as she became free.

Gable's own tangled love life, which still included Elizabeth Allan, took a jolting twist when Loretta Young turned out to be pregnant. To break the news, she summoned Gable to a meeting at the home of her mother, interior decorator Gladys Belzer, a tough "stage hen" with two more actress-daughters (Polly Ann Young and Sally Blane). When Young told Gable of her condition, his first reaction was to turn to her mother and say, "I thought she knew how to take care of herself. After all, she had been a married woman."

The exact details of what happened next will probably never be known, but the pregnancy had to be kept secret while plans were formulated as to how to deal with it. In a few more months Young's condition would become obvious.

More than likely Gable suggested an abortion. He'd been through one with Joan Crawford. The only alternative for Gable was to marry Young, which he certainly couldn't do without first divorcing his present wife.

Like many men in the same predicament, Gable also probably wondered whether he really was the father. Young had a long history of affairs. In any case he didn't completely turn his back on her. They had more secret meetings and telephone conversations until Young finally clamped down.

"He kept calling and calling, wanting to see me, and I kept telling him to go away, go away. I was so terrified someone would see us together. All I could think of was keeping him away," Young later recalled.

Young needed to do something fast or her career would be ruined. In those days single motherhood was a social taboo. As a devout Roman Catholic, abortion was not an option. If she took legal action against Gable to prove paternity, the scandal would destroy his career as well as hers.

Before her condition started to show, Young decided to leave Hollywood on what she announced to the press would be a "long rest cure" after working nonstop for the past year. In June she and her mother entrained to New York and then sailed to Europe on the *Ile de France*.

Meanwhile Gable finished *China Seas* and landed in his first squabble with Irving Thalberg, who wanted to continue the association with *Mutiny on the Bounty*, based on the best-selling novel about the British Royal Navy in the eighteenth century. For historical accuracy, the role of first mate Fletcher Christian required Gable to wear knee breeches, to have his hair styled with a pigtail at the back, and to shave off his by-now-trademark mustache.

Fearing that he'd come across like a big sissy, Gable refused the assignment, an act that, according to his contract, could by punished by suspension without pay while the movie was made with another actor in the role. Thalberg finally called him to his office for a talk. "Do this for me," he pleaded. "If it isn't one of your greatest successes, I'll never ask you again to play a part you don't want to do."

"Given that it's you, Irving, I'll do it," Gable said. "But if it was Selznick sitting in that chair, I'd tell him to go fuck himself."

The ongoing rivalry between the production units of Thalberg and David Selznick had recently exploded into war. Selznick complained to Loew's board chairman Nicholas Schenck that Thalberg was getting first choice of the contract stars and directors, as well as the original scripts, books, and plays that were acquired by the story department.

When Schenck refused to intervene, Selznick took the drastic step of handing in his resignation. He intended to form an independent production company as soon as he completed two MGM projects that were already filming: *Anna Karenina,* with Greta Garbo and Fredric March, and *A Tale of Two Cities,* with Ronald Colman and Gable's playmate, Elizabeth Allan.

Thalberg's resurgence had also caused William Randolph Hearst to quit MGM and to transfer his Cosmopolitan Pictures unit to Warner Bros. Thalberg had broken Marion Davies's heart by taking two choice roles away from her and giving them to Norma Shearer. The first, in *The Barretts of Wimpole Street,* won Mrs. Thalberg an Oscar nomination. The second was the title character in *Marie Antoinette,* a project still in preparation. Hearst's departure literally left a hole at MGM. Davies's fourteen-room dressing villa was dismantled into nine sections and transported by truck to the Warner studio in Burbank, fifteen miles away.

Costing nearly $2 million, *Mutiny on the Bounty* was MGM's most expensive production since the silent *Ben-Hur* in 1925. By the time Thalberg became interested in the novel by Charles Nordhoff and James Hall, freelance director Frank Lloyd had already taken an option on the screen rights, so MGM bought him out and agreed to place him at the helm. A former actor, the Scottish-born Lloyd had been one of Hollywood's top directors since early silent days; in the short history of the Academy Awards, he'd already won two Oscars, for *The Divine Lady* (1929) and *Cavalcade* (1933).

Mutiny on the Bounty was actually a trilogy of novels taking off from a true incident involving the H.M.S. *Bounty,* which had sailed from England to the South Pacific in 1787 to bring back breadfruit trees for cultivation in the Caribbean colonies. Scriptwriters Talbot Jennings, Jules Furthman, and Carey Wilson also drew from the other two *Bounty* books, *Men Against the Sea* and *Pitcairn Island.*

Thalberg ordered them to boil everything down to a searing conflict between the two main characters: Captain William Bligh, a villainous sadist who cruelly mistreats his crew, and first mate Fletcher Christian, an idealistic champion of the abused who leads them to mutiny. After the mutineers dispose of Bligh by setting him and his cohorts adrift in an open boat, the story turns into a classic manhunt as the captain vows to survive and to chase Christian to the ends of the earth if necessary to make sure that he hangs for violating naval law.

For the role of Bligh, Thalberg chose Charles Laughton, who was not only a master at playing despicable characters but in real life the complete opposite of Clark Gable. Thalberg expected them to hate each other's guts, which would surely spill over into their performances and make the animosity between Christian and Bligh more explosive and palpable.

For the past year director Frank Lloyd had been preparing the production, starting with the building of full-size replicas of the *Bounty* and Bligh's subsequent ship, the *Pandora*. Taking a camera crew with him, Lloyd sailed both ships fourteen thousand miles to Tahiti and back to shoot atmospheric background scenes at sea and on the island itself. When they returned to Hollywood, most of the footage had been ruined due to faulty storage under extreme weather conditions, so the whole trip had to be repeated.

One of Gable's favorite fishing haunts, Catalina Island, became MGM's equivalent of the South Seas. Twenty-two miles from mainland California, Catalina had a small resort area with hotels and rooming houses that could accommodate the company, and it was otherwise a natural paradise with beaches, tropical forests, and the vast Pacific Ocean beyond. One thing lacking was an equivalent of the waterfront of eighteenth-century Portsmouth in England, where the *Bounty*'s voyage began, so art director Cedric Gibbons built one, meticulously copied from old drawings and paintings.

For certain scenes that required hundreds of extras, MGM had to import them by the boatload from Hollywood. They were provided with free meals and lodging (in tents or Quonset huts) for as long as their services were required. Due to a shortage of real Polynesians, some of the "natives" in the scenes set on Tahiti were from whatever similar-looking ethnic groups that the casting department could find.

The twelve-week production schedule kept Gable occupied throughout the summer of 1935. Surprisingly he became close friends with Franchot Tone, his longtime rival for the affections of Joan Crawford. Tone had the key role of midshipman Roger Byam, one of the few mutineers whom Bligh eventually captures and takes back to England to be court-martialed. Gable and Tone discovered a mutual interest in booze and floozies, both of which were abundantly available in Avalon, Catalina's famous pleasure town.

Gossip circulated that Gable and Tone were also romantically involved with the two beautiful starlets whom Frank Lloyd picked to play their Polynesian sweethearts and eventual wives. Billed in the movie's credits only by their first names, they were Movita Castenada and Mamo Clark.

Gable and Charles Laughton became instant enemies. Gable couldn't stand being around homosexuals, or at least those who were overt enough for him to recognize them as such. Laughton had a sham marriage with the lesbian actress Elsa Lanchester, but he left her at home and brought a muscular male with him to Catalina as his personal "masseur." They were an obviously devoted couple and went everywhere together. Gable turned away in disgust whenever he saw them.

Only a year and a half older than Gable, Laughton had a complex about his pugdog homeliness and corpulent figure, so handsome coactors always made him surly. In Gable's case he was also still seething over being bested by him in the 1934 Academy Awards competition. Gable won for *It Happened One Night,* but Laughton didn't even get nominated for his highly acclaimed performance as the tyrannical father in *The Barretts of Wimpole Street.*

Off the set Gable and Laughton avoided each other totally. When working together, Gable tried to be civil, but Laughton deliberately avoided eye contact. When he was addressing dialogue to Gable, he looked anywhere but at the man facing him. Gable put up with it for a few days but finally complained to Frank Lloyd: "He's not playing to me. He's ignoring me!"

When the director couldn't get Laughton to cooperate, he phoned Thalberg, who flew out to Catalina by seaplane. He ordered both Laughton *and* Gable to stop behaving like prima donnas.

Tensions eased enough for Gable and Laughton to gang up on Frank Lloyd, whom they accused of paying too much attention to the backstory of the miseries of life on the high seas. They claimed that the director wasn't giving them the guidance that they needed. Thalberg again flew to Catalina to investigate. He found tempers raging and tried as best he could to pacify everyone. Personally he wasn't that bothered. The rushes that he viewed every morning at the studio were terrific. The conditions that Gable and Laughton complained about weren't evident on the screen. The tensions between them may have improved their performances, so he would let them go on squabbling if it contributed to a better movie.

During the filming news came of two major developments in the Hollywood industry. Darryl Zanuck and Joseph Schenck left United Artists and merged their 20th Century Pictures with Fox Film Corporation to become 20th Century–Fox. Zanuck and Schenck obtained the studio and distribution facilities they needed to become a major force in the industry. Louis B. Mayer and Nicholas Schenck remained secret investors in the new enterprise, which had Mayer's son-in-law, William Goetz, continuing as Zanuck's chief aide.

Mayer's other son-in-law, David Selznick, formed Selznick International Pictures, with financial backing from multimillionaire John Hay Whitney and two other members of the Whitney family. The independent company, with *Little Lord Fauntleroy* as its first production, would release its output through United Artists, filling the void left by the departure of 20th Century Pictures.

At the completion of *Mutiny on the Bounty,* Thalberg rushed it into the editing process for release as MGM's Thanksgiving holiday attraction. Gable meanwhile had some free time, so Howard Strickling asked him to make a cross-country publicity tour. Since it again required traveling in the company of his wife, Gable refused. But Strickling finally talked him into it by promising a two-week extension to South America that he could do on his own. Though written off as a publicity expense, it would be primarily a pleasure trip, with MGM's top executive in each country showing Gable the sights and making sure that all his needs were satisfied.

By the time Gable and Ria left Los Angeles by train in October 1935, *The Call of the Wild* and *China Seas* had been smash hits. He was running neck-and-neck with Shirley Temple for the number-one spot in box-office popularity. His female fans were the most demonstrative since Rudolph Valentino's in the mid-1920s. In every city that he visited, women and girls turned out by the thousands. They packed train terminals to overflowing. Police escorts were needed to get him to appointments.

During a press interview Gable expressed astonishment: "This power that I'm supposed to have over women was never noticed when I was a stage actor on Broadway. I don't know when I got it. And by God, I can't explain it."

When the tour ended in Baltimore, Ria returned to Los Angeles and Gable flew on to Mexico City, then to Bogotá, Lima, Santiago, Buenos Aires, and Rio de Janeiro. Though his hosts tried to keep the pleasure trip secret, he was mobbed and followed in the streets whenever he went out.

From Rio Gable took the ocean liner *Pan America* back to New York, where he would arrive in time for the premiere of *Mutiny on the Bounty*. The cruise was intended to be a rest after two weeks of over-indulgence, but he hadn't counted on Mexican spitfire Lupe Velez being on board. The movie sexbomb and stage entertainer, who'd just completed a vaudeville and nightclub tour, craved companionship, and Gable happily obliged.

When the *Pan America* arrived in New York, Velez's husband, Johnny Weissmuller, star of MGM's *Tarzan* series, was waiting for her at the Munson Line terminal. When he spotted her coming down the gang-way arm in arm with Gable, the MGM press agents who'd brought him there had to restrain him from making a scene. No doubt the "Battling Weissmullers," as gossip columnists called them, had another of their notorious slugfests when they reached the privacy of their hotel suite.

Gable stopped over in New York to attend the opening of *Mutiny on the Bounty* at the Capitol Theater, scene of his vaudeville stint eighteen months before. By now the Capitol ran movies only: a feature and selected shorts. In the continuing economic depression, the costs of stage productions were too high for the theater to earn profits.

Prior to the gala premiere performance, Gable did press interviews during the day and socialized at night. By prearrangement, he rendezvoused with Elizabeth Allan before she sailed to England for her annual Christmas visit with her husband. Gable also dated socialite Mary Taylor, the niece of his Hollywood friend Countess Dorothy di Frasso, an American of inherited millions who bought the title by marrying an impoverished Italian noble.

It was the first time the public had seen Gable out and about with women other than his wife. MGM publicists told inquisitive reporters that Ria Gable had influenza and couldn't travel from California.

On November 6 Gable was getting dressed to go out for the evening when a hotel bellhop delivered a telegram. Unsigned, it said, "Beautiful blue-eyed blond baby girl born 8:15 this morning." He walked into the bathroom, tore the telegram into shreds, and flushed them down the toilet.

Two nights later the new father attended the premiere of *Mutiny on the Bounty*. MGM arranged a motorcade, escorted by police on horses and motorcycles, to transport him across town from the Waldorf-Astoria Hotel on Park Avenue to the Capitol on Broadway. In a Lincoln Zephyr convertible sedan with the roof down, Gable sat perched atop the backseat, waving to the crowds that gathered on the sidewalks. Scores of hysterical women and girls chased after the procession, numbering in the thousands by the time he arrived at the Capitol, where thousands more were waiting to greet him. A hundred policemen formed a human wedge to get him into the theater.

Two and a half hours later, when the screening ended, the huge mob was still outside. The theater's manager wanted to sneak Gable out a rear exit, but he refused. "Nothing doing," Gable said. "They came here to see me, and I'm going out the same way I came in. The day they stop coming around is the day when I'm going to be through in this business. I owe them the decency of making an appearance. They deserve it. I'm going out there."

Needless to say, Gable survived the pandemonium. The next day, *Mutiny on the Bounty* received rave reviews and drew record-breaking crowds. Later that week he returned to Los Angeles by plane. It was his first trip on TWA's new DC-1s, which could travel at high speeds of up to 150 miles per hour and cut the transcontinental travel time to a mere twenty hours (including stopovers for refueling).

Gable must have done a lot of soul-searching during the flight. As soon as he got home, he told his wife that he was moving out.

Hearst gossip columnist Louella Parsons, who prided herself on "exclusives" that were always hand-fed to her by studio publicity chiefs, reported on November 19, 1935, that the Clark Gables had separated but had no immediate plans for a divorce. When some of Parsons's rivals tried to get Gable to comment, his only reply was "Let the lady tell it."

And so she did. In a statement written for her by Howard Strickling, Ria Gable said, "Clark has been working very hard in recent months and has been quite temperamental. Little differences, ordinarily of minor consequence, arose between us, which under stress assumed grave proportions. These things sometimes happen in a marriage and I hope that we can work them out. There is no other woman involved."

But in fact there were too many women involved. Gable's carousing had reached proportions that could no longer be kept secret. He had again given MGM grounds to terminate his contract for immoral behavior. If he wanted to continue chasing around, he'd be better off single. Not that bachelors could run rampant, but society tended to judge them less harshly than married men who'd made a legal commitment to love, honor, and obey only one woman.

For Gable a separation was preferable to a divorce. Though he would have to pay Ria maintenance, he was spared the whopping community property settlement that would be due her in a divorce.

Ria went along with it. She knew that he'd eventually have to settle with her if he found someone else he wanted to marry. In the meantime she remained Mrs. Clark Gable and was still entitled to all the perks and social status that went with being a spouse of Hollywood royalty.

Gable also had the Loretta Young situation to contend with. Immediately upon returning from New York, he phoned her about the baby. But all that Young would reveal was a name—Judith—and that the delivery took place at the maternal grandmother's beach house in Venice, near Santa Monica.

Gable asked to see the child, but Young told him that she'd sent her far away in temporary care. She said that her only concern right now was to recuperate and resume her career as if nothing had happened. She pleaded with him to leave her alone. Many rumors were circulating about them, including some that linked Young to Gable's separation from Ria.

He moved to a suite at the Beverly Wilshire Hotel in the heart of the Beverly Hills business district. The nine-story Beaux-Arts building had a separate residential wing where he could come and go without mixing with the tourist trade, not that there was much of it in those Depression times. Built in 1928, the Beverly Wilshire was in such desperate straits that MGM made a deal for Gable at $150 per month, which included a three-room apartment and full hotel services.

At the end of November, Gable started his third movie of the year. *China Seas* had been such a hit that exhibitors demanded a rematch with Jean Harlow. Producer Hunt Stromberg decided to try something different by adding Myrna Loy to the starring cast and making it a guessing game as to which woman would finally win Gable at the fade-out.

Based on a novel by romance specialist Faith Baldwin, *Wife Versus Secretary* had Loy as Gable's spouse and Harlow as his devoted office assistant. Through a series of misunderstandings, Loy becomes convinced that Gable and Harlow are having an affair. When Loy decides to leave Gable, Harlow is tempted to grab him for herself. But it soon becomes obvious that Gable will never love anyone as much as Loy, so Harlow engineers a reconciliation and settles for marriage to a longtime admirer. The latter provided a small role for twenty-seven-year-old James Stewart, who'd joined MGM that year on a trial contract.

During the filming Gable forgot whatever it was that had been causing him to snub Myrna Loy. "He was very sweet, very warm," she remembered. "He brought me coffee in the morning, and we began to be friends. We had lots of fun working with Harlow. The script was such a reversal of the types we usually played. Clark was supposed to be the faithful, steadfast husband. Jean was the other woman but played it very prim and proper. I was the sexiest wife that I'd ever been allowed to play."

Directed by Clarence Brown, *Wife Versus Secretary* finished production just before Christmas. By that time *Mutiny on the Bounty* was the number-one box-office hit in the nation and was landing on many critics' lists as the best film of 1935.

As the new year of 1936 began, the Hollywood industry was showing signs of recovery from the Depression. Average weekly theater attendance, which had sunk as low as 60 million in 1932, had increased to 80 million. But profit margins were still low due to an average admission price of twenty-five cents. Loew's, parent company of MGM, remained the most successful company in the business, with 1935 profits of $7.6 million.

On January 11 Gable attended the funeral of his friend and drinking companion John Gilbert, who had died from a heart attack at age forty. Publicized as the "the Perfect Lover," Gilbert had been MGM's undisputed king during the silent era. His alcoholism and battles with L. B. Mayer finally caused his downfall. Though he had reason to dislike Gable, who'd replaced him as MGM's top male, Gilbert had always been cordial and encouraging to him.

A week later Gable received his first assignment of the year—to Irving Thalberg's unit for *San Francisco,* which would start filming February 17 with W. S. Van Dyke as director and Bernard Hyman as associate producer. When told that his costar would be musical diva Jeanette MacDonald, Gable exploded. The redheaded singer had become Mayer's special pet since her smash hits in *The Merry Widow* and two teamings with Nelson Eddy in *Naughty Marietta* and *Rose Marie*. Mayer had ordered *San Francisco* written to her specifications so that she could prove her worth as a dramatic actress. Studio gossip had it that she'd gone down on her knees before Mayer to obtain Gable as her leading man.

Gable detested all prima donnas and shuddered at the prospect of scenes where he would have to sit still while MacDonald sang to him. He told Eddie Mannix, his usual studio defender, to find another actor, but Mannix failed him this time. Mayer was determined to have Gable, who surrendered to escape being placed on suspension. Besides losing about

$35,000 in salary, Gable would also have had to dip into savings to pay his estranged wife her weekly maintenance.

In the meantime Gable was enjoying his married bachelorhood. On January 25 he attended the first Mayfair Club social of the year, a formal dress ball at the Victor Hugo Restaurant in Beverly Hills. The spectacular dine-and-dance spot's main room resembled a rococo, Spanish Mediterranean–style movie palace, but with a backlighted ceiling of opaque glass instead of twinkling stars and floating clouds.

David Selznick, the current president of the Mayfair Club, had asked Carole Lombard to organize the ball and choose its theme. She was famous for throwing wacky parties for her pals, like one where everybody came dressed as doctors or nurses and dined in a replica of a hospital operating room. But with 350 of Hollywood's elite invited and the proceeds going to the industry's favorite charity, the Motion Picture Relief Fund, she realized that something more dignified and elegant would be required.

Lombard decided it would be a White Mayfair Ball. The women were requested to wear white gowns, the men white tie and tails. Decorative arrangements were made from every type of white flower available, including roses, orchids, gardenias, camellias, stocks, sweetpeas, and lilies of the valley. Footmen in powdered wigs, white jackets, and red satin knee breeches attended to the guests as they arrived. Tickets were twenty dollars per couple, including dinner, dancing, and a floor show (booze extra!).

Among the first to arrive were Merle Oberon and David Niven, followed by Jeanette MacDonald with Henry Fonda, Johnny Weissmuller and Lupe Velez, Bing Crosby and Dixie Lee, as well as hordes of couples with only one famous name in them, including Gloria Swanson, Janet Gaynor, Harold Lloyd, Buster Keaton, Adolph Zukor, Barbara Stanwyck, Claudette Colbert, Irving Berlin, Darryl Zanuck, Alice Faye, Jerome Kern, Louis B. Mayer, Fredric March, Irene Dunne, Ernst Lubitsch, Dolores del Rio, Stan Laurel, and Humphrey Bogart.

Gable brought along Eadie Adams, a blond singer who frequently did dubbing for some of the MGM stars. They came as guests of Marion Davies and William Randolph Hearst, who'd also invited Louella Parsons and her doctor-husband, Harry Martin, to share their table.

Carole Lombard was escorted by actor-friend Cesar Romero, but she was too busy running the party and turned him loose in the crowd. When the Hearst group arrived, she rushed over to greet Davies and "Lollypops," which was her pet name for Hollywood's number-one gossiper. Lombard looked ravishing in a clinging white silk gown. Gable was obviously impressed. He gave her a big smile and winked. She winked back and then pranced off to attend to business.

The Irving Thalbergs had just arrived, with Norma Shearer dressed in a bright crimson gown designed by MGM's Adrian. Up to now there had been two violations of Lombard's white dictate, with Jeanette Mac-Donald in mauve and Mrs. Joe E. Brown in powder blue. Lombard considered the colors pale enough to tolerate, but Shearer stood out like a fire engine. Lombard wanted to order her to leave, but Louella Parsons talked her out of it.

"That's just Norma's way, dear. She can't be dictated to. Don't make a scene. I don't want to see Irving get upset. He might have another heart attack," Parsons said.

Lombard went to the powder room to calm down. Lupe Velez, Anita Louise, Patsy Kelly, and several others were already gathered there and condemning Shearer's behavior. Lombard joined in with some obscene comments about Shearer's rise to stardom, which was allegedy as mistress to L. B. Mayer before she ever met Thalberg.

The party had nonstop dancing; Cab Calloway's swing orchestra alternated sets with Eduardo Durant's rumba band. After Gable punished the proverbial parquet with his date, Eadie Adams, and their hostess, Marion Davies, he decided that Lombard would be next. He found her just as Cab Calloway gave the downbeat for "Cheek to Cheek."

"I go for you, Ma," Gable said, grinning.

Lombard stared at him, puzzled until she suddenly remembered it was one of the nicknames that their characters in *No Man of Her Own* had used for each other after they married.

"I go for you too, Pa," she said, though just to humor him. Assuming that he wanted to dance, she took his hand and let him lead her to the floor.

Gable was no Fred Astaire, but he tried. He held Lombard so tightly that he could feel that she wore nothing under her gown. The closeness of their bodies and the scent of her Chanel Number Five were arousing him.

Lombard couldn't help noticing. She laughed out loud, causing Gable to turn red with embarrassment. She suggested that they stop and have a drink until he cooled down.

Gable had a better idea. He needed some fresh air, so how about a quick ride in his new Duesenberg convertible? Lombard pleaded party obligations, but he talked her into it by promising to bring her back in ten minutes. As they left, they passed Ria Gable, who had come with her lawyer and his wife.

"Doesn't that old bag belong to you?" Lombard asked.

"Yeah," he replied. "And from the look in those eyes, I figure that her asking price for a divorce just went up by about a hundred grand."

Gable drove Lombard on a quick tour of Beverly Hills to show off his new sixteen-thousand-dollar acquisition, which had been designed to his own specifications and, he boasted, was a foot longer than another customized Duesenberg owned by Gary Cooper. As Gable made his third circle around the block of the Beverly Wilshire Hotel, Lombard asked, "Are you trying to suggest something?"

"I live here. Would you like to see my apartment?"

"Who do you think you are? Clark Gable?" she quipped.

That was all that he needed—a reminder of a public image that had become a sore spot for him. Angered by her sarcasm, he stepped on the accelerator and delivered her back to the ball in less than a minute, thanks to the Victor Hugo being just a block away on Beverly Drive.

Gable and Lombard had been absent long enough for anyone who'd seem them leaving together to jump to a wrong conclusion. Actor Lyle Talbot, standing at the bar drinking, made a snide remark when they walked by. Gable looked about to punch Talbot, but Lombard restrained him and they ended up back on the dance floor, where they quickly forgot their tiff.

But tempers flared again when Lombard spotted the Thalbergs getting ready to leave. She told Gable that she was going to fix it so that a waiter dumped a tray of dirty dishes on Shearer and ruined that red dress. Gable advised her not to, they argued, and he left in a huff. He returned to his apartment, drank half a bottle of scotch, and went to bed.

The next morning Gable awoke with what seemed a severe hangover if not delirium tremens. A plump white dove was perched on his chest. Rubbing his eyes to make sure that he wasn't dreaming, he looked around the room. On one of the tables stood a gilded birdcage, with its gate wide open. Sudden cooing noises from the chandelier revealed a second dove on the loose.

In the wee hours of the morning, Lombard had summoned a pet store owner from bed and ordered a pair of doves to be delivered to Gable as a peace offering. She then bribed a hotel clerk to release the doves in Gable's apartment while he was still sleeping.

Gable wondered who could have played such a dumb trick on him. An hour later, after he'd caught the doves and was putting the second one back in the cage, he discovered a message tied to its leg: "How about it? Carole."

Gable laughed and phoned Lombard. Apologizing for his behavior the night before, he thanked her for the doves but wanted to know what he was supposed to do with them. He certainly couldn't keep them in his apartment, which already smelled like the birdhouse at the zoo.

Lombard offered to keep the doves at her house, which Gable interpreted as an invitation to bring them straight over. But when he asked for driving directions, she replied, "Oh, no, don't bother. I'll send someone to pick them up. Thanks for calling."

Gable didn't give up. The next day he called Lombard for a date, but she put him off. After two more attempts and the same response, he lost interest and found companionship elsewhere. Since word had gotten around about his move to the Beverly Wilshire, half of the phone calls coming through its switchboard were for him. He'd accumulated such a stack of messages with return numbers that he didn't need to keep a "little black book."

On February 1 Gable turned thirty-five. When he received a beautifully wrapped package containing three dozen French ticklers—including one for good luck—he guessed that Lombard was the sender. A gift card said "The rest of the present will be delivered at 9 P.M. Be there!"

At nine exactly Gable heard a knock on the door. When he opened it, standing there in a long mink coat, and carrying two bottles of champagne in her arms, was Merle Oberon.

The brown-eyed, dark-haired Eurasian beauty was hardly the Carole Lombard that Gable had been expecting, but she was certainly no birthday present to reject. Oberon swept in and proceeded to give him a party to remember.

An affair developed that raged on and off for several months. Twenty-five years old, the former Queenie O'Brien was a Hollywood newcomer but an established star in England, where she was (and continued) the mistress of producer Alexander Korda. Through another affair with Joseph Schenck while he still headed United Artists, she wrangled a contract with one of UA's top producers, Samuel Goldwyn. She longed for a place in the pantheon of Hollywood love goddesses, and landing Clark Gable seemed a giant step toward getting there. Her only public romance so far had been with David Niven, another alien from England, who'd worked as an extra in *Mutiny on the Bounty* and was just starting to make a name for himself in supporting roles.

Oberon was the first of Gable's paramours to take advantage of his new-found freedom as a married-but-separated man. Although he'd been involved with far more famous women, like Crawford and Harlow, the affairs had had to be kept secret from the public. Oberon kept him hopping, encouraging him to take her to movie premieres and nightclubs, where there were always plenty of photographers and journalists around.

On February 7 Gable escorted Oberon to an outdoor gathering that he and scriptwriter-friend Donald Ogden Stewart had dreamed up during a recent drinking spree. They had decided that something must be done to celebrate Mrs. Stewart's recent release from a sanitarium after apparently successful treatment for manic depression.

Her psychiatrist ordered her to take it easy and to avoid nocturnal socializing, so Stewart, who was famous for his prankish wit, suggested to Gable that they arrange a daytime party with a screwball twist. Though Bea Stewart's Annual Nervous Breakdown Party was to start at high noon, guests were requested to wear formal evening clothes. Invitations were issued by word of mouth. Being on a Sunday, the turnout could be in the hundreds, so Stewart persuaded his multimillionaire friend John Hay Whitney to loan his mansion-estate and to provide the refreshments.

Gable and Oberon arrived early. As cohost with Donald Ogden Stewart, he was supposed to welcome the guests after they'd gotten past the security guards at the front gate. Oberon, meanwhile, mingled as more and more guests accumulated.

Around twelve-thirty Gable was greeting Robert Taylor when they suddenly heard a siren wailing. Coming up the drive was a white ambulance, which stopped right in front of the house. Two uniformed attendants jumped out from the rear doors and proceeded to remove a stretcher bearing a figure wrapped in a white sheet. Only the face was showing: Carole Lombard's. Her eyes were shut, and she seemed to be unconscious.

Horrified, Gable cleared the entrance so that Lombard could be carried into the house. The attendants took her into the Whitneys' drawing room and gently lowered the stretcher to the floor. A crowd quickly gathered around her. Everybody thought she must have been in a terrible accident en route to the party.

But suddenly Lombard sat up and started laughing hysterically. Few people were amused, least of all Gable. Noticing the disapproval on their faces, Lombard shouted, "What the fuck's the matter with everybody? Can't you tell a gag when you see one?"

Gable glared at her and marched away. He could hear her cursing: "I always knew Gable was a stuffed shit—I mean shirt."

He turned around and pushed his way back through the crowd. By this time Lombard had unwrapped herself from the sheet and was standing there in the white evening gown that she had worn underneath. He dragged her by the hand and led her to an empty corner of the room.

It became a battle royal that neither could win. Gable told her that the prank went too far and that she needed a psychiatrist. Lombard countered that he must have lost his sense of humor while married to a woman old enough to be his mother. She'd obviously done some homework on Gable or she wouldn't have brought it up so abruptly.

As Gable and Lombard shouted at each other, Merle Oberon moved in and dragged him away. "That cunt can have him," Lombard told Wallace Beery. "Where's the nearest john? I feel like I have to puke."

Later in the afternoon Lombard spotted Gable and Oberon in cozy conversation, so she barged over and asked if she could borrow him for a round of tennis on the Whitneys' court. Since both were wearing formal evening clothes, Gable thought she really was nuts, but the idea was so outrageous that he decided to oblige her.

Gable removed his jacket and loosened his shirt collar, while Lombard hitched up the skirt of her gown so it looked like she was wearing pantaloons. Borrowing rackets and tennis shoes from the Whitneys' groundskeeper, they proceeded to play. Lombard won the first two sets. Watching them, Merle Oberon grew bored, realizing that the match could go on forever because Gable seemed determined to end his losing streak. She finally left, pleading an early call at the studio the next morning.

The Whitneys had yet to invest in an outdoor illumination system, so the competition ended at sundown, with a score of 8–0 in Lombard's favor. Gable looked so unhappy that she rewarded him with a sloppy kiss before she departed. Driving home alone, he might have whistled "Bewitched, Bothered, and Bewildered," except that the song hadn't been written yet.

As if Gable didn't have enough to cope with among Lombard, Oberon, and his estranged wife, Loretta Young had finally emerged from seclusion. In fact, she had returned to public view at the White Mayfair Ball, escorted by Janet Gaynor's ex-husband, production executive Lydell Peck. Gable had steered clear of Young that night, and she of him.

But Gable phoned her the next day and demanded an update on the baby. When Young confessed that Judith had been at the Venice beach house all along, being tended by a full-time nurse, Gable insisted on making a visit.

Late one night Gable and Young drove there separately to avoid being spotted together. Because of Young's fears of detection, she had refrained from ordering furnishings for the baby's room. Gable found Judith sleeping in a bureau drawer. Before he left, he pulled a wad of money from his pocket and handed Young four hundred-dollar bills. "The least you can do is buy her a decent bed," he said.

Many years later Young would tell Judith of Gable's reaction when he first saw her that night: "Oh! He couldn't keep his hands off of you, he just kept holding you; he couldn't stop."

Young would also claim that except for that four hundred dollars for bedding, Gable never again gave her any money toward Judith's upkeep. She allegedly opened a bank account for Judith and told Gable how to make donations without their being traced. When he didn't, she began to suspect that Gable loved neither mother nor daughter and wanted no part in their futures.

On February 15 Gable started working in *San Francisco*. When he arrived at MGM that morning, he found a belated valentine waiting for him. Parked outside the main gate was an old Model T Ford that had been sprayed white and then liberally painted all over with large red hearts.

A note attached to the steering wheel—"You're driving me crazy!"—suggested the work of Carole Lombard, and this time Gable guessed right. She'd bought the car in a junkyard for fifteen dollars and spent another five hundred having it decorated and restored to working order.

Gable was delighted and arranged for the jalopy to be parked in the space next to his Duesenberg. When he reached his dressing room, he phoned Lombard to thank her. Since he'd neglected to send her a valentine, he told her that he'd take her dancing that night at Café Trocadero.

Lombard spent the rest of the day preparing. She decided to wear a beaded champagne-colored gown, topped by a white chinchilla jacket. She envisioned pulling up to the Troc in Gable's Duesenberg and dazzling Hollywood society. But she didn't figure on Gable picking her up in the valentine Model T. Chugging along at ten miles per hour, it seemed like forever before they reached the night spot on the Sunset Strip. Once inside they made up for lost time, to the music of Phil Ohman's band.

Lombard was also about to start a movie at Paramount—*The Princess Comes Across*—with Fred MacMurray as costar. She told Gable that she would be unavailable for the next six weeks, and she meant it.

Meanwhile Gable had Jeanette MacDonald to contend with in *San Francisco,* plus his hard-drinking friend from Broadway days, Spencer Tracy. Gable and MacDonald were the movie's only stars, with Tracy listed below the title for his supporting role.

San Francisco had originated with MGM's resident idea man, Robert "Hoppy" Hopkins, who, during a meeting of the story department, suggested "Earthquake! San Francisco! Gable! A dame! A priest! Can't you see it? A box-office goldmine!" Contract scriptwriter Anita Loos, a native Californian who'd lived through some of its history, took on the construction job.

Gable became Blackie Norton, owner of a saloon-cabaret in the notorious Barbary Coast district and less of a crook than his Blackie Gallagher in *Manhattan Melodrama.* Loos modeled Norton on her friend Wilson Mizner, a legendary gambler and con man who dated back to the Gold Rush era and had died in 1933. Jeanette MacDonald portrayed Mary Blake, an aspiring opera singer forced to support herself by performing in Gable's den of iniquity. Loos also dipped into *Manhattan Melodrama* for Spencer Tracy's Catholic priest, Father Mullin, who has been Blackie Norton's friend since childhood but grew up to be his exact opposite in moral virtue.

The story built to a spectacular twenty-minute climax that re-created the devastating 1906 earthquake and fire with the gritty realism of a newsreel. Special effects wizards A. Arnold Gillespie and James Basevi showed the earth opening up and streets collapsing, which they achieved with hydraulic platforms pulled apart by cables, with hoses underneath gushing water to simulate broken mains. Sound engineer Douglas Shearer (brother of Norma) devised a way of literally shaking theater audiences by using nothing more than the simple monophonic amplification systems that were standard in those days.

To accommodate Jeanette MacDonald, *San Francisco* featured several operatic and pop numbers, including a rousing title song (by composers Walter Jurmann and Bronislau Kaper and lyricist Gus Kahn) that eventually became that city's unofficial anthem. Gable's fears about being sung to by MacDonald proved groundless. His only problem was working up the required tears of joy in the finale, when he discovers that his beloved has survived the quake.

The script called for Gable to drop to his knees and pray, in a low quavering voice, "Thanks, God. Thanks! I really mean it!" Gable considered it too unmanly, and director W. S. Van Dyke agreed, so they figured out a way for him to turn his back to the camera while uttering the soppy lines.

By the time of her collaboration with Gable, Jeanette MacDonald's temperament had earned her the studio nickname "the Iron Butterfly." Perhaps because he'd been forced into working with her, he never tried to find out if she deserved her reputation. He just ignored her when they were off camera.

According to Gable's agent, Phil Berg, his pique was over a clause in MacDonald's contract that permitted time off for menstruation. "That infuriated Clark, who had to put in a full day even when his hemorrhoids flared up," Berg recalled.

Prior to filming their first romantic scene, Gable deliberately ate spaghetti for lunch. When he had to kiss MacDonald, his breath so reeked of garlic that she looked ready to faint when he released her from the embrace. Director Van Dyke was delighted because the audience would see it only as proof of Gable's power over women.

Gable developed a more complex relationship with Spencer Tracy, who'd joined MGM the year before, after a discouraging five years at Fox and other studios. Though only ten months older than Gable, Tracy was shorter and stockier, with a mature aura that suited character parts better than romantic leads. Gable and Tracy were such distinctly different star actors that they could be friends, if not close buddies. They were not competitors for the same roles, and they had a common bond in their fondness for booze. But there was an underlying edge of jealousy. Gable considered Tracy a far better actor and was always afraid that Tracy would steal scenes from him. And Tracy resented not being as handsome or attractive to women as Gable was.

Consumption of alcohol was officially forbidden at MGM during working hours. But Gable and Tracy kept bottles in their dressing rooms and regularly got together during production breaks to gab and to have a few nips. Whether they ever discussed their relationships with Loretta Young is unknown, but it seems likely since they once made a surprise visit to a neighboring soundstage where she was working.

As luck would have it, 20th–Fox had loaned Young to MGM for *The Unguarded Hour.* Being filmed at the same time as *San Francisco,* the melodrama teamed her with Franchot Tone, who by that time had become Mr. Joan Crawford. One day Gable and Tracy sneaked onto the set while Young was in the midst of a scene with supporting actors Roland Young and E. E. Clive. When she spotted Gable and Tracy, she blew her lines and director Sam Wood ordered a retake. While the cameras were being reloaded, the visitors teased Young about her loan to MGM in exchange for Wallace Beery, whom 20th–Fox needed for *A Message to Garcia.* She got very upset and told them to scram. Being seen with two of her ex-lovers would only rekindle gossip and rumors.

While filming *San Francisco,* Gable received his second consecutive Oscar nomination, this time for his performance as Fletcher Christian in *Mutiny on the Bounty.* Also nominated for Best Actor of 1935 were Charles Laughton and Franchot Tone for the same movie, plus Victor McLaglen for *The Informer.* The Academy had decided to retain the write-in option on voting in all categories, so there was the possibility for winners who were not official nominees.

Mutiny on the Bounty also earned nominations for best picture, director, screenplay, music score, and film editing. The most important category, best picture, again had a dozen nominees, the others being *Alice Adams, Broadway Melody of 1936, Captain Blood, David Copperfield, The Informer, Les Misérables, The Lives of a Bengal Lancer, A Midsummer Night's Dream, Naughty Marietta, Ruggles of Red Gap,* and *Top Hat.*

Since the last Oscar presentations, the Hollywood industry had been engulfed in disputes between the studios, who *were* the Academy of Motion Picture Arts and Sciences, and labor unions that were trying to organize the workers. This year three of the most disgruntled, the Actors Guild, the Writers Guild, and the Directors Guild, were urging all their members to boycott the ceremonial banquet. As a result, fewer than the usual galaxy of stars and celebrities attended the gathering at the Biltmore Hotel on March 5.

But Gable was among those who did turn out. Not that he disapproved of the guilds, but he'd made a promise to escort one of his current flames, Merle Oberon, who'd been nominated in the best actress category for her work in independent producer Samuel Goldwyn's *The Dark Angel.*

Fans who had gathered outside the Biltmore applauded as the two nominees arrived arm in arm, Gable in tuxedo and Oberon in a sable-trimmed gown. Once inside they sat at the table of Samuel Goldwyn and his wife, Frances, a sort of neutral zone for Gable, who usually graced one of the MGM tables.

Frank Capra, the Academy's newly elected president, changed the order of some of the presentations. The two acting awards would be the very last to be handed out, so Gable and Oberon were in for a long wait. It would be the climax to a special tribute to the father of American cinema, director D. W. Griffith. After the best picture award, Griffith was to receive an honorary Oscar and then announce 1935's best director, actor, and actress.

It was well after midnight when Harry Cohn, producer of the previous year's winner, *It Happened One Night,* mounted the podium to present the best picture Oscar. By that time, *Mutiny on the Bounty* had won nothing, defeated by *The Informer* for best screenplay and music score and by *A Midsummer Night's Dream* for film editing. Gamblers in the audience were betting that *The Informer,* director John Ford's critically acclaimed drama about the Irish Rebellion, would take the best picture trophy. But *Mutiny on the Bounty* clocked its first win of the evening.

Irving Thalberg accepted the award, his first since *Grand Hotel* in the 1931–32 competition. His disparagers would claim that *Mutiny on the Bounty* won because of its astonishing box-office success. By this time it had become MGM's highest grosser since the silent *Ben-Hur,* with world film rentals of $4.5 million.

Gable had to be content with being star of the best picture for the second consecutive year. He did not repeat as best actor, which went to Victor McLaglen for *The Informer.* The nomination of Gable, plus Charles Laughton and Franchot Tone for the same movie, had apparently divided the voters. Insiders claimed that a write-in candidate, Paul Muni for *Black Fury,* came in ahead of the three *Bounty* nominees.

Merle Oberon was also disappointed, defeated by Bette Davis, whose Oscar for *Dangerous* was interpreted as a sympathy vote over her failure to win the previous year for *Of Human Bondage.* Ironically, the film for which Oberon had been nominated, *The Dark Angel,* was based on the play in which Gable had triumphed during his Houston stock company days. The role of the blinded aviator was acted on screen by Fredric March, who failed to get nominated for his performance but may have received some write-in votes.

The big winner of the evening turned out to be David Wark Griffith, who hadn't been able to get a job since the flop of his last movie, *The Struggle,* in 1931. The master innovator was all but forgotten by the mass public by the time Henry B. Walthall, one of his actors in *The Birth of a Nation,* handed him the honorary Oscar. After the ceremony Irving Thalberg hired Griffith to do some rescue work on *San Francisco,* which wasn't living up to the producer's expectations.

"Our director, 'One-Take Woody,' was sometimes too fast for his own good," Anita Loos recalled. "His dramatic scenes with Gable and the others were fine, but Woody rushed through some of the spectacle. Parts of the earthquake and fire looked stagey and unimaginative. D. W.

Griffith, who was once Woody's boss back in the silent days, came in and reshot some of the scenes that had mobs of extras. He gave some of them little bits to do and urged everyone to improvise. 'Pretend it's a real earthquake,' he shouted at them through a megaphone. 'Run for your lives! Try to help your friends!' I truly think that Griffith helped to make what might have been a disappointment into a classic."

San Francisco took fifty-two days to shoot and cost $1.3 million to produce, or almost $700,000 less than *Mutiny on the Bounty.* Although *San Francisco* had a shorter script, the big savings came from staying home. Everything was filmed on the MGM soundstages and backlot, whereas *Mutiny* had gone on location to Catalina Island and had second-unit photography in the South Pacific.

Gable's next assignment was one of those horse-trading deals that he loathed. But as a favor to Thalberg, he assented to a swap to Warner Bros. so that Paul Muni could come to MGM to play the lead opposite Luise Rainer in *The Good Earth.* Gable considered himself lucky in escaping that project, which had a predominantly Caucasian cast portraying Chinese peasant-farmers.

Before Warner Bros. could decide what to do with Gable, Marion Davies demanded him for her next project there. Her box-office popularity had sunk so low that only Clark Gable seemed man enough to restore it.

Clark Gable's repertoire of screen characters had yet to include a prizefighter, but *Cain and Mabel* took care of that. Before production began in April 1936, he spent two weeks with professional trainer Allen Pomeroy to get into physical shape and to learn enough moves to pass for a heavyweight championship contender. To please Marion Davies, who claimed to be allergic to mustaches, he went clean-shaven for the first time since *Mutiny on the Bounty.* When he was suddenly called back to MGM to do a day of retakes for *San Francisco,* he had to paste on a fake.

Based on a short story by H. C. Witwer published in Hearst's *Cosmopolitan* magazine, the facetiously titled *Cain and Mabel* found boxer Joe Cain involved with Mabel O'Dare, ex-waitress and aspiring musical comedy star, in a phony public romance designed to land them in the headlines and to boost their careers. They really loathe each other, but needless to say, they end up lovebirds in a vine-covered cottage in New Jersey.

Scripted by Laird Doyle, the combination of screwball comedy and musical spectacle had Lloyd Bacon, director of *42nd Street,* at the helm. In lieu of choreographer Busby Berkeley, who was committed to other Warner projects, Davies picked Broadway veteran Bobby Connolly to stage the production numbers. The songwriting team of Harry Warren and Al Dubin, and costume designer Orry Kelly, two more components of *42nd Street,* were also assigned to the project, which, of course, had financial backing from Hearst's Cosmopolitan Pictures.

The day before shooting began, Davies invited all the principals to Sunday brunch at her beachfront estate in Santa Monica. She also decided to play matchmaker and urged Gable to bring Carole Lombard.

After a fast start their acquaintance seemed to have cooled, which bothered Davies. She adored Lombard and considered her the best suited of the women whom Gable had been running around with.

Gable did bring Lombard. They had a wonderful time, dancing to the music of the four-piece band that Davies kept on retainer and also brought to her movie sets to create a relaxed atmosphere during the breaks between takes. Still in a mood for fun when the party ended, Gable and Lombard decided to visit the amusement pier at nearby Venice. Lombard had once rented the entire place for one of her wacky parties, so the owners had shown their appreciation by giving her a lifetime pass. She took Gable for free rides on the roller coaster, bumper cars, Ferris wheel, and other attractions. They held hands and necked like teenagers.

It was the beginning of a serious affair, but one that developed slowly due to their preoccupations with their careers. Lombard especially could not be actress and playgirl simultaneously. When she was filming, she had to rise at dawn every morning to get to the studio for makeup and wardrobe. She tried to get to bed by nine P.M. to conserve her energy as well as her looks. Most of Hollywood's glamour pusses kept the same regimen, though few were as strict about it as Lombard.

Nearly eight years younger than Gable, the former Jane Alice Peters was born on October 6, 1908, in Fort Wayne, Indiana, which is about three hundred miles from his hometown of Cadiz, Ohio. Unlike Gable, she came from an affluent family (hardware and home appliances) and had two older brothers. Her parents separated when she was six. The mother and three children moved to Los Angeles, where they lived quite comfortably if not luxuriously on a four-hundred-dollar-per-month allowance from the father (a substantial sum in 1914).

Growing up with two older brothers, Lombard became a highly competitive tomboy who excelled in athletics. At age twelve the scrappy blue-eyed blonde was spotted by movie director Allan Dwan, who happened to be visiting friends in the neighborhood and considered her ideal for a small part as Monte Blue's kid sister in *A Perfect Crime*. With her mother's permission she worked for three days and earned fifty dollars. From then on she never wanted to be anything but a movie star like her favorites, who included Mary Pickford, Gloria Swanson, Colleen Moore, and Norma and Constance Talmadge.

Her formal education ended with junior high school, after which she attended several professional schools to study acting, singing, and dancing. At age sixteen she landed a starlet's contract at Fox Films, where she debuted as Edmund Lowe's romantic interest in *Marriage in Transit*. Fox considered her name too plain, so Jane Peters became Carol Lombard. (The *e* was added in 1930 to conform to a typographical error in the credits for *Safety in Numbers,* her first successful film.)

By the time of her Fox contract, Lombard had already developed quite a vocabulary of obscenities that she learned while growing up with two older brothers. As a starlet, she soon discovered that she could use profanity to protect herself against "casting couch" seductions. "If you're a young blonde around this man's town," she once said, "you have to keep the wolf pack off somehow. If you know all those words, they figure you know your way around and they don't act quite so rough. It's better than having a blacksnake whip in your hand."

Throughout her life she used crude language, though never in the presence of her mother or young children. Strangers meeting her for the first time were usually shocked, but people who knew her accepted it as part of her lusty personality. As a friend put it, "Carole could say, 'I don't give a shit,' and it sounded as innocent as 'Isn't it a nice day?' " Ironically, though she peppered her speech with vulgarisms, she never told dirty jokes, but she loved to hear them from others.

Starting her career in 1925, Lombard was very much a product of silent movies. Unlike Gable she never worked on the stage, which is the test of a real actor. All she had was beauty and charisma, but not enough to make her stand out from hundreds of other starstruck novices. She did three more Fox films, including two westerns with the legendary Buck Jones, and then had the bad luck of being seriously injured in an automobile accident.

In 1926, while out driving with wealthy playboy Henry Cooper in his Bugatti roadster, Lombard got hurled against the windshield during a bumper-to-bumper collision with another car. The impact of her head shattered the glass, causing a deep gash on the left side of her face, from the upper lip to the top of the cheekbone. The wound required fourteen stitches. During the operation no anesthetics could be used because relaxing the facial muscles might cause permanent disfigurement. The healing of the wound and subsequent plastic surgery took almost a year.

Lombard stayed in seclusion but received no sympathy from Fox, which dropped its option when her contract came up for renewal.

Lombard would always have a faint scar, but she learned how to conceal it with makeup and by studying photography and the art of light and shadow. At nineteen she tried a comeback at comedy producer Mack Sennett's studio, where a face wasn't as important as a shapely figure that could fill a bathing suit. In 1927–28 she appeared in thirteen Sennett two-reelers, including *The Swim Princess, The Bicycle Flirt,* and *Matchmaking Mamas.* She developed the comedy style and sense of timing that were integral to her later "screwball" phase. She also acquired a lifetime friend in Madalynne Fields, an obese amazon who provided comic relief from the bathing beauties. "Fieldsie" later became Lombard's personal secretary and live-in companion, which started rumors that they were lesbian lovers.

Lombard's work for Mack Sennett earned her a few offers for features, starting with a supporting role in the independently produced *The Divine Sinner* in 1928. Pathé, which distributed the Sennett shorts, signed her to a standard player's contract, starting with a minor part in *Power.* The next, *Show Folks* and *Ned McCobb's Daughter,* were Lombard's last silents, but both were released with sound effects and dubbed-in bits of dialogue to cash in on the new craze for talkies.

Her distinctively resonant voice saved her from getting lost in the shuffle during Hollywood's transition to sound. She had not been famous enough during the silent era to become identified with it, so she could take advantage of the demand for new personalities. Bounced by Pathé when it was integrated into RKO Radio, she wrangled a trial contract at Paramount in the spring of 1930. After her impressive performance in *Safety in Numbers,* Paramount signed her to a seven-year contract, starting at $375 per week.

Up to then Lombard's romantic life had been a series of flings with society playboys and movie people. Like Joan Crawford, with whom she often competed in dance contests at the Cocoanut Grove and Montmartre, Lombard played fast and loose, but she kept the details to herself. She allegedly had affairs with Howard Hughes, Charles Chaplin, and Joseph P. Kennedy (who then controlled Pathé), among many others.

But early in 1931, during the filming of her fourth Paramount film, *Man of the World,* she became seriously involved with costar William

Powell, who was sixteen years her senior. The sexual chemistry was so evident that Paramount rushed them into another teaming in *Ladies' Man*. After living together for several months, they got married on June 26. It was the second time for Powell, who had a son, now six years old, by his first wife, actress Eileen Wilson. Powell, then one of the highest-paid Hollywood stars at six thousand dollars per week, was also erudite and ultrasophisticated. Under his influence Lombard gained poise and culture, but she was too much of a free spirit to mesh with the formal and orderly lifestyle that he preferred. The marriage lasted twenty-eight months. After they divorced in 1933, they remained pals, largely because Lombard, who could have wiped Powell out in the property settlement, liked him too much to demand even one penny.

Lombard had also lived in Powell's professional shadow. After the divorce her career seemed to soar, starting with the 1934 comedy hit *Twentieth Century,* in which director Howard Hawks and costar John Barrymore helped to bring out the magical screwball that had been lurking in Lombard all along. Paramount, which loaned her to Columbia for that film, took notice and started to give her a big buildup as well as a glamorizing by its resident fashion genius, Travis Banton. She quickly became regarded as one of Hollywood's best-dressed women, both on and off the screen.

While Gable was working on loan-out to Warner Bros. in *Cain and Mabel,* Lombard had a similar booking at Universal for *My Man Godfrey,* teamed with ex-husband William Powell, who'd been borrowed from MGM. Ironically, director Gregory La Cava had selected one of Gable's ex-mistresses, Alice Brady, to portray Lombard's mother in the screwball comedy.

Gable's costar in *Cain and Mabel* was also an ex-flame. But in the four years since their brief affair during the filming of *Polly of the Circus,* he and Marion Davies had developed into such devoted friends that both probably realized that it was best to keep it platonic. Why risk spoiling a beautiful friendship?

Cain and Mabel was the apotheosis of William Randolph Hearst's infatuation with Davies, whom he had plucked from the chorus of the *Ziegfeld Follies of 1916* before she ever had a chance to prove that she had the talent and charisma to become a star on merit alone. Mabel O'Dare personified the Broadway queen that the onetime Marion

Douras might have become without the support of her sugar daddy. By the time of *Cain and Mabel,* Hearst had spent about $10 million toward the production of his mistress's films, plus countless millions more on building her homes and providing her with a regal lifestyle.

Gable had never before worked in such a sumptuous production and rarely would again. He didn't figure in any of the musical numbers except in separately filmed reaction shots that were edited into the scenes, showing Joe Cain applauding and cheering Mabel's perform-ances from a box seat in the theater. For a tap-dance number built around the song "Coney Island," Hearst spent $35,000 on a full-scale replica of a famous carousel at the Brooklyn resort's Luna Park. After the filming the carousel was moved to Davies's Santa Monica estate and permanently installed in a tent near the tennis courts and swimming pools.

Soundstage number seven, the largest at Warner Bros., wasn't high enough to accommodate some of the sets, so Hearst paid $100,000 to have the roof raised by thirty-five feet. The movie's grand finale, to the music of "I'll Sing You a Thousand Love Songs," occupied nine minutes of screen time, took two and a half weeks to shoot, and cost $400,000. The settings shifted from the canals of Venice, Italy, complete with float-ing gondolas, to the palace of Versailles. In the course of the action, Davies changed costumes five times, ending in a magnificent satin and lace wedding dress with hundreds of yards of train. As she married her prince charming, a ninety-foot-high pipe organ in the background sud-denly swung open at the middle and spewed forth 160 chorus girls dressed as bridesmaids.

After he completed *Cain and Mabel,* Gable took a hunting trip on the Kaibab Plateau in northern Arizona, near the Grand Canyon. Since Carole Lombard had also finished *My Man Godfrey,* he tried to per-suade her to join him, but she declined. As much as she liked Gable, she knew that he was a fast operator. She didn't want to be rushed into any-thing that she might regret later.

Since divorcing William Powell, Lombard had been involved in three unhappy relationships. The first, with Russ Columbo, the immensely popular radio and recording crooner, had ended on September 2, 1934, when he was fatally wounded while visiting a close friend who collected antique pistols. A police investigation concluded that one of the guns had gone off accidentally, sending a bullet ricocheting off a desk and tearing through Columbo's left eye into his brain.

Lombard was vacationing at Lake Arrowhead at the time. When she returned for the funeral, she dressed and behaved like Columbo's widow, sobbing to reporters, "His love for me was the kind that rarely comes to any woman."

Lombard found consolation with a swarthy Russ Columbo look-alike, George Raft, a fellow Paramount contractee who'd been attentive since they worked together earlier that year in *Bolero*. Paramount went on to reteam them in *Rumba,* which gave them plenty of opportunities for a dressing-room romance. Since Raft was married, the affair had to be kept secret, but Lombard fell hard for the forty-year-old actor. She once told a friend that Raft was the best lover she had ever had, but also the randiest. He wanted sex many times a day and had a harem of women around town who satisfied his needs.

Lombard was repelled by Raft's close alliance with Benjamin "Bugsy" Siegel, a childhood friend from New York and now the head of organized crime in Hollywood. Raft employed a full-time bodyguard to protect himself against rival gangsters. Mixing in such sinister company could ruin Lombard's reputation.

After George Raft, Lombard became involved with scriptwriter Robert Riskin, a longtime admirer who'd campaigned unsuccessfully for her to be cast in *It Happened One Night* before Claudette Colbert got the role. For Riskin's birthday Lombard threw a surprise party, transforming the interior of her home into a barn, complete with bales of hay, roaming livestock, and a hillbilly orchestra. On Christmas Day 1935 Riskin proposed marriage, but Lombard turned him down because he didn't want to have children. She told him that making babies was the only reason to get married, so why bother.

Before Gable left on his hunting trip to Arizona, Lombard had jokingly told him to bring her back a wildcat or two. She wasn't prepared for a cougar cub, which weighed seventy-five pounds and had sharper teeth and claws than any of the cats in her collection of pets. Keeping it at home was impossible, so she persuaded Gable to donate it to MGM's backlot zoo.

In June Gable started a profitable sideline of guest appearances on national radio broadcasts. Agent Phil Berg and his associate Cornwell

Jackson obtained permission from MGM, which granted the right to do a maximum of four per year, provided that mention was made on the air of Gable's latest movie.

Jackson set five thousand dollars as Gable's fee, which was more than he earned in a week at MGM and involved far less work. On June 1 Gable appeared on the premiere broadcast of the soap-sponsored *Lux Radio Theatre,* which was hosted by director Cecil B. DeMille and quickly became an every-Monday-night "must" for forty million listeners across America.

The sixty-minute CBS program, which presented dramatizations of popular movies, marked Gable's return to the stage. Broadcasts were live from the Music Box Theater in Hollywood, in front of an audience of about a thousand people. A radio play, of course, required no costumes or scenery, but a full orchestra played background music and technicians supplied sound effects.

Radio gave Gable opportunities to work with stars whom he never would in films. He teamed with Marlene Dietrich in *The Legionnaire and the Lady,* which was based on the 1930 *Morocco,* her first Hollywood film (with Gary Cooper as costar). By this time Dietrich had been declared box-office poison and was getting ready to leave for England to work for Alexander Korda in *Knight Without Armour.*

Gable scored such a hit on *Lux Radio Theatre* that offers poured in for the three remaining guest shots that he could do that year. Since the demand exceeded the supply, Cornwell Jackson upped Gable's fee to $6,500, which R. J. Reynolds Tobacco was happy to pay. It bought all three commitments for its *Camel Caravan,* a weekly series that alternated between variety shows and dramas based on movies or plays.

That summer MGM released *San Francisco,* which turned out to be an even bigger hit than *Mutiny on the Bounty,* earning $5.3 million in world rentals and a profit of $2.2 million for the studio. Critics raved about the teaming of Gable and Tracy, which made another one mandatory when a suitable script could be found. Jeanette MacDonald's histrionics were less well received. The studio decided thereafter to restrict her to musicals, which effectively scratched her from the list of Gable's potential leading ladies.

Another hit that summer, though far below *San Francisco* in box-office receipts, was Universal's *My Man Godfrey,* which also made a deep impression on Gable when he saw it. He always told friends that Lombard's delightfully daffy performance as a society debutante in love with an apparent hobo was what finally made him realize that he'd fallen in love with her.

Like thousands of other people, Lombard spent part of the summer reading a 1,037-page novel entitled *Gone With the Wind*. She not only loved it but envisioned herself and Gable playing the main characters, Scarlett O'Hara and Rhett Butler, in the movie version, which was already in preparation. In a prepublication deal, David O. Selznick had purchased the rights for fifty thousand dollars for his independent production company.

Lombard spent three dollars for another copy of the book and sent it to Gable, inscribed with the message "Let's do it!" He immediately mistook it for a sexual invitation and phoned to make a date. When she set him straight and happened to mention Selznick's ownership of *Gone With the Wind*, Gable lost interest. He took the two-and-a-half-pound volume into the bathroom and placed it at the bottom of a pile of reading material that he kept next to the toilet.

On August 14 Gable started working in his third film of the year, *Love on the Run*. When he first joined MGM, the studio had jump-started his career by teaming him with its biggest stars. Now it was his turn to help one who'd also been his lover. Joan Crawford's popularity had sunk to an all-time low, due partly to a long career that now dated back eleven years and partly to stinkers like her most recent, *The Gorgeous Hussy*. In the historical fiction about an alleged mistress of President Andrew Jackson, Crawford had five male costars—Robert Taylor, Lionel Barrymore, Melvyn Douglas, James Stewart, and Franchot Tone—but it turned out a turgid turkey.

Since 1933 Crawford's only hits had been the three films she made with Gable, the last *(Forsaking All Others)* nearly two years ago. Producer Joseph Mankiewicz decided that a rematch was urgently needed, so he picked writer John Lee Mahin to concoct a script attuned to the current vogue for screwball comedies. The result was a cross between *It Happened One Night* and the very public private life of Woolworth heiress Barbara Hutton.

In *Love on the Run* Gable was again a flippant newspaper reporter, this time based in Europe and assigned to cover the Paris wedding of a spoiled American heiress to Prince Igor of Taluska. Crawford changes her mind at the last minute and bolts, with Gable and another reporter from a rival paper in hot pursuit. Not surprisingly, that rival was played by Franchot Tone, now in his tenth month as Crawford's real-life husband after a long affair.

Anticipating a bumpy ride among the three principals, Mankiewicz handed the direction to "One-Take Woody" Van Dyke, who'd never yet failed to live up to his reputation and seemed capable of overcoming any tensions on the set. But Gable and Tone had become buddies during the making of *Mutiny on the Bounty,* and the only problems that developed were between Crawford and her husband. Tone had reached the end of his tether. His once-promising career had been reduced to supporting parts in Crawford's films. He was disheartened and also envious of all the attention that she received. He'd started sleeping away from home, and Crawford was furious.

On September 14 thirty-seven-year-old Irving Thalberg died at home after a siege of lobar pneumonia. On the set of *Love on the Run,* Woody Van Dyke was called to the phone. He returned with tears in his eyes and announced the news. L. B. Mayer declared an official day of mourning. The studio would be closed on September 16, the day of the funeral.

Gable and other MGM male stars were asked to be ushers at the services at the B'nai B'rith Temple on Wilshire Boulevard. Gable, who'd never been close friends with Thalberg, at first refused but got talked into it by Howard Strickling. The press would surely notice Gable's absence and interpret it as an insult to Thalberg and his widow.

Gable hadn't spoken to Thalberg since an angry encounter earlier that year. He thought Thalberg had flipped his lid when the producer asked him to team with Norma Shearer in *Romeo and Juliet.* When Gable caught his breath, he told Thalberg, "I don't look Shakespeare, I don't talk Shakespeare, I don't like Shakespeare, and I won't do Shakespeare." He also made some rude remarks about Shearer's unsuitability and walked out. Thalberg finally hired Leslie Howard for the movie, which he completed several weeks before his death.

Thalberg's passing had no effect on Gable's status at MGM and brought no sweeping changes in the studio power structure. L. B. Mayer dismantled the Thalberg unit and assigned whatever projects it had under development to other staff producers. Though she was minus a husband, Norma Shearer still wielded power. She and their two children inherited Thalberg's substantial stock holdings in MGM's parent company, Loew's, Inc.

After *Love on the Run* Gable found himself with time to kill while the studio readied his next project, an expensive historical drama based on the scandalous love life of the Irish political rebel Charles Parnell. Carole Lombard also happened to be between assignments, so they became a steady item. There were few movie premieres or nightclub show openings that they missed. Both loved sports. They went to the racetrack, played tennis and golf, and attended boxing and wrestling matches.

As news reporters and gossip columnists started to take notice, the general public got its first whiff of the liaison. Fan magazines described it as the grandest star-crossed romance since Mary Pickford and Douglas Fairbanks. Due to the strict moral climate of the time, bold words like *lovers* and *affair* were never used, but they were implied between the lines.

Gable still had an apartment at the Beverly Wilshire, but was a frequent guest at Lombard's house on the residential western end of Hollywood Boulevard. Lombard had been sharing it with her best friend and secretary, Madalynne Fields, so Gable's comings and goings were becoming a bit awkward. The house was also so centrally located that someone might easily come knocking at the door or peeping through the windows.

Lombard decided to rent another house for herself and to leave Fieldsie in charge of the Hollywood place. To keep Lombard's participation secret, Fieldsie made the rounds of real estate agents and found a rental in a secluded part of Bel-Air, well north of Sunset Boulevard. She took a two-year lease in her own name and then swapped houses with Lombard.

Gable's affair with Lombard affected some of his other relationships. Ria Gable hired a private detective to tail Gable to collect evidence for a divorce action. Merle Oberon decided to move on to the married Gary Cooper. Elizabeth Allan reconciled with her producer-husband, who had moved to Hollywood from England to manage her career.

And Loretta Young gave up waiting for Gable to show some interest in their daughter. When the baby was nine months old and getting too cumbersome a secret, Young smuggled her to San Francisco and placed her in a Roman Catholic facility that was both an orphanage and a home for unwed mothers. Unless she could find a way to explain the baby's existence that wouldn't cause scandal for herself and Gable, she'd decided to put Judith up for adoption.

On November 9 Gable started working in *Parnell*. A week later Lombard began *Swing High, Swing Low* at Paramount. The unplanned overlap taught them a lesson: if they arranged their breaks to coincide, they would be able to spend more of their leisure time together.

Parnell was a pet project of L. B. Mayer, who envied Warner Bros.' success with *The Story of Louis Pasteur* and thought MGM should be making more movies of social and historical significance. The New York story department recommended *Parnell*, a highly acclaimed first play by Elsie Schauffler, a middle-aged Kansas homemaker who had died shortly before its November 1935 premiere on Broadway. Two esteemed writers, John Van Druten and S. N. Behrman, were hired to collaborate on the screenplay.

Mayer entrusted the production to freelance director John M. Stahl, who had a vivid visual style and was meticulous about research and preparation. Stahl spent nine months assembling the required seventy-four sets, including a replica of the interior of the House of Commons in London, which occupied almost a square mile of space on MGM's vast backlot.

Rather than a whole-life biography, *Parnell* focused on the last years of Charles Parnell, who became known as "the Uncrowned King of Ireland" for his efforts to obtain home rule for Ireland and to relieve the sufferings of its impoverished populace. Unfortunately he becomes romantically involved with Katie O'Shea, the wife of one of his adversaries. When her husband finds out, he files for divorce, naming Parnell as corespondent. The scandal destroys Parnell's political power. While campaigning to restore it, he suffers a heart attack and dies convinced that he betrayed his country for love of a woman.

Although it was against his usual type, Gable liked the role and saw a chance to prove his versatility. L. B. Mayer wanted Joan Crawford to play Katie O'Shea, but she'd developed such a phobia for historic costume roles after her huge flop in *The Gorgeous Hussy* that she begged to be excused. In a classic example of MGM's factory system, Mayer simply switched Crawford to the upcoming *The Last of Mrs. Cheyney* and moved Myrna Loy from that to *Parnell* to play opposite Gable.

Gable immediately locked horns with director John Stahl, who, for historical accuracy, wanted him to grow a beard. Gable refused. He wanted no more natural adornment than his mustache, but he finally agreed to augment it with the longer and fuller sculpted sideburns that were fashionable in the 1880s.

Stahl was the reverse of W. S. Van Dyke and other MGM speed demons. He had a slow, meticulous approach to directing, often insisting on ten or twelve takes of a scene before he was satisfied. L. B. Mayer, an old friend of Stahl's from the early silent days, was well aware of that tendency and made allowances for it in the shooting schedule. At 108 days it was the longest shoot of Gable's films so far. *Mutiny on the Bounty* had taken eighty-eight days, and *San Francisco* only fifty-two.

Charles Parnell is described in history books as frail, nervous, haughty, and sensitive—everything that Clark Gable wasn't, but he tried to create a believable character. "The best love scene Clark ever played was in that picture," Myrna Loy recalled. "It's the first meeting between Parnell and Katie, when he talks about having seen her in a white dress at the opera. It's a beautiful scene. You can feel the beginning of this love that would rock the British Empire."

Gable dreaded filming the death scene, in which he expires in Loy's arms. In his methodical way John Stahl took a week to rehearse and shoot it. To keep Gable and Loy in a somber mood, he had a phonograph on the set, playing sad, funereal music. One night Gable complained to Carole Lombard that he couldn't stand much more of it. The next morning she made a surprise visit to the set to cheer him up. At the same time she bribed a prop man to put a different record on the phonograph. When Stahl gave the signal to start the music, the jazzy "I'll Be Glad When You're Dead, You Rascal You" blasted through the air. Bedlam followed, with Lombard making a swift exit.

Parnell would eventually disappoint Gable and Loy fans alike, who sent thousands of complaints to the studio following its release. "Clark gave a subdued, sustained performance, which apparently was the problem," Loy remembered. "He had been so typed as those red-blooded Blackie Nortons that people didn't want to be reminded he was an actor.

They wanted the macho stuff. And I was breezy Nora Charles of the *Thin Man* series. They didn't want to see me in Adrian's nineteenth-century finery and creating a more sober characterization. But we were actors, for God's sake. We couldn't be Blackie and Nora all the time."

During the filming, showman Sid Grauman invited Gable to officially become a Hollywood immortal by leaving his footprints in a block of concrete in the forecourt of the world-famous Chinese Theater on Hollywood Boulevard. Thousands turned out for the klieg-lighted ceremony, in which Gable also had to get down on his knees to scrawl an autograph and to add an impression of his enormous hands to his footprints. Two men were needed to restrain him from falling face forward into the fast-drying cement. Carole Lombard later joked that he should have registered a "cockprint" as well.

On February 1, 1937, the eighty-fourth shooting day of *Parnell*, Gable turned thirty-six years old. The studio arranged a birthday party that truly surprised Gable when a grand piano was rolled onto the set, trailed by songwriter Roger Edens and a chubby teenager named Judy Garland. While Edens sat down at the piano to accompany her, Garland climbed up onto the refreshment table next to the three-tiered birthday cake and beckoned to Gable to come over. When he was within kissing range, she burst into song with "You Made Me Love You," an old favorite introduced by Al Jolson in 1913. It was usually sung as a love song, but this time Roger Edens had turned it into a fan letter by writing a new opening verse:

> *Dear Mr. Gable . . .*
> *I guess I'm just another fan of yours,*
> *And I thought I'd write and tell you so.*
>
> *You made me love you,*
> *I didn't want to do it,*
> *I didn't want to do it . . .*

Gable was moved to tears. When Garland finished, he lifted her down into his arms and kissed her. Only fourteen at the time, Garland came near to swooning as Gable whispered, "Thanks, honey, that was a real thrill."

L. B. Mayer and other executives present were so impressed by Garland's performance that they decided that the recent contractee should repeat "Dear Mr. Gable" in *Broadway Melody of 1938* (dated a year ahead to extend its release life). The scene proved a showstopper and launched Garland to stardom at MGM.

The adult Garland remembered: "Mister G. was one of the finest men I ever knew, a truly gentle man. He gave me a bracelet that I still cherish. But the funny thing is that whenever I sang that song, that big, wonderful man wept. And he always stood up while I sang. Years later, during a chance meeting, he told me, 'Judy, I had a birthday the other day, and I hid. I was afraid that you'd pop up from somewhere and sing that song again.' "

Soon after Gable's birthday, the nominations for the 1936 Academy Awards were announced. Four Gable films were released that year—*San Francisco, Wife vs. Secretary, Cain and Mabel,* and *Love on the Run*—but for the first time since 1934 he failed to get nominated. He stood no chance of a write-in because the Academy had decided to drop that option after a two-year trial. But *San Francisco* did get nominated for best picture, the third year in a row that one of his films landed in that category.

Gable was miffed over Spencer Tracy's nomination for best actor for *San Francisco.* He wasn't jealous and thought that Tracy deserved it, but another new change in the Academy Awards that year was the creation of two more male and female acting awards, for best supporting performances. Gable and many others felt that Tracy should have been nominated in that category. Tracy's billing had been below the title, which was the accepted dividing line between a star and the supporting performers.

A surprise nominee was Carole Lombard for best actress for *My Man Godfrey.* For his performance in the same film, her ex-husband, William Powell, was nominated for best actor. Ironically, Gable's ex-mistress, Alice Brady, got a supporting nomination for her portrayal of Lombard's mother in *My Man Godfrey.* It promised to be a big night for Gable after all.

Lombard's very first Oscar nomination thrilled her and left her a bit gaga by the time of the ceremonial banquet on March 4. She vacillated between two new evening gowns but finally decided to wear one that Travis Banton had designed for her for *My Man Godfrey.*

Gable agreed to Lombard's suggestion that they make it a double date with William Powell and Jean Harlow, who'd been an unmarried couple for going on two years now. Press photographers had a field day when the foursome arrived at the Biltmore Hotel. Harlow, who'd been depressed and boozing heavily since Powell got her pregnant and then forced her to have an abortion, looked bloated and slightly dazed. Lombard took her to the powder room several times to help her repair her makeup.

No one in the quartet went home with an Oscar, though Powell's *The Great Ziegfeld* was voted Best Picture of 1936. Lombard, who was up against Irene Dunne *(Theodora Goes Wild),* Gladys George *(Valiant Is the Word for Carrie),* Norma Shearer *(Romeo and Juliet),* and Luise Rainer *(The Great Ziegfeld),* saw the last-named be declared best actress. Paul Muni won the best actor award for *The Story of Louis Pasteur.*

Lombard may not have won an Oscar to put on a shelf next to Gable's, but the nomination and the success of *My Man Godfrey* enabled her agent, Myron Selznick, to get her a new three-year contract at Paramount. The deal was nonexclusive and guaranteed Lombard at least two pictures per year at Paramount for $150,000 each. In addition, she had the freedom to work elsewhere as long as it didn't conflict with the Paramount shooting schedules. In other words, Paramount could no longer loan her to another studio or profit from it. Whatever monies she earned from non-Paramount projects were hers alone.

Gable became envious. He was still MGM's exclusive property and had little choice in the movies he made or the people he worked with. In comparison with Lombard's $150,000 per picture, he earned $4,000 per week, or $160,000 per year. If he made two pictures a year, that worked out to only $80,000 per picture, or $53,333 per in the case of three (all figures predicated on a studio calendar year of forty weeks).

But at MGM Gable did receive fringe benefits that partially made up the difference. In times of crisis the studio's publicity machine, legal department, and police force were always available, at no charge for their services. In April 1937 Gable needed all three when he became the central figure in a paternity case.

For nearly a year a woman calling herself Mrs. Violet Norton had been writing to Gable in care of MGM, claiming that he was the father of her daughter Gwendolyn. At first Gable thought it might be a plot by

Loretta Young or by someone who knew of their lovechild and was try-ing to profit.

But that guess turned out wrong when a private detective retained by Mrs. Norton contacted MGM and demanded $150,000 in hush money. If the studio didn't pay, the world would be told that Clark Gable was really Norton's ex-lover, Frank Billings, who abandoned her after she became pregnant in 1922. It all supposedly happened in Norton's native England, where Gwendolyn was born in 1923.

MGM's lawyers turned the matter over to the U.S. attorney gen-eral's office for investigation. When the story leaked out to the press, Gable's name was emblazoned in newspaper headlines everywhere: MOTHER TELLS GABLE TO CONFESS; IS THIS GABLE'S CHILD?; WILL GABLE COME CLEAN?; GABLE PATERNITY MYSTERY ROCKS HOLLYWOOD. Ironically, some of it *was* true, though a different woman and child were involved.

After studying all the evidence, the federal government indicted Violet Norton for using the mails to defraud. The public trial was assigned to the Los Angeles federal court, with Gable to be called as the key witness for the prosecution. MGM's attorneys were confident of winning the case if they could prove that Gable had never been in England in the year prior to the date on the child's official birth certifi-cate. Gable had, in fact, never visited England in his entire life.

The pretrial preparations forced Gable to recall a romance that he would rather have forgotten—with the young actress Franz Dorfler, whom he dumped when he became involved with Josephine Dillon. His affair with Dorfler in Oregon in 1922–23 coincided with the time that he had allegedly impregnated Norton in England.

Gable told his lawyers that he was sure that Dorfler would testify in his behalf. He knew that she'd moved to Hollywood to find acting work in movies, without any luck. He'd last seen her about three years before, when he'd bumped into her at MGM, where she was en route to inter-view for a secretarial job. Asked if he'd offered to help her, Gable said that it had never occurred to him. The lawyers wondered if that might cause Dorfler to refuse to be a defense witness. Bewildered, Gable asked, "Why?"

Ironically, Dorfler was found currently employed as a domestic in the mansion of Bert Allenberg, the partner of Gable's agent, Phil Berg. Before that she'd worked as a shop clerk. Her parents, who'd once sheltered Gable when he was sick and jobless, had been wiped out in the Depression and lost their farm. Yet Dorfler willingly agreed to testify for Gable at the trial. She seemed to bear him no grudge for never doing anything to help her, despite his own enormous success.

In advance of the trial, Gable's image polisher, Howard Strickling, decided that Franz Dorfler would make a stronger impression on the jury if she was introduced as a successful movie actress rather than as a struggling domestic servant. She was signed to one of MGM's stock contracts, starting at sixty-five dollars per week, which placed her in a talent pool used for minor roles in B features and short subjects. She continued working there for seven years, but as she later recalled, "Clark would walk right past me, pretending that he didn't see me. I never saw him again on a friendly basis."

The trial started on April 20, 1937, with Judge George Cosgrove presiding. During the selection of the all-male jury, seven candidates were dismissed when they admitted to being Gable fans. Another was excused when he confessed to being a childhood friend of Jean Harlow's father.

Hundreds of women, most of them middle-aged or older, started lining up the night before for spectator seats. By morning the line stretched completely around the courthouse. Street vendors were hawking peanuts, hot dogs, and eight-by-ten glossy photos of Clark Gable.

Gable arrived in the courtroom via a secret entrance. Through narrowed eyes he took his first look at buxom and ruddy-faced Violet Norton, who wore a dark blue dress and black hat. When she spoke, which would be often, she revealed a thick cockney accent and false teeth that rattled whenever she got excited. Obviously Norton and Gable did not go to the same dentist.

Mae West, who'd received a letter from Norton begging her to be the godmother of "Clark Gable's child," had been sought as a witness but managed to elude the subpoena servers. The first witness was columnist Jimmy Fidler, who'd also received letters from Norton and described them as "the work of some kind of a nut."

A representative of the U.S. Passport Agency testified that there were no records of Gable leaving or reentering the country during the period in question. Four men who'd known him in Oregon testified to his residing there during the time Norton placed him in England.

MGM went to work on Franz Dorfler before she took the stand, sending her to the beauty parlor for a permanent wave and facial and outfitting her in an expensive dress and hat. When her name was called, Gable bounded from his seat and escorted her to the witness box.

Dorfler spoke discreetly of her relationship with Gable, never mentioning that they were lovers but hinting that they had been on the verge of getting married. When she finished, Gable again got up and led her by the arm back to her seat. He kissed her on the cheek and whispered thanks. Many of the women spectators were weeping. It could have been a scene from a Gable movie and in fact had been deliberately planned that way by the MGM lawyers.

When Gable was finally called, his testimony coincided with that of the previous witnesses. But Violet Norton leaned forward as if she were hearing it all for the first time. When he finished, she shouted defiantly, "I still think Clark Gyble is the dad of me kid." Unable to restrain himself, Gable laughed out loud, along with the rest of the spectators.

In her own testimony Norton claimed that Gable, or Frank Billings as he called himself then, had seduced her while humming the tune "I'm Forever Blowing Bubbles." She said that she never saw him again until years later, when "I went to the pictures and there he was mykin' love to that Joan Crawford—just the syme as 'e did to me."

After deliberating for an hour and fifty-five minutes, the jury found Violet Norton guilty of using the U.S. mails to defraud. She was sentenced to a year in jail. Six months later she was released for good behavior but deported to Canada together with her daughter, who'd been staying with a court-appointed guardian in the meantime. Both were forbidden to ever return to the United States.

Carole Lombard thought that the Violet Norton trial was the funniest thing that ever happened, though she had to follow it from Gable's reports and the press coverage. MGM insisted that she stay away. It would have hurt Gable's case if his latest sweetie were in the audience while he was trying to prove himself innocent of another woman's paternity charges.

At MGM's urging the lovers tried to avoid being seen together during the period of the trial, but as soon as it was over they were back on the social circuit. On April 29 they attended a costume party in honor of William Randolph Hearst's seventy-fourth birthday. Marion Davies threw one every year at her Santa Monica estate. This time the theme was "the Circus." The five hundred guests could come in appropriate outfits or select one when they got there from a truckload of things that Davies rented for the evening from the Western Costume warehouse.

Gable and Lombard stretched it a bit by going as rodeo riders, wearing their favorite blue jeans and western shirts but augmenting them with new boots and Stetsons. Among the other celebrants were Bette Davis as a sideshow bearded lady, Leslie Howard as a penguin, Cary Grant and housemate Randolph Scott as acrobats, Humphrey Bogart as a hot dog vendor, and Ernst Lubitsch as a cigar-smoking Indian chief. Marion Davies was a bareback rider and the guest of honor a clown without greasepaint.

Everybody took rides on the carousel that Hearst had built for *Cain and Mabel,* trying to catch brass rings that were redeemable for bottles of vintage champagne. Two of Hearst's star columnists, Louella Parsons, costumed as a lion tamer, and Walter Winchell, dressed as himself, wandered around trying to gather scoops. Lombard whispered into Winchell's ear that she and Gable were expecting triplets and dared him to report it. Winchell didn't.

Gable had just started working in *Saratoga*, another brainchild of idea man Robert Hopkins. "Horse racing!" he extemporized at a story conference. "We'll call it *Saratoga*, a town as famous as San Francisco. There's this society girl so hoity-toity that she's got polka dots on her toilet paper. Might be ideal for Gable and Crawford." Bernard Hyman, producer of *San Francisco*, agreed and again assigned Anita Loos to write the script.

Meanwhile Joan Crawford Tone tested pregnant and took off on a maternity leave that eventually ended in a miscarriage. Hyman replaced her with Jean Harlow, who was overdue for a rematch with Gable. In their last, *Wife vs. Secretary,* she had turned out the romantic loser to Myrna Loy.

Anita Loos again used Wilson Mizner as a model for Gable's character, Duke Bradley, a racetrack bookmaker who gets involved with a snooty socialite whose late father ran a horse-breeding farm and lost everything to gambling. She blames Duke for her father's misfortune and tries to ruin him by fixing a big race on which he's staked his bankroll. Although they behave as if they despise each other, there's an obvious attraction between them. What might have been a drama of revenge turns into a romantic comedy with a happy ending.

Harlow, who'd been in frail health in recent months, requested her favorite director, Jack Conway, to make things easier for her. What exactly ailed Harlow may never be known, but it seemed a combination of years of heavy drinking, which had permanently damaged her kidneys and liver, and a blood infection that developed during an operation for either impacted wisdom teeth or an unwanted pregnancy. It was the era before antibiotic drugs. There was no way of stopping the infection from spreading throughout her already-impaired system.

Thanks to an extra hour in the makeup chair each morning, Harlow looked reasonably healthy when *Saratoga* started production. Jack Conway ordered the camera crew to go easy on the close-ups and lighting. Unfortunately, Harlow tired quickly and usually couldn't work past the early afternoon. What had been scheduled as a thirty-day shoot promised to take twice as long.

On May 29 Gable and Harlow were preparing for a boudoir scene. He was supposed to pick her up in his arms and then drop her onto a chaise longue. But as Gable started to lift Harlow, he sensed that something was wrong. Her body felt limp, and her brow was beaded with sweat. Calling for help, he gently lowered her onto the chaise. She started to get up, mumbled that she felt sick, and then fainted. An assistant director revived her with smelling salts and then carried her to her dressing bungalow. Jack Conway phoned for Harlow's chauffeur and arranged for a studio nurse to take her home.

The filming of *Saratoga* continued without Harlow, concentrating on scenes in which she didn't appear. Whenever Gable or anyone else phoned to check on Harlow's condition, her mother always answered and said that the patient was much better and would return to work soon.

But after a week of such calls, producer Bernard Hyman decided to go to the house, and he asked Gable, who'd known Mama Jean for years, to accompany him. When they arrived, Mama Jean tried to turn them away, but they barged past her and found Harlow semiconscious in bed. Since they'd last seen her, she had ballooned to twice her size. When Gable greeted her with a peck on the lips, her breath smelled like urine. "It was like kissing a rotting person," he later recalled.

Mama Jean was a devout Christian Scientist who believed that only God and prayer could cure her daughter. She refused to permit Gable and Hyman to call for a doctor. Hyman finally phoned Eddie Mannix, who sent *two* doctors, but it was too late. They diagnosed acute nephritis, or kidney failure. Unable to urinate normally, Harlow was excreting waste in her saliva and perspiration.

She was rushed by ambulance to Good Samaritan Hospital and placed on life support. Early the next morning, June 7, the retained fluids triggered a cerebral edema, or swelling of the brain. When she slipped into a coma, the hospital called the inhalation squad of the Los Angeles fire department. They pumped four tanks of oxygen into her but to no avail. At 11:38 A.M. Jean Harlow died. Three months before, she had celebrated her twenty-sixth birthday.

Gable was deeply shaken. Though Harlow was affectionately known around MGM as "the Baby," he'd always called her "Sis." Lovers or not, they had been great friends for going on seven years. He would miss her, both as a pal and as a coworker. They had made six films together.

MGM announced that out of respect for Harlow's memory, the unfinished *Saratoga* was being scrapped, at a loss to the studio of nearly a million dollars. No mention was made of the fact that most of that sum would be recouped from production insurance.

Gable was selected to serve as a pallbearer and usher at the funeral on June 9. MGM, which had a habit of controlling its stars' lives right up to the grave, planned the rites like a superproduction. The setting was Forest Lawn Memorial Park, which occupied two hundred acres near Glendale and advertised itself as "a place for the living to enjoy." Several decades later Bob Hope would describe it as "the Disneyland of cemeteries."

Gable took Carole Lombard with him to the service, which was held in the park's Wee Kirk of the Heather, a replica of the legendary church in Scotland where Annie Laurie worshiped. Lombard sat in the rear of the chapel and held a place for Gable so that he could join her after all the guests were ushered in. Within minutes the crowd swelled to over 250 and seemed like a Who's Who of Hollywood, with Greta Garbo the only notable absentee.

Jeanette MacDonald warmed things up with "Indian Love Call," one of Harlow's favorite songs. After an organ interlude Mrs. Genevieve Smith, the Christian Science practitioner who had advised Mama Jean against seeking medical help for her daughter, read several selections from the Bible. Then the Lord's Prayer was recited in unison by the mourners, followed by Mrs. Smith reading the Scientific Statement of Being from Mary Baker Eddy's *Science and Health*.

At the end of the twenty-three-minute service, Nelson Eddy joined Jeanette MacDonald for a rendering of "Ah, Sweet Mystery of Life."

Halfway through, MacDonald broke down in tears and Eddy carried on alone. His baritone was momentarily drowned out by the sound of a single-engine plane that had been hired to shower the roof of the church with Harlow's favorite white gardenias.

Gable appeared grim as he helped to carry Harlow and her five-thousand-dollar bronze-and-silver casket to the hearse for transport to the Sanctuary of Benediction in Forest Lawn's Memorial Court of Honor. Harlow's lover, William Powell, paid $25,000 for a nine-by-ten-foot crypt, which had a stained-glass window and two eternally burning candelabra and would be named "the Jean Harlow Room."

Two days after the funeral L. B. Mayer announced that *Saratoga* would be released after all, claiming that Harlow had finished most of her scenes before she died. In response to what Mayer termed "overwhelming popular demand," the movie would be completed and distributed as soon as possible. But the real reason for the decision was pressure from theater owners, who felt that the unprecedented news coverage of Harlow's passing would turn her final movie into a blockbuster.

Harlow's unfilmed scenes were more numerous than MGM was willing to admit. Director Jack Conway remembered a former Harlow stand-in named Mary Dees, who looked enough like her to be a twin sister. With the hiring kept secret, Dees was assigned all the scenes in which Harlow figured prominently and had dialogue. To save time another double, Geraldine Dvorak, was used in some of the background shots and crowd scenes where even the real Harlow would have been hard to spot.

Mary Dees's scenes were rewritten so that she could be photographed with her back to the camera or wearing a large floppy hat that put her face in shadow. Unfortunately, her voice had none of Harlow's unique shrillness, so radio actress Paula Winslow later had to redub the dialogue.

"I feel like I've been holding a ghost in my arms," Gable said after his first day of working with Mary Dees.

Some of Harlow's key scenes couldn't be faked. Anita Loos deleted them from the script and filled the gaps by writing new ones using the superior supporting cast, which included Walter Pidgeon, Frank Morgan, Una Merkel, and Gable's old friend Lionel Barrymore (as Harlow's grandfather!).

A beneficiary of the rewrite was hefty, dark black Hattie McDaniel, who played Harlow's maid. Loos added some showy comic moments for her character, Rosetta, who becomes smitten with Gable and at one point exclaims, "If he was only the right color, I'd marry him!" Their delightful scenes together would later be remembered when another major movie was being cast.

Saratoga wrapped on June 29 and hit theater screens on July 23, just six weeks after Harlow's death. Most critics declared it far from the best of the Gable-Harlow teamings but a satisfying enough send-off for a great star. At the box office *Saratoga* was Gable's biggest hit since *San Francisco*, earning $3.3 million in world rentals and a profit of $1.1 million over its production cost.

The success more than compensated for the failure of *Parnell*, which entered release on June 4, three days before Harlow's death. Negative reviews and public word of mouth acted like a stink bomb in emptying theaters. MGM suffered a loss of $637,000 on its investment. Gable blamed it on the historical subject matter and vowed to never do another costume epic.

During the production of *Saratoga*, Gable figured in another headline story, but only he and those personally involved knew about his role. The day after Harlow's funeral gossip columnist Louella Parsons announced to the world that Loretta Young had become a mother—through the adoption of two adorable blondes, Jane and Judy, aged three and nearly two. Young refused to explain where or how she found the children. "That is a secret I hope I never have to reveal," she told Parsons. "I want to forget as soon as possible that they are not mine. For I feel that they really belong to me."

But the revelation was just the unmarried mother's opening gambit. In order to keep her own daughter, Loretta Young had created a hoax that required her to lie to the child as well as to the world. When Young ran out of lies, she kept inventing new ones to confuse and to prevent the truth from exposure.

A month later, on July 4 no less, she released another bombshell, announcing that she was returning the older girl, Jane, to her real mother because the latter had relented and demanded her back. But "Jane," in fact, had never been adopted by Young; nor did she even exist.

The younger girl, Judy, would remain with Young. Her age was reported as twenty-three and a half months, although it was actually only twenty months. That was to discourage anyone from figuring out the true birth date and connecting it with Young's "temporary retirement" during her pregnancy.

Baby Judy's nurses were instructed to keep her overlarge ears, which seemed inherited from Gable, covered with a bonnet or hat whenever they took her out. If Judy did go bareheaded, her curly hair was to be brushed over the ears to make them less conspicuous. Intentionally or not, by erasing clues that might connect them, Young made it easier for Gable to distance himself from both her and their daughter.

After Gable finished *Saratoga,* MGM had no project ready for him, so he spent the summer loafing. He tinkered with his cars, made several hunting and fishing trips with friends, and spent as much time with Carole Lombard as she could spare him.

Lombard was in the midst of her first "outside" job since signing her new nonexclusive contract with Paramount. Agent Myron Selznick had sold her services to his brother, David, for *Nothing Sacred.* Scripted by Ben Hecht, the screwball comedy costarred Fredric March and had William Wellman as director. Lombard earned $18,750 per week, which was what her $150,000 fee broke down to over the eight-week shooting schedule. She was ecstatic. In addition to the high pay and excellent script, it was her first movie to be photographed in color. She also saw it as a chance to ingratiate herself with David Selznick and become a contender for *Gone With the Wind,* which was still in the early stages of preparation.

Since Gable disliked David Selznick, he wasn't too happy about Lombard working for him. Gable sensed that Selznick might try to use her to persuade him to play Rhett Butler in *Gone With the Wind.* In the year since Selznick had acquired the property, the producer had been keeping interest alive by running frequent public opinion polls about the casting of the leading roles. Gable was consistently the number-one choice for Rhett Butler, followed by Ronald Colman, Gary Cooper, and Errol Flynn.

By this time Gable had read Margaret Mitchell's novel and liked it. But his aversion to costume roles as well as to David Selznick made him dead set against being involved with the movie.

Gable wanted to take Lombard on a hunting trip to Mexico when she finished *Nothing Sacred,* but Paramount immediately put her to work in *True Confession.* The screwball comedy was Lombard's fourth teaming with Fred MacMurray; they were becoming Paramount's equivalent of MGM's Myrna Loy and William Powell.

To spend some recreational time with Lombard, Gable had to settle for accompanying her to Lake Arrowhead for the filming of a motorboat chase and other outdoor scenes for *True Confession.* Director Wesley Ruggles was an old friend, having worked with them both on *No Man of Her Own* and having found jobs for Gable during his stretch as an extra in silent days.

At the fashionable resort in San Bernadino County, Gable and Lombard squeezed in some swimming and horseback riding while staying at the Arrowhead Springs Hotel. On October 6 they celebrated Lombard's twenty-ninth birthday by going dancing at the High Hat Club. As a surprise, Gable gave Lombard a ring—one that he found in a box of Cracker Jack candy-coated popcorn.

Lombard loved Gable, but she often wondered about the intensity of his feelings for her. After more than a year of shacking up, she thought he should be working on a divorce so that they could be properly married.

Gable was also smitten with Lombard. He often boasted to friends that she was a woman in a billion, that he wanted to spend the rest of his life with her. "You can trust that little screwball with your life or your hopes or your weaknesses, and she wouldn't even know how to think about letting you down," he once said. "She's more fun than anybody, but she'll take a poke at you if you have it coming and make you like it. If that adds up to love, then I love her."

Gable's stalling was mainly financial, the fear of being wiped out by a divorce settlement. He was a miser, hardly unusual for someone who suddenly becomes rich after a lifetime of hard struggle. He was afraid that his luck wouldn't hold, that he'd eventually end up as a garage mechanic or a farmer. Whatever he managed to save after his weekly maintenance payments to his wife, he hoarded in cash in a safe-deposit box. He had no investments in stock, real estate, or other enterprises that involved any risk. He liked his money where he could put his hands on it. He always carried several thousand dollars in cash, divided between his wallet and a money belt.

In November 1937 management of the affair became more complicated when MGM summoned Gable back to work and Lombard started
another freelance deal, this time at Warner Bros. Producer-director
Mervyn LeRoy hired her for *Fools for Scandal,* a romantic comedy that
teamed her with Fernand Gravet, a suave European import being
groomed as the next Charles Boyer.

Gable had the title role in *Test Pilot,* which returned him to the skyways for the first time since *Night Flight* in 1933. Budgeted at $2 million,
the action adventure was Hollywood's most expensive aviation movie
since *Hell's Angels.* MGM made a deal with the army air force to use
March Field, near Riverside, California, as its base of operations for the
filming of the aerial scenes.

Director Victor Fleming and producer Louis Lighton were assigned
to the project after a big success earlier that year with *Captains Courageous,* which finally established Spencer Tracy as one of MGM's top
stars. After the smash of *San Francisco,* L. B. Mayer wanted another
teaming of Gable and Tracy, so *Test Pilot* was the result. Also starring
was Myrna Loy, who in the past year had become the studio's number-
one female attraction due to the continuing decline of Crawford and the
death of Harlow.

Based on a story by Lieutenant Commander Frank Wead, who
came up with the idea for Gable's earlier *Hell Divers* and many other aviation movies, *Test Pilot* drew liberally from the legend of Don Quixote
as well as *What Price Glory?*. Gable was a daredevil pilot who tests
planes and himself to the limits of endurance. Tracy played his mechanic
and best friend. When skirt-chaser Gable decides to settle down into
marriage with Myrna Loy, Tracy gets upset but eventually becomes pals
with Loy before sacrificing his life for Gable's in a plane crash. Gable
and Tracy both had such masculine images that there was no chance of
their *Test Pilot* relationship being interpreted as homosexual, if that was
even the intention of scriptwriters Vincent Lawrence and Waldemar
Young.

In real life Gable and Tracy made for an odd couple. "They weren't
great pals, but they respected each other and worked well together,"
Myrna Loy recalled. "They had a lively banter, which seldom went on
with many coactors during filming. Clark sort of envied Spence's acting
reputation. Spence coveted Clark's standing with the public and the

studio, so their raillery had an edge to it. Spence was the first to call Clark 'the King,' and also 'Your Majesty.' Clark dubbed Spence 'the Iron Duke' and always called him a 'Wisconsin ham' when he pulled one of his scene-stealing tricks. It was just macho against macho, but it sometimes got a bit out of hand."

One night in the air force officers' mess hall during the location filming at March Field, the pilot of one of the new B-17 bombers offered to take Gable, Tracy, and Victor Fleming on a short flight over Catalina Island. When Tracy declined, Gable and Fleming called him a coward and worse. After they left, Tracy felt so humiliated that he went off by himself on a drinking spree. The next morning he didn't show up for work. Finally around noon he strolled onto the set looking like hell. "I don't know where he'd been," Myrna Loy remembered, "but he'd let them suffer and taken his revenge."

The scriptwriters emulated the poetic imagery of aviator-writer Antoine de Saint-Exupéry for some of the dialogue, but Gable hated his and had most of it changed. One bit that remained had him talking about his love for flying and using "a girl in a blue dress" as a metaphor for the sky.

"That scene terrified him, scared him to death," Myrna Loy recalled. "He got so upset when he shot it that I had to keep reassuring him, comforting him. Not that he was incapable of doing the scene—he did it beautifully—but he was afraid it would make him appear too soft. He had this macho image strapped on him, and he couldn't get out of it. The studio kept reminding him that this was what he had to do. He happened to be an actor, a damned good one, and nobody knew it, least of all Clark. He always deprecated his ability, pretending that it didn't matter. He was really a shy man with a terrible inferiority in him somewhere. Something was missing that kept him from doing the things he could have done."

Paul Mantz, a onetime copilot and navigator for Amelia Earhart, served as Gable's technical adviser. For many of the aerial scenes, cinematographer Ray June used eighteen camera operators simultaneously, nine working on the ground and the others in the air. Cameramen were stationed in the open side doors of planes, in the noses, and even out on the wings (safely fastened, of course). In one scene more than a hundred aircraft filled the skies. Among them were many new models of military and commercial aircraft that, in those pre-TV times, would be seen by the general public for the first time when the film was released.

Test Pilot finally finished production in February 1938, shortly after Gable's thirty-seventh birthday. That month he was also elected "the King of Hollywood" in a national contest conducted by Ed Sullivan, then the movieland gossip columnist for the *Chicago Tribune–New York Daily News* syndicate. While visiting the set of *Test Pilot* one day, Sullivan heard Spencer Tracy calling Gable "King" and had a brainstorm. Sullivan asked the editors of all the newspapers that carried his column to poll their readers to select a King and Queen of Hollywood movies.

The idea was inconceivable because Hollywood in those days had dozens and dozens of truly big stars, but the very absurdity of it caught the imagination of the public. More than twenty million people voted. By a huge majority, Gable was elected "King" and Myrna Loy "Queen." That they just happened to be costarring in the soon-to-be-released *Test Pilot* smacked of a fix by MGM, but nobody demanded a recount.

Ed Sullivan staged an official coronation ceremony on his weekly NBC radio program. Mock crowns, made from tin plate and purple velvet, were inscribed with the regents' names. In true Hollywood fashion they were too big to wear, but thanks to the audio-only medium of radio Gable and Loy had only to pretend that Sullivan had placed them on their heads.

The honorific "the King of Hollywood" became permanently linked with Gable's name, but he grew contemptuous of it in later life. "This 'King' stuff is pure bullshit," he once said. "I eat and sleep and go to the bathroom just like everybody else. There's no special light that shines inside me and makes me a star. I'm just a lucky slob from Ohio. I happened to be in the right place at the right time, and I had a lot of smart guys helping me—that's all."

To capitalize on the coronation, MGM rushed out *Test Pilot*, which by that time could boast of an additional winner in its trio of stars. Spencer Tracy had just received an Oscar for Best Actor of 1937 for *Captains Courageous*. *Test Pilot* opened to smash business and eventually earned world rentals of $3.9 million. Despite the success, earnings were over a million dollars less than those of *San Francisco*, the last Gable-

Tracy teaming. MGM blamed it on the war jitters in England and Europe, where movie attendance had dropped sharply in the twenty-one months between release dates.

Meanwhile Gable's private life was undergoing public scrutiny as fan magazines began publishing articles like "Can the Gable-Lombard Love Story Have a Happy Ending?". Now entering its third year, the relationship had developed into sort of a substitute marriage, with Gable still legally tied to another woman. But for all practical purposes, Lombard had assumed the role of Gable's wife.

In the process both changed considerably. Gable seemed more relaxed and self-confident. During his relationships with much older women, he became somewhat of a fuddy-duddy, but Lombard's youth and vivaciousness cured him. He gained zeal and showed a greater interest in other people.

Lombard became less of a social butterfly and adapted herself to Gable's fondness for the outdoor life. She took lessons in riflery, skeet shooting, and fly casting. She'd been a superb athlete in her youth, so she became as proficient as Gable and probably could have excelled him if she'd wanted. But for the sake of his ego, she opted not to.

One weekend they decided to go to a private hunting club near Bakersfield. Gable was a member of the all-male group, which up to then had never permitted women to stay overnight, if only because there were no separate facilities for them. Lombard solved that problem by renting a small trailer for herself, complete with kitchen and bathroom. She had it hauled to the campsite and parked about fifty feet from the shack that served as the men's dormitory. She and Gable spent most of the first day hunting by themselves, but when they returned that evening, the men, who were sitting around drinking and playing cards, tensed up at the woman in their midst. Lombard heard so much mumbling and grumbling that she kissed Gable goodnight and retreated to her trailer.

About an hour later the smell of baking bread and the tinkle of ice cubes started emanating from the trailer. Within minutes every man in the camp was at Lombard's door. A party was soon in progress. Gable had to drive into Bakersfield for more liquor.

When bedtime came around, the men teased Gable about where he would sleep that night. Lombard made it clear that it wouldn't be with her. She said, "Goodnight, boys, it's been swell," and shooed everybody out, including her lover. Her only companion that night was her Pekingese, Pushface.

Gradually Lombard so endeared herself to Gable's hunting buddies that they treated her like one of the gang. She never demanded delicate handling. She did whatever was expected of a hunter, whether it was lying flat on her stomach with her face in the mud or lugging heavy guns and equipment on her back. It was quite a change for a glamour symbol, but she seemed to revel in it.

Gable was still sneaking in and out of Lombard's Bel-Air home at odd hours of the day and night, but he also now had a house of his own. His residency at the Beverly Wilshire Hotel had become too well known to Gable fans, who daily crowded the lobby, so he rented a hacienda in North Hollywood that once belonged to silent film star Alice Terry and her director-husband Rex Ingram. Lombard never visited him there; Ria Gable's spies had it under constant surveillance.

The Gables were in a cat-and-mouse game that seemed as if it could go on forever. Since Ria had wealth of her own, getting divorced from Gable wasn't a matter of urgency. The law was on her side. If he wanted a divorce, he would have to pay for it. The longer he delayed, the more he'd have to surrender. But he was such a miser that he kept avoiding the issue, as if it might eventually evaporate.

In May King Clark reported to MGM for another teaming with Queen Myrna, their sixth since *Men in White* in 1934. The frothy melo-drama entitled *Too Hot to Handle* was specially written for them by Laurence Stallings and John Lee Mahin, who borrowed liberally from Pearl White serials, Buster Keaton comedies, and the life of Amelia Earhart. The story spanned three continents, including exterior scenes in China and the Amazon jungle, but director Jack Conway filmed it entirely on the MGM backlot in six weeks.

Gable played a newsreel cameraman who will stop at nothing to get a scoop, even if he has to invent one. Loy, a world-famous pilot, is nearly killed when he causes her to make an emergency landing in which the plane crashes and explodes. After he rescues her and romance blossoms, she persuades him to join the search for her long-lost brother, also a pilot, who disappeared during a flight over Brazil.

On the first day of production, Gable received a surprise package from Carole Lombard with a label marked "Too Hot to Handle." Inside were a pair of asbestos gloves and a large envelope filled with graphic photos of sex orgies.

During the filming of Loy's plane crash, a mishap on the set made news headlines. Gable reportedly saved Loy's life when a pipeline carrying "controlled fire" to the cockpit where she was supposedly trapped got turned on ten seconds too soon. If Gable hadn't yanked her out, she would have been burned to death. Many years later Loy said, "It could have been pure publicity. You do a lot of risky things when you're making pictures, but it all happens so fast, and you're usually well protected. I don't recall feeling extreme heat or anything. I can't honestly say if Clark really saved me or not. Such was the power of Howard Strickling and the MGM publicity department."

Another day two of Gable's pals in the technical crew begged a favor. One had a starstruck teenage niece who was dying to meet Gable. Would it be possible for her to come to his dressing bungalow to have lunch with him one day? Gable agreed. When it took place and he found himself alone with the girl, she proved far less innocent than she looked. She threw herself at Gable, unbuttoned the fly of his trousers, and reached inside. "You ain't got much, have you?" she squealed, and then made a fast exit. Gable was still standing dumbfounded and unbuttoned when his friends arrived to tell him it was all a joke. The girl was actually a hooker whom they had hired from a call service. Gable roared with laughter.

Over the years he'd acquired cronies whom he enjoyed working with and would always request for his movies. When a favorite electrician fell for one of the bit players in *Too Hot to Handle,* Gable let them use his dressing quarters as a trysting place. Ida Koverman, L. B. Mayer's snoop-nosed secretary, found out and had the electrician fired. Gable then phoned Koverman and told her, "My boys can do anything they want in my bungalow." The dismissal order was immediately rescinded.

While Gable was making *Too Hot to Handle,* Mayer and son-in-law David Selznick were in serious negotiations over *Gone With the Wind.* Selznick, in behalf of his independent production company, wanted to "borrow" Gable for the role of Rhett Butler. But Mayer made a counterproposal of a package deal in which MGM would provide Gable and other stars, as well as production funding, in exchange for the distribution rights to *GWTW* and a fifty-fifty share of any profits.

That was more than Selznick wanted or was prepared to give away. But on June 17 he tested the waters by announcing to the press that he was having talks with MGM and that Norma Shearer and Clark Gable were being considered for the roles of Scarlett and Rhett. The overwhelming public reaction proved two things: Gable was the right and only choice; Shearer, who was a close friend of Selznick's and had been hounding him for the part, a wrong one. Letter writers and gossip columnists complained that Shearer was too mature, too much the *grande dame* to play the young vixen.

Shearer got so upset that she not only issued a public statement of withdrawal from the competition but also joked about it. "Scarlett is a thankless role. The one I'd really like to play is Rhett," she said.

Gable, meanwhile, neither wanted nor liked the role. "The public interest in my playing Rhett puzzled me," he later recalled. "I was the only one, apparently, who didn't take it for granted that I would. I found myself trapped by a series of circumstances over which I had no control. It was a funny feeling. I think I know now how a fly must react after being caught in a spider's web."

He also didn't think that he should play that sort of character. "Scarlett doesn't always love Rhett," Gable complained to story executive Samuel Marx. "It's the first time that the girl isn't sure that she wants me from the minute she sets eyes on me."

With Scarlett still uncast, a deal was finally made between MGM and Selznick International on August 24. Selznick received Gable's services plus $1.25 million to put toward production costs. In return Loew's, Inc., parent company of MGM, got world distribution rights to *GWTW* for five years and 50 percent of the profits. Loew's was also entitled to 15 percent of film rentals for handling the physical distribution.

Selznick would pay Gable his current MGM contract rate of $4,500 per week "for a period reasonably necessary to complete the role." Since Rhett Butler figured in about 50 percent of the scenes, Selznick's estimators figured that Gable would be needed for twelve weeks, for a total payout of $54,000. Needless to say, Gable's agent, Phil Berg, threw a fit. In those days stars who worked independently of the studio contract system got upward of $75,000 per picture and the top ones got at least $150,000 and sometimes a percentage of the profits as well.

Gable considered it the equivalent of slave labor and threatened to go on strike. The worst that could happen if he did was that MGM would suspend him without pay for the time that it took to make *GWTW* with another actor. But the whole deal had been predicated on Gable, so Mayer and Selznick finally agreed to pay him a bonus of $50,000 when he signed the contract. Selznick's share was $16,666, with MGM picking up the rest.

Remuneration of slightly more than $100,000 still seemed like peanuts for a production as important as *Gone With the Wind,* but Gable decided it was better than landing on suspension. The contract stipulated a starting date of January 5, 1939. Before that, Gable had one more picture to make for MGM to fulfill his 1938 obligations.

As the worldwide search for Scarlett O'Hara continued, Carole Lombard also signed a deal with Selznick International, but hers was for two pictures at $150,000 each. It was more reason for Gable to be angry, but not at Lombard. She was in the forefront of freelance stars who were helping to increase the pay standards for all actors. In 1937 she earned $465,000 for working in three movies, an average of $8,942 per week and nearly twice what Gable made at MGM.

Lombard's one-shot deal with Selznick for *Nothing Sacred* had proved a box-office hit, so he was eager to continue the relationship. Lombard, however, had become sick of making screwball comedies, so she requested a dramatic vehicle to start off the new pact. The result was *Made for Each Other,* an episodic story of a young couple in the first years of marriage. Selznick borrowed James Stewart from MGM to portray the husband.

Meanwhile, to free Gable for *Gone With the Wind,* MGM cranked up *Idiot's Delight,* one of the last properties acquired by Irving Thalberg before he died in 1936. The Broadway smash by Robert E. Sherwood, which won a Pulitzer Prize, had been a showcase for Alfred Lunt and Lynn Fontanne. The distinguished married couple's first attempt at moviemaking (*The Guardsman* for MGM in 1931) turned out such a flop that they vowed never to try again. When Thalberg bought *Idiot's Delight,* it was understood that Norma Shearer would take Fontanne's role, just as she had done in the case of *Strange Interlude.* Shearer idolized Fontanne and considered herself Hollywood's equivalent.

To make up for Shearer's embarrassment over *Gone With the Wind,* L. B. Mayer promised her that she could have Gable for *Idiot's Delight.*

They hadn't been teamed in the five years since *Strange Interlude,* which was made before Gable reached his present popularity. Shearer's latest film, *Marie Antoinette,* which had Tyrone Power (borrowed from 20th–Fox) thrown in for a romantic subplot, was a costly flop that indicated that Shearer could no longer draw crowds on her name alone.

Taking its title from a slang expression for the card game solitaire, *Idiot's Delight* focused on a group of world travelers who find themselves stranded in a ski resort–hotel in the Italian Alps on the eve of what could be World War II. Chief among them are an American song-and-dance man and a Russian countess who turns out to be an ex-performer whom he once romanced during a vaudeville stand in Omaha, Nebraska.

Producer Hunt Stromberg hired playwright Sherwood to do the film script, which moved the original play's pacifist theme and antifascist preachments into the background. To spare the movie from being heavily censored or banned in its European release, all references to Italy and Benito Mussolini were removed. Soldiers who had spoken Italian in the play had their dialogue changed to Esperanto. To further confuse, the setting was switched to the Swiss Alps.

Gable had seen the Lunts in *Idiot's Delight* in Los Angeles during the play's national road tour, so he knew what he was in for. He had to sing and dance as well as crack jokes like a stand-up comedian. In preparing for it, Alfred Lunt had taken coaching from Milton Berle, Sophie Tucker, and Harry Richman.

Director Clarence Brown enrolled Gable in two weeks of dance lessons with George King, a hoofing instructor of the old school. For Gable's first day, Carole Lombard sent him a billowy tutu that had a black velvet bodice with the initials *CG* in silver sequins, plus a pair of size 11-C ballet slippers.

In the beginning Gable couldn't lift his feet six inches off the floor. His instructor took the routines apart step by step and put them back together. As Gable gained confidence, it came easier. Fortunately his character, Harry Van, wasn't supposed to be a supertalent like Fred Astaire. After Gable mastered the footwork, he learned how to use a straw hat and cane for props.

Harry Van's act consists of him and a troupe of six chorus girls known as Les Blondes. For a flash finish, they perform Irving Berlin's "Puttin' on the Ritz," which required Gable to collapse into the girls' arms and be carried offstage in a horizontal position. Gable was afraid that they might drop him, so it was the very last scene filmed in case he broke his back. Carole Lombard came to the set to watch. When Gable managed it in one take, she said, "I've seen it, but I still don't believe it."

Throughout the whole production Lombard visited Gable frequently. She had spies who told her that Shearer and at least one of Les Blondes had designs on Gable. Since Shearer had ended her mourning period for Irving Thalberg, she'd become known around Hollywood as "the merry widow." Her most frequent companion was one of Lombard's exes, George Raft. Very privately she was also involved with the sex-mad teenager Mickey Rooney, whose mother finally found out and ended it.

When the two costars reported to the studio's photo gallery to pose for publicity and advertising stills, Gable noticed that Shearer wasn't wearing panties underneath her tight-fitting evening gown. In the clinches she kept thrusting herself at him until he couldn't stand much more. When she went to powder her nose, Gable told the photographer, "I wish this broad would get the hell out of here."

Gable finished *Idiot's Delight* on December 10, which left him with a month off until *Gone With the Wind* started in January. Carole Lombard had also completed *Made for Each Other,* so they took a skiing holiday in Sun Valley, Idaho. While they were away, they became central figures in a national scandal over an article just published in *Photoplay,* the most influential and widely read movie magazine of the time.

Gable and Lombard topped a list of "Hollywood's Unmarried Husbands and Wives," which also included such similarly paired lovebirds as Robert Taylor and Barbara Stanwyck, Charles Chaplin and Paulette Goddard, Gilbert Roland and Constance Bennett, and George Raft and Virginia Pine.

"Unwed couples they might be termed," the article said. "But they go everywhere together; do everything in pairs. No hostess would think of inviting them separately or pairing them with another. They solve one another's problems. They handle each other's business affairs. They build houses near each other, buy land in bunches, take up each other's hobbies, father or mother each other's children—even correct each other's clothes—each other's personalities. Yet to the world, their official status is 'just friends.' No more."

Author Kirtley Baskette wrote of Gable and Lombard that "For Clark, Carole stopped, almost overnight, being a Hollywood playgirl. People are expected to change when they get married. The necessary adaptation to a new life and another personality shows up in every bride and groom. All Clark and Carole did was strike up a Hollywood twosome. Nobody said 'I do!' . . . The altar record, in fact, among Hollywood's popular twosomes is surprisingly slim. Usually something formidable stands in the way of a marriage certificate when Hollywood stars pair up minus a preacher. In Clark and Carole's case, of course, there is a very sound legal barrier. Clark's still officially a married man. Every now and then negotiations for a divorce are started, but until something happens in court, Ria Gable is still the only wife the law of the land allows Clark Gable."

Although its points were made almost entirely through innuendo, "Hollywood's Unmarried Husbands and Wives" was the most candid article about the private lives of the stars that had ever been published up to that time. The piece was intended to test the stiff restrictions placed on the fan press by studio publicists and the movie industry's self-governed censorship organization. But it didn't work. *Photoplay* was forced to run a public apology the following month.

The "Unmarried" issue, dated January 1939, sold out within days of hitting the newsstands in mid-December 1938. The story crossed over into the gossip columns and daily tabloids, creating a public furor. Will Hays, the Hollywood industry's moral guardian, was bombarded with complaints from members of the National Catholic Legion of Decency, the Daughters of the American Revolution, the General Federation of Women's Clubs, the American Legion, and the Knights of Columbus. Their demands could be summed up in four words: "Get those tramps married!"

Since Gable and Robert Taylor were the only stars among the "unmarried husbands and wives" who answered to a single studio boss (the others were all freelancers), Hays went after them first. Conveniently for Hays, the boss in both cases was L. B. Mayer, who threatened his bad boys with contract termination and worse if they didn't do something fast. While Mayer couldn't force them to marry their sweeties, he made it plain that their only other option, if they wanted to continue working in the Hollywood industry, was to terminate the affairs.

Mayer was especially severe with Gable because of the possible negative feedback on *Gone With the Wind*. David Selznick had a double problem: Paulette Goddard, another of the "unmarrieds," was his number one choice for Scarlett O'Hara.

Due to Gable's years of procrastination over a divorce, he found himself trapped in a corner with no easy way out. Ria's lawyer was demanding a settlement of approximately $300,000, which amounted to 50 percent of the current value of Gable's MGM pension fund. Gable finally agreed when the studio offered to give him an advance on his contract, which still had three years to run and would escalate from $4,500 to $5,000 per week in July of 1939.

But Gable's capitulation wasn't enough to satisfy Ria, who considered herself the wronged party in the mess and wanted to make him squirm. Her insistence on divorcing him under California law meant that he would not be free to marry again until one full year *after* the decree was granted. Any plans that he had to wed Carole Lombard would have to be postponed indefinitely.

Carole Lombard believed in miracles, or at least in the possibility that Ria Gable might suddenly drop dead, so she started shopping for a house. The couple might have been able to swing a deal for her rented home in Bel-Air, but Gable wanted something larger and more removed from the increasingly urban sprawl of Los Angeles.

To Lombard, who grew up there, that meant traipsing over to the other side of the Santa Monica Mountains and the Hollywood Hills to the San Fernando Valley. Running several decades behind other areas of Los Angeles in development, the wide belt between Burbank and the eastern borderline of Ventura County still had plenty of open country at reasonable prices.

Through the studio grapevine Lombard heard that director Raoul Walsh wanted to sell a twenty-acre ranch in Encino that was no longer his primary residence. She and Gable had attended parties there and remembered its beautiful rustic setting, so they decided to take another look.

In the eyes of an Ohioan like Gable, the place was more like a farm than a ranch. The small two-story house of whitewashed brick was built in 1926 but had been artificially weatherbeaten by movie set designer Malcolm Brown to appear much older. There were several smaller buildings, including a barn, a stable, and a garage. The grounds were thick with trees—pepper, eucalyptus, avocado, plum, peach, apricot, and fig. A separate citrus orchard had orange, lemon, and grapefruit trees. Surrounding fields were reserved for alfalfa and oats.

The house's interior needed work, but it had possibilites, with lots of wood paneling, random-planked floors, and real fireplaces. After

Lombard dragged him around to point out all the changes she wanted to make, Gable said, "I've always wanted a place like this. It will be the first home I've had since I was a boy that I can really call my own. Ma, I think we're going to be very happy here."

But there was a major obstacle. Raoul Walsh wanted fifty thousand dollars for the place, all in cash in total. Gable doubted that he'd have any money left by the time that his wife finished divorcing him. Lombard didn't want to lose out, so she asked Walsh if her personal check for fifty thousand would do. It did, and she became owner of the property officially listed in Encino records as 4525 Petit Street.

Given the big scandal over the "Unmarried Husbands and Wives" article, there was no way that Gable and Lombard could occupy their home until they were legally wed. Not that they really wanted to anyway until renovations could be completed. Again, Lombard would have to pay the bills and also supervise the work while Gable concentrated on preparing for *Gone With the Wind*. Though an MGM release, production would be centered at the Selznick International studio, an old-timer in Culver City originally built and owned by Thomas Ince. Pathé had taken it over by the time Gable toiled there in 1930 in his first talkie, *The Painted Desert*.

By Christmas David Selznick had selected twenty-five-year-old Vivien Leigh, a client of brother Myron, to play Scarlett O'Hara, but the casting was still top-secret in anticipation of public outrage over a British actress being chosen instead of an American. Selznick's press agents also needed to do some sanitizing of Leigh's affair with Laurence Olivier, who was also in Hollywood making *Wuthering Heights*. Due to their recent arrival, the lovers had narrowly missed being mentioned in the "Unmarried Husbands and Wives" scandal.

On January 13, 1939, Selznick finally announced Leigh's signing, as well as those of Olivia de Havilland to play Melanie Hamilton and Leslie Howard for Ashley Wilkes. Gable first met his costars on January 20, when they all did makeup, hair, and costume tests for the Technicolor camera crew. The movie was Gable's first in color. Technicians found that bright lighting would have to be avoided because his dark brown hair and mustache took on a red sheen.

Production officially started on January 26, but Gable's first call was on January 31, the day before his thirty-eighth birthday. He arrived in an angry mood after spending most of the night reading a ninety-two-page memo from Selznick on how the producer envisioned him portraying Rhett Butler. The memo had been delivered by a motorcycle messenger just as Gable was getting ready to go to bed.

Gable's first scenes were complicated ones of a charity bazaar and dance, which required him to learn the Virginia reel and to be quite the dandy, something that he felt quite uncomfortable doing. His edginess, combined with his doubts about the role and his ability to play it, were intensified by the emotional climate on the set. Gable didn't relish the slow, methodical style of director George Cukor, which reminded him of his painful experience with John Stahl during *Parnell*.

Gable also felt excluded from the close relationship that had developed among Cukor, Vivien Leigh, and Olivia de Havilland. Between takes and even after work, Cukor spent a great deal of time coaching the two actresses. Cukor's efforts with Gable were mainly at loosening him up and trying to get him to add some mocking, tongue-in-cheek elegance to the role.

But Gable couldn't relate to Cukor or to his work methods; their personalities and temperaments were poles apart. At MGM Gable had become accustomed to fatherly veterans like Woody Van Dyke and Victor Fleming who knew exactly what they wanted from him and showed him how to do it. The thirty-nine-year-old Cukor, however, was a fussy, intellectual type whom Gable found maddeningly vague in his instructions. Gable wanted to be told specifically what he did wrong and how to correct it, and he thought that Cukor wasn't delivering.

Cukor was also homosexual, which in those ultracloseted times he tried to conceal but couldn't completely stop from creeping out in effeminate mannerisms. Though not as blatant as Charles Laughton's, it was enough to ignite Gable's intolerance of gays and make it even more difficult for him to work with Cukor.

Gable started complaining about Cukor to David Selznick, who was already unhappy with the director for other reasons. After only two weeks of shooting, the schedule was already five days behind schedule, which Selznick blamed on Cukor's perfectionism and fondness for retakes. The producer also thought that Cukor concentrated too much on performances and that most scenes lacked the visual excitement that the public expected in a historical epic.

Unfortunately for Cukor, MGM shared Selznick's opinion. L. B. Mayer was disappointed by the rushes and insisted that one of the MGM contract directors take over. Since Gable had been so unhappy with Cukor, Selznick asked him if he had a preference. Gable nominated Victor Fleming, who was just finishing *The Wizard of Oz*. In exchange, MGM set Cukor to directing a sophisticated comedy that seemed more suited to him—*The Women,* with an all-female cast headed by three one-time Scarlett candidates, Norma Shearer, Joan Crawford, and Paulette Goddard.

Cukor's dismissal on February 13, politely announced to the press as a "withdrawal," became a hot topic of discussion and stayed one for decades to come. Although it was plainly a matter of creative differences and financial necessity, Gable's involvement got blown up to incredible proportions. Gossip that started with claims that Gable had Cukor fired because he hated homosexuals grew ever weirder. It was later suggested that Cukor knew of a homosexual episode in Gable's past and that Gable was so terrified of Cukor tattling that he couldn't look the director in the eye or stand being in his company.

The story, which first surfaced in Kenneth Anger's 1985 sequel to *Hollywood Babylon,* claimed that Gable, while still an extra and bit player, had tried to advance his career through a passive quickie with the gay MGM star William Haines. But Gable had been aware from the time he signed his *GWTW* contract in August 1938 that Cukor would direct. If he was that petrified of exposure, he could easily have demanded another director then, rather than in the midst of production.

Selznick had an unexpected shock when Victor Fleming took over. "David, your fucking script is no fucking good," the director said. Selznick panicked and on February 18 shut down production for two weeks while he consulted with his favorite script doctor, Ben Hecht. Selznick paid Hecht fifteen thousand dollars to do an instant rewrite. It was strictly a technical job: Hecht cut and pasted his way through Sidney Howard's "final" screenplay and several more written by others in the three years since Selznick had purchased the property. Hecht tried to give more focus to the personal story of Scarlett and Rhett and to eliminate some of the sprawling historical background.

During his unexpected holiday Gable hired a new lawyer who finally succeeded in reaching an agreement with Ria over the divorce. In addition to the $300,000 settlement, Gable would pay any income taxes that were levied on the amount. In return, Ria Gable promised to drop her California case and to obtain a quickie divorce in Nevada instead.

Gable also gave an okay to Carole Lombard's plans for the new house. She then commissioned Tom Douglas, a freelance scenic artist whom she knew from the studios, to design the interior. To supervise the contracting work, she hired a new secretary, Jean Garceau, as a replacement for her best pal Fieldsie, who had quit to marry director Walter Lang.

By this time Lombard had recovered from her disappointment over not playing Scarlett O'Hara (she had never even been invited to make a screen test) and also had forgiven Myron Selznick for helping another of his clients to get the part. Myron had redeemed himself by setting a deal for Lombard at RKO Radio for four pictures at $150,000 each, plus a share in the profits. Lombard still had a commitment with David Selznick for one more film, but he was too obsessed with *GWTW* at the moment to discuss projects with her.

On March 2 Selznick restarted *Gone With the Wind* with Victor Fleming at the helm. Unhappy with the subdued color scheme favored by cinematographer Lee Garmes, Selznick replaced him with Ernest Haller, whom he ordered to strive for more vivid effects. There were some 650 scenes to be filmed. To finish in time for the movie's planned Christmas release, Fleming would have to shoot at least three pages of script, or about two minutes of screen time, per day.

With Victor Fleming in charge, Gable's attitude and demeanor changed completely. He relaxed, and under Fleming's attentive handling he even began to enjoy the role.

On March 8 Gable had more reason to be happy. In Las Vegas Ria Gable was granted a divorce in a court hearing that lasted all of four minutes. Afterward she told reporters that "Clark knew he could have a divorce anytime, but he never seemed to want one. I think a marriage between a movie star and a society woman has a better chance of succeeding than one between two stars."

The Gables had been separated for so long that the exact duration of the marriage was debatable. But nearly twelve years had passed since Gable first became involved with Ria in 1927.

Louella Parsons phoned Carole Lombard when the divorce news

broke. Up until then Lombard had never gone public about her feelings for Gable or their plans to marry. But now she didn't hesitate to tell "Lollypops" as much as she knew at the moment. "When Clark gets a few days off, perhaps we'll sneak away and have the ceremony performed," she said.

Lombard's hint of an elopement caused newspaper reporters to establish a day-and-night watch on her house in Bel-Air. In the next few days she and Gable received piles of telegrams and letters from resort hotels, chambers of commerce, and justices of the peace that suggested times and places for the wedding. Lombard feared it would develop into "a fucking circus" unless they found a way to sneak off quietly without anyone knowing about it.

Gable asked Otto Winkler, the MGM staff publicist who handled all of his dealings with the press, to find some remote spot that was a bit nearer to Hollywood than Timbuktu. Winkler finally hit on Kingman, Arizona, a small town with a population of two thousand and located about four hundred miles northeast of Los Angeles. Winkler was so nervous over whether he'd made the right choice that he put it to the test by actually getting married there to his fiancée Jill Jordan, a singer-starlet at Warner Bros.

On March 25 Gable learned that he would have six days off due to a sudden rescheduling of scenes in which he didn't appear. Otto Winkler urged him and Lombard to get married then, due to a lucky coincidence: most of the Hollywood press corps would be away on a junket to San Francisco for the world premiere of 20th–Fox's *The Story of Alexander Graham Bell*. Joining the contingent were the movie's stars, including Loretta Young.

Otto Winkler's boss, Howard Strickling, wanted the newlyweds to be available for a press conference in Los Angeles on the morning after the elopement. To accomplish that, they would have to make the eight-hundred-mile round trip to Kingman by car in one day.

They left Los Angeles at dawn on March 29, with their wedding clothes packed in a suitcase. Both were wearing old shirts and dungarees; Lombard skipped making-up and had her hair tied in pigtails. They traveled with Otto Winkler in his blue DeSoto coupe, well supplied with sandwiches and Thermoses of hot coffee and ice water. Gable took turns driving with Winkler, who would serve as best man at the wedding.

Whenever they stopped for gas, they first pulled off to the side of the road so that Gable could hide under a blanket in the rumble seat and not be spotted.

Reaching Kingman in the late afternoon, they drove straight to the town hall. The clerk on duty in the marriage bureau recognized Gable and became so flustered that she couldn't speak when she handed him the license application forms. Gable gave his age as thirty-eight and his occupation as "actor." Lombard subtracted a year from her age and claimed to be twenty-nine.

Without revealing the couple's names, Otto Winkler had arranged for the minister of the First Methodist-Episcopal Church to perform the ceremony. When Gable and Lombard arrived at the rectory, neither the minister nor his wife showed any signs of recognition as they escorted them to separate rooms to change into their wedding clothes. Gable put on a blue serge suit, white shirt, and printed tie. Lombard's complete outfit, including a tapered gray flannel suit and a polka-dotted blouse, was designed by her close friend Irene Gibbons, who was better known as Irene in the fashion and movie worlds.

If the wedding had taken place in Hollywood, it surely would have been another MGM spectacular, but in Kingman not even the local newspaper knew about it. Lombard cried her eyes out. Gable was so choked up that he handed the minister the platinum wedding band before he was even asked. After the ceremony Lombard phoned her mother in Los Angeles. Gable got on the line and said, "This is your new son-in-law, Mom." It all seemed as normal as an *Andy Hardy* family comedy.

Otto Winkler dropped the newlyweds back at Lombard's house in Bel-Air at three the next morning. When they retired, they discovered that one of Lombard's brothers had hung a shotgun on the wall over the bed.

After a few hours of who knows what, the Gables redonned their wedding clothes for the press conference that Howard Strickling had arranged in Lombard's living room. Six members of the MGM police force surrounded the house to make sure that only authorized reporters, photographers, and newsreel cameramen got in.

Gable and Lombard entered down a staircase from the second floor. Smiling broadly, they clutched each other nervously as photographers barked requests in a posing session that preceded the interview portion.

When reporters started firing questions, Gable fielded the first one. Due to the couple's movie commitments, there would be no honeymoon trip, but they hoped to visit the soon-to-open New York World's Fair before it closed. Lombard claimed that she could cook: "Damn well, too, but I don't know what Pappy's favorite dishes are yet." Giggles and embarrassed expressions were the Gables' only replies to queries about having children and about Hollywood's high divorce rate in marriages between stars.

Louella Parsons considered herself above attending press conferences, so Lombard phoned her afterward and received a tongue lashing for not giving the gossip queen a scoop on the elopement. To pacify her, Lombard spoke frankly about the future: "I'll work for a few more years, and then I want a family. I'll let Pa be the star, and I'll stay home, darn the socks, and look after the kids."

News of the wedding devastated Loretta Young, who'd never given up hope that Gable might eventually come to his senses and marry *her* if he ever broke loose of Ria. Now going on four, their daughter, Judy, had started asking "Daddy" questions. Young decided that it was best to tell her that he was dead. Judy already knew that she was "adopted" but not that Young was her real mother.

Gable moved into Lombard's house while renovations continued on the ranch property. A week after he resumed working in *Gone With the Wind,* she started the first film in her new deal with RKO Radio. The romantic melodrama *In Name Only,* in which Lombard costarred with Cary Grant and Kay Francis, had unintended parallels to her own life: she falls in love with an unhappily married millionaire whose money-mad wife refuses to give him a divorce.

Meanwhile Gable tried to keep calm as problems with *Gone With the Wind* continued. Early in April Selznick started running out of money and got caught in a squeeze play with MGM, which offered to provide the required $1.25 million in exchange for 100 percent ownership of the movie. Rather than submit, Selznick arranged a straight loan for the amount from the Bank of America. Due to his shaky finances, the loan had to be guaranteed by his Whitney family partners, which meant giving them a bigger share in the earnings of Selznick International.

Gable was delighted to be working again with Hattie McDaniel, who on his recommendation had been selected for the role of Mammy over Louise Beavers. Due to her hefty poundage, McDaniel looked much older than Gable, but only five and a half years separated them. Born in Kansas and raised in Colorado, she had to be taught by dialogue coach Susan Myrick to speak in the dialect of a black slave from northern Georgia.

One of the major scenes between Gable and McDaniel showed them having a celebration drink together after the birth of Bonnie Butler. Substituting for alcohol in their glasses was colored water. As the takes multiplied, McDaniel complained, "I sure am tired of drinking this stuff." Without telling her, Gable arranged a switch for the next retake.

"It was real scotch, and the best, or so he told me after I took a big swig," McDaniel recalled. "But I didn't know because it burned my mouth so. It was the hottest afternoon I had seen in many a day, and the sun wasn't shining either. The next morning he had the audacity to whiz past me and holler, 'Mammy, how's the hangover?' "

Gable found himself caught in the middle of an ongoing battle between Vivien Leigh and Victor Fleming. He'd grown fond of Leigh and sympathized with the problems she was having in her affair with Laurence Olivier, who by this time had left Hollywood to work on the Broadway stage in *No Time for Comedy*. The temporary separation was driving Leigh wacky. One day she told Selznick that she was pregnant and would need a week off to have an abortion. It turned out to be a false alarm.

Since taking over the direction, Fleming had been pushing Leigh to the limit, trying to get her to inject more fire and bitchiness into Scarlett O'Hara, contrary to the more genteel concept that she'd worked out with George Cukor. Gable tried to stay out of their squabbles, but as an old friend of Fleming's, he had to listen to his complaints every day at cocktail time.

Fleming was also under constant pressure from Selznick, whom he despised and called "the Jew producer" behind his back. In his anger and agitation, Fleming nearly drove off a cliff while on his way to work one morning.

On April 29 Fleming finally cracked while rehearsing a scene with Vivien Leigh, who kept resisting his orders to put more venom into her lines. "I can't be a bitch," she said. Fleming glared at her for a moment, then rolled up his copy of the script and threw it at her, shouting, "Miss Leigh, you can shove this up your royal British ass."

Fleming went straight home to Malibu and phoned in sick the next day, claiming that he needed a complete rest and would be out for two weeks. Selznick appealed to MGM for help and got director Sam Wood to take over temporarily. When Fleming finally returned, Selznick retained Wood and kept both directors working on different scenes to make up for lost time.

Gable refused to work that way, so Selznick promised him that Fleming would direct all of his remaining scenes. Coming up was one that Gable had dreaded since he first read the script. It required Rhett Butler to break down in tears when he learns that Scarlett has suffered a miscarriage in an accident that he provoked.

Gable was embarrassed, believing it unmanly to cry. He was so adamant that no amount of persuading from Fleming could change his mind. David Selznick finally appealed to Carole Lombard for help. The night before the scheduled filming, she spent hours trying to persuade Gable that there was nothing wrong about an actor crying and that it would be a memorable scene if he did it convincingly.

On the day Olivia de Havilland, who shared the scene with him, also tried to calm his fears. But when he continued to fuss and fume, Victor Fleming diplomatically offered to shoot the scene twice and to let Gable decide which one would be used. They did it Gable's way first, without tears, and then he turned on the waterworks for a retake. After viewing the rushes he reluctantly agreed that the weepie version was better. "Print it!" he told Fleming.

Production of *Gone With the Wind* finally ended on June 27. Although the scenes had been shot randomly rather than in the order that they appeared in the script, the last one to go before the cameras was Rhett's farewell to Scarlett. Selznick had been unhappy with it since the first draft screenplay and kept revising and rewriting it right up to the morning of the shoot.

While Victor Fleming was rehearsing Gable and Leigh, Selznick had one more inspiration and insisted on changing Rhett's reply to Scarlett's "If you go, where shall I go, what shall I do?" Rhett's "My dear, I don't give a damn" became "Frankly, my dear, I don't give a damn." It added a lilt that made for as classic a catchphrase as Scarlett's fade-out "After all, tomorrow is another day."

Gable, by now yoked to *Gone With the Wind* for six months, had his agony prolonged when Selznick insisted on shooting an alternate version of the scene in anticipation of problems with the enforcers of the industry's Production Code. The word *damn* hadn't been used in American movies since the Code's adoption in 1933. For the alternate take, Selznick changed Gable's line to "Frankly, my dear, I just don't care."

Expurgated or not, those were Gable's own feelings when he cleared out his dressing suite. He and Victor Fleming pledged to each other over a bottle of scotch that they would never have dealings with David Selznick again. Fleming predicted that *GWTW* would be "the biggest white elephant of all time" and Selznick's ruination.

By this time Carole Lombard had completed *In Name Only,* and the Gables were preparing to move to the Encino ranch. The main house's gabled roof caused Hollywood punsters to call the place "the House of the Two Gables." By movie-star standards, it was quite ordinary: no tennis court, no screening room, not even a swimming pool. When asked why, Lombard always said, "If we put in everything at once, we'd have nothing to look forward to."

She instructed decorator Tom Douglas to make it a home fit for a king: not for "the King of Hollywood" but for a man of Gable's exceptional size. Every piece of furniture that Gable might sit in or sleep on was custom made to be a third larger than ordinary. Even the bar glasses were king-sized, suited to Gable's giant paws as well as to his unquenchable thirst.

The interior decor was Early American, and the focal point was Gable's gun room on the main floor. A glass case covered one wall and displayed about fifty antique pistols and rifles. The collection was constantly expanding as Gable's friends and fans sent additions. The parlor was done very simply in a green-and-yellow color scheme, with two large sofas and several wingback chairs. The dining room resembled a "ye olde" tavern, with a long narrow table and an electrified chandelier of antique oil lamps.

Upstairs, traditional Hollywood emerged in the two separate but adjoining bedroom suites. Lombard's included a dressing room and bath with mirrored walls and ceilings, white marble fixtures, and controlled lighting. She called it "the most elegant shithouse in the San Fernando Valley."

Gable's huge bed had a headboard of brown tufted leather. Built into the wall behind it were bookshelves and a small but fully stocked bar. His beige marble bathroom had a stall shower but no tub, which he considered unsanitary. In his study an empty space awaited delivery of an antique desk used in *Gone With the Wind,* which David Selznick gave the Gables as a wedding present.

Lombard promoted her personal secretary, Jean Garceau, to also assist Gable and to manage the household as well. The married Garceau resided elsewhere but had an office on the premises.

The Gables hired three live-in servants, all blacks. Two were carry-overs from Lombard's staff in Bel-Air: Jessie, a cook whose down-home southern specialities were famous on the celebrity dining circuit: and Juanita, a maid. Rufus Martin was butler-valet. When Gable was film-ing, Martin accompanied him to the studio to take care of his wardrobe and to be in charge of his dressing bungalow.

Lombard brought a flock of pets with her from Bel-Air, including dogs, cats, and offspring of the two doves that she had sent to Gable after the White Mayfair Ball. Their wedding gifts to each other were horses. His was named Sunny, hers Melody. The area was so rural that they could saddle up and ride across the hills to Santa Monica without passing another house.

With no work commitments the Gables spent their first summer of married life at the ranch, just settling in and relaxing. Their relationship continued pretty much as it had for the past three years, the major differ-ence being that they were now legally married. Sex wasn't as basic or all-consuming as might have been expected of two of Hollywood's hottest love idols, but they both had healthy appetites.

Lombard tended to be the romantic, while Gable wanted fast grati-fication. "I love the guy, but to tell you the truth, he's not a hell of a good lay," she once said, referring to his technique and not to his physical equipment. She blamed his inexpertness on his two marriages with con-siderably older women, types who were starved for sex and just wanted to be screwed as often as possible.

One morning while Lombard was away shopping and Gable was in the garage puttering with his cars, a male teenager broke into the house and the gun room. Secretary Jean Garceau heard noise and shouted for Gable, who came running and easily overpowered the youth as he tried to escape. In the struggle a loaded pistol snatched from Gable's collection went flying, but luckily it did not go off. Lombard got queasy when she returned and found out. It reminded her all too vividly of Russ Columbo's accidental death in 1934.

Lombard herself landed in Cedars of Lebanon Hospital that summer, but the reason is somewhat of a mystery. According to a hospital spokesperson, Lombard had an emergency operation for acute appendicitis. But some of her friends claimed that she was pregnant and had suffered a miscarriage. Whatever the case, Gable was so worried that he arranged to stay in the room next to his wife's, where he slept every night until she was released.

Strangely, only days after that, on August 8, 1939, Lombard executed a new will. It may have been only what any wealthy person would do after a recent marriage. She left her entire estate to Gable, but additionally provided a $100,000 trust fund for her mother and a smaller one for best friend Madalynne Fields, who by now had a son in her marriage to director Walter Lang.

Lombard's convalescence forced a month's postponement of her next RKO project, *Vigil in the Night*. Ironically, she portrayed a nurse in the hospital drama, which was based on one of novelist A. J. Cronin's exposés of the failings of the British medical system.

Gable was also due to start working at MGM in *Strange Cargo*, but on September 1 Hollywood stuck to its radios as news came of Nazi Germany's invasion of Poland. Britain's and France's prompt declarations of war against Germany caused fright if not panic. The isolationism of most Americans toward European politics seemed to increase in a westward direction. The movie colony's main concerns over a European war were financial. How could the industry compensate for lost markets?

Meanwhile, production continued as usual. Lombard started *Vigil in the Night* on September 5, Gable *Strange Cargo* two weeks later. His return to working on the MGM lot after a long stretch at Selznick was less than happy. Joan Crawford, whose box-office popularity had sunk to an all-time low, had talked L. B. Mayer into teaming them for the first time since the 1936 *Love on the Run*, which was also Crawford's last hit.

Gable was still miffed at Crawford for weaseling out of *Parnell*, which turned into his biggest flop. He also disliked the script for *Strange Cargo*, which was originally titled *Not Too Narrow, Not Too Deep* and dealt with a group of convicts trying to escape from a penal colony on New Guinea island in the South Pacific.

Gable's main objection was the story's heavy dose of religious allegory, which seemed likely to repel fans who went to Gable-Crawford movies for the sex and romance. Gable played the least evil of a group of fugitives that include a mysterious Christ-like character who leads them to repent their sins. Crawford played a stranded trollop who latches on to the group in hope of getting to Australia to ply her trade.

The contemporary drama was the seventh and most unglamorous of the Gable-Crawford vehicles. He wore prison garb throughout and became increasingly unwashed and unshaven as the action progressed. Crawford insisted on going without makeup and false eyelashes. Her wardrobe amounted to two cotton dresses and a tacky evening gown, all purchased by the costume department at a bargain boutique for forty dollars.

Directed by Frank Borzage and produced by Joseph L. Mankiewicz, *Strange Cargo* had a prestigious supporting cast, including Ian Hunter as the mystic, Paul Lukas, Albert Dekker, Eduardo Ciannelli, and J. Edward Bromberg. Peter Lorre played an informer, Monsieur Pig, whose name matched his repulsiveness.

Since Gable last worked with Crawford, she had divorced Franchot Tone. Given the long-ago Gable-Crawford affair, Carole Lombard kept teasing him, threatening a double murder if it resumed.

The saving grace of *Strange Cargo* for Gable was MGM's backlot jungle, which spared everybody an expedition to New Guinea and back. The same tropical forestry had doubled for Indochina in *Red Dust* and Brazil in *Too Hot to Handle*. Gable's farthest travel was 150 miles north to Pismo Beach, near San Luis Obispo, for a week of exterior scenes. The clam lovers' paradise was the nearest spot to Los Angeles with a shoreline similar to New Guinea's.

Bad weather caused a one-day extension and forced Joan Crawford to cancel a trip to San Francisco to attend the opera with some wealthy friends. Newspaper columnist Whitney Bolton, who happened to be visiting the Pismo Beach location at the time, remembered her complaining to Gable: "Joan had bought a whole new outfit to wear," he said. "She went on to describe it in elaborate detail, starting with her tiara and going straight down to her shoes. She left nothing out, not even the lingerie."

Unfortunately, Gable was in a miserable mood, nursing a hangover from the previous night's boozing and consumption of three dozen pismo clams in sauce. After Crawford finished, Gable turned to Bolton and did a mock imitation: "Whitney, I have brand-new dancing pumps, a white Sulka tie, a gorgeous dress shirt, a blue plush suit, and a pea-green opera cloak, and where am I? At the San Francisco Opera? No! Down here in this very, very unsocial Pismo Beach? Yes!"

Bolton was shocked. "Any other star talking like that would not have surprised me. But I'd known Clark for years, and that was the only time I heard him say or do anything that was mean or ungracious."

Friends believed that Crawford deeply resented Gable's recent marriage. "I will never forget the bitterness between them," her longtime hairstylist, Sidney Guilaroff, recalled. "Although there were no outbursts of emotion, she must have been whispering things that irritated him, because he would walk away from her, furious. She would remain cool until she reached her dressing room, and then she'd burst into laughter. The tension between them was so thick that everyone on the set found it almost unendurable, and I finally asked to be taken off the picture because it upset me so."

During the filming of *Strange Cargo,* Howard Strickling brought Gable up to date on publicity plans for *Gone With the Wind,* which would have its world premiere in Atlanta, the hometown of author Margaret Mitchell, on December 15. The governor of Georgia had declared a state holiday, which would be surrounded by three days of parades, parties, dances, and other festivities.

Needless to say, Gable, as well as Vivien Leigh, Leslie Howard, and Olivia de Havilland, were expected to attend as part of a large Hollywood contingent being put together by David Selznick, who'd chartered a plane from TWA for transport. Victor Fleming, angrier than ever at Selznick due to a recent dispute over his directorial credit, decided to boycott the event. He urged Gable to join him.

By December 1939 the average American Joe and Jane Public were probably more interested in *Gone With the Wind* than in the wars raging in Europe and China. The novel had been at the top of best-seller lists for three and a half years; preparation for the movie had been making news headlines for almost as long.

Except for Margaret Mitchell, no one had become as identified with *Gone With the Wind* as Clark Gable, so his absence from the world premiere threatened to ruin it. Hundreds of thousands of people from Georgia and surrounding states were expecting him. MGM was flying in press from all over the United States and Canada, as well as from England and other countries where it was still able to conduct business.

Gable's allegiance to Victor Fleming and their mutual loathing of David Selznick were the main obstacles. Luckily for the MGM and Selznick camps, Mrs. Gable and Mrs. Fleming thought their husbands were behaving like children. Both women were eager to attend and had already ordered new outfits to wear. Lombard told Gable to imagine it as the honeymoon trip that they'd yet to take.

Gable and Fleming finally agreed, but they refused to travel with the Selznick group on its chartered TWA flight. Howard Strickling contacted TWA's upstart rival, American Airlines, which happily contributed a DC-3 in exchange for all the publicity it would receive.

As everybody packed for the trip, fate gave Victor Fleming an excuse to cancel. On December 12 his best buddy and onetime mentor, Douglas Fairbanks, died in his sleep of a heart attack at age fifty-six. Fleming was devastated and insisted on being a pallbearer at the funeral. The rites would be held at Forest Lawn at the same time as Atlanta staged its massive welcoming parade for the *Gone With the Wind* celebrities.

Before leaving Los Angeles, Gable and Lombard drove to Fairbanks's oceanfront estate at Santa Monica to pay their respects to the widow, the onetime Lady Sylvia Ashley. Gable had known the earlier "King of Hollywood" well. After Gable's coronation Fairbanks jokingly gave him an alternate title as "the Toothless Wonder."

American Airlines stenciled "MGM's *Gone With the Wind*" across the exterior of the DC-3 that carried the Gables and some of the movie's supporting actors to Atlanta. Otto Winkler, the publicist who served as best man at their wedding, again chaperoned the couple. Since he'd never flown before, he was extremely nervous. During the takeoff Lombard sat next to him and held his hand until he calmed down. Teasingly she said, "If we're going to crash, we might as well go together."

The flight was timed to land in Atlanta soon after the TWA charter carrying the Selznick group, which included the producer and his wife; Vivien Leigh and her lover, Laurence Olivier; and Olivia de Havilland. Leslie Howard, who'd returned to his native England to help in the war effort, cabled his regrets.

Among other cast members flown in were Ona Munson, Laura Hope Crews, Evelyn Keyes, and Ann Rutherford. None of the black actors were represented. David Selznick had at least attempted to bring Hattie McDaniel, but MGM advised him not to because of Georgia's segregationist laws, which would have required McDaniel to stay in a colored-only hotel and prevented her from sitting in the theater with her white peers.

Most of Atlanta's 300,000 population—white, black, and whatever—crowded the route of the seven-mile motorcade that conducted the Hollywood visitors from the airport to the Biltmore Hotel. Seventy-four years after the end of the Civil War, the South still seemed unvanquished. Street musicians played "Dixie." Aged veterans wore their Confederate uniforms. For weeks newspapers had been urging the public to wear things that might have belonged to their parents or grandparents.

Gable and Lombard sat in the back of an open Packard convertible, waving to the spectators. A woman in an old-fashioned gown peeled off one of her long gloves and hurled it at Gable. His wife bet him five dollars that someone's pantaloons would be next. She won.

That night the Gables attended a formal dress ball, patterned after the charity bazaar sequence in *Gone With the Wind*. Gable, Vivien

Leigh, and Olivia de Havilland wore their original costumes, which had been shipped in from Hollywood. Carole Lombard, gowned in black velvet, sat on the sidelines next to a tuxedoed Laurence Olivier, whose unmarried alliance with Leigh had yet to cause any ripples of censure.

On December 15 *GWTW* had its premiere showing at Loew's Grand, a 1932 art deco conversion of the 1898 Grand Opera House. The facade of the 2,500-seat theater was transformed into a replica of Twelve Oaks, the Wilkes family mansion, which was more typically Old South than Scarlett's beloved Tara. When Gable and Lombard arrived, many in the enormous street crowd let loose with the Confederate rebel cry.

Gable waved his huge hands in the air to quiet them. Though he hadn't intended to make a speech, he took the microphone from the sidewalk emcee and said: "Ladies and gentlemen. Tonight I am here just as a spectator. I want to see *Gone With the Wind* the same as you do. This is Margaret Mitchell's night and the people of Atlanta's night. Allow me, please, to see *Gone With the Wind* just as a spectator."

Gable had previously rejected Selznick's offers of an advance screening, so he wasn't lying. That night he and Lombard were seated next to Margaret Mitchell and her husband, John Marsh, who were also first-time viewers. While watching the scene where Scarlett is nursing wounded Confederate soldiers and the camera view expands to include thousands of invalids, Mitchell leaned over and whispered to Gable, "Mah Gawd, if we'd-ah had as many soldiers as that, we'd ah won the woah."

On the third and final day of the celebration, "Peggy" Mitchell gave a cocktail party for the Hollywood visitors at the Atlanta Women's Press Club. So many female admirers swarmed around Gable that he found it impossible to chat with Mitchell. Finally losing patience, he lifted the tiny author off the floor and carried her in his arms to an adjacent room, where he closed the door behind them.

Fifteen minutes later Gable and Mitchell emerged, smiling but refusing to answer questions about what had transpired. Not even Carole Lombard ever found out, though she made several ribald guesses to pals. But most likely it was nothing more than Gable trying to verify the famous rumor that Mitchell had used him as the model for Rhett Butler when she wrote the book.

Mitchell had often said publicly that she would never discuss it with anyone but Gable himself. The research of Mitchell scholars suggests that Gable was *not* her inspiration. Evidence points to *San Francisco* as the first Gable movie that Mitchell ever saw in her life, but by the time of that film's release in June 1936, *GWTW* was already in bookstores. Of course, Mitchell could have been subliminally influenced by press coverage of Gable, who'd been world famous since 1930–31.

The Gables flew home from Atlanta the next day. Minutes after they checked out of the hotel, a woman approached the reservations desk and requested the suite that Clark Gable had just vacated. The clerk took the reservation but told the woman that she couldn't go up until housekeeping made the rooms ready.

"Will it be the same bed that Mr. Gable slept in?" she asked.

"Well, I wasn't there, madame, but I presume so," came the reply.

"In that case, please tell them not to change the sheets," the woman said.

The Atlanta premiere was just the first step in the launching of *GWTW.* Due to its unprecedented running time of three hours and forty-two minutes, MGM and Selznick had to buck tradition to ensure a profit on their $4 million production investment, an all-time record for an American film. Rental terms were the highest ever, with exhibitors required to cough up 70 percent of box-office receipts (in other words, 70 cents of every dollar taken in). In those days, the distributor's share of first-run engagements was usually 35 percent and occasionally 50 percent for blockbusters like *San Francisco* and *Snow White and the Seven Dwarfs.*

At a time when the average price of a movie ticket in the United States was 23 cents, admission to *GWTW* was fixed at 75 cents at matinees and $1.10 at night. The lengthy running time also demanded a comfort break (aka "intermission") of at least ten minutes, so one complete showing took about four hours. Theaters could run no more than three performances per day. Smaller ones of fifteen hundred seats or fewer had the option of a "hard-ticket" policy like a stage play, with one matinee and one evening performance daily and all seats reserved. In those cases, prices also started at 75 cents but graduated to as high as $2.20 for the best seats on a weekend night.

All newspaper advertising carried an advisory that *GWTW* would not be shown anywhere at lower prices "at least until 1941." At the end of its first-run bookings, *GWTW* would be temporarily withdrawn from release instead of moving on to subsequent-run theaters that charged lower prices. In 1941 *GWTW* would reenter release at regular or "popular" prices and cover the entire route, starting again in first-run theaters but going straight on to all the lesser ones.

After Atlanta only two more openings were held in 1939, to qualify *GWTW* for nominations for that year's critical awards and Oscars. Coming just four days after Atlanta, the New York premiere at the Capitol Theater on December 19 was comparatively peaceful, but Olivia de Havilland represented the cast, with many movie and Broadway stage notables attending as well.

The Hollywood premiere was held at the Carthay Circle Theater on December 27, two days after the Gables celebrated their first Christmas at the ranch. Lombard bought the biggest evergreen that she could find, then had it sprayed white and decorated it herself with red lights and silver ornaments. Her gifts to Gable that year were white silk pajamas and a matching robe, designed by her friend Travis Banton. The precious fabric was some of the last to leave China before the Japanese invasion.

Gable surprised his wife with an elegant necklace designed by jeweler Paul Flato. A huge heart-shaped ruby dangled from a solid gold chain.

Gable grouched that attending the Atlanta premiere of *GWTW* was more than enough, but the Hollywood gala promised to be the most glittering event of the decade soon to end. Lombard refused to stay home. Without telling him, she had invited Will Gable and his wife to join them. Gable was furious, but there wasn't much he could do about it since she'd already splurged on new outfits for her in-laws. Gable's father refused to wear a tuxedo, so Lombard bought him a navy blue suit instead. She took Edna Gable to Irene's salon and helped her to select a gown.

For herself, Lombard picked out a tight-fitting gold lamé number that had a matching overcape to protect her against the December chill. Gable wore white tie and tails. When the Gable party arrived at the theater, pandemonium broke out among the thousands of fans and sightseers who were packed into temporary grandstands that MGM had erected on both sides of the entrance and across the street.

A reporter cornered Will Gable and asked him what he thought of his son's acting ability. "I like him whatever he does. He don't have to be Rhett Butler to please me. He's a good boy, and always has been" was the diplomatic response.

The all-star turnout included some surprising couplings. Loretta Young was escorted by Lombard's ex-husband, William Powell. Joan Crawford came with Cesar Romero, Norma Shearer with George Raft. Vivien Leigh and Laurence Olivier again made the scene, arriving in the company of the recently married Merle Oberon and Alexander Korda.

At intermission Gable decided that he couldn't sit through the rest of the movie. While his father and stepmother remained, he took Lombard to the lobby, where they ran into Marion Davies, who, in the absence of W. R. Hearst, had come with director Raoul Walsh and his wife. Gable thought that they could all stand a drink, so he requisitioned the manager's office and sent an usher for two bottles of Chivas Regal that he'd stashed in the chauffeured limousine that MGM had put at his disposal for the evening. Everybody got tiddly, and Davies and the Walshes missed the second half of *GWTW*.

When the screening finally ended at past one in the morning, the festivities were only half over. David Selznick's partner, John Hay Whitney, had taken over the Trocadero for a supper-dance that Gable feared would drag on for at least as long as *GWTW*. He wanted to go home to bed. No amount of pleading from Lombard or from MGM's and Selznick's publicists could change his mind.

The party was intended as a sort of final victory celebration for everybody involved with *GWTW*, so Selznick was hurt and offended by Gable's nonattendance. They never worked together again.

Gable's hostility toward Selznick also affected the producer's working relationship with Lombard, who still had a contract with him for one more film. Selznick soon wrote her a letter expressing his feelings: "Are you sure, Carole, that we should make another picture together? I know from countless sources how highly you think of me, both as a person and as a producer, and this is a source of great gratification to me. And I shall always look back on our past associations as among the most pleasant of my career. Certainly I have always held you up as the shining example of what a joy it can be to work with a star when that star appreciates a producer's problems and cooperates in their solution. But I must face the fact that you are married to Clark, and that Clark obviously feels quite differently about me."

Selznick went on to say, "I certainly recognize the awkward position you are in, and cannot expect to come out on the right side when your loyalties are divided. And perhaps some day in the future, attitudes may change, as they do in this business, and it will again be possible for you to do a picture for me with the wholehearted pleasure that we once both knew in our endeavors. The decision, however, is entirely yours. You would suffer much more from the repercussions in your personal life than would I; and I can stand it if you can."

Meanwhile *GWTW* turned into a box-office record-breaker in its first three openings and began to spread nationwide. Even with only 250 prints in circulation for the limited first-run release, it would gross an astounding $26 million in its first six months. No movie in history had ever come near that except possibly the mother of all Civil War epics, the 1915 *The Birth of a Nation,* which producer-director D. W. Griffith sold outright to a flock of independent regional distributors who often never reported box-office takings. In MGM's record book *GWTW* was four times ahead of the silent *Ben-Hur* and was doing six times better than Gable's previous top grosser, *San Francisco.*

In late January 1940 the Gables finally took off on a honeymoon trip, heading for a hunting club in Baja California, about seventy miles south of the U.S.-Mexican border. Gable had recently bought a specially equipped Dodge station wagon with four-wheel drive and a sixty-five-gallon gasoline tank. The couple loaded up with a tent, guns and fishing tackle, groceries, cooking equipment, and the like. Lombard had a new sleeping bag, fully lined with skins from an old mink coat that was no longer in fashion.

Before the Gables left home, Otto Winkler asked if he could drive down to Baja later in the week with a staff photographer to shoot some stills that *Photoplay* had requested for a feature layout about the couple's leisure interests. Gable hated such intrusions on his privacy, but he was so fond of Winkler that he agreed. He promised to phone Winkler to confirm arrangements when they reached their destination.

The hunting club was situated in a remote mountainous area, served only by rutty, unpaved roads. When the Gables arrived, they were

TOP: At sixteen, Clark Gable was already a high school dropout and chain-smoker (HOWARD FRANK/PERSONALITY PHOTOS). ABOVE LEFT: Gable, seated at table, made his Broadway stage debut in 1928 in the dramatic shocker *Machinal* (CULVER PICTURES). ABOVE RIGHT: Clark and Ria Gable attending a Hollywood gala in the company of Irving Thalberg and Norma Shearer (CULVER PICTURES).

RIGHT: In *Susan Lenox: Her Fall and Rise* (1931), Greta Garbo was one of the first Hollywood love goddesses who would be matched with MGM's new star (CULVER PICTURES).

BELOW: William Boyd, right, had yet to become immortalized as Hopalong Cassidy when he played the hero to Gable's villain in the latter's first major movie, *The Painted Desert* (1931) (CULVER PICTURES).

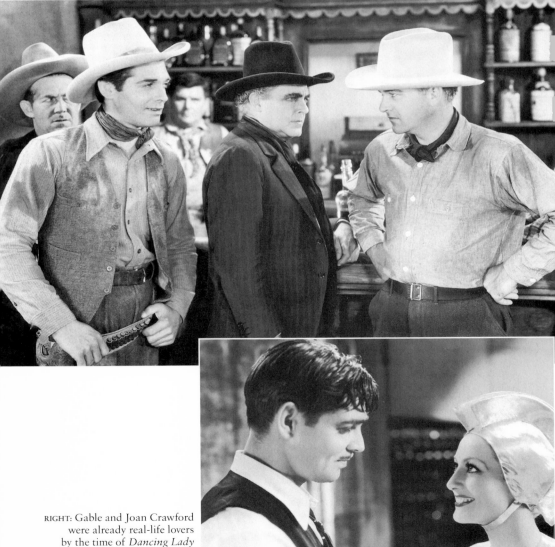

RIGHT: Gable and Joan Crawford were already real-life lovers by the time of *Dancing Lady* (1933), their fourth movie together (CULVER PICTURES).

TOP: The rain-barrel scene in *Red Dust* (1932) helped to make Gable and Jean Harlow the most sexually provocative of MGM's star teams (CULVER PICTURES). ABOVE: Gable and Claudette Colbert both won Oscars for *It Happened One Night*, which was also voted the best film of 1934 (HOWARD FRANK/PERSONALITY PHOTOS).

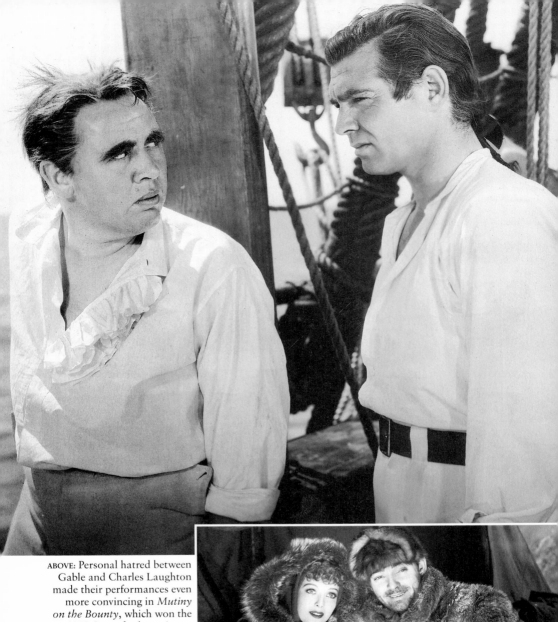

ABOVE: Personal hatred between Gable and Charles Laughton made their performances even more convincing in *Mutiny on the Bounty*, which won the 1935 Oscar for best picture (CULVER PICTURES).

RIGHT: Nine months after the filming, Gable's teaming with Loretta Young in *The Call of the Wild* (1935) had an unexpected result (CULVER PICTURES).

TOP: Gable and Spencer Tracy, here with Myrna Loy in *Test Pilot* (1938), made a great screen team but were never close friends off the set (CULVER PICTURES). ABOVE: In *Idiot's Delight* (1939), Gable stopped the show with his rendition of Irving Berlin's "Puttin' on the Ritz" (CULVER PICTURES).

ABOVE: Acting opposite Gable in *Gone With the Wind* (1939) helped Hattie McDaniel to win an Oscar, the first ever to be presented to a person of color (HOWARD FRANK/PERSONALITY PHOTOS).

RIGHT: Gable's marriage to Carole Lombard ended in tragedy and became one of the touchstones in the history of Hollywood romances (CULVER PICTURES).

LEFT: Gable romanced Lana Turner in four films, starting with *Honky Tonk* (1941), where one of his costumes was a favorite lounging robe that he kept from *GWTW* (CULVER PICTURES).

ABOVE RIGHT: Gable later claimed that he must have been drunk when he proposed to his fourth wife, who in previous marriages had been Lady Sylvia Ashley and Mrs. Douglas Fairbanks (CULVER PICTURES). ABOVE: Gable was teamed with MGM's new box-office queen, Greer Garson, and reunited with *GWTW* director Victor Fleming in his first post-WWII movie, *Adventure* (1945). Nonetheless, it proved to be a fiasco (CULVER PICTURES).

LEFT: Gable and Grace Kelly, then still in the supporting-actress phase of her career, became involved in an intimate romance during the African location filming of *Mogambo* (1953), a remake of his earlier *Red Dust*, with Ava Gardner in the role originated by Jean Harlow (HOWARD FRANK/PERSONALITY PHOTOS).

BELOW: *The Misfits* (1961) would prove to be both Marilyn Monroe's and Gable's final film; here they posed in a group photo with the other "Misfits": director John Huston, Eli Wallach, and Montgomery Clift (HOWARD FRANK/PERSONALITY PHOTOS).

ABOVE: Gable's fifth wife, Kay Williams, was young enough to bear him an heir, but "The King of Hollywood" died four months before John Clark Gable was born (CULVER PICTURES).

so exhausted that they went straight to bed and forgot to call Otto Winkler. The next morning there were few ducks flying, so they decided to drive farther south to an area where brant geese had been reported. They stayed at a lodge that was really no more than several dingy shacks and a cantina that would never pass a health inspection. Lombard came down with diarrhea and spent most of the time running back and forth to the communal privy.

For Gable's thirty-ninth birthday on February 1, Lombard decided that they should drive to Ensenada, a town on the Pacific coast, to celebrate. En route they were caught in a thunderstorm. Their station wagon skidded off the slippery mountain road and got stuck in deep mud. With darkness approaching, they gave up hope of finding help and spent the night in their sleeping bags in the back of the vehicle.

Meanwhile the Gables were unaware that they were causing headlines back in the United States. Newspapers throughout the country had front-page stories like GABLE MISSING WITH CAROLE and SUSPECT GABLE AND BRIDE KIDNAPPED BY MEXICAN BANDITS. When they failed to phone Otto Winkler as promised, he had become concerned and chartered a plane to Ensenada, which had Baja's only airport, to try finding them. Upon arrival he asked around and learned nothing, so he cabled Howard Strickling for authorization to hire a search party. A copy of the telegram somehow got into the hands of the press, which immediately went wild with speculative coverage.

After being stranded overnight, the Gables were rescued by the driver of a passing truck. By the time they finally reached Ensenada, Otto Winkler had the whole town on the alert, so they were quickly spotted. Their friend was terribly embarrassed because he'd unintentionally started an international incident. The Mexican government was furious about the news coverage, claiming that the country had been maligned as backward and lawless. An official complaint to MGM resulted in Otto Winkler's dismissal. Gable exploded and immediately had him reinstated.

While the Gables were in Mexico, the Academy of Motion Picture Arts and Sciences announced the nominations for the 1939 Oscars. To no one's surprise, *Gone With the Wind* topped the list with an all-time record of thirteen nominations, including one for Gable as best actor. It was his first nomination since 1935's *Mutiny on the Bounty*.

By now, rave reviews from critics had Gable half-believing that he could win. He thought that he certainly stood a better chance than Mickey Rooney, who was up for *Babes in Arms,* but he wasn't so sure about Robert Donat (*Goodbye, Mr. Chips*), Laurence Olivier (*Wuthering Heights*), or James Stewart (*Mr. Smith Goes to Washington*). Stewart won in the New York Film Critics Awards, which always had a powerful influence on Oscar voters.

To please his wife, Gable agreed not only to attend the February 29 ceremonies but also to accept the hospitality of his hated producer. David and Irene Selznick held a cocktail party for the *GWTW* nominees at their home in Beverly Hills and then took everyone in chartered limousines to the banquet at the Cocoanut Grove at the Ambassador Hotel.

In those simpler times before the Oscars became a world media circus, the Academy always supplied a complete list of winners to major newspapers *before* the event so that they could appear in the next morning's early editions. Editors, of course, were sworn to secrecy, but there were occasional leaks. Perhaps in celebration of Leap Year Day, *The Los Angeles Times* jumped the gun with its last evening edition, which hit newsstands at eight-forty-five P.M., more than two hours before the start of the awards ceremony.

The news quickly reached the banqueting guests. The winners and losers all knew who they were, but it was too late for any of the disappointed to leave without being considered rude and cowardly.

Among the twelve hundred diners was supporting actress candidate Hattie McDaniel. Besides being the first black ever to be nominated for an Oscar in *any* category, she was also one of the first of her race to be admitted to the Cocoanut Grove (except for entertainers or others who might be working there). McDaniel and her escort, performer-friend Wonderful Smith, had a table to themselves at the rear of the nightclub but were invited to move to Selznick's table when the ceremonies began.

Darryl Zanuck handed out a slew of technical awards, including three for *GWTW,* before Mickey Rooney came on to present an honorary miniature Oscar to seventeen-year-old Judy Garland for "best performance by a juvenile" in *The Wizard of Oz.* In lieu of an acceptance speech, Garland crooned "Over the Rainbow," which minutes before had been named 1939's best song.

The first major award of the evening, for best director, went to Victor Fleming for *GWTW*. The well-informed groaned audibly as David Selznick marched to the podium and announced that Fleming was too "ill" to attend. After accepting the award from Mervyn LeRoy, Selznick tried to repair his breach with Fleming by rhapsodizing at length about the director's genius.

GWTW next gained the unsought distinction of being the first movie in history to receive a posthumous Oscar. Screenplay writer Sidney Howard had died the previous August at his Massachusetts farm, in a freak accident involving a runaway tractor.

With best director and best script in hand, *GWTW* seemed destined to win best picture, and it did. The other nominees, in a year of exceptional movies, were *Dark Victory, Goodbye, Mr. Chips, Love Affair, Mr. Smith Goes to Washington, Ninotchka, Of Mice and Men, Stagecoach, The Wizard of Oz,* and *Wuthering Heights.* (It should be noted that beginning with the 1944 Oscars, the best picture category was permanently reduced to five nominees and the presentation moved to the grand finale of the program. Prior to that, the acting awards were always the very last handed out.)

When David Selznick came to the podium for the second time that night, emcee Bob Hope cracked, "David, you should have brought roller skates." A few minutes later Selznick returned to accept the Irving Thalberg Memorial Award, an ironic twist to the bitter rivalry between the two men during Selznick's tenure at MGM.

As the evening narrowed down to the four acting awards, Thomas Mitchell, who was featured in *GWTW* but got nominated for his performance in *Stagecoach,* won best supporting actor. When presenter Fay Bainter announced Hattie McDaniel as best supporting actress, the crowd went wild.

"The ovation will go down in history as one of the greatest ever accorded any performer in the annals of the industry," Louella Parsons reported. "En masse the entire audience, stars in every place, stood and cheered the beloved Hattie McDaniel."

McDaniel's face was wet with tears by the time she reached the stage. "This is one of the happiest moments of my life," she said in a short prepared speech. "I sincerely hope that I shall always be a credit to my race, and to the motion picture industry. My heart is too full to express just how I feel, so may I say to each and every one of you, thank you and God bless you."

McDaniel rushed off crying. When she got back to Selznick's table, Gable vigorously shook her hand. Selznick, meanwhile, grabbed her other hand and kissed it.

As soon as the room quieted down, Spencer Tracy, the previous year's best actor (for *Boys Town*), presented the remaining two awards. Though Tracy might have been rooting for his chum Gable, the Oscar for best actor went to Robert Donat for *Goodbye Mr. Chips*, produced by MGM at its studio in England. Tracy accepted the award for Donat, who was working in a stage play in blitz-torn London.

Another Briton won best actress for *GWTW*. Vivien Leigh's competition was Bette Davis (*Dark Victory*), Irene Dunne (*Love Affair*), Greta Garbo (*Ninotchka*), and Greer Garson (*Goodbye, Mr. Chips*). In her acceptance speech, Leigh hailed David Selznick as a "composite of energy, courage and very great kindness." One can only guess what Gable would have said in his speech if he'd been a winner.

GWTW won a total of eight Oscars, the most ever given to a single movie up to that time. The previous record-holder was *It Happened One Night* with five, including Gable's for best actor.

Gable's loss in the case of *GWTW* was reportedly caused by MGM putting its considerable voting strength behind Robert Donat to boost attendance at *Goodbye, Mr. Chips,* which up to then had been a box-office disappointment. Perhaps, but an Academy official told *Variety* that Gable came in third to Donat and James Stewart, who was only a few votes short of winning for *Mr. Smith Goes to Washington*.

On their way back to the ranch that night, Mrs. Gable tried to cheer up her husband: "Don't be blue, Pappy. I just know we'll bring one home next year."

"No, we won't," he said. "That was it. That was my last chance. I'm never gonna win again."

"Not you, you self-centered bastard," Lombard answered. "I mean me!"

No public uproar had been raised over Gable's use of "damn" in *Gone With the Wind,* but his next movie, *Strange Cargo,* landed in deep

trouble when released in March 1940. It was the first Hollywood production since the introduction of the industry's self-regulated censorship
system to receive a "condemned" rating from the Catholic Church's
Legion of Decency. Attending a condemned movie constituted a venial
sin and was forbidden to those of the Catholic faith. In places with a
large Catholic population, the Legion had a proven power over theater
box offices.

Governed by a board of bishops, the Legion charged that *Strange
Cargo* presented "a naturalistic concept of religion contrary to the
teachings of Christ and the Catholic Church." Cited as offensive were
the movie's "irreverent use of sacred scripture" and "lustful implications
in the dialogue and situations."

In a panic MGM suspended distribution of *Strange Cargo* and did
some deleting and re-editing, mainly on scenes involving the Christ-like
fugitive enacted by Ian Hunter. After another look, the Legion softened
its rating to AII ("morally objectionable in part" and for adult viewing
only). Even so, Catholic strongholds like Detroit and Providence still
banned the film.

The controversy may have increased the film's domestic takings, but
due to wartime conditions in the foreign market, *Strange Cargo* earned a
profit of only $21,000 on its $1.3 million investment. Gable never
worked with Joan Crawford again.

In fact, it was the last of Gable's films with any of the MGM queens
with whom he had been reared. Except for the deceased Harlow, they
were still on the contract roster, but Gable wanted a change from the
constant rotation of costars that had been going on for nearly ten years.
His success with Vivien Leigh, though not the happiest of working relationships, indicated that the public wanted to see him with newer and
younger stars rather than the older ones, some of whom, like Crawford,
Garbo, and Shearer, had been around since silent days.

Strange Cargo wasn't what fans expected of Gable after *GWTW*, so
MGM assembled a superproduction for his next. *Boom Town* marked a
reunion of two teams, Gable and Spencer Tracy, and Gable and Claudette
Colbert, with the new European sexpot, Hedy Lamarr, tossed in as an
additional romantic complication. With such a powerful combination of
stars, L. B. Mayer saw no need for the extra expense of color photography.

Boom Town returned Gable to the make-believe world of black and white. Besides being his first color movie, *GWTW* would also turn out to be his last for more than a decade.

Some of Gable's own memories of working in the Oklahoma oil fields were woven into the script of *Boom Town,* which was written by his close friend John Lee Mahin from a story idea by James Edward Grant. To pacify Spencer Tracy, who'd become a huge star in his own right and no longer fancied being cast as Gable's sidekick and moral conscience, the plot had them competing romantically for the first time.

Gable and Tracy portrayed wildcatting buddies who make and lose several fortunes, with bust-ups and reconciliations along the way. Both men fancy Claudette Colbert, who starts out as Tracy's fiancée but winds up Gable's wife. After she provides him with a son, Gable, by now an oil tycoon, falls into the clutches of industrial spy Hedy Lamarr, but Tracy helps to set everything right by the end.

Directed by Jack Conway, the action-packed drama included several punch-ups between Gable and Tracy, one of them so fierce that they demolish most of the furniture in the business office in which it takes place. Needless to say, stunt doubles were frequently used, intermixed with the stars. One day while Gable had to face the camera and was working with Tracy's double, the latter got carried away and truly pummeled him. Gable sank to his knees. His false teeth were broken, his mouth and lips bleeding. He needed three weeks to recuperate while production continued around him.

When Gable returned, he was still wearing temporary dentures while new permanent ones were being made. Unfortunately, his first scene was a romantic one with Claudette Colbert. She kissed him so hard that the temporaries cracked. Gable was rushed to the studio's resident dentist for repairs.

Carole Lombard trusted Gable around Colbert, who happened to be lesbian, but when he shot his love scene with Hedy Lamarr, she made a surprise visit to the set. The Austrian brunette had acquired a notorious reputation for appearing in the nude in the Czech-made *Ecstasy,* but in *Boom Town* she was well covered by a gorgeous wardrobe designed by Adrian.

When Lombard arrived, she was a walking advertisement for Irene, her own favorite designer. A set worker recalled that Lombard "looked like four million bucks," wearing a fur stole, tailored suit, and hat. If she was trying to prove that she could outclass Hedy Lamarr, she succeeded.

If Mrs. Gable had visited on another day, she might have found cause for worry. A new fan magazine writer and aspiring gossip columnist kept badgering Otto Winkler for an interview with Gable. When an appointment was finally arranged, she arrived at the studio wearing a suit, but en route to Gable's bungalow she stopped in a rest room and changed into a slinky, low-cut cocktail dress that she'd packed in her briefcase.

An attractive, big-busted redhead, she made quite an impression on Gable when Winkler introduced them. "I think I can handle this one on my own," Gable said as he ushered the publicist to the door. The interview, if that's what it could be called, lasted two hours. From then on May Mann always got whatever Gable stories and tidbits she wanted.

As the king of Hollywood's romantic idols, Gable was constantly being pursued by women, especially at the studio, where he was most accessible. His powers of resistance being virtually nil, he was always bedding down with some starlet, extra player, or secretary.

Such behavior would be intolerable for any wife who expected fidelity from her husband, but Carole Lombard was more liberal and usually gave him a long leash. She took the attitude that sex was an automatic and often uncontrollable impulse. She knew that she couldn't have stopped Gable even if she tried. As long as he kept his escapades simple and didn't get emotionally involved with the women, knock them up, or catch the clap, she tended to ignore his philandering.

Boom Town turned out to be the last of Gable's collaborations with Spencer Tracy, though L. B. Mayer tried for at least one more. One day he summoned both men to his office to discuss it. Mayer had just made a deal with Katharine Hepburn for the rights to *The Philadelphia Story*, the hit Broadway play that had been specially written for her by Philip Barry. Hepburn had quit moviemaking in 1938 after exhibitors branded her box-office poison, so she felt that she needed two red-hot costars to offset her tarnished reputation. She requested Gable and Tracy, but neither saw a chance to shine in what was essentially a Hepburn vehicle. She had to settle for freelancer Cary Grant and MGM's own James Stewart.

Meanwhile *Gone With the Wind* continued to smash box-office records and to aggravate Gable every time it added another million dollars to the grosses. For what was surely turning into the biggest moneymaker of all time, he'd earned comparative peanuts for his labor, and he owned not even the tiniest of shares in the profits. It was now too late to do anything about that, but agent Phil Berg made L. B. Mayer aware of Gable's unhappiness, stressing the fact that the actor's current salary of $4,500 per week was on the low side for major stars.

Mayer finally agreed to renegotiate Gable's contract, which still had two years to run. It was extended another three years, with an immediate increase to $7,500 per week and escalators to $10,000 weekly by the end.

Newspaper reports of Gable's new contract spurred celebrated humorist J. P. McEvoy into calculating that the star now earned more money in ten weeks than President Roosevelt did in a year. McEvoy declared that unfair, "since FDR is a much better actor."

Gable's raise brought him up to $300,000 a year, about equal to Carole Lombard's earnings, which came from an average of two free-lance deals per year at $150,000 each. Their combined annual income from moviemaking was around $600,000. Between them, they earned another $50,000 or so from guest appearances on radio programs. Of course, all that made them subject to the highest rate of federal income tax, which was about 60 percent in those days.

By the time Gable finished *Boom Town* in May 1940, Lombard was ending a work sabbatical that had started when she completed *Vigil in the Night* the previous November. Though she still had two projects remaining on her four-picture deal with RKO, the studio wanted to judge the box-office results of the first two before deciding on scripts. *In Name Only,* with Cary Grant and Kay Francis as costars, did well, but *Vigil in the Night,* in which Lombard was supported by Brian Aherne and Anne Shirley, bombed. RKO blamed the failure (and loss of $327,000) on director George Stevens and production chief Pandro Berman, both of whom left the studio under pressure from company president George Schaefer. Berman's successor, Harry Edington, was a former agent who adored Lombard. He was eager to keep her at RKO but thought that more care should be taken in casting her.

During the lull while scripts were being considered, Lombard discovered that she was pregnant. She intended to break the news to Gable on their first wedding anniversary, but in the interim she suffered a miscarriage and never told him. In her doctor's opinion, physical exertion may have been the cause. He urged her to give up all strenuous activities, which wasn't the easiest thing for a movie star and rancher's wife to do.

By June Lombard and RKO had settled on *They Knew What They Wanted* as her next project. Gable groaned when she told him that her costar would be his onetime nemesis Charles Laughton, but she'd worked with him before (at Paramount in 1933 in *White Woman*) and believed that she could cope again. Laughton's career had faltered after *Mutiny on the Bounty,* but he'd recently made a sensational comeback in *The Hunchback of Notre Dame,* one of the few blockbusters in RKO's ten-year history.

Gable had acted in *They Knew What They Wanted* in his stock days, so he could understand Lombard's enthusiasm for the drama, which in 1925 won a Pulitzer Prize for Sidney Howard (later the Oscar-lauded scriptwriter of *GWTW*). The story of an Italian immigrant grape grower and his mail-order bride had already been filmed twice, as the silent *The Secret Hour* with Pola Negri and Jean Hersholt, and then in 1930 as *A Lady to Love* with Vilma Banky and Edward G. Robinson. In 1956 it would become the basis for Frank Loesser's Broadway musical *The Most Happy Fella.*

Because of the play's bold content and notorious reputation, Hollywood censors had forced cuts and title changes on the first two film versions, but by 1940 the Production Code authority had become more liberal. Director Garson Kanin and scriptwriter Robert Ardrey received approval for a version that retained much of the original work but took a harsher view of the Lombard character's affair (and pregnancy) with one of her husband's workers.

Gable usually stayed away from Lombard's projects, but she persuaded him to accompany her during the three weeks of outdoor location work in the wine vineyards of the Napa Valley, about fifty miles north of San Francisco. The production manager found accommodation for the couple in a private home in the small town of Saint Helena. The sheriff posted a public notice that anyone caught pestering the Gables for autographs or anything else would be jailed for the balance of the visitors' stay.

By the time of the location shooting, Charles Laughton was feuding with everyone, and Lombard had dubbed him "Captain Blubberlips." Traveling with wife Elsa Lanchester, he never socialized with the Gables, nor they with the Laughtons. Gable went hunting and fishing, taking Lombard with him whenever her schedule permitted. One day they attended a local harvesting festival and learned how to stomp grapes with their bare feet.

During the semivacation Lombard hoped that she might get pregnant. As soon as the Gables got home, she went for a test, which proved negative. She wondered if her doctor might be right. Perhaps she did need to slow down or even to stop working entirely. She decided that when she finished the next and last of her RKO commitments, she would take a year off.

Clark Gable seemed untroubled by his wife's childbearing problems. Some of their mutual friends later claimed that having a family was Lombard's dream, not Gable's, but that he wasn't opposed if it did happen. His experience with Loretta Young validated his virility and suggested that Lombard's "failures" weren't his fault. But Gable was now nearly forty and his wife was thirty-two, so they couldn't be expected to be as fertile as a couple in their twenties.

Their life together centered on the ranch in Encino, which they were trying to put on a self-sustaining basis. Their first efforts were discouraging. After purchasing a cow and a milking machine, they found that the product was costing them $4.50 per quart to produce.

Lombard decided that they could make a fortune by raising chickens and selling eggs. They bought six hundred New Hamphire Reds to get started. Lombard designed a carton labeled "The King's Eggs," illustrated with a rooster wearing a crown. But production costs averaged a dollar per egg, so the project was quickly abandoned.

For a couple earning upward of $600,000 per year, the Gables lived quite conservatively. Their annual living expenses were about $16,000, including household help, groceries, utilities, and property taxes. Besides their two riding horses, they owned only a mule and a gang of dogs and cats.

When the spirit moved him, Gable worked hard around the place, taking care of the fruit trees, cultivating the soil with mule and plow, or mowing the lawns. Lombard bought him a little yellow tractor to use. He also did most of the mechanical repairs on the couple's fleet of cars and station wagons.

In July 1940 Loretta Young married Tom Lewis, a vice president in the radio division of the Young and Rubicam advertising agency. They bought a home in Beverly Hills and started an instant family with her "adopted" daughter. Lewis wanted to officially adopt Judith as well, but Young talked him out of it. Secretly she feared that in the legal process Lewis might discover Judy's true parentage. But she had no objections to Judy being raised as Judith Lewis. Up until then she'd been known as Judith Young.

Gable's reactions to all that are unknown. We sometimes share our personal secrets with no one, and they may be difficult even for ourselves to live with. Carole Lombard must have known of his lovechild, which had been underground gossip for years, but it may have been too sensitive a subject for them to discuss.

In September both Gables started new movies. When Lombard finished hers, she intended to take a year off to have a baby. After three dramatic films for RKO, she decided to round out the four-picture deal with a comedy, her first since the flop *Fools for Scandal* in 1938.

With RKO's approval, Lombard packaged most of *Mr. and Mrs. Smith* herself, starting with an original screenplay by Norman Krasna that had once been planned as her final project for David Selznick. Lombard persuaded Selznick to sell the script to RKO and also talked him into loaning one of his contract directors. Alfred Hitchcock was delighted because he'd always wanted to do a romantic comedy. Prior to and since leaving England in 1939, he'd become identified with suspense and melodrama.

Mr. and Mrs. Smith concerned a happy but constantly bickering couple who suddenly discover that they were never legally married. For her costar Lombard wanted Cary Grant, but when he turned out to be solidly booked for the next three years, she requested his debonair equal, Robert Montgomery, whom RKO had to borrow from MGM for $13,750 per week.

Meanwhile Gable was back in the arms of Hedy Lamarr, if only in the romantic romp entitled *Comrade X*. The sexual chemistry between them in their few scenes together in *Boom Town* had been so potent that L. B. Mayer ordered an instant rematch. Walter Reisch, one of the scriptwriters of *Ninotchka,* came up with the idea, which was then transformed into a screenplay by Ben Hecht and Charles Lederer.

Not surprisingly, *Comrade X* had certain similarities to the recent Greta Garbo–Ernst Lubitsch hit that spoofed Russian communism. Gable portrayed a Moscow-based American reporter who, under the alias Comrade X, has been dispatching stories that criticize the corrupt Soviet regime. While trying to avoid capture by the secret police, he falls in love with a gorgeous streetcar driver who is a believer in *pure* communism and thus was in deep trouble with the current leadership.

Producer Gottfried Reinhardt assigned the direction to King Vidor, maker of such classics as *The Big Parade* and *The Crowd,* who would hopefully be able to whip a performance out of Hedy Lamarr. Prior to her surprisingly effective cameo in *Boom Town,* she had proved inept in the two MGM vehicles that introduced her to the American public.

"Hedy prided herself on being Viennese, but she was far more naive than sophisticated. She was a peasant type, really. She had one of the most beautiful faces ever seen, but not the figure to go with it. She didn't have any natural talent and was inclined to be nervous. You had to nurse her along," King Vidor recalled.

Gable tried to be patient with her. To conceal Lamarr's deficiencies, nearly every exchange of dialogue between them was punctuated by at least one smoldering kiss.

At the end of their first day, Gable squeezed Lamarr's hand and said, "You're doing great, kid. You're gonna knock 'em dead."

"What do you mean? Knock who dead?" asked Lamarr, who wasn't versed in American slang.

"The paying customers," Gable said. "You're gonna lay them in the aisles."

Lamarr thought a moment, then started giggling and finally howling. When Gable asked her what was so funny, she said, "I was just thinking how it would look, a lot of dead people lying in the aisles."

Due to the conflict with her own production schedule, Lombard never found time for a surprise visit to MGM to check out gossip about an affair between her husband and Lamarr. But if one did occur, Lamarr failed to mention it in her 1966 memoir *Ecstasy and Me,* in which she candidly detailed thirty years of passionate encounters with both sexes.

While both Gables were filming, their prior works reached theater screens. *Boom Town* was another blockbuster, the highest grosser of 1940 except for the continuing *GWTW.* But *They Knew What They*

Wanted was Lombard's second flop in a row, recording a loss of $291,000 and thus negating her profit participation. In her disappointment she tweaked Gable that if MGM had given him points in *Boom Town,* he would have earned a tidy sum from the movie's $1.9 million in profits.

At the conclusion of *Mr. and Mrs. Smith,* Lombard officially started the year's sabbatical that she'd promised herself. Though she intended to cut back on strenuous activities, she couldn't pass up the opening of the duck-hunting season, when the Gables always assembled a group of friends and drove to Baja California for a couple of weeks.

This time the party included Gable's agent, Phil Berg, and actress-wife Leila Hyams; actor William "Buster" Collier and wife Marie Stevens, an ex–Ziegfeld Follies showgirl; and Harry and Nan Fleischmann, owners of a gun club near Bakersfield. When they reached Ensenada, the hunting proved disappointing, so they decided to go higher up into the mountains to Laguna Hanson, a small lake where flocks of the wild ducks known as canvasbacks had been sighted.

To get them there, Gable phoned Los Angeles and spoke to aviator Paul Mantz, who'd become a buddy since serving as technical adviser on *Test Pilot.* Mantz agreed to fly down in his twin-engine amphibian to spare them the long and arduous road trip. A hunter himself, he would also join the party for the duration of their stay.

"Clark and Carole were down-to-earth people," Mantz later recalled. "I was glad to be a part of their gang. They didn't act like movie stars. I loved being with them."

Lombard promptly dubbed the Sikorsky S-38 plane "Nellie the Goon." After landing on Laguna Hanson, the group found an old cabin occupied by Mexicans and paid them handsomely to take temporary leave. The interior had a coal stove and decrepit furnishings, so everybody bedded down on the floor in sleeping bags.

The duck hunting proved excellent, marred only when Lombard was stung by a yellowjacket and contracted a bad case of poison ivy rash. When she returned home, she took to bed for several days, completely naked except for the white ointment that she used to quell the itchy blisters that covered most of her body.

Laguna Hanson was surrounded by dense forest, and taking off from such a limited space was more difficult than landing on it. Paul Mantz recalled, "The surface of the lake was smooth as a mirror, so I taxied in a circle in order to rough it up and create a few waves. We were carrying two cases of ammunition and a heavy spare battery, however, and when I'd reached the point of no return, I aborted the takeoff, and we had to start over again."

The overweight was first unloaded, to be picked up later when Gable could make arrangements. The second takeoff was successful, but Nellie the Goon barely made it over the treetops. Lombard, watching the near mishap through a plane window, clutched Gable's arm and said, "Please, let's never travel in separate planes. Whenever I fly, I want you with me."

Their next trip together, right after Christmas 1940, was by train to Baltimore for a visit to the esteemed Johns Hopkins Medical Center. When the couple left Los Angeles, MGM announced that Gable needed treatment for back pain that had been plaguing him since he got thrown from a horse in 1933. But the real reason for the journey was for both Gables to undergo tests in the hospital's gynecology division, which was considered the best in the nation. In those days such intimate matters were never reported in the press. Gable and Lombard were also such sex symbols that raising public doubts about their potency could only dent their images.

The results of the Johns Hopkins tests were known only to the Gables and their doctors, but friends of the couple later claimed that no major medical problems were discovered. Lombard did have a minor flaw in her uterus that could be corrected in a simple operation, but she was advised to wait. The Gables' sexual routine might well be the culprit. They were urged to experiment with positions and to increase their couplings during Lombard's monthly period of ovulation.

Before returning to California, Gable and Lombard hopped by limousine to Washington, D.C., for a short vacation. Mrs. Gable had never been to the national capital, so Carter Barron, MGM's lobbyist with Congress, arranged a VIP tour of the must-see places of interest, plus restaurants and nightclubs.

When President Roosevelt learned that the Gables were in town, he invited them to the White House on December 30 for his next Fireside Chat with the nation. The radio broadcasts were so popular that many movie theaters paused for an intermission and piped them through the sound system so that people wouldn't stay home to listen.

Gable wore a chalk-stripe gray suit that night, Lombard a black silk dress and a matching hat with a veil. When they arrived at the Oval Room, they were ushered to front-row seats next to Secretary of State Cordell Hull and the president's mother, Sara Delano Roosevelt. Chairs for fifty guests faced the president's desk, on top of which were several microphones that would feed the broadcast to five hundred radio stations around the country.

Watching FDR pull up behind the desk in a rubber-tired wheelchair came as a bit of a shock to the Gables. His disability from polio was usually concealed in press photographs and newsreels, for fear that it might lessen the public's confidence in the leader of what many considered the mightiest nation on earth.

President now since 1933 and recently reelected for a third term, Roosevelt hoped to steer the United States away from its isolationist policies into greater support of England and its allies in the war against Nazi Germany. In the fifteenth of his periodic "chats," he envisioned the U.S. role in the war as "the great arsenal of democracy."

In a somber voice FDR said, "Never before has our American civilization been in such danger as now." He accused the Nazis of attempting "to dominate all life and thought in their own country . . . to enslave the whole of Europe . . . to use the resources of Europe to dominate the rest of the world."

The president continued, "If Great Britain goes down, all of us in the Americas would be living at the point of a gun. The vast resources and wealth of this hemisphere constitute the most tempting loot in the world." He urged the nation to step up its armament and defense efforts and hinted that the rationing of consumer and luxury goods might soon become necessary.

After the broadcast FDR brightened up. Along with his wife Eleanor, he chatted with the Gables for half an hour. A great movie fan, he fired questions at Gable about *Gone With the Wind*. He also thanked Lombard for a headline-making stunt that she had pulled back in 1938, when she endorsed the federal income tax system and claimed to be delighted with the way the government spent her money.

The president told the Gables that the movie industry must play a major role in the current emergency. He reminded them of World War I, when the studios had produced propaganda films and stars had helped to sell bonds and entertained the troops. The couple promised their support.

Back home again Lombard realized that her work sabbatical was ticking by and that she and her husband should be spending more time trying to make a baby. Close friends were advised not to drop by the ranch without phoning first. "Clark and Carole burned up the sheets," a chum recalled. "They tried every position known to humans. They would have done it hanging out a window if somebody said you could get pregnant that way."

On February 1, Gable turned forty. Lombard held a surprise party at the ranch, catered by the Brown Derby. Owner Robert Cobb provided a huge buffet of forty appetizers, entrées, and desserts, including Gable's favorites of corned beef hash, stew, pot roast, and baked beans.

Two weeks later Gable reported to MGM for the start of *They Met in Bombay,* with Clarence Brown as director. To comply with Gable's demands for new leading ladies, producer Hunt Stromberg selected Rosalind Russell, who'd been promoted to a full-fledged MGM star since her supporting roles in Gable's *Forsaking All Others* and *China Seas* back in 1934–35.

Anita Loos, who'd become a specialist in creating con man characters for Gable, collaborated with Edwin Justus Mayer and Leon Gordon on the script for *They Met in Bombay.* Gable and Russell played rival jewel thieves who have trailed a British duchess to India to steal her fabled diamond necklace. Russell succeeds, but Gable catches her and persuades her to become his partner in crime.

The comedy-adventure was the first of Gable's movies to recognize current world conditions. During another caper he disguises himself as a British Army captain and is accidentally assigned to command a battalion that is being sent to defend an outpost against the Japanese. The fake officer proves himself a hero and gets decorated with the Victoria Cross, which helps to win him a light prison sentence when he decides to take the rap for his and Russell's misdeeds.

Rosalind Russell had become famous for a rapid-fire delivery that had been clocked as high as four hundred words per minute. Fortunately Gable's wife spoke almost as fast all the time, so he had no problems adjusting.

"Clark was a delight to work with," Russell remembered. "He

always shared, never upstaged his marks or the other performers. There was nothing small or petty about him. He was as big as he was physically. . . . No director ever had to tell him how to do a love scene. He was tremendously graceful. Much like a ballet dancer, he had rhythm and timing. There wasn't all that enormous clinching and awkwardness that some actors put you through."

During the filming of *They Met in Bombay,* the Gables reached their second wedding anniversary. Carole Lombard threw a surprise party on the set, again catered by the Brown Derby. Spencer Tracy stole the show, arriving in his fright makeup for *Dr. Jekyll and Mr. Hyde,* which was being filmed next door.

Counting their three-year affair, Gable and Lombard had been a couple now for five years, refuting the Hollywood belief that marriages between movie stars couldn't last because of the pressures of the business and the inevitable clashes of ego.

The Gables may have endured because they were so well matched. Both were at the zeniths of their careers, and neither had reason to be jealous of the other's success. In personality and temperament they were synchronized opposites: Gable quiet and easygoing, Lombard boisterous and high-strung. As a couple, they struck a happy medium between the two extremes. Astrologically speaking, they were also ideally suited as air signs (Aquarius and Libra).

But the most important bonding agent seemed to be Lombard's determination to make the marriage a lasting success. From childhood she had always wanted to be the best and to have the best in everything. After she achieved that as an actress, she went after it in her private life, setting her sights on one of the most desired men in the world and netting him. If their marriage didn't work, Carole Lombard would be a loser for the first time in her life.

She succeeded by subordinating herself to Gable yet never giving up her own identity or individuality. As a friend recalled, "She was so vital, so full of the joy of living, that she carried everything and everybody along in her lighthearted wake. The atmosphere of love and companionship, the 'Clark comes first' attitude in all her thinking, had its effect on Clark. With Carole he began to relax, to be free, to shake off the old fears and depressions."

By the completion of *They Met in Bombay* in April, MGM had released *Comrade X,* which proved another hit, though hardly in a class with *GWTW* or *Boom Town.* But *Comrade X* did substantially better than its Russian cousin *Ninotchka,* which was probably due to the declining popularity of Greta Garbo with American moviegoers. Her films had long earned their profits from Europe, but release there had now become minimal due to the spreading war.

Carole Lombard also enjoyed a success with *Mr. and Mrs. Smith,* not a large one but enough to indicate that she'd made the right choice in returning to the type of comedy roles that made her so popular. For the moment, of course, she didn't want to work, but she started phoning around and asking writer and director friends to send scripts that might suit her.

Four months had passed since the trip to Johns Hopkins, but Lombard still wasn't the least bit pregnant. She thought maybe she'd been trying *too* hard. When Gable proposed a fishing trip, she decided that it couldn't do her any harm as long as she didn't overexert herself. They loaded up the station wagon and drove to the Rogue River in southern Oregon.

Unfortunately, locals discovered the Gables' campsite and started coming around to gawk. After a few days the couple lost patience and drove home. Gable still wanted a break, so he arranged for Paul Mantz to fly them to Lake Mead in Nevada. The couple rented a cabin cruiser and spent several days sailing around and getting acquainted with the artificial wonder, which had been formed in 1936 with water from the brand-new Boulder Dam (later renamed Hoover Dam).

On June 2, 1941, Gable reported back to MGM to start *Honky Tonk,* which was deliberately titled to resemble that of the smash hit *Boom Town* and teamed him with the studio's hot new star, Lana Turner. Jack Conway, who directed *Boom Town,* would again be at the helm, with Pandro S. Berman, former studio head of RKO, as producer.

Scripted by Marguerite Roberts and John Sanford, *Honky Tonk* was Gable's first western since *The Painted Desert,* though it was more like *San Francisco* transferred to a small town on the prairie. Blackie Norton was now Candy Johnson, a fugitive con artist who lands in lawless Yellow Creek and rapidly takes control of its gambling, vice, and politics. Along the way, he falls for and marries the innocent Boston-reared Lucy Cotton, who has a powerful influence on turning him honest for the inevitable happy ending.

Twenty-one-year-old Lana Turner had joined MGM in 1938, so Gable knew her casually from around the studio. In fact, the natural brunette owed her current golden hair to a dye job for *Idiot's Delight,* in which she was supposed to play one of the six Les Blondes. But an emergency operation for a pelvic infection (from a previous botched surgery for appendicitis) landed her in the hospital instead, and another starlet took the role. Since then MGM had moved Turner along from supporting parts in the *Andy Hardy* and *Dr. Kildare* series to one of the title roles, along with Judy Garland and Hedy Lamarr, in *Ziegfeld Girl.* In the process the well-stacked Turner also received a publicity buildup as "the Sweater Girl" and made personal headlines by marrying and then quickly divorcing clarinetist-bandleader Artie Shaw, who was the king of pop music at the time.

In *Ziegfeld Girl,* Turner was romanced by James Stewart and Ian Hunter. In the subsequent *Dr. Jekyll and Mr. Hyde* she was courted by the good side of Spencer Tracy, while Ingrid Bergman grappled with the evil. But *Honky Tonk* was Turner's first shot at a full-fledged star vehicle. She received equal billing with Gable above the title. It was the most that any costar could hope for, since Gable's contract guaranteed him first position.

Since breaking with Artie Shaw, Turner had been involved with attorney Greg Bautzer and millionaire Howard Hughes. Gossip columnists had her pegged as a climber of the famous and influential, so all were watching to see what happened when she started working with the King of Hollywood.

The curious included Mrs. Gable, who turned up on the set while her husband and Turner were rehearsing their first love scene. When Turner spotted Lombard, she later remembered that "my knees went watery, and I became so flustered that I excused myself and fled to my dressing trailer. I stayed there, trying to collect myself, until a knock came on the door. 'They're ready to shoot, Miss Turner,' a voice said. When I peeked out, there was no sign of Carole Lombard.

"I assume that Clark must have asked her to leave, saying that the kid was nervous. I apologized to him for running off, pretending that I'd left something in my trailer. That famous smile lit up his face. He said simply, 'I understand.' ''

During the six weeks of production, rumors flew of a Gable-Turner fling. Years later Turner described her relationship with Gable as "a closeness without intimacy. There was a dear loving for him but never an affair. No way."

Gable and Turner had four bedroom scenes, where she wore revealing negligées or black lace undergarments designed by Robert Kalloch, a new addition to the studio's costumers. Working under such intimate conditions, it wouldn't be surprising if some personal interaction did take place.

In any case, Gable treated Turner tenderly, realizing that she was an untrained actress and barely out of her teens. Whenever she fluffed a line, he'd say, "That's all right, baby. Don't you worry about it." Then he'd blow one of his own lines so that she wouldn't feel so bad.

But there were limits to his patience. One day Turner turned up several hours late, keeping everyone waiting on the set. Gable growled at her, "The next time you do that, you won't find me here, and I won't be back. They'll have to start over with some other poor bastard in my boots."

With *Honky Tonk* and *They Met in Bombay,* Gable fulfilled his contractual requirement of two pictures per year. He had the balance of 1941 free except for being on call for publicity, press interviews, and the like. With Lombard also on sabbatical, the couple divided their time between the ranch and treks into the great outdoors.

It was an odd existence for two symbols of Hollywood glamour, but they loved it. "We die if we have to go out of an evening," Lombard once said. Their favorite parlor games were backgammon and showdown poker. Both were avid readers. Gable favored mystery novels and pulp detective magazines. Lombard tried to keep up with all the latest novels, usually with an eye toward their movie potential.

Once or twice a year Lombard staged a "fun party" for the Gables' friends and coworkers. The gatherings were never as wacky as some she had arranged in the early days when she was trying to make a name for herself, but they always had a gimmick. One night arriving guests found the Gables' patio set up for a twelve-piece orchestra, with all the necessary instruments, but with no musicians to play them. Lombard urged everybody to choose something and to form a band. Gable sat in on drums, Fred MacMurray on saxophone, and Buster Collier at the piano. Spencer Tracy played bass, while Robert Taylor and Dick Powell joined the brass section. Lombard took up the trumpet and also did an impersonation of Ina Ray Hutton, the blond bombshell bandleader.

Late one afternoon the Gables were sitting in the yard, sipping drinks and watching the sun go down. Mellowed by several scotches, Gable said, "Ma, we're lucky people. We've got this ranch, and while it's not going to support us, it feels like a ranch, it smells and looks like a ranch. It's not just animals and hay. We've got the house fixed just to suit us, we've both got good jobs, friends, money in the bank, and our health. God's been good to us. Can you think of anything you really want that you haven't got?"

Lombard sucked on the straw of her Coca-Cola before answering. "Pa, to tell you the truth, I could use a couple of loads of horseshit to spread around the rosebushes."

Always very close with her mother and two brothers, Lombard tried to improve relations between Gable and his father, but both men seemed too stubborn to change. Though Gable supported his father and stepmother financially, the elder kept telling him that his MGM salary was "just whistling and tobacco-chewing money" compared to what he could have earned if he'd become an oil wildcatter instead.

In Will Gable's view, his son could never do anything right. One weekend Gable and buddy Al Menasco had just finished putting up a new fence at the ranch when Will Gable happened to drop by. Looking the job over, Will told his son, "Now, Kid, I taught you how to build fences better than that." He ordered "the Kid" and his friend to tear down the fence and nail it back together the right way. Lombard, who'd been watching, shrieked with laughter.

As much as the Gables enjoyed their twenty-acre enclave, they were finding it increasingly difficult to maintain any privacy. The ranch's location was included on the maps of movie stars' homes that were purchased by tourists and locals alike. Sight-seeing buses drove by several times daily. Fans often tried to scale the high chain-link fence that surrounded the property.

Since most of the climbers were female, ranging in age from seventeen to seventy, Clark Gable seemed the main cause of the problem. The

MGM police force sometimes had to be called to eject them, though every effort was made to do it quietly and gently. The couple's secretary, Jean Garceau, kept a "crazy woman file" on all incidents, in case the intruders ever tried to retaliate with a lawsuit.

During hunting and fishing trips that summer, the Gables looked at properties in California, Oregon, Nevada, and Arizona. Business advisers urged them to buy a working cattle ranch of about a thousand acres, which would be self-sustaining. Lombard, still intent on parenthood, was all for retiring from acting. Gable could commute to MGM for his two pictures per year.

But by September, as Lombard neared the end of her self-imposed sabbatical for baby-making, she was still not pregnant and was becoming increasingly depressed over her failure. She and Gable decided that the best thing for her to do was to resume working. It would put her mind on other matters and didn't mean that the couple had to stop trying.

During her year off Lombard had dropped agent Myron Selznick and encouraged one of his associates, Nat Wolff, to open an office and to take her on as his first client. To shake loose from Myron Selznick, Lombard had to pay him $27,500, which equaled his estimated commissions on the balance of their contract. But Lombard thought it was well worth it because Selznick's boozing, womanizing, and gambling had become more important to him than taking care of business. Lombard was the first of many dissatisfied Myron Selznick clients to desert him before he died from alcoholism in 1944 at age forty-five.

Nat Wolff quickly made two deals for Lombard, the first for *To Be or Not to Be,* an Ernst Lubitsch production for United Arists release, and the second for Columbia Pictures' *They All Kissed the Bride.* Due to the disappointing box-office takings of her four RKO movies, Lombard had to lower her asking price. For the opportunity to work with Lubitsch, she agreed to take $75,000, with another $75,000 to be paid later from the movie's profits. Columbia would pay her a flat $112,500 for what would amount to a maximum of six weeks' work.

Before Lombard started filming, the Gables and their friends Harry and Nan Fleischmann headed for South Dakota for the opening of the duck-and-pheasant-hunting season. Due to bad weather their plane flight from Los Angeles got grounded in Albuquerque. To make new connections they had to take a train to Kansas City and stay overnight at the Muehlebach Hotel. The manager and staff gave them such a fawning welcome that Gable couldn't stand it, so he phoned the airline and demanded that his party be flown to South Dakota immediately. The airline had only one of its big transcontinental planes available. The Gables and Fleischmanns were its only passengers, but due to its size, it had to land at Omaha, Nebraska, where they were shifted to a Piper Cub for the final flight to Watertown, South Dakota.

The two couples rented rooms in a private home. Within two days they had bagged their full quota of birds and were ready to return to Los Angeles. More bad weather threatened a repeat of their earlier flying problems, so Gable went to the local Ford dealer and bought another station wagon to add to his fleet of vehicles. He and Harry Fleischmann took turns driving on the twelve-hundred-mile trip back across portions of Nebraska, Colorado, and Arizona.

Along the way the Gables saw some beautiful country and talked again of resettling. As a first step Lombard consulted several real estate agents about selling the Encino ranch. Purchased three years before for $50,000, it could probably fetch $85,000 in the current market. Some private viewings were arranged, though never with the Gables present. When they learned that a prospective buyer had also propositioned the servants to come to work for him, whether he bought the place or not, they decided to take it off the market.

On October 29 Lombard reported for *To Be or Not to Be,* which Ernst Lubitsch had organized independently with producer Alexander Korda for distribution by United Artists after all the major studios rejected it as too controversial. Set in Nazi-occupied Poland, the satiric comedy told of two married stage stars who are trying to put on a production of *Hamlet* while constantly being harassed by the Gestapo. Jack Benny, the ultrapopular radio comedian who dabbled at moviemaking, portrayed Lombard's husband.

Ironically, Ernst Lubitsch had been the first movie director with whom Clark Gable ever worked, albeit as a lowly extra in the silent *Forbidden Paradise.* When Lombard invited Lubitsch to the ranch for dinner one evening, he jokingly proposed remaking the sex farce with Lombard as Catherine the Great and Gable as her hussar-lover.

On Sunday morning, December 7, Gable was in the stable grooming the horses, when Lombard came bursting in with news that she'd just heard on the radio. Japanese planes had attacked and bombed the U.S. Navy base at Pearl Harbor near Honolulu, Hawaii. The Gables returned to the house and stuck close to the radio to follow the breaking story. For reasons of security and public morale, the broadcasts were censored and the details were sketchy, but it became plain that the death toll and loss of American ships and planes were catastrophic.

Lombard was due to make a guest appearance that evening on Jack Benny's weekly radio show to promote *To Be or Not to Be*. But she received a call from NBC that all of its regular programming had been suspended and that the broadcast would be rescheduled for a later date.

The ongoing news bulletins indicated that the U.S. would declare war on Japan within twenty-four hours and that the country would also soon be dragged into the European conflict due to Japan's Axis pact with Germany and Italy. Lombard got so fired up that she persuaded Gable to join her in writing a letter to President Roosevelt, reminding him of their promise to help in the war effort.

By the end of the week the United States had officially entered World War II on all fronts. On the set of *To Be or Not to Be*, Ernst Lubitsch, a German-born Jew directing an anti-Nazi film, was personally embarrassed by a visit from FBI agents who were investigating his German-born butler. The man turned out to be the paymaster for a ring of Nazi spies and was promptly arrested.

Despite his role in the world crisis, President Roosevelt somehow managed a prompt answer to the letter from the Gables. It was just a short note that thanked them for their support but said that they could best serve their country by continuing to make movies, which were essential to boosting public morale in a very worrying time. "You are needed where you are," FDR wrote.

Lombard, who usually agreed with the president, thought him wrong this time. She wanted Gable to enlist in military service. For herself, she envisioned joining the Red Cross or one of the anticipated female auxiliaries of the army and navy.

Verging on forty-one, Gable was well above draft age and had no wish to give up his exceedingly comfortable existence. Lombard kept badgering him, but she also had to contend with MGM. The studio's stars were its most important assets. L. B. Mayer wanted to hold on to as many as he could. He had already lost James Stewart and Robert

Montgomery, who had enlisted even before Pearl Harbor. He was currently fighting the 1-A draft classification of twenty-one-year-old Mickey Rooney, on the grounds of essentiality.

To counter Mrs. Gable's efforts to persuade her husband to enlist, Mayer asked Lowell Mellett, FDR's newly appointed liaison with the motion picture industry, to intervene. Mellett told Gable that he could best serve the war effort by providing entertainment, keeping up public morale, and paying his gigantic income tax. After the meeting Mellett stated to columnist Walter Winchell that "Gable's one of the people's daily habits. We don't want to rob them of their steady habits all at once. That's the one thing we've copied from Goebbels's propaganda machine."

MGM immediately announced that Gable's next movie would be a patriotic flag-waver entitled *Somewhere I'll Find You,* in which he would portray a war correspondent caught up in the Japanese invasion of Indochina. Lombard bemoaned the casting of Lana Turner as Gable's costar, but she had to admit that it made box-office sense. Except for *GWTW,* which continued to amaze in its switch-over to general release at ordinary admission prices, *Honky Tonk* was MGM's biggest grosser of 1941. *Life* magazine had declared Gable and Turner an "electric combination" that deserved repeating.

One day while Gable was at the studio for wardrobe fittings, he received a rare summons to the office of L. B. Mayer, with instructions to first take a gander at a tall brunette sitting in the waiting room. Gable was so impressed that he gave a wolf whistle as he glided into his audience with Mayer, who wanted him to make a screen test with the young woman.

"Do me a favor," Mayer said. "Her name is Esther Williams. She's a swimming champion that we've just signed to a contract. She doesn't think that she can be an actress. Convince her that she can."

Needless to say, Gable did. He patiently guided the eighteen-year-old through a test that gave her enough confidence to attempt a tiny part in *Andy Hardy's Double Life.* A slow learner, she would not be cast in a starring role until 1944, when she was finally permitted to do what she did best, in *Bathing Beauty.*

Through the intervention of MGM, "King" Gable was appointed chairman of the Screen Actors Division of the Hollywood Victory

Committee, an industrywide group set up to organize all activities supporting the war effort. The first meeting of Gable's division was held on December 22 at his onetime residence, the Beverly Wilshire Hotel. The gathering was one of the last displays of Hollywood glitz, which would be put into mothballs for the sake of wartime austerity. Most everyone came dressed to the nines, the women in furs and dripping with jewels. Lombard wore a black silk ensemble and told everyone that she was disguised as a blackout.

Gable was elected to head a committee of fifteen that would select and book talent for bond rallies, camp shows, and hospital tours. Serving under him on the committee were Myrna Loy, Claudette Colbert, Charles Boyer, Bob Hope, Rosalind Russell, John Garfield, Bette Davis, Tyrone Power, Gary Cooper, Ginger Rogers, Ronald Colman, Cary Grant, Irene Dunne, and Jack Benny. As the chairman's wife, Lombard was the first to pledge her cooperation. She was quickly followed by Marlene Dietrich, Jeanette MacDonald, Henry Fonda, George Raft, Merle Oberon, Rudy Vallee, Carole Landis, and Kay Kyser.

Two days later, on Christmas Eve, *To Be or Not to Be* finished filming. At the wrap party on the set, Carole Lombard doled out gifts to everyone and then left, announcing that "I've had a swell time, but Clark and I have a more important job to do now. We're going to entertain a bunch of soldiers for Christmas." She drove to MGM, where Gable served as host to several busloads of men from bases in the area. Judy Garland, Mickey Rooney, Red Skelton, Eleanor Powell, and other studio stars put on a special Christmas revue, with Wallace Beery as Santa Claus.

The Gables' personal holiday celebration was subdued that year. Lombard had no time for decorating the house or shopping, so most people on the couple's gift list received an engraved card indicating that a donation had been made in their name to the Red Cross. Their gifts to each other were also simple, but not paper. Gable gave Lombard a pair of ruby-and-diamond clips to match the previous Christmas's ruby heart. She presented him with an ultrathin gold cigarette case inscribed, "Pa, dear—I love you—Ma."

But Christmas took second place to the war news, none of it happy. Wake Island and Hong Kong had fallen to Japan. London was under heavy bombardment by Germany. Right at home fears were increasing of Japanese sneak attacks on the Pacific coast. Public air-raid drills were being held. The Gables loaned their horses to the mounted squadron of air-raid wardens that patrolled the San Fernando Valley.

Lombard still wanted Gable to enter military service. A new bill just passed by Congress could accomplish that if he didn't enlist first. All men between eighteen and sixty-four were required to register for the draft. But at present only those from twenty to forty-four were being called, with the youngest first.

MGM was being pilloried in the press for its efforts to defer Mickey Rooney, so the studio decided to tread more carefully with Gable. If he really wanted to serve, he should, but under conditions appropriate to "the King of Hollywood." His chief image polisher, Howard Strickling, envisioned him as an officer, with a posh desk job in Washington. L. B. Mayer agreed. He didn't fancy such a box-office asset becoming an ordinary soldier or sailor and possibly getting killed.

Lombard raised another ruckus, telling Strickling that "the last thing I want for Pappy is one of those phony commissions." She believed that his enlisting as a private would set a good example and inspire other men into doing the same.

As 1942 began, MGM set January 15 as the starting date for *Somewhere I'll Find You*. In the meantime Gable continued working for the Hollywood Victory Committee. When a request came in from Indiana for a star to launch the state's participation in the national campaign to sell war bonds, Gable naturally thought of his Hoosier-born wife. She was thrilled by the prospect and instantly agreed to make the trip.

Lombard wanted Gable to accompany her, but his commitment to *Somewhere I'll Find You* made that impossible. Instead she insisted on taking her mother, who hadn't been back to Indiana for many years. Gable arranged for their MGM publicist-friend, Otto Winkler, to go along as tour manager and chaperon to the two women.

Though Lombard's final destination was Indianapolis, she would travel from Los Angeles by train, making short stopovers at Salt Lake City and Chicago en route and at Kansas City and Albuquerque on the return trip. The tour was to be entirely by rail, which was less prone to weather delays than plane flights. At each stop there would be a public reception at the train station, with Lombard delivering a pep talk on war bonds. (These interest-bearing seven-year bonds, as well as small-denomination stamps that could eventually be converted to bonds, were sold by the Treasury Department to raise funding for the war effort.)

Prior to Lombard's departure on January 12, she and Gable tiffed over his upcoming work reunion with Lana Turner, which was due to start on the same day that she arrived in Indianapolis. She warned him against any hanky-panky with Turner and also threw in the names of two MGM starlets whom she considered husband-stealers. According to several of the couple's friends, a fierce argument erupted. Gable got so agitated that he finally stormed out and spent the night elsewhere.

Whatever happened, Gable was conspicuously absent when Lombard and party entrained from Union Station in downtown Los Angeles. Before Lombard left the house, she handed secretary Jean Garceau some sealed envelopes containing notes to Gable, which were to be given to him at the rate of one a day. Upstairs, in Gable's bed, she'd placed a naked blond dummy, with a tag tied around its neck: "So you won't be lonely." Where Lombard got it is unknown, but the prank obviously required advance planning and must have been in the works before she and Gable quarreled.

He returned to the ranch the next day. When he found the dummy blonde in his bed, he howled with laughter. To even the score, Gable phoned a friend in the MGM prop department and asked him to prepare a male dummy, with a huge erect phallus, to surprise Lombard when she got home.

Lombard tried to call Gable whenever she could get to a phone. They finally connected and, according to secretary Jean Garceau, sounded like lovebirds.

Despite freezing and snowy weather, Lombard attracted large crowds at her first stop in Salt Lake City. By the time she reached Chicago, she was so bursting with patriotic fervor that she telegraphed Gable: HEY PAPPY, YOU'D BETTER GET INTO THIS MAN'S ARMY.

Together with her mother and Otto Winkler, Lombard arrived in Indianapolis in the early morning of January 15 and was rushed by motorcade to the statehouse for a flag-raising ceremony. She gave the thousands of spectators the V-for-Victory sign and shouted, "Heads up, hands up, America! Let's give a cheer that will be heard in Tokyo and Berlin!"

For the next eight hours, Lombard held court at a desk in the rotunda of the statehouse, selling bonds and signing autographs for everyone who purchased some. "I'm like a barker at a carnival," she laughed. The Treasury Department had given her a quota of $500,000. By lunchtime sales had passed $1 million. At the end of the day they totaled $2,017,513.

That evening, garbed in a strapless black velvet gown, Lombard was the epitome of Hollywood glamour as she participated in a patriotic pageant on the stage of Cadle Tabernacle. Three military bands and choirs from Indiana and Purdue Universities performed. At the finale Lombard commanded the groups and the audience to join her in "The Star-Spangled Banner." Overcome by the excitement, she broke into tears.

Lombard and party were supposed to stay in Indianapolis overnight and take a train back to Los Angeles the next day. Two more bond-promoting stops were scheduled for Kansas City and Albuquerque.

But Lombard suddenly decided that she wanted to go home immediately—by plane. She told her mother that she was too exhausted to continue the tour, but she had additional reasons as well. She was eager to get back to Gable, especially now that he had actually started working with Lana Turner. She'd also been informed of a sneak theater preview of *To Be or Not to Be* on January 18, which she hoped to attend.

Bessie Peters, who'd never flown before and was terrified by the prospect, tried to dissuade her daughter. Otto Winkler also balked because it meant canceling the remainder of the Treasury Department–sponsored tour. Lombard still insisted but finally agreed to settle it with the toss of a coin. Heads they'd go by train, tails by plane. Winkler took a nickel from his pocket and flipped it in the air. Lombard won.

Due to the wartime emergency, all flights were heavily booked, but Otto Winkler succeeded in getting them on a TWA service that left Indianapolis at four in the morning and was scheduled to arrive at Burbank Airport in Los Angeles that evening. It had originated in New York and made numerous stops, but it was the best that Winkler could do. He cabled Howard Strickling with the details and told him to advise Gable of the change in plans.

Lombard's mother was an avid believer in numerology. En route to the airport, she did some figuring and grew even more frightened and nervous about the trip. The date had advanced to January 16, and the number sixteen was an omen of accident or death. The TWA flight was number three and the aircraft a Douglas DC-3, three being another number that Mrs. Peters considered unlucky. Furthermore, they were a traveling party of three, and one of them—the movie star—was thirty-three years old. Bessie begged her to reconsider and to go later by train, but Lombard only laughed. She told her mother that if she kept it up, she'd have her committed to a lunatic asylum when they got home.

After a smooth takeoff, Bessie Peters calmed down and fell asleep. Three stops later, in Wichita, Kansas, the touring concert violinist Joseph Szigeti, also bound for Los Angeles, became another passenger. At the next landing, in Albuquerque, he was among four who agreed to take a later flight so that some army pilots and soldiers headed for West Coast bases could be accommodated.

The chief TWA pilot, Wayne Williams, also asked Lombard to relinquish her seats because three more servicemen were waiting. Though never one to pull rank, Lombard was concerned about her mother and insisted that she had priority due to her mission for the Treasury Department. If they disembarked at Albuquerque, it would mean staying overnight and trying to get on one of the next day's flights.

Due to the changes in the passenger list, departure from Albuquerque was delayed. The next and last stop before Burbank was supposed to be Boulder, Colorado, where the landing field had a daylight-only restriction. Since night was already falling, TWA diverted the flight to Las Vegas, which had a more modern airport with full service. In either case, the main reason for the stopover was to refuel the aircraft. At full capacity the dual-engine plane consumed gasoline faster than when flying at less.

Flight number three landed at Las Vegas at 6:30 P.M. After servicing, it took off again at 7:07. Expected arrival time in Los Angeles was 8:45.

I t'll sure be nice having Ma back. Life without her around ain't hardly worth living," Clark Gable said as he helped the servants to decorate the dining room with red, white, and blue balloons and crepe-paper streamers. He'd arranged a surprise party for the returning war bonds trio. Joining in the celebration were his two brothers-in-law, Stuart and Frederick Peters; Fred's wife, Virginia; and Otto Winkler's wife, Jill. Bouquets of red roses graced every room. Gable wanted the house to be lit only by candles when the travelers arrived.

Upstairs in Lombard's bedroom, that other surprise awaited her. Gable had brought it home from the studio that afternoon and placed it in her bed under a quilt so that its protuberance created a tentlike effect.

Aware that Lombard's airport arrival would attract a mob of reporters and photographers, he deliberately stayed away. Proud of her for undertaking the bond tour, he didn't want to be accused of trying to steal some of her glory. MGM publicist Larry Barbier and a studio limousine had been dispatched to pick up the trio and to deliver them to the ranch. Barbier promised to telephone Gable as soon as the plane landed.

A call finally came, but the voice was that of Eddie Mannix, Gable's best friend in the MGM hierarchy. "Can I get back to you?" Gable asked. "I'm expecting word on Ma's arrival any minute."

"King, that's why I'm calling," Mannix said. "Larry Barbier just phoned from the airport. Carole's plane went down just a few minutes after it left Las Vegas."

Gable blanched. "How bad do you think it is?"

"Nobody knows yet," Mannix said, "but we'd better get over to Vegas right away. Howard Strickling's chartering a plane. We're sending a car over in a few minutes to take you to the airport."

Gable insisted on taking Jill Winkler and Lombard's favorite brother, Stuart, with him. By the time MGM's chartered flight reached Las Vegas, rescue operations were well under way, so there was nothing to do but wait. The night sky over the Nevada desert was still as clear and star bright as when flight number three took off. In the outline of distant mountains, Gable could see a glowing crimson spot that was believed to be burning wreckage from the plane.

MGM booked everyone into the El Rancho Vegas Hotel, with Gable getting an individual bungalow. He wanted to join the next rescue group that left, but Eddie Mannix talked him out of it and went instead. Mannix feared the worst and wanted to spare his friend an agonizing sight. "Suppose the first party brings Carole back and you're not here to greet her," Mannix said, trying to keep his hopes up.

Gable spent the rest of the night in the bungalow. The hotel management surrounded it with security guards as an ever-enlarging crowd of press and radio reporters, photographers, and curiosity seekers swept into town. It was one of the first major mishaps in the short history of large multipassenger planes.

Although Howard Strickling stayed with him, Gable spoke hardly a word. He just paced the floor, trembling, and smoking one cigarette after another.

Rescuers were headed for Mount Potosi, thirty miles southwest of Las Vegas. Better known to locals as Table Rock Mountain, it rose to a peak of 8,500 feet. There were no roads up, only trails buried beneath several feet of snow. An Indian guide leading the expedition guessed that it would take twelve to fifteen hours to reach the site of the crash.

Early the next morning, Gable received a telegram from Eddie Mannix, who'd sent it from a miners' way station on the mountain: NO SUR-VIVORS. ALL KILLED INSTANTLY.

Gable crushed the message in his hand and walked out onto the porch. In the bright daylight he could see Table Rock Mountain clearly. No tears came to his eyes, but sorrow was written all over his face. He went back inside and plunked down in a chair. By this time his and Lombard's close friends, Al Menasco and Buster Collier, had arrived by car from Los Angeles. They tried to get him to eat some breakfast, but he refused. He even passed up offers of scotch and bourbon, claiming that he felt numb already.

"Why did Ma have to go?" Gable kept asking. "Did you ever see anyone more beautiful? There was never a person in the world who was so generous, so full of fun. God damn it, why Ma?"

Flight number three had collided headlong into a rock cliff about 730 feet below the summit of the mountain, splitting in two upon impact. The front section, in which Lombard, her mother, and Otto Winkler were among those seated, was compressed into a mass about ten feet long and was partly consumed in the ensuing explosion.

When Eddie Mannix reached the wreckage, he found the mountain snow splattered with blood. The air reeked of what an Indian guide said was the aroma of burnt human flesh. The bodies were charred beyond recognition. Some, including one believed to be Lombard's, had been decapitated prior to the fiery explosion. Twenty-two people had perished, including fifteen army pilots and soldiers and the TWA crew of three.

Tangled in a piece of debris, Mannix found a few strands of light-blond hair that he thought were Lombard's. Someone also discovered a portion of a diamond-and-ruby clip that Mannix immediately identified as from the pair that Gable gave to Lombard last Christmas. The matching heart-shaped ruby pendant was never found. A legend grew that it had been embedded in Lombard's own heart by the force of the crash.

When Mannix returned to the bungalow at El Rancho Vegas, he handed the clip remnant to Gable, half-expecting him to break down. Gable faltered, but caught himself. "Do you think she knew just before?" he asked.

"No," Mannix said. "It happened too quickly." He refrained from describing the horrors he'd seen. He told Gable that the trail to the accident site was so narrow and treacherous that it would take two or three days to bring down all the remains. In the meantime there wasn't much that they could do but wait.

Gable asked to be driven to the foot of the mountain. When he got there, he walked off by himself to look for signs of the crash. They weren't hard to spot. The burning plane had ignited a forest fire in a ravine directly below. The flames and smoke had left a huge black smudge on the rocky cliffs surrounding the wreckage. Gable stood staring for several minutes. It was the final confirmation that he needed.

Meanwhile Carole Lombard's death was being treated like a

national tragedy. President Roosevelt sent Gable the following telegram: "Mrs. Roosevelt and I are deeply distressed. Carole was our friend, our guest in happier days. She brought great joy to all who knew her and to millions who knew her only as a great artist. She gave unselfishly of her time and talent to serve her government in peace and in war. She loved her country. She is and always will be a star, one we shall never forget nor cease to be grateful to. Deepest sympathy."

Later FDR awarded Lombard a medal as "the first woman to be killed in action in the defense of her country in its war against the Axis powers."

In Hollywood on January 19, the first working day since the tragedy, every studio paused at noon for the playing of taps and two minutes of silence in Lombard's honor. Gossip columnists Louella Parsons and Hedda Hopper were in rare agreement, urging readers to remember Carole Lombard by buying more bonds for victory.

Gable's longtime employer placed full-page ads in Hollywood's two daily trade papers, featuring an ultraglamorous recent photograph of Lombard juxtaposed with a caricature of its registered trademark. Dressed in a formal black mourning suit, Leo the Lion stood with his head bowed and held a large wreath in one paw.

The Civil Aeronautics Board had started an investigation of the crash. Due to the fifteen servicemen aboard, the War Department and the FBI were also studying the possibility of enemy sabotage. Twelve of the victims were pilots and would be sorely missed at a time when the United States was underprepared and suffering heavy combat losses.

But the CAB finally found overwhelming proof of "pilot's error," meaning that Captain Wayne Williams had failed to "follow the proper course by making use of the navigational facilities available to him." After taking off from Las Vegas, Williams had allegedly changed direction in order to make up for lost time. If he'd been flying only another 750 feet higher, he should have made it over the mountain.

Gable refused to leave Las Vegas without taking three caskets with him. What exactly they contained may never be known due to the charred and/or incomplete corpses of the twenty-two victims. But possibly something of Carole Lombard Gable, Elizabeth Peters, and Otto Winkler ended up in the oblong boxes bearing their names.

Gable returned to Los Angeles by train, with his cargo in the baggage car. To escape the herd of reporters and photographers at the terminal, he was sneaked on board to his private compartment from the opposite side of the platform. To avoid the same kind of hassle at L.A.'s Union Station, MGM arranged for Gable to disembark at the stop ahead at Colton, where a limousine awaited him and a mortuary van took the caskets to temporary storage until funeral arrangements were made. Gable couldn't face going back to the ranch, so he'd arranged to stay at the home of his friends, the Al Menascos, in San Gabriel.

Since Lombard had been on a patriotic mission, the War Department wanted to give her a full-scale military funeral. A rifle squad, marching band, and troop of men were already being drilled at the army camp that now occupied part of sprawling Griffith Park. Gable, however, declined the War Department's offer when he discovered that his wife had requested something quite different in her last will and testament.

As a precaution against such public spectacles as the one for Jean Harlow, Lombard had insisted on a simple private service, limited to family and very close friends. She left exact instructions for the texts to be read and the music to be played. She also wanted to be buried in a white gown designed by Irene.

Gable tried to comply, but there was one major change that his wife could never have anticipated when she made the will. It would be a double funeral: for Carole Lombard Gable and for her mother, Elizabeth Knight Peters.

The services were held on January 21 at the Church of the Recessional at Forest Lawn Memorial Park. In keeping with Lombard's wish, reporters, photographers, and the public were barred, but a few longtime press friends like Louella Parsons, Adela Rogers St. Johns, and Lloyd Pantages made the invitation list. Lombard's first husband, William Powell, was part of the star contingent, along with Spencer Tracy, Myrna Loy, Jack Benny, Fred MacMurray, and Dorothy Lamour.

Gable sat in a private family room, flanked by his father and stepmother. Lombard's two brothers and their wives shared a pew with Bess Peters's three sisters. All told, there were forty-six mourners in a chapel that could hold 150.

The two dark-gray steel coffins were closed and covered with blankets of gardenias and orchids. Before sealing Lombard's, a mortician added the white Irene gown to the contents.

Gordon Chapman, a Methodist minister, conducted the service, which exactly followed Lombard's instructions. Readings were from the Old and New Testaments and some of Lombard's favorite poetry. At the conclusion Reverend Chapman recited two lines from the teachings of Persian philosopher Baha Ullah that reflected the mother's and daughter's lifelong infatuation with the religion of Baha'i: "I have made death even as glad tidings unto thee. Why dost thou mourn at its approach?"

Interment was in the Sanctuary of Trust in the Great Mausoleum at Forest Lawn. In her will Lombard specified a "modestly priced crypt." Gable purchased three adjoining wall vaults. Lombard was entombed in the center vault, with her mother to the right. The vault to the left of Lombard was reserved for Gable when his time came.

After the funeral Gable returned to the ranch for the first time since his wife's death. Secretary Jean Garceau, who still had one note remaining from the batch that Lombard wrote for Gable before she left on the bond tour, decided that he should have it.

After Gable read whatever was contained therein, he broke down, with tears in his eyes. "Up until then," Jean Garceau recalled, "Clark had borne himself with fortitude and courage, had been stronger than any of us throughout the entire ordeal. After he calmed down, he was again in perfect control, his grief masked. He asked no sympathy, wanted none, was unapproachable."

The next day Gable had one more funeral to attend. In some ways it was the hardest because he loved thirty-six-year-old Otto Winkler like a brother and considered himself responsible for his death. They first met in 1937, when Winkler was a *Herald-Examiner* reporter assigned to cover the Violet Norton paternity trial. Gable liked Winkler's coverage and got him a publicist's job at MGM. Winkler became Gable's contact with the press and had been his best man at the wedding.

Gable escorted widow Jill Winkler to the religious service and to the burial at Hollywood Memorial Cemetery. He promised Mrs. Winkler that he would do everything he could to provide for her future. The couple had no children.

He now had to make some decisions about his own future. MGM had suspended production of *Somewhere I'll Find You,* which had started filming the day before Lombard's death. Depending on how Gable felt about it, the studio was considering replacing him with

Robert Taylor, who'd just proved very compatible with Lana Turner in *Johnny Eager.*

Lombard's death also affected two other films. United Artists postponed the release of *To Be or Not to Be* for one month to permit "a suitable period of public mourning." Director Ernst Lubitsch also decided to cut a line of dialogue in a scene where Lombard and Jack Benny are making plans to escape from Warsaw and she says, "What can happen in a plane?"

Joan Crawford volunteered to take over Lombard's pending project, *They All Kissed the Bride.* MGM, which had just about given up on Crawford as a box-office magnet, was happy to loan her to Columbia Pictures. Not to be outdone by Lombard's bond tour, Crawford promptly donated her $112,500 fee to the Red Cross and other war-related charities. When her agent refused to waive his commission and billed her for $11,250, she fired him.

Clark Gable's past romantic history with Crawford was not forgotten by Hollywood gossips, who interpreted her takeover of Lombard's film role as a first step toward becoming the next Mrs. Gable. Crawford had never kept it a secret that she regretted not marrying Gable when they first became involved back in 1931.

Gable finally decided to continue in *Somewhere I'll Find You,* provided that he could first take a month off to rest and adjust. L. B. Mayer agreed. Director Wesley Ruggles would "shoot around" Gable so that all the scenes in which he didn't appear were finished by the time he returned. As luck would have it, Ruggles had directed Gable and Lombard in *No Man of Her Own,* their only film together.

With friends Harry and Nan Fleischmann, Gable headed for the Rogue River in Oregon to do some hunting and fishing, but without Lombard as catalyst the two-week trip didn't brighten his mood. When he returned to the ranch, he was still in a state of shock. He often spoke of Lombard as if she were a living person whom he expected to pop into the room at any moment.

Since the tragedy Gable had lost twenty pounds. He spent hours roaming around the ranch, alone except for Lombard's little dachshund following in his trail. Prior to her death, Commissioner had always ignored Gable, but now he wouldn't leave his side.

Gable's walks often finished in the garage, where he meditated while sitting behind the steering wheel of the Dodge station wagon that the couple had used on so many of their trips together. He never took it out on the road again, but always kept it in immaculate condtion and perfect working order.

Gable instructed the household staff to keep Lombard's bedroom suite exactly as it was on the day she left. Prior to Gable's return, they decided to spare him grief by disposing of the male dummy that he had planted there as a joke. When the rooms were cleaned, every bottle on her dressing table, every article of clothing in her closets, had to be put back in the same place. Even a book that Lombard had been reading, *The Cloud of Unknowing,* was left open to a page that she had marked.

But for all his sorrow, Gable displayed his usual frugality during the legal settlement of Lombard's estate. Clothes that she purchased from the wardrobe that Irene designed for her for *To Be or Not to Be* were returned for a full refund.

Although the press reported that Gable decided to waive his widower's right to sue TWA so that there would be fewer claimants and Otto Winkler's wife would be able to get a bigger cash settlement, the opposite was true. Gable persuaded Jill Winkler to waive *her* right to sue the airline by promising to build her a house and to also provide her with a $100,000 annuity after he settled with TWA. Years later Mrs. Winkler would sue Gable, claiming that he reneged on his promise and never gave her anything more than a house that cost $7,500 to build.

Lombard willed her entire estate to Gable. Separately she had also established trust funds for her mother and for best friend Madalynne Fields Lang. Due to Bessie Peters's death, her $30,000 fund would be divided equally between her two surviving children, Stuart and Frederick. Gable's brothers-in-law were furious and felt cheated. They believed that Gable had coerced their sister into cutting them out of the will. Gable, who'd always barely tolerated them and considered them leeches, broke contact and never spoke to them again.

For a star who'd long been one of the highest paid in Hollywood, Lombard's estate seemed modest. The tax appraiser fixed its value at $300,000, including savings, investments, and personal property such as jewelry and furs. (Some of the most expensive, unfortunately, were uninsured and lost with her in the plane crash.) Not figured in was the Encino ranch, which Lombard had paid for but was purchased in Gable's name. She also left him an annuity of $125,000, as well as her contractual rights in the five movies that she made with a profit participation. None of the four for RKO had done well enough to earn her any royalties, while *To Be or Not to Be* had yet to be released.

On February 23 Gable returned to *Somewhere I'll Find You*. When he realized how the title might be equated with his personal dilemma of the moment, he demanded a change. Producer Pandro Berman selected *Red Light*, which signified absolutely nothing in the movie but put at least a temporary stop to Gable's objection. The original title, which had been in place *before* Lombard's death, seemed a guaranteed crowd-puller and would be restored by release time.

Scripted by Marguerite Roberts, who also wrote *Honky Tonk*, the romantic melodrama gave Gable a younger brother, played by the studio's up-and-coming star, Robert Sterling. While working together as war correspondents for a New York newspaper, they both fall in love with a beautiful cub reporter who is about to be promoted to the foreign desk. When she disappears during an assignment in Indochina, they try to find her. All three eventually wind up on Bataan at the onset of the Japanese invasion. Sterling dies heroically, leaving Gable and the girl, by now a Red Cross nurse, to confront a possibly tragic ending.

Since last working with Gable, Lana Turner had been named "the Girl We'd Most Like to Be Marooned on a Desert Island With" by the student body of the U.S. Naval Academy at Annapolis. In *Somewhere I'll Find You,* she did her bit for the war effort by introducing (with help from hairstylist Sidney Guilaroff) the short "Victory Bob," which hopefully would be widely copied because it saved time and precious bobby pins (which were no longer being manufactured due to war-industry demands for metal).

On Gable's first morning back the cast and crew were nervous and apprehensive. But as a coworker recalled, "If you didn't look closely and ignored his thinness, he was the usual Gable, with the flashing smile and the jaunty wisecracks."

Gable's only deviation from his normal routine was at lunchtimes. He'd always gone to the studio restaurant and sat with friends at one of the communal tables. But now he retired alone to his dressing bungalow and had his meals delivered from the commissary's kitchen.

Just before Gable returned, L. B. Mayer summoned Lana Turner to his office and reminded her to be respectful of her costar's bereavement. "You must be very patient with him," Mayer said. "If his mind should wander, you just be ready at all times. If he wants to come in earlier, you be there before him. If he wants to work past five, do it. A lot of the pressure of this picture is going to be riding on your shoulders. We're trying to arrange for people to go home with him for dinner. If he should ask you, go. Agreed?"

"But I don't know him that well," Turner said.

"Never mind. Just do as I say," Mayer insisted.

"I'll try with all my heart," she promised.

According to Turner, an invitation did come from Gable. "A studio limousine delivered me to the house he had shared with Carole," she remembered. "His butler served the meal. As we ate, I chattered brightly, trying to ease the sorrow that lined his handsome face. But he never mentioned it. He was courtly and cordial and far too private for that."

After dinner, Turner recalled, "Clark showed me his gun collection. He had been polishing some of the pieces—a cherished hobby, I thought, that gave him comfort now. Then the studio limousine arrived to take me home."

In her autobiography, *Lana*, she called that evening "the first and only social occasion" that she ever shared with Gable. "My esteem for him grew even greater," Turner said. "His willingness to finish the film at all showed his decency. And although some say they could see a difference in the way he performed before and after the tragedy, I for one was not able to detect it. He was the consummate professional. No wonder they called him the King."

Joan Crawford, who kept phoning Gable's secretary for updates on his emotional health, finally invited him to dinner at her house in Brentwood. "He needed someone to talk to, and I just listened until three in the morning. He knew I would never repeat anything he said. The next day I received twelve dozen red roses with the longest stems I'd ever seen," she recalled.

When Gable started visiting Crawford several times a week, rumors circulated that they'd resumed their long-ago affair. But Crawford's later memories of those meetings painted a different picture. "He wasn't the gay, romantic Clark I'd first known. He was a moody man who needed friendship. I was afraid that he might drink himself to death. One night

I told him, 'You have a guilt complex because you didn't go with Carole on that trip. You couldn't go, you were working! You've had your grief, Clark, now pull yourself out of it.' "

But it wasn't that easy for Gable. The release of *To Be or Not to Be* brought more public tributes to Carole Lombard, this time directed at her sparkling performance and lamenting that Hollywood had lost an irreplaceable treasure. Though more of a critical success than a box-office smash, the movie was the first and only of her five percentage deals to make money. As Lombard's sole heir, Gable eventually received $57,307 as her share of the producer's profits.

A souvenir pictorial magazine entitled *Carole Lombard's Life Story* suddenly flooded newsstands. Carrying no credit to either author or publisher (allegedly Adela Rogers St. Johns and Hearst Magazines), the thirty-six-page special sold for a dime and was printed in sepia tone with a full-color cover. The text started with a vivid account of Gable taking his wife to the train station for the bond tour and sending her off with a sizzling kiss "of which the Hays Office would not have approved." The scene, of course, never happened. Gable may have wished now that it had.

By this time a Hollywood guessing game had started that will probably never end. If Lombard hadn't died, would the marriage have lasted? Given the discouraging track records of star-crossed marriages, probably not. But Lombard might have *made* it endure because she wasn't the sort to give up easily or to admit defeat. Going through a divorce would have been too humiliating for her. And Gable certainly had no reason to divorce Lombard. He loved her. She made his life perfect and tolerated his philandering.

One thing is certain: Gable spent the rest of his life with Carole Lombard's ghost. Many of the women whom he became seriously involved with resembled her in some way or another. Whether he was consciously seeking *another* Carole Lombard or not, it made stirring romantic fodder for the gossip columnists and fan magazines.

Gable was obviously devastated by the tragedy. It seemed as if his own life had ended when Lombard died. Despite doctors' warnings, he was drinking heavily. He couldn't sleep and often sat up all night watching Lombard's old movies or thumbing through the many scrapbooks that she had kept of their life together. The couple had never gotten around to building a screening room, but Lombard once gifted Gable with a sixteen-millimeter sound projector and folding screen for Christmas. By the time of her death, she had coerced the studios into giving them prints of many of their films.

On May 29 Gable was shattered by the death at sixty of John Barrymore, a longtime drinking buddy and also one of Lombard's best friends since she had worked with him in *Twentieth Century*. Though Barrymore succumbed to a heart attack, he was hospitalized at the time for acute alcoholism, cirrhosis of the liver, and gastric ulcers. Gable took it as a warning and managed to stay sober until Barrymore's wake on June 2, when hosts Errol Flynn and Raoul Walsh made sure that everyone got plastered.

MGM had started sending Gable scripts for his next project. His relationship with Joan Crawford turned sour when he rejected one that would have reteamed them for the first time since *Strange Cargo*. Due to the wartime drain on its contract roster, the studio had to hire freelancer Fred MacMurray to team with Crawford in *Above Suspicion*. The espionage thriller marked the end of her seventeen years with MGM. Her contract was not renewed, and she left to freelance.

Victor Fleming, who hadn't directed Gable since *GWTW,* proposed a biography of Eddie Rickenbacker, the onetime racing car driver who became America's number one fighter pilot in World War I by downing twenty-five German planes and blimps. The patriotic air spectacle would be MGM's answer to Warner Bros.' *Sergeant York,* which won an Oscar for Gary Cooper as the First World War foot soldier who singlehandedly captured 132 Germans. Gable decided to pass, but the idea was later taken up by 20th Century–Fox, which made *Captain Eddie* with Fred MacMurray in 1945.

Meanwhile MGM was secretly negotiating with the draft authorities to get a deferment for Gable on the grounds that his immense popularity made him essential to the studio's efforts in behalf of the war. When Gable found out, he was at once embarrassed and stirred into action. For months he'd been deliberating over his talks with Lombard about enlisting. Holding him back were fears that he might be rejected or unable to get through basic training.

Scriptwriter-friend Sy Bartlett, now a captain in the army air force, put Gable in touch with Colonel Luke Smith to discuss possibilities.

Smith realized what having Clark Gable in the air force could do for recruitment, so he urged him to consider applying for training as an aerial gunner, one of the jobs that few men seemed interested in. "Everyone wants to be a pilot," Smith told him. "Your becoming a gunner would help to glorify the plane crews and the grease monkeys."

Gable agreed. When he asked Eddie Mannix to pass on his decision to L. B. Mayer, the latter blew his stack, but that was about all that he could do. If MGM tried to prevent Clark Gable from enlisting, the resulting publicity would blacken the studio's reputation.

Mayer wanted to suspend Gable's contract for the duration of his military service. Agent Phil Berg deemed that unfair because the contract was due to expire in another year. Berg had been expecting to make a new deal for Gable at a considerably higher rate than his present $7,500 per week. After much bickering, they compromised: the contract would continue to term, but Gable would take a 50 percent salary cut to $3,750. Added on to the $66 per month that he would earn as a buck private, he should be able to manage comfortably.

Howard Strickling wasn't sure that Gable could pass the entrance physical, so he urged him to go for medical and dental checkups first to avoid public humiliation later. Not surprisingly, Gable's teeth, or lack of real ones, proved the only problem. He needed a new set of dentures, this time in triplicate. He was advised to take extra pairs with him. Once he reached the combat zones, it would be difficult if not impossible to get repairs or replacements.

Enlistment spared Gable from making a final decision about the ranch. He'd been considering selling it and had even looked at houses in Beverly Hills and Bel-Air. But deep down he knew that he couldn't part with it. "It would be like letting Ma go forever," he told a friend.

With his $150,000 a year from MGM, he could afford to maintain it, but he scaled it down for wartime. Valet Rufus Martin and some of the other servants found jobs in defense plants but promised to return when Gable did. A caretaker couple remained, as did daytime secretary Jean Garceau. Chickens and other farm animals were sold. The horses were to be kept but sent out to graze in the fields every day to save on mowing.

Before leaving, Gable gave gold ID bracelets—the latest wartime fad—to some of his friends as a farewell gift. When he delivered one to Jill Winkler, he told her, "I'm going in, and I don't expect to come back, and I don't really give a hoot whether I do or not."

On August 12, 1942, the King of Hollywood became Private Clark Gable in an induction ceremony at the Federal Building in downtown Los Angeles. MGM and the War Department conspired to make it a front-page event, with more than a hundred reporters, photographers, and newsreel cameramen covering.

Dressed in the same dark suit that he had worn to his wife's funeral, Gable listened attentively as Colonel Malcolm Andruss read the army oath, which concluded with "You, Clark Gable, a citizen of the United States, do hereby volunteer to enlist as a soldier in the Army of the United States of America for the duration of the war plus six months." Gable raised his right hand and pledged, "I do."

In a news conference afterward, Gable said, "I don't want to sell bonds, I don't want to make speeches, and I don't want to entertain. I just want to be sent where the going is tough."

Jimmy Fidler, a gossip columnist who tended to be more prying than some of his rivals, questioned Gable's intention to become an aerial gunner. Fidler thought that his sheer physical size would make that impossible. Before Gable could respond, an army officer interjected, "He's not too large for the rear turret of a bomber. It takes a big man to handle one of those guns."

Gable's dogtag bore the identification number 191-257-41. He wore it around his neck with a second chain that held a small gold locket containing the remnant of Lombard's clip found in the crash wreckage.

He applied for admission to Officers Candidate School and was posted to Miami for the thirteen weeks of training. Graduates became second lieutenants, mockingly called "ninety-day wonders" by career men. Traveling with Gable was another new inductee, Andrew McIntyre, a junior cameraman at MGM. The War Department had secret plans for them that would later be revealed. Meanwhile they were to be treated like any other newly enlisted men.

En route to Florida by train, Gable had no peace as word spread ahead of him along the line that he would be passing through. Passengers pleaded for his autograph, and fans clogged the platforms at every stop. When he reached New Orleans on August 15, a crowd of five thousand—mostly hysterical females—packed the terminal and caused him to miss a connecting train. He arrived in Miami a day late.

Nearby Miami Beach had been converted from a tourist mecca into a restricted military zone. Most of the hotels were now vertical barracks or apartment houses for career officers and their families. It was more posh than most army bases, but the climate was hotter and more tropical than Gable had grown accustomed to in Los Angeles.

His first day was upsetting. The army had invited wire service photographers to cover his mandatory session in the barber's chair. Gable balked but finally agreed to go halfway. The photographers were permitted to click away as the world's most famous mustache (except for Hitler's!) was removed. Gable then insisted on privacy as his thick mop of hair was reduced to a crew cut. As he feared, his ears took on added prominence and made him look like Dumbo, the flying elephant. He requested no more photographs unless he was wearing a cap or hat.

Residing in a third-rate hotel that had been renamed the Liberty Arms, Gable had a lot of adjusting to do. With Andy McIntyre he shared a three-bunk room with a former soda jerk from Davenport, Iowa. Though he'd gotten used to rising at six in the morning to go to work at MGM, reveille was at four-fifteen and was followed by a brisk two-mile march before breakfast. Now pushing forty-two years of age, he was twice as old as the majority of rookies.

Most of his fellows were skeptical. When they first discovered Clark Gable's presence, they thought he was only there to make a movie. They couldn't believe that a superstar with his connections would start at the bottom in Officers Candidate School. VIPs usually went straight to Officers Training School, and some entered the service as commissioned officers.

But Gable quickly ingratiated himself. One morning in the communal washroom, he removed his upper plate of false teeth and waved it at the other men. "Look at the King of Hollywood," he laughed. "Sure looks like the Jack now, doesn't he?"

Raymond Green, a younger OCS classmate of Gable's, later remembered, "We began to realize he was the real McCoy. But still you'd say to yourself, 'Only an actor can act the way he does.' He was the all-American hero, the energetic superman gonna do it the hard way; a flag-waver of the first order. We were all, all those things, but he was Clark Gable. The day he arrived he had more military bearing than most of the men had when they left, partly because of his natural posture, and partly because he was an actor, I'm sure."

Gable was nearly defeated by the academic side of his training. A high school dropout in the tenth grade, he found it extremely difficult to adapt to a routine of seven to eight hours of classes daily. In ninety days the potential officers were expected to learn everything from military law to aeronautical science. If Gable flunked out because he did badly on the daily barrage of written tests, he would not only be reduced to the ranks as an ordinary soldier, but when the test results were inevitably revealed by the news media, he would also become a national joke.

Gable solved the problem by treating the lessons like movie scripts. At the beginning of every class, mimeographed sheets were distributed that contained the information to be covered in the lecture. Gable took them back to quarters and memorized them page by page. After the lights-out call at night, he often tucked a bundle under his robe and walked to the lavatory. Locking himself in a booth, he sat down on the closed toilet lid and proceeded to cram for several hours.

One day while chatting with fellow candidate Edwin Wilber, Gable said that if he didn't know the answers to test questions, which were always multiple-choice or true-or-false, he left them blank. "I was shocked, because most people, myself included, will make the best guess that they can if they don't know the answer," Wilber later recalled. "But this very straightforward man thought that guessing was cheating! When I set him straight, Gable thanked me for the advice and said he would do the smart, self-protective thing in the future."

Several weeks later Gable ran into Wilber again and told him that he'd taken his advice and was getting much higher grades on the tests.

In his few spare moments Gable corresponded with secretary Jean Garceau. "The courses are getting as stiff as a groom on his wedding night," he wrote in one of the letters. He complained of the army chow and requested parcels of his favorite gingerbread and cookies.

At the end of October Gable passed the final exams and finished seven hundredth in a class of 2,600. At the request of his mates, who no doubt were put up to it by army PR, the now–Second Lieutenant Gable gave the graduation address.

"I've worked with you, scrubbed with you, marched with you, worried with you over whether this day would ever come," he said. "The important thing, the proud thing I've learned about us is that we are men. Soon we will wear the uniforms of officers. How we look in them is not very important. How we *wear* them is a lot more important. Our job is to stay on the beam until—in victory—we are given the command to fall out."

H. H. ("Hap") Arnold, commanding general of the army air force, presided at the commencement and later met privately with Gable to discuss the future. After another thirteen weeks of training, Gable and fellow graduate Andy McIntyre would work for a documentary film unit attached to the Eighth Air Force in Europe. They would attend the Air Force Gunnery School at Tyndall Field in Panama City, Florida, for six weeks and then finish their training at Fort Wright, near Spokane, Washington.

Gunnery school was partly a breeze for Gable because of his long experience as a hunter and marksman. But Lombard's death left him plane shy. It took many hours of flight time before he was able to overcome his anxieties. At the completion of the courses, he was promoted to first lieutenant.

Prior to his transfer to Spokane, Gable was granted a Christmas furlough. He hitched a ride to Los Angeles on an air force freighter and experienced a momentary scare when the plane developed engine trouble over Texas and had to make an emergency landing at a small field in the desert.

Back at the Encino ranch for the first time since August, Gable relaxed and caught up with friends. Now that he'd become an officer, he decided to let his mustache grow back. He also visited his longtime tailor, Eddie Schmidt, to be measured and to place an order for uniforms. Officers were permitted to have them custom-made provided that they conformed to the regulation design.

At a small dinner party given by Jill Winkler, Gable became reacquainted with twenty-five-year-old Virginia Grey, an MGM contractee who'd been a special pet of his since playing blond temptations in *Test Pilot* and *Idiot's Delight*. Carole Lombard had managed to stifle the romance, but the widower had no restrictions on him now. It was a new beginning for an intimate relationship that lasted many years.

But his remorse over Lombard's death was still apparent. When he left for Spokane, he told secretary Jean Garceau, "I have everything in the world anyone could want, but for one thing. All I really need and want is Ma."

At Fort Wright Clark Gable's female constituency became a problem. Women who worked or lived at the base kept following him around and passing him their phone numbers. The commandant finally posted an official notice: "Lieutenant Gable will appreciate it if the public will not interfere with his training. He wishes to be treated like every other member of the Service."

Yet Gable didn't resist some of the advances when the spirit moved him. Some of his buddies were surprised when he had a tryst with a matronly secretary who looked like Wallace Beery in drag. When asked what attracted him, Gable said, "She makes no trouble. Sometimes the homely ones are the best kind, easy to please and very grateful afterward."

In the last week of January 1943, only days before his forty-second birthday, Gable finished training and received his silver wings as an aerial gunner. Hollywood newsreel coverage of the event showed him stepping forward from the ranks, getting his badge pinned on, and saluting. The unseen commentator for MGM's *News of the Day* boomed, "Watch out, Mr. Hitler, Lieutenant Clark Gable is headed your way!"

Although Clark Gable often posed for air force publicity photos in the garb of an aerial gunner, wearing a goggled helmet and with a bandolier of bullet shells draped around his broad shoulders, he never actually served in that capacity. But he did see action and participated in numerous bombing missions over Germany and the Nazi-occupied countries of Europe.

From Spokane, Gable and Andy McIntyre, now also a lieutenant, were dispatched to Pueblo, Colorado, to join the 351st Heavy Bombardment Group, which was commanded by Colonel William Hatcher and would soon be based in England. Gable and McIntyre were ordered to form a small crew and to make short films that could be used for the recruitment and training of new men. Members of the 351st would be the "stars" as Gable's group filmed their day-by-day activities. Gable's role would be strictly behind the cameras, as director and voice-over narrator.

Gable needed a creative sidekick and arranged a transfer for his scriptwriter-friend Lieutenant John Lee Mahin, who'd been serving as an instructor at Combat Intelligence in New Mexico. Andy McIntyre rounded up two more ex-studio camera operators, Mario Toti and Robert Boles, and sound technician Howard Voss. The sextet became known as "the Little Hollywood Group."

John Mahin, who hadn't seen Gable in the fourteen months since Lombard's funeral, found him "far more serious than he used to be. Quieter. He looked a little stunned. He didn't know whether he was going to be any good at what he was committed to do," Mahin remembered.

As before, Clark Gable's arrival in a new setting aroused suspicion in the younger "real" soldiers who knew him only as the King of

Hollywood. "None of the kids believed he was going to do anything at all," Mahin recalled. "They never thought he was going to expose himself to any kind of danger. They said it was a lot of bullshit. It nearly killed Clark that the kids shunned him. All the brass was crazy about him, naturally, because they wanted their pictures taken with him. Press correspondents would come around in a group, and of course the colonel would be in everything. The boys resented that."

At the time the operations of the 351st Heavy Bombardment Group (mostly four-engine B-17s) were a closely guarded secret, but in late April 1943 its base was moved to Peterborough, England, about eighty miles north of still heavily bombarded London. By that time Gable had received an automatic promotion to captain. Due to heavy losses in all the Allied forces, officers were being moved rapidly up the ranks.

To win the friendship of the 351st's regulars, Gable rejected Colonel Hatcher's offer of special housing. Instead he moved into the officers' barracks and took an eight-by-fifteen-foot room next door to John Mahin. Sharing a bathroom, they quickly learned each other's quirks.

"Clark had a cleanliness fetish," Mahin remembered. "He shaved his chest and armpits. At first sight it shocked me, and I said, 'By God, you shave.' And he said, 'Yeah, I can't stand hair. You smell with it. It makes you sweat more.' "

Gable also abhorred taking baths. "How can you sit in that tub, with all that dirty water coming off of you?" he asked Mahin. The next day Gable drove into the town of Peterborough and bought hardware to rig up a portable shower for himself.

Colonel Hatcher and other superior officers were always inviting Gable to their houses for dinner to show him off to their guests. He got annoyed and tried to limit it to once a week. At other times he bypassed the officers' mess and ate with the regular guys. "They got the worst food—brussels sprouts and potatoes, Spam and beans. Godawful. We all put on pot bellies," Mahin recalled.

Gable's weight soared from 198 pounds to 230. Although he was qualified to fly in planes as high as 30,000 feet (when oxygen masks were required), he twice suffered the bends and had to go on a strict diet.

Although the 351st dropped bombs instead of eggs, the group was nicknamed "Hatcher's Chickens." Nazi Intelligence was obviously well informed of its activities. Over the radio one night William Joyce, an Anglo-American fascist who called himself "Lord Haw Haw" and made propaganda broadcasts to Britain from Berlin, sent greetings: "Welcome to England, Hatcher's Chickens, among whom is the famous American cinema star, Clark Gable. We'll be seeing you soon in Germany, Clark. You will be welcome there too."

Now that he'd crossed the Atlantic and was within easy reach, Gable had been added to Nazi Germany's list of most-wanted "war criminals." Although MGM, for obvious reasons, never publicized the fact, Adolf Hitler once said that Clark Gable was his favorite Hollywood actor. Some of the fondness allegedly came from Gable's part-German ancestry. When relations between the United States and Germany began to frost in the late 1930s, MGM's publicity department quietly changed the word *German* to *Dutch* in all of Gable's biographical data.

A movie fanatic, Hitler had a huge collection of American and British films, many of them recent releases and stolen from troop ships and military bases. He allegedly saw *Gone With the Wind before* it premiered in England in April 1940.

Gable seemed a Nazi obsession. A German film magazine suggested that he might be related to the man who controlled the nation's screens, Propaganda Minister Joseph Goebbels. *Gable* supposedly was derived from *Goebel* or *Gobel,* American bastardizations of a proud German name.

Air Minister Hermann Goering posted a cash reward equivalent to five thousand dollars for the pilot who shot down Gable's plane. If Gable survived the crash and was captured, the pilot would also receive a promotion and a free vacation trip on his next furlough.

Gable fretted but tried to laugh it off. "If Hitler catches me, the sonofabitch will put me in a cage like a gorilla and send me on a tour of Germany," he told a friend. "If a plane that I'm in ever gets hit, I'm not bailing out."

His first taste of action came on May 4, 1943, in a B-17 with Group Commander Hatcher himself as chief pilot. Gable and his crew of five were on board to film a bombing raid on the factory district in German-occupied Antwerp, Belgium. During the flight Gable was nearly killed when a twenty-millimeter shell from an attacking Focke-Wulf ripped through the plane, knocked the heel off one of his boots, and went out just a couple of inches over his head.

After a couple more missions in which Gable took over for gunners who were wounded during the flights, the noncommissioned "kids" started to take him seriously. "They adored him," John Mahin recalled. "They couldn't stay away from him. And he was proud that they accepted him."

In one huge multiplane raid into Germany, Gable flew on a B-17 nicknamed "Ain't It Gruesome?" One of his cameramen had been grounded by the flu, so Gable substituted and spent most of the seven-hour trip taking pictures from over the shoulder of the top turret gunner. The bomber survived five attacks by German fighters and returned to base with fifteen gaping flak holes in the fuselage.

Sergeant Mario Toti recalled that "Clark always worked very hard and was all business. He had his whole heart and soul in it. He said he was going to get all the pictures he wanted, even if Jerry [battle slang for the Germans] dropped a grenade down the back of his neck."

As officer in charge of the film unit, Gable made periodic trips to London to screen some of the footage when it came from the processing lab. He used the projection room at MGM's offices on Tower Street and usually stayed overnight at the Savoy. Despite the hotel's perpetual sold-out sign, it could always find a room for Captain Clark Gable.

During his London visits Gable socialized and possibly did more with his pre-Lombard sweetheart Elizabeth Allan, now thirty-five and a mother of two but still stunningly beautiful. Since returning to England in 1938, she had become one of its major movie and stage stars. Allan's reportedly open marriage with producer Wilfred O'Bryen made it possible for her to resume her affair with Gable.

Gable also renewed his friendship with David Niven, which had started back in Hollywood in 1934 when Niven, then a struggling bit player, was working part time as a deckhand on a fishing boat that Gable once chartered for a weekend. Niven was verging on stardom by the outbreak of war in 1939, when he left to join the army in his native England. By now Niven had a young wife, Primula, and a baby, David, who were living in a rented cottage near the royal castle in Windsor. Niven visited from his army base whenever he could.

"I came home one night to find a large American air force officer sitting in *my* chair; on his knee was *my* son; serving him from my *last* bottle of whiskey was *my* wife," Niven later remembered. "It was a great reunion. From then on our cottage became Clark's refuge from military life. With Carole's death, he had been dealt the cruelest of blows, but on the surface at least, he was making the best of it. In his own deep misery he found it possible to rejoice over the great happiness that had come my way, and he became devoted to my little family, always showing up with unheard-of goodies, such as concentrated orange juice and nylons from the bountiful American PX."

Niven also recalled that as the months passed, "Clark's personal wound seemed to be healing, but Carole was never far from him, and the very happiness of our little group would sometimes overwhelm him. Primmie found him one evening on an upturned wheelbarrow in the garden, his head in his hands, weeping uncontrollably. She held the huge bear of a man in her arms and comforted him."

At the 351st base in the Midlands, Gable had his usual problems with females. Women from neighboring farms and villages congregated at the gates, hoping to get a glimpse of him. Officers' wives flirted with him and sometimes scored. "Clark never talked about his conquests, but he was a sucker for anything," John Mahin remembered. "I imagine that he was a pretty vital guy sexually. He had to have that stimulation, it didn't really matter with whom."

One weekend Gable and the film crew followed a group from the 351st to the seaside resort at Blackpool to shoot scenes of the men spending R&R leave (rest and recreation). Local police tried to keep the public from crowding around, but a middle-aged woman finally broke through and jumped on Gable, piggyback. "Her skirt was up and her shanks were hanging out," John Mahin recalled. "It was all so silly that the crowd started to laugh. Clark shouted to me, 'Get this son of a bitch off me, get her off.' He was almost crying. I grabbed her, and a constable also grabbed her, and she kept yelling, 'I found ya! I found ya!' It looked so awful. I felt so sorry for him."

Gable bought a secondhand motorcycle to ride around the base. He got to know everybody and became very upset whenever anyone got killed or wounded. He wrote condolence letters to widows and made frequent visits to the base hospital to stroll around the wards and chat with patients.

One day while Gable was standing at the bedside of a mortally wounded turret gunner, a doctor-colonel happened by and proceeded to give a report on the patient, whom he claimed was too doped up with morphine to hear. As the doctor went into gory detail and predicted death within hours, Gable glanced at his friend and saw tears in his eyes. He grabbed the doctor by the arm, pulled him out into the hallway, and shoved him against the wall. "If you ever do anything like that again, I'll kill you," Gable blustered, then stormed away.

"Clark was a human with heart," a sergeant-buddy remembered. "When Bob Hope and his troupe came to the base to put on an outdoor show, there were thousands of guys in the audience, with Clark tucked in there somewhere. Hope stood at the mike, trying his damnedest to get Clark on the stage. Hope kept joking, 'I know there's a celebrity out there. Where is he?' But he couldn't get him to even stand up. The guys laughed, and some sitting near Clark shouted 'Here!' and started to applaud and whistle. Clark half got up, smiled and gave half a wave, and then put his head down. The applause and whistling went on, gee, it must have been ten minutes. Everybody thought he was great."

Gable's fraternizing and frequent flights on bomber missions worried his superiors, who believed that he was setting a bad example for an officer. Some thought he had a death wish and was deliberately trying to get killed so that he could join Carole Lombard. Colonel Hatcher reportedly couldn't wait for Gable to finish his project. He didn't want to be remembered as the colonel who sent Clark Gable to his death.

In October Gable was awarded the Distinguished Flying Cross and the Air Medal, the latter for "exceptionally meritorious achievement while participating in five separate bomber combat missions." It may have been a kiss-off. Colonel Hatcher had been pulling strings to get him removed from his command.

In any case, by that time Gable and crew had shot fifty thousand feet of film. The coverage included aerial combat, as well as scenes of daily life at the base and interviews with a cross-section of the 351st's personnel. In November the Little Hollywood Group was reassigned to the air force's photographic division in Los Angeles to begin the editing.

En route Gable had orders to stop in Washington to confer with General Arnold. He thought it would be a private briefing, but upon his arrival at the Pentagon, he discovered that the War Department had also scheduled a press conference to welcome him home. Hundreds of government employees provided a cheering section as he confronted reporters and photographers.

John Mahin, who accompanied Gable, remembered that "Clark was furious, but he amazed me in the way that he rose to the occasion. He was simply magnificent—charming, gracious, and modest. He said he didn't deserve a hero's reception and that other men were doing so much more."

Gable received a shock during his meeting with General Arnold, who'd forgotten what he'd sent him overseas for! "To make a film, sir," Gable said. "There was a problem recruiting gunners."

He turned pale when General Arnold replied, "Oh, we've licked that." Gable tried to explain that he'd shot fifty thousand feet of film and that something had to be done with it. The general finally told him, "Do anything you want. I'm sure that you must have the basis for a documentary that will do the air force proud. As soon as you're finished, we'll talk about the next project."

Until further notice, Gable would be stationed at "Fort Roach," the Hal Roach Studios in Culver City, which had been taken over by the Army Signal Corps as West Coast headquarters for all activities related to the production of training and recruitment films. As Captain Gable, he had the officers' privilege of living off the base, but he was required to report every day and to wear his uniform whenever he left home.

Friends noticed that Gable had grown thinner and more solemn, and that his hair was turning gray at the temples. He often spoke of his combat experiences. "I saw so much in the way of death and destruction that I realized that I hadn't been singled out for grief—that others were suffering and losing their loved ones just as I love Ma," he once said.

He had no sooner returned than his longtime hunting buddy, Harry Fleischmann, died of a heart attack. Gable attended the funeral in Bakersfield and tried to console the widow, who was also a cherished friend.

In December Gable's contract with MGM expired. Agent Phil Berg wanted him to become a freelance, which seemed the wave of the future and had proved a bonanza for Cary Grant, Gary Cooper, John Wayne,

Fred MacMurray, Charles Boyer, and others. But Gable had been turned off freelancing by Lombard's disappointments and decided that he preferred a guaranteed weekly paycheck as well as the fringe benefits. Although he hated L. B. Mayer, he revered Eddie Mannix and Howard Strickling, who between them gave him the caring protection that he could never get bouncing from studio to studio. He also didn't want to lose his hefty rights in MGM's pension plan.

Phil Berg struck a new deal with MGM that was actually a seven-year extension of the old one, but with additional benefits. For the balance of his military service, Gable would collect half pay. When he resumed working, the salary would return to $7,500 per week for every forty-week calendar year. He would make a maximum of two pictures a year but still get paid if it turned out to be only one. His new perks included the right to quit work at precisely five P.M. and a minimum of twelve weeks off between assignments.

When Gable returned to MGM for the contract signing, he lunched in the commissary for the first time since he joined the service. He'd always had a special chair at the head of a table. When he left, they put it upside down on top of the table so that no one else could use it. When he arrived that day, wearing his captain's uniform, he put the chair back in place and sat down as if he'd never been away.

"Everybody got up and applauded and cried. Richard the Lion-Heart didn't get a better reception when he came back from the Crusades," publicist Eddie Lawrence recalled.

On January 15, 1944, the second anniversary of the last full day of Carole Lombard's lifetime, Gable was guest of honor at a ship christening ceremony at the Terminal Island docks near Long Beach, California. Henry Morgenthau, U.S. Secretary of the Treasury, had recommended that the latest vessel built from the sale of war bonds be named the Liberty Ship *Carole Lombard*.

The event kicked off the fourth major bond drive of the war. More than fifteen thousand shipyard workers and their families attended the ceremony, which was covered by press and newsreels and staged with help from MGM. Louis B. Mayer served as emcee and freelance star Irene Dunne, currently working in an MGM film, was the christener.

Mayer eulogized Lombard, emphasizing that her record of more than $2 million in bond sales had yet to be surpassed. The uniformed widower listened with head bowed and fists clenched at his sides. When it came Gable's turn to speak, his voice broke as he mentioned his wife's name. He said that the 10,500-ton vessel was the 318th of its kind to be built at the yards.

Gable snapped to attention and saluted as Irene Dunne smashed a bottle of champagne against the prow. Tears streamed down his face as he watched the ship glide from its perch into San Pedro Bay. It was the first and only time that he ever made a public display of his grief. He would later be heartened by the *Carole Lombard*'s record in the Pacific, which included rescuing hundreds of survivors of sunken ships and returning them to safety.

Gable's own war job now was to produce something worthy from the nine and a half miles of documentary film that he had brought back from England. Although still officially posted at "Fort Roach," he got permission to do all the work at nearby MGM, which had superior technical facilities. Eddie Mannix arranged for Blanche Sewell, one of the studio's best editor-cutters, to help him. Captain John Mahin continued as idea man and scriptwriter.

Gable and team eventually put together five short films that could be used for training and recruitment purposes. Unfortunately, by the time the films were routed through Pentagon and air force channels, they had become outdated and were never widely shown. But much of the footage ended up in government film archives and got mixed in with stock that has been perpetually recycled for World War II documentaries.

While Gable worked on the films, he also made guest appearances at bond rallies and visited military hospitals to cheer patients who were constantly arriving from the Pacific combat zone. Inevitably, he got drawn back into the Hollywood social scene, which focused on the war effort with star-studded parties and premieres for various charities.

Gable had resumed his prewar relationship with Virginia Grey, one of many that Carole Lombard had considered too trivial to worry about. Grey had moved to a rented house near his in Encino, but he was also dating two blondes from MGM's stable of starlets: singer-actress Marilyn Maxwell and ex-model Kay Williams.

He had no contact with Loretta Young, whose army major husband was stationed in Los Angeles producing programs for the Armed Forces

Radio Service. The Lewises were expecting their first child in August. Judy Lewis, now going on nine years old and attending an all-girls' Catholic school, had undergone plastic surgery to reduce the oversize ears that reminded her friends not so much of Clark Gable as of Disney's cartoon character Dumbo.

In May he was promoted to Air Force Major Clark Gable. Nearly finished with his film project, he awaited new orders and expected to be sent to the Pacific. By June he was still waiting. Upon first learning about the D-Day invasion of Europe from a newscast on the radio, he became discouraged and felt discarded.

On June 12 he requested a discharge from active service, which was his right as a volunteer well above draft age. Since being inducted in August 1942, he'd served 670 days, or a year and ten months. His application was quickly approved by Captain Ronald Reagan, the air force personnel officer at "Fort Roach."

Out of respect for the millions who were still risking their lives daily, Gable decided to postpone his return to moviemaking until an Allied victory seemed assured. He would continue to promote the war effort and do whatever was requested of him, but otherwise he wanted to put his personal life back together.

Since his wife's death, Gable had developed a problem that he didn't see as one but that troubled his friends and associates. He consumed at least a quart of alcohol per day, much of it vintage scotch that he had bought by the truckload before the war and hoarded at the ranch.

"He must have had twenty pounds of blotting paper in his stomach," Al Menasco recalled. "He *had* to be drunk because of his enormous intake, but he never fuzzed words. His speech did not become erratic. He did not become bad-tempered. The only way you could tell he was stoned was when he tried to get through a doorway. He would always walk sideways then."

Fortunately or not, Gable drank alone or in the company of close friends, so the public never saw him intoxicated.

After his discharge from the air force, Gable stuck to the ranch and relaxed. He tinkered with his cars and joined the Bel-Air Country Club to play golf. One of his caddies was a neighborhood youth, Robert John Wagner, nicknamed "R.J."

"Clark was my idol. I worshiped him and was always asking him questions about the picture business," Wagner remembered. "He talked to me, advised me, and helped me. When he saw that I was really serious about an acting career, he took me to MGM to meet the head of casting. I eventually made my debut there with a bit part in a movie about a boys' school, but I had to wear a baseball catcher's mask and nobody saw my face."

One evening director Howard Hawks and wife Nancy, or "Slim" as everyone called her, tried playing matchmakers by inviting Gable to their house for dinner. Their fourth guest was Hawks's twenty-year-old protégée Lauren Bacall, who was then going through a difficult patch in her affair with the married Humphrey Bogart.

"Howard and Slim did everything to distract me," Bacall remembered. "They said, 'We've got the most dazzling man. Once you meet him, you'll forget all about Bogie.' The man was Clark Gable—one of those larger-than-life people that you pay your carefully saved money to see. He *was* dazzling, but he stirred me not a bit. I tried to flirt a little, tried to be attracted to him—but it didn't work. He was just a terrific-looking man without an overabundance of humor who had incredible dimples and was named Clark Gable. There were no sparks flying."

After dinner Gable insisted on driving Bacall back to her apartment building in Beverly Hills. "He walked me to the foot of the stairs," she recalled. "In the moonlight he kissed me goodnight, smiled, and walked away. Nothing, but nothing." A year later she married Humphrey Bogart after he finally divorced actress Mayo Methot.

In September 1944 Gable took some of his short films to Washington to show to Pentagon brass and then went to New York for his first visit there since 1935. Nicholas Schenck, president of the Loew's-MGM empire, and his wife, former showgirl Pansy Wilcox, threw a supper party for him at the Stork Club. Among the guests was socialite Dolly O'Brien, who quickly became one of Gable's favorite companions.

Nicknamed for her blond, blue-eyed beauty, the onetime Laura Hylan was a celebrated gold digger who'd collected millions in divorce settlements from her three ex-husbands. Her one big mistake was divorcing yeast tycoon Julius Fleischmann too quickly. Soon after she settled for $5 million, he died in a polo accident and his entire $66 million fortune might have been hers if she'd waited.

Dolly O'Brien was six years older than Gable but exceptionally youthful. Witty and unerringly elegant, she undoubtedly reminded him of Carole Lombard. A romance developed, subject to O'Brien's dislike for California. She preferred New York and Palm Beach, where she lived like a queen in an oceanside villa. In December Gable spent two weeks with her there, the first of many such visits.

By New Year's Eve Gable was back home and celebrating the arrival of 1945 at a dinner-through-breakfast party thrown by Jack Benny and wife Mary Livingstone in their Beverly Hills backyard. For the formal dress gathering, a huge tent had been erected, with room enough for a dance floor, full orchestra, and tables for a hundred guests.

When she spotted Gable arriving, Judy Garland, there with future husband Vincente Minnelli, insisted on singing "Dear Mr. Gable." The red-eared honoree gave her a big hug afterward and moved on to chat with Joan Crawford and her latest husband, actor Phillip Terry. Crawford enthused about signing with Warner Bros. for *Mildred Pierce*, which would be her first work since leaving MGM two years ago. It had taken that long to find a worthy script that suited the now-middle-aged legend.

Gable faced a similar dilemma as MGM started sending him scripts for his return to the screen. His last effort, *Somewhere I'll Find You*, had been released in August 1942 and earned world rentals of $4 million, slightly ahead of *Honky Tonk*, his previous hit with Lana Turner. They seemed a winning combination worth repeating again, except that during Gable's absence the studio had committed Turner to several major productions, none of which could easily be altered to fit Gable as costar. Until Turner made those films, she was off the list of Gable's potential leading ladies.

In addition to Joan Crawford, most of Gable's prewar teammates had also flown the MGM coop. Greta Garbo and Norma Shearer had permanently retired; Myrna Loy, Hedy Lamarr, and Rosalind Russell were freelancing; and Jeanette MacDonald had switched to opera and concerts.

Besides Lana Turner, the current female star roster included Greer Garson, Judy Garland, Katharine Hepburn, Esther Williams, Ann Sothern, and moppet Margaret O'Brien, as well as newcomers Kathryn Grayson, June Allyson, Gloria DeHaven, Jane Powell, and Elizabeth Taylor. Some were automatically ruled out as too young, too musical, or too wet to be matched with Clark Gable.

Gable personally favored Ann Sothern, a flippant doll-faced blonde in the Harlow mold but with more heart and soul. But Sothern had become too valuable to MGM as star of its highly popular *Maisie* series, which was being expanded into a weekly CBS radio program as well. She stood slight chance of being teamed with Gable or, for that matter, with any of the studio's top male stars.

Gable had already rejected an attempt to cast him with Katharine Hepburn, in *The Philadelphia Story.* Since then MGM had struck gold by teaming her with Spencer Tracy, who'd also become her lover in private life. They'd just finished their third collaboration. Due to the longtime rivalry between Gable and Tracy, it seemed likely that a Gable-Hepburn teaming would create more problems than it was worth.

That left the Irish-British redhead Greer Garson as the only choice for Gable's costar. Brought over from England in 1939 after an auspicious debut in *Goodbye, Mr. Chips,* she rapidly became MGM's box-office queen and was second only to 20th–Fox's Betty Grable in the Hollywood industry. The 1941 *Mrs. Miniver* won Garson an Oscar and earned MGM a staggering $8.9 million in rentals. Her three subsequent films brought in another $18.3 million. Three of her hits were with Walter Pidgeon, and one with the long-established Ronald Colman. She had just completed *The Valley of Decision* with newcomer Gregory Peck, which would go on to earn $8 million for MGM.

L. B. Mayer practically drooled over the box-office potential of a Gable-Garson teaming, but the story department couldn't find a property that suited them. Garson, who had Mayer's ear and yearned to do something on the grand scale of *Gone With the Wind,* suggested John Galsworthy's *The Forsyte Saga,* the story of a wealthy English family during Victorian and Edwardian times. Gable sniffed another *Parnell* in the wind and refused to be involved.

Since the outbreak of the war, MGM had done its bit to uplift public morale by switching much of its output to lighthearted fluff like slapstick comedies with Red Skelton or Abbott and Costello and Technicolor musicals with Judy Garland, Gene Kelly, Frank Sinatra, and Esther Williams. With Gable and other romantic leads like Robert Taylor, James Stewart, and Robert Montgomery away in the service, the studio had neglected to build an inventory of scripts for them.

Meanwhile Gable was adamant about not filming *anything* until the war ended. By February 1945 that seemed within reach as Allied forces continued to pound Germany and Italy and also started bombing raids on Japan.

In March Gable's heavy drinking finally caught up with him. While driving home from a party celebrating the American victory on Iwo Jima, he lost control of the car as he passed through the Bristol Circle, a dense tree-filled traffic island on Sunset Boulevard in residential Brentwood in West Los Angeles. It being around four o'clock in the morning, there may have been no eyewitnesses to what actually happened. But MGM publicists and security chief Whitey Hendry got to the accident scene before it was reported to the police or press.

Howard Strickling later claimed that Gable crashed into a tree on the front lawn of the home of Harry Friedman, a talent agent for MCA. According to Strickling, Friedman knew enough about the industry's penchant for secrecy to phone MGM instead of the cops.

"It wouldn't have been good if a photographer arrived and snapped Clark Gable lying on the lawn covered with blood and his car all cracked up," Strickling said. After a studio doctor arrived to patch up Gable, he was taken to Cedars of Lebanon Hospital, and the wrecked car was quickly towed away.

At the hospital Gable required ten stitches for head and shoulder wounds and was detained for "observation." He was in a drunken stupor and kept threatening to walk out, so all his clothes were taken away to lessen the chances. He spent the next three days in isolation, being thoroughly dried out.

The press had so many informants at Cedars of Lebanon that Gable's presence became known within minutes. Amusingly, the story handed out by MGM was that Gable's car had been sideswiped by a drunken driver who immediately sped away! Nobody believed it, but it got printed and also started rumors of what really happened. One of the more extreme had Gable killing a pedestrian and MGM persuading one of its minor executives to take the rap for him! After "confessing" that he had really been driving the car and Gable was only a passenger, the exec supposedly served a year in jail for manslaughter, after which MGM rehired him with a whopping pay increase and pension plan.

Some of Gable's friends blamed his drinking on loneliness and boredom. Eddie Mannix believed that once Gable got back into harness and started working again, it would be all the therapy he needed. End of the war or not, Mannix wanted Gable back in front of the cameras as soon as possible.

Gable's close friend Victor Fleming, a veteran of thirty-five years in the business who now considered himself semiretired and had directed only three films since *GWTW,* offered to take over the Gable-Garson project, with Sam Zimbalist as producer. L. B. Mayer wanted something with the inspirational, heart-tugging qualities of *Mrs. Miniver* and *Random Harvest,* in which Greer Garson had portrayed, respectively, the matriarch of a war-torn family and the loyal wife of an amnesiac soldier.

Mayer recommended one of his favorite books, a long-ago weeper entitled *The Rosary* that had also been adapted to a stage play and silent movie, but sanity prevailed and the final choice was *This Strange Adventure.* The novel by Clyde Brion Davis was originally purchased by MGM in 1935 as a potential vehicle for child star Freddie Bartholomew, who would have played the son of the two main characters.

Four writers were assigned to do a rush job on the screenplay, but Victor Fleming disliked the result and asked John Lee Mahin to take over. Mahin, who was still in the air force and assigned to the signal corps at "Fort Roach," accepted but had to work secretly and without screen credit.

Mahin had been involved in all the Gable-Fleming scripts since the first, *Red Dust,* so he tried to please them as well as Greer Garson, for whom he'd never written before. To begin with, he shortened the title to *Adventure,* meant simply in the generic sense of the word as an exciting or very unusual experience.

Gable portrayed a career merchant marine bosun with a sweetheart in every port. When his ship is torpedoed by the Japanese, he and several others escape in a lifeboat and are eventually rescued, possibly due to the prayers of an old Irish sailor who believes in miracles. While stopping over in San Francisco for his next assignment, Gable falls for public librarian Greer Garson, a prim spinster who considers him a brute but finally gets swept away by passion and marries him. Garson tries to reform him and to persuade him to give up his wandering ways, but he soon ships out again, and she files for divorce. Gable eventually realizes his mistake and returns, just as Garson, who'd never told him that she was pregnant, is about to have their baby. The child is apparently still-born, but Gable suddenly remembers his old sailor friend and prays for another miracle. Needless to say, he gets it.

Prior to his military service, Gable had become acquainted with Greer Garson in chance meetings at MGM, but they had never mixed socially. She belonged to the "English aristocracy" circle that he and Carole Lombard had always avoided. In 1941, during the filming of *Mrs. Miniver,* Garson became romantically involved with actor Richard Ney, who was fourteen years younger and portraying her son. They married in 1943, though Ney was currently serving with the U.S. Navy in the Pacific.

Budgeted at $3.5 million, *Adventure* started production on May 21, 1945, thirteen days after Victory-in-Europe Day. Gable could relax in the fact that he'd at least kept part of his pledge to lay off moviemaking until the war ended.

Since Gable was now forty-four years old and Garson nearly forty-two, Victor Fleming and cinematographer Joseph Ruttenberg had to use their ingenuity to conceal the encroachments of middle age. Gable's face had filled out, especially around the jowls. To keep his weight down, he was dieting and taking the appetite suppressant Dexedrine, which made him sweat a great deal and often gave him the shakes. Fleming would call "Cut!" until he got himself under control.

Garson infuriated Gable with her Garbo-like fetish for closed sets and for acting out love scenes behind folding screens with only a minimal technical crew present. Every afternoon at four Garson insisted on a break for the traditional English tea of light refreshments. Gable always went to his bungalow for a few shots of scotch or bourbon while Garson played hostess on the set. He would no sooner return than five o'clock came around and he left for the day, one of the perks of the new contract that went into effect with *Adventure.*

"Gable and Garson never hit it off," MGM publicist Emily Torchia recalled. "He'd look at her as if she wasn't even there. It was the same with Jeanette MacDonald in *San Francisco.* With warm, earthy girls like Jean Harlow and Lana Turner, he was his usual charming self. With others he could be as cold as ice."

More to Gable's liking was bubbly, down-to-earth Joan Blondell, who, rather incongruously, played Garson's best friend and roommate. The fortyish blonde, now freelancing after a long affiliation with Warner

Bros., had recently divorced singer-actor Dick Powell, who dumped her for the considerably younger June Allyson.

Gable and Blondell started dating and became fast friends, if not more. "Clark *adored* women—not in a lechy way. He loved beauty," Blondell remembered. "His eyes would sparkle when he saw a beautiful woman. And if he liked you, he let you know it. He was boyish, mannish, a brute—all kinds of goodies. When he grinned, you'd have to melt. If you didn't want him as a lover, you'd want to give him a bear hug. He affected all females, unless they were dead."

Blondell found Gable a welcome change from most movie actors. "That's a bad profession for men. They become picky and fussy and do a lot of talking to themselves in the mirror," she said. "Clark wasn't like that, ever. He was so unaffected. He never took advantage of that marvelous appeal he had. He handled himself very well. He was completely real in every sense of the word."

Gable finished *Adventure* in July. Three weeks later the world's first atomic bomb was dropped on Hiroshima. By September 2 the war had ended in a total victory for the Allied nations.

In the interim Gable lost a romantic tug-of-war that had been raging with one of his steady girlfriends. Hoping to incite Gable into a marriage proposal, starlet Kay Williams had started dating the much-married playboy Adolph Spreckels, whose superwealthy family owned sugar plantations, refineries, and shipping lines. When Spreckels proposed, Kay gave Gable the chance to make a counteroffer. He told her to buzz off, so she proceeded to become the fifth Mrs. Adolph Spreckels, with homes in Beverly Hills and the dynasty's business headquarters in San Francisco.

Still keeping company with Virginia Grey and Dolly O'Brien, Gable soon found a replacement for Kay Williams in an even more beautiful blonde, Anita Colby. One of the first professional models to become a major celebrity, Colby was known as "The Face" and had been featured on scores of magazine covers. In addition, she currently had a $100,000-per-year contract as beauty-and-fashion consultant to David Selznick's independent production company.

Gable seemed to be window shopping but in no mood yet to buy. Whenever he went salmon fishing on the Rogue River in Oregon, he always consorted with Carol Gibson, a willowy brunette whose father owned the landmark We Ask U Inn. On golfing trips to Phoenix, Arizona, he played the links and house-guested with blond Betty Chisholm, a war widow who was immensely wealthy in her own right as an heiress to oil and meat-packing fortunes.

"All of his old friends wanted to see Clark married again because we knew that he hated the loneliness," Adela Rogers St. Johns remembered. "One day, as someone who could take certain liberties with him, I mentioned a possible candidate, and he said, 'Look, let's face up to something. I have a hole in me that's never going to be filled up. It wouldn't be fair to anybody. I haven't anything more to give.' "

By December 1945 even Santa Claus at the North Pole must have known that "Gable's back and Garson's got him!" For months MGM had been running a teaser campaign for *Adventure* with newspaper and magazine ads, radio spot commercials, theater trailers, and roadside billboards. The slogan was even painted on the exterior walls of the Culver City studio and the Loew's home office building in New York's Times Square. Though no one was ever given credit, it was the handiwork of master song lyricist Howard Dietz, who also happened to be vice president in charge of advertising, publicity, and exploitation for Loew's, Inc.

It may not have been the first time in industry history that stars' names were linked in such catchy fashion, but it caught on as no advertising lines had before and started a new era in movie marketing where a movie's slogan became as important as its title and cast. "Gable's back and Garson's got him!" was picked up and parodied by so many radio comedians and newspaper humor columnists that it earned a million dollars' worth of free publicity for the movie.

Adventure opened quietly in Los Angeles in mid-December to qualify for the 1945 Academy Awards; the big guns were reserved for the January 1946 premiere at New York's six-thousand-seat Radio City Music Hall, "the Showplace of the Nation," where a stage show always supported the movie. No Clark Gable film had played there since *It Happened One Night* lasted all of one week in 1934, but in recent years Greer Garson had become its box-office queen. Her *Mrs. Miniver* set a new long-run record of eleven weeks, but she soon shattered her own mark with *Random Harvest,* which ran for thirteen weeks. It should be noted that in that era movies were not mass-distributed as they are today. A brand-new film usually opened in a limited number of theaters around the country and played there exclusively until the bookings ended, at which point it moved on to other theaters. While *Adventure* played at Radio City Music Hall, for example, it couldn't be shown at any other theater within a sixty-mile radius of New York City.

Except for reissues of some of his oldies, Clark Gable had been absent from theater screens for over three years, so legions of fans turned out and helped *Adventure* to break all box-office records in its first week at the Music Hall. But attendance rapidly declined due to mixed critical reviews and unfavorable word of mouth from patrons.

Bosley Crowther, then the most influential movie critic in the nation by virtue of his byline with *The New York Times,* wrote: "By all the laws of Hollywood, some sort of nuclear fission should have occurred when Metro brought Greer Garson and Clark Gable together in a film. For those two names joined on a marquee have the potential, in a box office way, of the atom splitting equation used by the scientists at Oak Ridge. But something went wrong in Metro's handling of these two cosmic elements, and their *Adventure,* which should have been a bombshell, is about as explosive as a slightly ancient egg."

Crowther thought Gable might have have been trying too hard after three years away. "He talks too loudly, shouts 'Ha!' contemptuously too many times, and persists in keeping his hat on to an irritating extreme," said Crowther, who was also put off by the actor's "dark, leering, leathery face."

James Agee of *Time* magazine took a kinder view: "*Adventure* was clearly carpentered to fit the old Gable formula; and former aerial gunner-photographer Gable himself fits the formula as smoothly and as agreeably as ever. If he is a little chubbier around the jowls, he is still able to sling his weight around—and in his bright eye is the same old wicked fire."

Photoplay, the only fan magazine taken seriously by the Hollywood industry, said, "What use for us to cite the flaws and bemoan the story, for it's Gable's first postwar picture, and movie fans, if for no other reason than that, will send its rating sky high. What we can't understand, however, is the vociferous and he-mannish Mr. Gable consenting to mouth the innocuous and at times whimsical dialogue that means just nothing. Words, words, words. Nevertheless, it rates a best because it brings back Gable to the screen and will please Miss Garson's fans to have her young and gay for a change."

When *Adventure* reached the hinterlands, where people tended to be more demonstrative than in sophisticated big cities, many audiences actively loathed it—hooting and talking back at the screen. Nonetheless the movie was a commercial success, eventually earning world rentals of $6 million and a profit of half a million. From Gable's standpoint, it took in $2 million more than his last film, *Somewhere I'll Find You,* but from Garson's it was a big drop from some of her previous heights. The teaming did Gable no great harm but Garson's career went into a sudden and irreversible decline. *Adventure* was the last hit picture she made for MGM in an association that lasted until 1954.

Needless to say, *Adventure* received no nominations for the 1945 Academy Awards, though Garson did earn one for best actress for her prior work in *The Valley of Decision,* released in June of that year. But ironically the Oscar went to Gable's old chum, Joan Crawford, for *Mildred Pierce.* Billy Wilder's *The Lost Weekend,* with Ray Milland, won the Oscars for 1945's best picture, actor, and director.

At the awards ceremony on March 7, emcee Bob Hope had fun with "Gable's back and Garson's got him," claiming that it was being set to music for Bing Crosby's next record. Hope also joked that Gable's next teaming would be with MGM's canine star and advertised as "Clark's bark makes Lassie sassy!"

While hardly the disaster of *Parnell, Adventure* became even more of a sore spot to Gable, who turned forty-five during its release. Critics' gibes about his maturing looks and the ill-suited vehicle made him squirm and caused depression about the future. He wondered if he should quit before he made even more of a fool of himself. Given his MGM contract, that would be next to impossible without a costly litigation, but he kept turning down scripts. It would be another year before he regained enough confidence to try again.

Meanwhile MGM was trying new ways of finding material for its stars. Spencer Tracy, who was even more difficult to cast than Gable because of his preference for character roles, wanted to return to the Broadway stage for *The Rugged Path,* a World War II drama specially written for him by Robert E. Sherwood. MGM agreed, in exchange for the screen rights if the play was a success. Unfortunately, it received mixed to negative reviews, and not even Tracy's popularity could keep it running more than eighty-one performances.

Besides Gable and Tracy, MGM needed vehicles for its third prewar star, Robert Taylor, who had just returned from three years as a flying instructor with the navy air force. Taylor's comeback film, *Undercurrent,* in which he was illogically teamed with Katharine Hepburn, proved an even bigger fiasco than *Adventure.*

Gable's freelancer friend David Niven had also returned from the war, accompanied by wife Primmie and young David, as well as a recent addition, Jamie, now six months old. After the Nivens settled into a rented house in Beverly Hills, Gable began making regular visits. "As in England, he always arrived loaded with goodies for the children and played with them for hours and, as before, he found great peace and comfort in the calm serenity of Primmie," Niven remembered.

One night Gable attended an informal dinner party for the Nivens at the home of Tyrone Power and his French actress-wife, Annabella. After the backyard barbecue everyone went inside to play parlor games, starting with hide-and-seek. Unfamiliar with the house, Primmie Niven opened what she thought was a closet door and plunged twenty feet down a steep flight of stairs to the concrete cellar floor. She was rushed to the hospital but never regained consciousness and died the next day, at the age of only twenty-five. Niven, left with two young sons, was devastated.

"During that long period of utter despair, Clark was endlessly thoughtful and helpful, and he checked up constantly to see if I was all right," Niven recalled. "Without my realizing it, Clark was drawing on his own awful experience to steer me through mine, and for the next eighteen months I saw a great deal of him, being one of the small handful that his houseman, Martin, automatically buzzed through the electrically controlled gate at the ranch."

By the summer of 1946 Gable had become more relaxed and sociable. Victor Fleming and best friend Howard Hawks talked him into buying a motorcycle and joining a small gang they had called the Moraga Spit and Polish Club, which met every Sunday morning at Hawks's hilltop home on Moraga Drive in Bel-Air. Members, who were constantly changing and sometimes absent, included Gary Cooper, Robert Taylor, John Wayne, Van Johnson, Keenan Wynn, Ward Bond, Andy Devine, William Wellman, and John Huston.

Gable had a Harley-Davidson model, the Square 4 Aerial. The Sunday group spent a couple of hours zooming around the surrounding hills and then returned to Howard Hawks's place for lunch. "Afterward we sat around drinking beer and polishing our bikes—spit and polish, you know," Andy Devine recalled.

Once a month Gable and gang loaded their motorcycles into station wagons and drove to open roads in the Mojave Desert to race and have a picnic. On his bike Gable was known as a "hot shoe," capable of creating sparks by letting the steel heel of his boot scrape against the pavement.

Gable continued to pal around with Virginia Grey, Anita Colby, Betty Chisholm, and Dolly O'Brien, though hardly simultaneously. A new companion was Standard Oil heiress Millicent Rogers, a fortyish, thrice-divorced leader of the fashion pack who reportedly spent half a million dollars a year on designer wardrobes. She was the most smitten of Gable's consorts. When he dated others, she often turned up at the restaurant or nightclub at an adjoining table. She paid service employees handsomely for information and even tried bribing Gable's secretary with some twenty-four-carat gold jewelry.

For a time Gable also resumed his relationship with Joan Crawford, which had been more off than on since they first became involved fourteen years ago. Crawford was suddenly single again after her three-year marriage to actor Phillip Terry ended in her third divorce. She and Gable tried playing house together, but it didn't work out. According to some of Gable's friends, he still fancied Crawford but found it impossible to cope with her career obsession, now intensified by her recent Oscar, or her adoption of two young children through possibly illegal channels. No paragon of parenthood himself, Gable didn't want to be dragged into it.

Gable's romantic affairs were well covered in the gossip columns and fan magazines, keeping him in the public limelight at a time when he had no new films in release. Although Bing Crosby, Van Johnson, and Gary Cooper topped the most recent industry poll of male box-office stars, he was still affectionately regarded as the King, and nobody tried to challenge the title.

Early in 1947 he tarnished it a bit when he got arrested for allegedly violating California hunting laws while shooting for ducks at a gun club near Bakersfield. Gable and actor-friend Frank Morgan went there with about twenty buddies, including director Frank Capra.

"Clark couldn't get up with us at four A.M. because he was stewed or something," Capra later recalled. "The ducks were plentiful that morning, and some of the guys shot more than they were supposed to. When they brought the ducks in, they put the extra ones on Clark's empty strap. Maybe twelve or thirteen, though the legal limit per hunter was ten. I think they meant it as a joke. Well, when Clark finally got up, he went out and shot a full strap. When he returned to the lodge, the game wardens happened to be making their rounds. They said, 'Mr. Gable, you've shot way over the limit.' He said, 'How is that?' They said, 'You exceeded the limit this morning. Here's your strap.' He didn't hesitate a minute. He said, 'If they're on my strap, they're my ducks.' "

Frank Morgan got angry and tried to help by claiming that some of the ducks were his, which only resulted in both men being arrested and taken to the local jail. "They had to pay five-hundred-dollar fines and also suffer the embarrassment of the damn thing getting into the newspapers," Capra remembered. "Clark was no game hog. He didn't hunt to kill. He went hunting because he liked to talk dirty with the guys, drink, and make passes at dames."

The arrest got reported on the radio and made banner headlines the next day: CLARK GABLE CITED ON GAME LAW CHARGE. Howard Strickling wanted to hold a press conference so that Gable could explain, but he refused. "It's not that important," he said. But he was incensed at some of his buddies for not coming forward to confess their prank. He never went hunting with that group again.

MGM finally found a property that Gable liked—a recent bestselling novel by Frederic Wakeman entitled *The Hucksters*. But the exposé of the new postwar phenomenon of high-pressure advertising and Madison Avenue agencies run by men in gray flannel suits contained too much sex and immorality for the enforcers of the industry's Production Code. Scriptwriter Luther Davis had to make many cuts and changes to win its approval. Jack Conway, who last directed Gable in *Boom Town* and *Honky Tonk,* took the helm, with Arthur Hornblow, Jr., as producer.

Gable portrayed Victor Norman, a prewar advertising executive newly discharged from the army who joins the Kimberly Tower Agency

to take charge of the Beautee Soap account. His first tasks are to produce a weekly radio program and to recruit twenty-five beautiful
socialites to endorse the product in a series of magazine ads. Making it
tough for Vic are the ruthless agency boss, the hard-to-please owner of
Beautee Soap, and a young widow who's the sole holdout in his endorse-
ment campaign.

After his experience with Greer Garson, Gable insisted on first making a screen test with the leading lady whom MGM had selected. Her
name was Deborah Kerr. She'd never worked in Hollywood before,
though MGM's British studio had signed her to a seven-year contract in
1945. American audiences had seen her sporadically since 1941 in imports
such as *Major Barbara, Colonel Blimp,* and *Vacation from Marriage.*
Despite her red hair and other resemblances to Garson, she was eighteen
years younger and had more zing and warmth. Gable liked her immediately and approved the casting. MGM started a publicity buildup: "Deborah KERR: Rhymes with STAR!"

The showy supporting role of a nightclub singer gave Gable his first
chance to work with Ava Gardner, who had joined MGM at age seventeen in 1941 as a bit player and had only recently started to show star
potential in a loan-out to Universal for a sexy featured part in *The
Killers.* Along the way, she had become a celebrated playgirl with numerous affairs and two disastrous marriages, to Mickey Rooney and Artie
Shaw.

In earlier days such a free spirit might have landed in Gable's personal harem, but the timing was always off and they never did connect
due to conflicting relationships. At the time of *The Hucksters,* Gardner
was still involved in a bitter divorce from Artie Shaw, and Gable already
had a overfull card of women.

MGM assembled an exceptional supporting cast for the $2.3 million
production, including Adolphe Menjou, Sydney Greenstreet, Edward
Arnold, and Keenan Wynn. Gable's scenes with the obese, thunder-
voiced Greenstreet, as the tyrannical soap manufacturer, were highly
charged and ended hilariously with Gable dumping a pitcher of water
over his head.

Due to the long gap since *Adventure,* MGM rushed *The Hucksters*
through production and released it in August 1947. Though some critics
complained that the original muckraking novel had been reduced to a

romantic satire on the advertising business, most enjoyed the movie and found it a vast improvement over *Adventure.*

"Clark Gable zooms back to the pre-eminent place he long held in Hollywood with his smash performance," claimed *The Hollywood Reporter.* "The Gable-Kerr team-up is ideal," said the *New York Herald-Tribune.*

A notable dissenter was James Agee of *The Nation,* who wrote that "Clark Gable seems well at ease, most of the time, but something soft and unfortunate has happened to his mouth. . . . I dislike the movie as I disliked what little I could read of the book: for I find uniquely nauseating the spectacle of incurable corruption laboring under delusions of honesty."

At the box office, *The Hucksters* fared less well than *Adventure* due to its total failure in the foreign market, which in those days knew nothing about American advertising or commercial broadcasting. But *The Hucksters* earned total rentals of $4.4 million and a final profit of $412,000 (against $478,000 for *Adventure*).

The Hucksters helped to place Gable in 1947's "Top Ten Box-Office Stars," his first appearance on the lists since military service. But a bigger contributor to his return was MGM's autumn rerelease of *Gone With the Wind,* which had been withdrawn from circulation in 1942 after bringing in an all-time industry record of $48.9 million in world rentals.

The 1947 reissue of *GWTW* brought in another $9 million in rentals in the United States alone, which was almost twice as much as any *new* film released by MGM or any other company that year! Most of the takings went to MGM, which now owned over 95 percent of the movie (two small interests were still owned by a member of the Whitney family and the estate of Myron Selznick).

Needless to say, Gable saw not a penny of the reissue millions. David Selznick sold his share in *GWTW* in 1942 for $400,000 to raise funds for his independent company. His only remaining stake was the right to produce a sequel to *GWTW,* something that Margaret Mitchell had yet to write.

In their discontent Gable and Selznick became friends again. No doubt they both realized that they would need each other if *GWTW II* ever came about.

In November, while attending a dinner party at L'Aiglon in Beverly

Hills, Gable renewed an old friendship with Douglas Fairbanks's widow, Sylvia, now married to but separated from England's Lord Stanley, baron of Alderly. The blue-eyed blonde quickly became part of Gable's rotating circle of consorts and the first one with *Lady* in front of her name.

But Dolly O'Brien seemed to have the inside track to Gable's affections. When she wed a considerably younger gigolo, Gable was devastated. But the marriage lasted not much longer than *GWTW*, and she soon returned to Gable's string of favorites. O'Brien's fondness for Palm Beach, New York, and the playgrounds of Europe was the main problem in the relationship. If Gable hadn't been so rooted to Hollywood, she would have married him in a flash, friends believed.

In January 1948 MGM finally came up with a vehicle for Gable and Lana Turner, whose last work together six years before in *Somewhere I'll Find You* had been interrupted by the death of Carole Lombard. Since then Turner had skyrocketed to sex goddess status and engaged in a very public private life, with a failed marriage to actor Steve Crane, the birth of their daughter, and a liaison with the married Tyrone Power.

The affair with Power was still blazing and had recently forced Turner to undergo an abortion to escape a scandal that could have ruined them both. If Gable and Turner had once been lovers, her current emotional commitment to Power seemed to stand in the way of reversing the clock.

Homecoming brought Gable full circle with director Mervyn LeRoy. In the eighteen years since LeRoy tried unsuccessfully to cast the unknown stage actor in a supporting part in *Little Caesar,* they'd never worked together. LeRoy had better luck with Lana Turner, whom he launched to stardom at age sixteen in *They Won't Forget* and later brought to MGM when he left Warner Bros.

The third Gable-Turner teaming had roots in his 1934 *Men in White,* which was based on the hit play by Sidney Kingsley. The struggling intern whom Gable portrayed might well have become the wealthy Park Avenue doctor of Kingsley's short story "The Homecoming of Ulysses," which Paul Osborn expanded into a screenplay with the less pretentious title *Homecoming.*

The story did have Homeric touches, with Gable's Dr. Ulysses Johnson leaving his wife and practice to serve in the medical corps during

World War II. In North Africa he meets temptation in the young army nurse who assists him. They start off hating each other but eventually fall deeply in love and have to confront the future. At the end of the war, will Dr. Johnson return to his wife, or will he try to make a fresh start with Nurse Jane? Her sudden death from combat wounds brings the answer and sends him home a sadder but wiser man.

Anne Baxter, a 1946 Oscar winner for her supporting performance in *The Razor's Edge,* played Gable's wife. Her real-life husband, John Hodiak, portrayed another doctor who was Gable's best friend in medical school.

Homecoming used flashbacks to cover Gable's courtship of Baxter and their early life together. Since Baxter was actually twenty-two years younger than Gable, she managed it with a minimum of help from the makeup department. But Gable looked grotesque in some of the scenes. A hemorrhoid cream was used to shrink the bags under his eyes. His jowls were pulled tight behind his ears with rubber bands.

Despite its tragic tearjerking finale, *Homecoming* contained enough torrid Gable-Turner love scenes to justify the advertising slogan, "The TEAM that generates STEAM!" Audiences would never know what Gable had to put up with.

"To keep my breath fresh for those clinches, I chewed gum," Turner recalled. "During a take I would stash the wad in the side of my mouth. One day Clark kissed me too forcefully. When he drew back, we were attached by a ribbon of sticky gum! I shrieked with laughter as he glumly picked the gum from his lips and mouth. From then on I rinsed with Listerine instead."

At the completion of *Homecoming,* Gable made another of his frequent fishing trips to Oregon to be with Carol Gibson. He chartered a cabin cruiser and took her along the Columbia River, retracing the route he once followed as a novice actor with the Astoria Players.

Before returning to Los Angeles, Gable treated Gibson to her first visit to San Francisco, where he'd also worked during his stage career. He showed Gibson all the sights and didn't let nearly constant rain deter them from riding the cable cars. Gable wore a hat and dark glasses, but when passengers spotted him, they didn't want to get off until he did. Once they started singing *San Francisco* and kept it up all the way from

Fisherman's Wharf to Market Street. Gable joined in and waved to gawkers on the street.

In April Gable started another film, the first time since 1941 that he'd made more than one in a single year. But his contract gave MGM the right to use him in as many as two per year, so he couldn't really complain of being overworked.

Command Decision was a radical departure for Gable, a psychological study of modern warfare, with no love story and an all-male cast. Based on a highly acclaimed play that ran for more than a year on Broadway, it also gave MGM a chance to revive the all-star dramatic genre that it had started with *Grand Hotel* and *Dinner at Eight*.

Although Gable had the leading role, he was supported by two of the studio's most valued stars, Van Johnson and Walter Pidgeon, plus such other notables as Brian Donlevy, Charles Bickford, Edward Arnold, and John Hodiak. Sam Wood, who left MGM in 1940 to freelance, was hired to direct. Gable last worked with him in *Hold Your Man* back in 1933. For old times' sake they requested the same cinematographer, Hal Rosson, who after that filming was briefly married to Gable's costar, Jean Harlow.

Written by army air force veteran William Wister Haines, *Command Decision* was adapted for the screen by William Laidlaw and George Froeschel. Ironically, the action takes place at an air force base in England not unlike the one where Gable served with Hatcher's Chickens. He brought a certain understanding to his portrayal of General Dennis, commander of a division flying B-17s deep into Germany to bomb aircraft and munitions factories. The story focuses on his moral dilmemma over executing orders that are equivalent to sending his men on suicide missions.

As a stage play, *Command Decision* was restricted to several interior sets. The movie was opened up with some stock footage of bombing raids and one big outdoor scene shot at March Field. It gave Gable his only chance to play hero as he uses a two-way radio to safely "talk down" a crippled Flying Fortress that has a crew member subbing for the dead pilot.

During the production, Gable's relationship with Anita ("The Face") Colby hit a snag when her consultant's contract with David Selznick expired and she decided to return to her native New York and the fashion-beauty business. According to Colby, Gable tried to stop her by proposing marriage.

"Clark came to my house to say good-bye," Colby remembered. "We were sitting by the fireplace looking at each other, and he started this strange conversation which had to do with the fact that I was a strict Catholic. He said he had been baptized a Catholic and would go to a priest about joining the Church and annulling his marriages. He said we could have a fine life together, have children, live any way I wanted. He told me later that my eyes got like saucers, and he thought I would say yes. What I was thinking was, 'How do you say no to Clark Gable?' I told him I wasn't ready for marriage and wanted to go home. I also told him he drank too much—he drank scotch in vases by that time—and he said, 'That's because I'm lonely.' "

Colby told Gable, "Please don't get married to anyone right now. You're so anxious, you might make a mistake." After she left for New York, he sent her a note, "The sun has gone from California." Colby recalled, "We did see each other after that, but the subject of marriage never came up again."

Elegant and thirtyish "Slim" Hawks, by now divorced from Gable's director-friend, filled some of the void. A California-born playgirl whose family owned fish canneries, she adored the outdoor life. Gable took her hunting and fishing, but as she soon told a friend, "He wants to get you over the hill and into the feathers." She found a more congenial companion in talent agent Leland Hayward, whom she married.

"I was in love with the *idea* of Clark Gable, with the attention he was lavishing on me, but never with Clark himself. In the end I was merely fond of him and wanted to keep him in my life as a friend. I always think you can do that with a man, but you really can't," the one-time Nancy Raye Gross recalled in her memoirs.

That summer another of Gable's blondes, Dolly O'Brien, persuaded him to holiday at her villa on the French Riviera. Since Carole Lombard's death he had developed a phobia about commercial airlines, so he entrained to New York and on July 12 sailed on the *Queen Mary* to Le Havre.

Dolly O'Brien met Gable at the dock and took him to nearby Deauville, where they stayed several days at the luxurious Hotel du Golf and played on the fairway. After motoring south to Cannes, they were dragged into the social whirl around gossip columnist Elsa Maxwell and her best chums, the Duke and Duchess of Windsor. Gable quickly tired of it and took off on his own to Paris, where the head of MGM's branch office arranged a deluxe tour of bars, bistros, and bordellos.

On August 4 Gable received a phone call from Los Angeles that his father had died suddenly from a heart attack. William Gable was seventy-eight and had outlived three wives, so his son reacted stoically but also a bit bizarrely. Gable ordered the funeral postponed until he returned, which would hardly be overnight due to his reluctance to fly.

In fact, the corpse landed in cold storage while Gable waited for the next ocean liner to New York, where, after five days at sea, he faced another three and a half days on the train to Los Angeles. MGM's publicity department kept the whole matter as secret as possible. Will Gable's passing never received more than a couple of lines in trade paper obituary pages.

The forty-seven-year-old son quickly sold the house that he had built for his father, for a price that was considerably below its market value. Given his miserliness, he seemed desperate to get rid of anything that reminded him of their cold and contentious relationship.

Meanwhile another of Gable's "fathers," Louis B. Mayer, lost power when Loew's-MGM president Nicholas Schenck hired Dore Schary to share the running of the studio as its first production chief since Irving Thalberg. Since the wartime boom in theater attendance had ended, the company's profits had dropped drastically, which Schenck blamed on weak product and Mayer's preoccupations with raising racehorses and courting young women. The forty-three-year-old Schary, who'd recently distinguished himself as production head at RKO, was considered more attuned to current audience tastes. Now sixty-three, Mayer had been running MGM since 1924 but still favored star-driven escapism at a time when the public seemed to become attracted more by stories and subject matter than by the names in the cast.

Mayer was outraged by Schary's appointment but accepted it to pacify Schenck, who had the power to oust him. Mayer still had the right of final decision on all projects. Schary's job was to choose them and to assign and to supervise the producers and directors who made them.

MGM, as well as the whole Hollywood industry, had reached a dangerous crossroads. Commercial television, the development of which had been retarded by the war, was on the verge of revolutionizing show business. By the end of 1948 nearly a million American households would have TV sets. While that was only a drop in the bucket for a nation of 130 million, most of the sets were concentrated in large cities, where it was easy to spot their potential for keeping people at home and emptying everything from theaters and nightclubs to sports arenas and bowling alleys. Once the technology reached the hinterlands, the fallout on competing forms of entertainment promised to be catastrophic.

Simultaneously, Loew's-MGM and four other majors (Paramount, Warner Bros., 20th–Fox, and RKO) were only a year away from having to comply with a federal antitrust decree that would end their monopolistic practice of controlling the production, distribution, and exhibition of their movies. If they wanted to continue as studios, they would have to dispose of their theater holdings or vice versa.

Dore Schary immediately announced plans to double MGM's production by the autumn of 1949. He held meetings with all the contract writers, directors, and producers to get their ideas. Thanks to the recent success of *Homecoming,* Clark Gable, as well as Lana Turner, figured to be major players in Schary's plans. The melodrama, which had yet to be released abroad, would eventually earn rentals of $5.6 million and a tidy profit of more than a million.

Eddie Mannix, Howard Strickling, and other longtime associates of L. B. Mayer disliked Schary and passed their resentments on to Gable, who knew him slightly from an earlier association with MGM as a scriptwriter and head of a low-budget production unit. Schary's work tended to have social or political messages, which earned him a reputation as a "pinko" among Hollywood's right-wingers. Gable eyed him with suspicion and mistrusted him as much as he once did David Selznick, who was a close friend of Schary's and had employed him for some of his independent productions.

Schary certainly came up with something different in his first project for Gable, which would be with MGM's most important producer, Arthur Freed. Though a specialist in musicals like *Meet Me in St. Louis* and *Easter Parade,* Freed did an occasional drama, so Schary put him together with writer Richard Brooks to prepare a vehicle for Gable. Brooks's novel *The Big Foxhole* had been the basis for *Crossfire,* the most controversial and profitable film that Schary made at RKO.

Brooks's scripts for *Brute Force* and *Key Largo* were tough and unflinching melodramas.

For Gable, Brooks and Freed picked *Any Number Can Play,* a novel by Edward Harris Heth that was already owned by 20th Century–Fox, which agreed to sell it to MGM for $50,000. While Brooks wrote the script, Freed arranged for his and Gable's longtime friend Mervyn LeRoy to direct. Freed, a onetime song-plugger and lyricist, got his production start as associate to LeRoy on *The Wizard of Oz.*

MGM was currently short on stars who suited the female lead, so Freed borrowed Alexis Smith from Warner Bros. To make it a pleasant working experience for Gable, the supporting cast included such past colleagues as Frank Morgan, Lewis Stone, Mary Astor, and Marjorie Rambeau, as well as first-timers Audrey Totter, Wendell Corey, and Barry Sullivan.

Richard Brooks devised a character for Gable that resembled Blackie Norton gone to pot. At forty, gambling casino–owner Charley King is rapidly falling apart. His devotion to business has alienated his wife and seventeen-year-old son. He's addicted to alcohol and cigarettes and suffers from angina pectoris. Doctors have prescribed pills and warned him to slow down and to stop drinking and smoking if he wants to live much longer. The role was the nearest thing to a "real" person that Gable had ever enacted, and it also mirrored some of his own personal problems of the moment.

Arthur Freed sandwiched the production of *Any Number Can Play* between two musicals, *The Barkleys of Broadway* with Fred Astaire and Ginger Rogers, and *On the Town* with Gene Kelly and Frank Sinatra. Shooting began on January 4, 1949, and took forty-three days at a final cost of $1.5 million. In line with new accounting procedures at MGM, part of Gable's annual salary was charged to the production, to the tune of $241,250.

On January 6 Gable took several days off due to the sudden death of his great friend Victor Fleming at age sixty-five. Since directing Gable in *Adventure,* Fleming had left MGM and made only one film, the disastrous *Joan of Arc,* with his longtime love, Ingrid Bergman. Out of respect to Fleming's widow and family, Bergman was conspicuously absent from the funeral, at which Gable served as a pallbearer.

While *Any Number Can Play* was filming, MGM launched *Com-*

mand Decision, which received mixed reviews and flopped at the box office. Some critics who'd seen the original Broadway production declared Gable's portrayal of General Dennis inferior to that of Paul Kelly on the stage. But the widest complaint was that the movie was a boring talkathon that lacked cinematic interest and seemed like a mere photographic record of a stage production. The drama eventually earned only $3.7 million in world rentals. Due to the absence of business in England and Europe, where World War II stories were still too upsetting for most of the public, *Command Decision* ended up in the red by $130,000, Gable's first loser since the 1938 *Idiot's Delight.*

Since *Command Decision* had been made before Dore Schary took charge of MGM production, he couldn't be blamed for its failure, but he learned something from it. He would give no more projects to Gable that didn't contain a strong thread of romance for his female fans, who wrote thousands of complaining letters to the studio. At some theaters they even marched out in the middle of *Command Decision* and demanded their money back.

While working in *Any Number Can Play,* Gable added a new blonde to his string of consorts with thirty-year-old Audrey Totter, who played his sister-in-law in the film. One night he took her to a dinner party where Lana Turner happened to be the center of attention, wearing a magnificent diamond ring and matching necklace and earrings.

Totter stared bug-eyed. Gable asked if she was admiring Turner's jewels. When she nodded, he said, "You have something far more important. You have jewels inside."

"That was just like Clark," Totter remembered. "He was a sensitive and considerate man, not at all like the rough-and-tumble roles he sometimes played."

Another new Gable companion was Paulette Goddard, the blue-eyed brunette who might well have played Scarlett O'Hara in *Gone With the Wind* if it hadn't been for her dubious alliance with Charles Chaplin. For a time it seemed like Goddard would become the next Mrs. Gable, as soon as her recent divorce from actor Burgess Meredith became final.

Now forty-three, Goddard had passed her peak as a Paramount star and ranked as box-office poison, but she was still exceptionally beautiful and vivacious. Gable had known her casually for years, but he became smitten when she started dating his close friend, director John Huston.

In the twinkling of an eye, Goddard switched from Huston to Gable, though the two men remained buddies and Huston returned to his wife, Evelyn Keyes (an actress who did appear in *GWTW* as Suellen O'Hara).

Gable and Goddard had a very public romance and went out dancing and dining almost every night. Columnist Dorothy Kilgallen dubbed them "Hollywood's atomic couple." One weekend they went to a resort hotel at Rosarita Beach, where they had a lovers' spat and ended up falling into the swimming pool fully clothed.

Unhappily for Gable, his miserliness quickly disillusioned Goddard, who'd been a celebrated gold digger since her early days as a Ziegfeld chorine and had received at least one fabulous piece of diamond jewelry from each of her many wealthy lovers. Goddard's collection was reportedly worth millions, but her first gift from Gable was a gold Saint Christopher's medallion, which he presented when she was due to fly to Mexico to make a low-budget independent film entitled *The Torch*.

Goddard's skin turned black when she wore the medal, which meant it couldn't be real gold. She told several friends, and the story landed in the newspapers, much to Gable's embarrassment. He'd already promised to drive her to the airport in his Rolls-Royce, but after delivering her to the departure gate, he literally gave her the kiss-off and never dallied with her again.

On April 26, 1949, Metro-Goldwyn-Mayer celebrated the twenty-fifth anniversary of its creation with a gigantic luncheon at the Culver City studio. Arranged in alphabetical order, eighty stars and featured players from the current contract roster sat at long tables and dined on the commissary's legendary chicken soup, roast beef, and Silver Jubilee cake. Sitting between Errol Flynn and Ava Gardner and two places away from Judy Garland, Clark Gable invited them to share his hip flask of brandy when coffee came around. They were all pleasantly tipsy by the time L. B. Mayer and Dore Schary delivered long-winded speeches on MGM's glorious past and hopefully golden future.

The next day Gable left for Palm Beach to stay with Dolly O'Brien. Afterward they went to New York for a charity ball being thrown by Elsa Maxwell at the Park Sheraton Hotel. Another of Gable's frequent companions, Lady Stanley, now divorced and back to calling herself Lady Ashley, happened to be there with banker Kingman Douglass and his wife, Adele, the sister and onetime stage partner of Fred Astaire. Adele Douglass had been a titled lady herself as wife of Lord Charles Cavendish, who died in 1944.

Elsa Maxwell selected an "Americana" theme for the party, with old-fashioned square dancing alternating with the usual ballroom favorites for couples. The snobbish Dolly O'Brien considered square dancing a bit beneath her dignity, so Gable spent part of the evening in the arms of Lady Ashley, who was dressed divinely in a sheer white strapless gown by Christian Dior.

O'Brien got jealous and finally asked Gable to take her home. He did but returned to the ball and stayed until the end with Lady Ashley.

What happened next can only be guessed at, but when Gable went back to Los Angeles, Lady Ashley soon followed and began spending more time there. She owned a mansion in Santa Monica that was part of her inheritance from Douglas Fairbanks and home for her married sister and family.

To top off MGM's silver anniversary production schedule, Dore Schary received approval for the most expensive film that any studio had made since *GWTW.* To establish a link, Schary wanted Gable to be the star of *Quo Vadis?,* based on the famous novel of Christian martyrdom in imperial Rome. Gable would play Marcus Vinicius, a dedicated centurion who falls for a young Christian woman and becomes converted during a time when the insane emperor Nero is fiddling with plans to burn Rome to the ground.

Gable, who'd seen the great silent version of *Quo Vadis?* made by Italian hands, took less than two seconds to reject the idea. "Me in short skirts, carrying a shield, and wearing a helmet with plumes? You've got to be kidding," he told Schary.

By this time Schary's first project with Gable, *Any Number Can Play,* had received several sneak previews around the country and aroused predominantly negative reactions. Comment cards said that the realistic story was too somber and confusing, that Clark Gable suffering blackout spells and striving to be a better husband and father was too much like the soap operas on radio and newfangled television. Bring back sex and romance!

For Gable, who was now almost twice as old as MGM, that demand presented a casting problem. But his friend Z. Wayne Griffin, a former Berg-Allenberg agent trying to better himself, found a promising script and sold Schary on a package deal with Griffin as producer. A romantic comedy by Robert Riley Crutcher, *Key to the City* told of two small-town mayors (one, of course, a woman) who meet and fall in love during a national mayors' convention in San Francisco.

For the publicity value Dore Schary thought that they should consider reteaming Gable with one of the stars from his prewar films. Schary suggested Loretta Young, a close friend since his RKO production *The Farmer's Daughter,* which had won her the 1947 Oscar for best actress. Schary, who knew of Gable and Young's secret, may just have been jesting and trying to provoke a reaction, but both stars accepted the proposal.

It can only be guessed why they accepted, but Gable and Young were both hardened professionals who believed in the old adage "The show must go on." If they declined to work together, it might revive old rumors and start new ones that could harm them as well as their child and other people in their current lives.

By this time Young and advertising executive Tom Lewis had two children of their own, Christopher and Peter, born eleven and a half months apart in 1944 and 1945. Bizarrely, during the recent production of *Come to the Stable,* in which Young played a Catholic nun, she became pregnant again, but she was still in the early stages and decided that she could cope with the six weeks required for *Key to the City.*

Schary assigned the direction to George Sidney, who, with help from a filial connection to a top Loew's executive, had quickly risen from making "B" programmers to major hits such as *Bathing Beauty, Anchors Aweigh,* and *The Three Musketeers.* Gable requested supporting roles for two of his old friends, Frank Morgan and Lewis Stone. Marilyn Maxwell, one of Gable's favorite contract players and also his occasional consort, got her first chance to work with him, as the proverbial "other woman."

Gable's first postwar romantic comedy found him as a tough-fisted ex-stevedore who ran for mayor to wipe out corruption in a small West Coast city. At a convention in San Francisco he meets his exact opposite in the spinster mayoress of Wenorah, Maine. During a series of mishaps, they nearly get arrested several times, but they manage to preserve their political reputations while falling in love. In the end they marry, with the mayoress happily quitting elected office and settling for being a mayor's wife.

Key to the City started shooting in July 1949. Fourteen and a half years had passed since its two stars had last worked together in *Call of the Wild* in snowbound Washington State. Now forty-eight, Gable showed all the ravages of age, but his thirty-six-year-old coactor still looked youthful due to her luminous eyes, sculpted bone structure, and strict physical regimen. For the teaming, MGM concocted a rather raunchy advertising slogan (for 1949!): "They click like a key in a lock."

Amusingly, the ex-lovers fought almost immediately over Gable's contractual right to quit work at five P.M. For some of their scenes together, Young was often left to film her close-ups without Gable standing behind the camera to feed her lines, which costars usually did. She resented having to work with an assistant director or script girl who read Gable's dialogue, so she threatened to quit if he didn't stick around. Director George Sidney feared Gable too much even to suggest it, so he persuaded Eddie Mannix to put the whole production on a nine-to-five schedule.

One day while filming a scene with simulated San Francisco fog, Young collapsed in Gable's arms. He carried her to her dressing room, from where she was rushed by ambulance to Queen of the Angels Hospital. Her personal publicist, Helen Ferguson, later told reporters that the vapors from the fog machines made Young sick and triggered a miscarriage. Young spent two weeks in the hospital and then returned to *Key to the City* for her remaining scenes.

On September 18 Young and her husband held an end-of-production party at their home in Beverly Hills. Gable was the first to arrive, so Tom Lewis fixed drinks for both of them and took him out onto the terrace to chat. Many years later Lewis confided to his son, Christopher, that he asked Gable if the rumors about his being Judy's father were true.

Gable allegedly replied, "Tom, if that were true, do you think I would let anything or anyone stop me from knowing my own child?" Gable may have just been covering up for Young, who apparently had never confessed to Lewis that she was Judy's real mother. She excused their strong resemblance by hinting that Judy was an indiscretion of her wayward actress-sister, Sally Blane.

The party had barely started when news arrived that Frank Morgan had died suddenly of a heart attack. Gable, who'd played golf with his fifty-nine-year-old friend that very morning, was devastated and left immediately to console the widow. *Key to the City*, in which Morgan portrayed Mayor Gable's fire chief, turned out to be his last movie, but he will always be most remembered for playing the title role in MGM's 1939 *The Wizard of Oz*.

By November Gable and Lady Sylvia Ashley had become a steady couple. Friends believed that after nearly eight years of widowerhood and chasing around, Gable finally wanted to settle down again. Lady Ashley, who'd once been a queen of Hollywood society as Mrs. Douglas Fairbanks, saw what might be her last chance to regain her former status.

In December Gable and Lady Ashley were observed holding hands and kissing during a party at the home of agent Charles Feldman. Several days later Gable phoned Howard Strickling and asked him to make arrangements for a private wedding ceremony. When Strickling hesitated and asked if he'd been boozing, Gable replied, "I know what I'm doing. Don't worry about it."

The wedding took place on December 20 in Solvang, a picturesque Scandinavian community in Santa Barbara County. Strickling had some friends there who loaned their living room and arranged for the pastor of the Danish Lutheran Church to officiate. Strickling stood in for the late Otto Winkler as Gable's best man, and Lady Sylvia's brother-in-law, Basil Bleck, gave the bride away.

The ceremony was kept secret from the press, but Strickling brought along an MGM still photographer to provide coverage for the next day's official announcement. The bride and groom wore seemingly color-coordinated outfits—she a tailored navy-blue wool dress and he a navy-blue suit. When they toasted each other with champagne after the ceremony, they were both so nervous that they spilled bubbly down their fronts and wilted her corsage and his boutonniere.

The marriage license listed Gable's age as forty-eight and Sylvia's as thirty-nine. More likely she was in her middle forties. In 1936, when she married Douglas Fairbanks, she claimed to be thirty-two, which in 1949 would have made her forty-five.

The wedding announcement took the news media by surprise and sent reporters rushing to the morgues to dig up background on the fourth Mrs. Clark Gable. Over the years she'd covered many of her tracks, but this much seems to be true: Born Sylvia Hawkes, the cockney Londoner was the daughter of a stable groom, though in later life she tried to dignify him by claiming he was a policeman. A willowy blonde with Wedgwood blue eyes and a rosy complexion, she blossomed early. As a teenager she worked as a lingerie model in designer showrooms and as a chorine in stage revues and nightclubs. Along the way she acquired a posh accent, a taste for jewels and high fashion, and a long string of wealthy admirers. In 1927 she married Lord Anthony Ashley, heir apparent of the Earl of Shaftesbury, and became the toast of Mayfair society. She philandered with playboys and business tycoons, and when she became involved with Douglas Fairbanks, by then a globe-hopping retired movie star in a disintegrating marriage to Mary Pickford, Lord Ashley finally divorced her. After Pickford also filed for divorce, Ashley and Fairbanks were married in 1936. He bought a house on Park Lane in London, and they traveled extensively until his death at their main home in California in 1939.

Before Fairbanks died, Ashley persuaded him to change his will to favor her instead of his only child, Douglas Junior, product of his first marriage to socialite Beth Sully. According to Douglas Junior, his father left a cash estate of $4 million, plus the homes in Santa Monica and London and a three-thousand-acre California citrus and cattle ranch known as Rancho Zorro. Junior claimed that Ashley got half of everything and that he ended up with about one-third after other bequests were taken care of. She also received first choice of tangible assets and took both houses, several Rolls-Royces, and Fairbanks's famous collection of Old West paintings and sculptures by Frederic Remington.

In 1944 Sylvia married another British aristocrat, Lord Edward Stanley, Baron of Alderly, who'd settled in New York for the duration of the war. They separated after eight months, allegedly due to his bisexuality, but she continued to circulate in high society as Lady Stanley until they were divorced in 1948.

After celebrating Christmas at the ranch in Encino, the newlywed Gables took a honeymoon trip to Hawaii, sailing from San Francisco on New Year's Eve on the S.S. *Lurline*. Overnight, the 1940s ticked into the 1950s. The couple woke up to a cablegram from Dolly O'Brien: "Happy leis, happy days!"

When the *Lurline* reached Honolulu, ten thousand Gable fans had gathered at the terminal to wish the honeymooners "Aloha." MGM had arranged for a police escort to whisk them to their rented villa in the swank Kahala section of the city.

Two weeks later the Gables returned home, looking tanned and deliriously happy. During their absence huge wooden crates had started arriving from England, filled with furniture, antiques, and more of

Sylvia's belongings that had been in storage for years. Gable urged her to take over running the household and to make whatever decorative and staff changes that she wanted.

On February 1, which just happened to be Gable's forty-ninth birthday, MGM released *Key to the City*. Like *Any Number Can Play* before it, the comedy received mixed to negative reviews and sold just enough tickets to earn a modest profit. Given the industry's current business depression, that alone was something of an achievement. The number of home TV sets and broadcasting stations had more than doubled in a year. Movie theater attendance had plunged to an average of 60 million per week, the lowest level since 1933. In large cities, which had the highest concentration of TV sets, attendance during the prime evening hours was down by as much as 90 percent! Many theaters were closing and would end up being demolished or converted to other use.

So far the Hollywood movie industry was treating TV like an enemy by withholding its product (old and new) and refusing to let its stars work in the medium. If the public wanted to see Clark Gable, it would have to go to a theater.

"Give them something they can't see at home" became the dominant philosophy at MGM and elsewhere. That meant not only big stars but "big" pictures like musicals, action-adventures, and historical epics with color photography and other technology that couldn't be found on fuzzy, small-screen black-and-white TV. (Tubes bigger than sixteen inches and color were still a decade away.)

MGM had some new male stars under development, most notably Stewart Granger, who'd been assigned to the African safari thriller *King Solomon's Mines,* and Mario Lanza, about to make *The Great Caruso*. But Schary and Mayer wanted the highly paid contract veterans to share the load. Spencer Tracy had found a niche in character vehicles like *Father of the Bride,* and Robert Taylor was taking over the role that Gable rejected in *Quo Vadis?*

Gable couldn't quarrel with two projects that were being prepared for him. *To Please a Lady* was a racing car drama with Barbara Stanwyck as costar. *Across the Wide Missouri,* based on the Pulitzer prize-winning frontier history by Bernard DeVoto, would be a $5 million epic and Gable's first movie in color since *GWTW*.

The first script required some location filming at the annual Indianapolis 500 in May, and the other would be made almost entirely in Colorado during the summer, when outdoor shooting days were longest. They would be produced back to back, after which Gable would have the rest of the year for leisure.

Meanwhile Gable and "Ducky Doodle," his pet name for the ex-Lady Ashley, started feathering their nest. She considered the house too small for entertaining, so Gable sanctioned the building of a second dining room and a two-bedroom guest cottage. Not surprisingly, Sylvia hated everything reminiscent of Gable's previous wife and marriage, but she shrewdly kept her feelings to herself and made gradual changes rather than doing anything drastic that might upset him.

In time the interior decor became more London Mayfair than California Rancho. English and French antiques replaced Early American pieces, but Gable's favorite sofas and chairs were simply smartened up with slipcovers. To gain a room for her hobbies of needlepoint and watercolor painting, Sylvia took over the office of secretary Jean Garceau, who would henceforth work from her home in nearby Sherman Oaks.

Two new additions to the household were Sylvia's personal maid, who'd been with her for years, and a toy terrier named Minnie. Sylvia wanted to replace Gable's longtime valet, Rufus Martin, with a British-trained butler, but he refused to consider it. He did agree, however, to a new cook. The present one, Jessie, originally hired by Carole Lombard, took an instant dislike to her new boss and seemed capable of spiking her morning tea with poison.

In May, Gable started *To Please a Lady,* working for the first time since 1941's *They Met in Bombay* with MGM's dean of directors, Clarence Brown, whose recent adaptation of William Faulkner's *Intruder in the Dust* (racial biogotry in the Deep South) had been critically aclaimed but a box-office flop. The title of Barré Lyndon and Marge Decker's original screenplay had been selected before Gable's marriage and was not intended to capitalize on the publicity it received.

Professional racing car driver Mike Brannon was the most hard-boiled character that Gable had played in more than a decade. Due to Mike's ruthless tactics on the track, several rival drivers have been killed or seriously injured. Crowds boo him, and he's finally reduced to stunt driving in carnival shows to earn a buck. Meanwhile Regina Ford, a gossip columnist and newscaster as powerful as Walter Winchell, has started a crusade against Mike to make sure that he never races again.

Gable's teaming with Barbara Stanwyck was another throwback to the past, the first time they'd worked together since 1931, when he was still only a featured player and had the villain's role in her Warner Bros. melodrama *Night Nurse*. Since then Stanwyck had opted for a freelance career and ping-ponged between studios while becoming a Hollywood legend and at least the peer of the strong, dominant types like Bette Davis and Joan Crawford. Now forty-three, she had to be careful about playing romantic roles, but the macho and six-years-older Gable seemed a good match.

Gable and Stanwyck were among those named in the notorious "Unmarried Husbands and Wives" scandal, though, of course, with other partners. Stanwyck's affair with Robert Taylor had also quickly been legitimatized through marriage. After eleven years they were still wed, but the relationship was currently being tested by Taylor's seven-month posting to Italy for *Quo Vadis?*

Gable's brutalizing of Stanwyck in *Night Nurse* was one of the first things that made him a romantic idol, so Clarence Brown and the scriptwriters included a scene in *To Please a Lady* as a sort of homage. When Gable first complains to Stanwyck about derogatory remarks in her syndicated column, he tells her, "I can handle you, baby. You're just another dame to me." Goaded by the caustic smirk that she gives him, he adds, "You better listen to what I'm saying, or I'll knock that smile off your face."

"Knock it off," Stanwyck snarls contemptuously, whereupon he does. Following the whack, he practically smothers her with a kiss and then struts out.

Needless to say, Stanwyck keeps coming back for more, though never again for anything quite that violent. When Gable tries a comeback by entering the classic Memorial Day race at Indianapolis, he redeems himself by giving up the lead in the race in order to save another driver's life.

The production of *To Please a Lady* was the new Mrs. Gable's first real exposure to the movie business. Douglas Fairbanks had retired by the time of their marriage, so she was unprepared for Gable getting up at five in the morning and being away at the studio all day. She didn't know what was expected of her as a star's wife. Was she supposed to be involved with his career or keep out of it? If anyone knew the answer to that, there might have been fewer Hollywood divorces.

Sylvia tried to be helpful and supportive. Although she was the reverse of an early riser, she managed to get to MGM several times a week to have lunch with Gable in his dressing bungalow. Afterward she would visit the set to chat with Stanwyck and featured actor Adolphe Menjou, both of whom she'd known socially for years.

The movie was one of the few that took Gable beyond the MGM backlots to film exterior scenes. His wife accompanied him on the three-week shoot in Indianapolis, which was tinged with sad memories for Gable. The city had been the final stop on Carole Lombard's bond tour, and she had left from there on her plane journey home. Gable visited the downtown places where she had made her last public appearances, but due to his insistence on train travel, he was able to avoid the airport.

Gable did some of his own driving in the raceway scenes, with stunt men doubling in the more dangerous moments. His longtime cinematographer and friend Hal Rosson used six camera crews to get what a *Variety* critic later called "some of the greatest racing footage ever put on celluloid."

The Gables stayed at the Marriott Hotel. Sylvia brought along her favorite nephew, seventeen-year-old Timothy Bleck, for companionship while Gable toiled. The youth was a bit too spoiled and "nancy" for Gable's liking, but he tried to tolerate him.

Before returning to Los Angeles, Sylvia wanted to go to England to confer with her money managers, but she hadn't figured on Gable's impending commitment for *Across the Wide Missouri*. His phobia against flying and the slow train-boat option made it impossible for him to accompany her. She took off in tandem with nephew Timothy and promised to be home in time to join Gable for the Colorado-based production.

Sylvia's trip was evidence of a serious problem in the marriage. All of Gable's wives had always paid their own way in terms of personal things like clothing and jewelry, cars, and health and beauty expenses. He expected Sylvia to do the same, but her case was complicated by her lack of ready cash. Most of her wealth was in British banks and securities.

Since the end of the war, the government had been protecting the economy by placing drastic limits on the export of local currency. Citizens, of which Sylvia was still one, could leave with no more than five hundred pounds at a time.

On this London trip Sylvia tried to outfox the authorities by dipping into one of her bank safe-deposit boxes for some diamond jewelry worth about 18,000 pounds ($90,000), which she intended to sell to her superrich friend Barbara Hutton back in Los Angeles. But Sylvia didn't escape the eagle eyes of a U.S. Customs inspector, who couldn't find the jewelry listed on her declaration form. He temporarily confiscated it for appraisal, and she was eventually fined $5,000 for customs evasion.

By the time that Sylvia returned in July, Gable had finished costume fittings and other preparations for *Across the Wide Missouri*, his first historical western since *Honky Tonk* but going further back in time to the 1820s. Dore Schary and producer Robert Sisk persuaded Gable to accept William Wellman as director, though the two had been estranged since battling over Loretta Young during the filming of *Call of the Wild* more than fifteen years before. But Gable had to admit that Wellman was one of the masters of rugged outdoor adventures. He also admired Wellman's recent World War II drama *Battleground,* the first smash hit of the Schary regime.

L. B. Mayer had approved a budget of $5 million for the Technicolor epic. Talbot Jennings, one of the scriptwriters of *Mutiny on the Bounty* and a specialist in literary adaptations, extracted the screenplay from Bernard DeVoto's nonfiction best seller, which had no plot or major characters in the dramatic sense. Jennings and William Wellman invented them but used real names and happenings from the book for authenticity.

Clad throughout in buckskin and leather, Gable portrayed Flint Mitchell, a Kentuckian leading an expedition of French and Scottish fur trappers through wild country controlled by a militant faction of the Blackfoot Indians. The story carries a trendy 1950s message for racial tolerance as Flint marries the granddaughter of the elderly chieftain so that he can continue the expedition and open the region to white settlement. He succeeds but in the process falls deeply in love with his bride and fathers a son. He decides to remain with them, but when other trappers start a war with the Indians, he winds up a widower with a baby to raise.

Talbot Jennings borrowed some of the mixed-race romance from *The Squaw Man,* a famous stage melodrama that had been filmed twice, most recently in 1931 by MGM, which still owned the rights. Sylvia Gable, who had a rather biased view of the world beyond her lily-white society circle, was appalled that Gable took the role and predicted it would ruin his career. He told her to butt out. If he rejected the job, he'd be suspended without pay, and they'd have to start economizing to compensate for the $250,000 that went to his replacement.

Not surprisingly, MGM had no Native American actors under contract; nor were there many in all of the Hollywood industry. The casting of the Blackfoot characters started with María Elena Marqués, a major star in her native Mexico, who was recommended for the role of Kamiah by her compatriot, Ricardo Montalban, an MGM contractee. Montalban (who happened to be the brother-in-law of Loretta Young) also landed in the cast as a warrior named Nippo Strongheart. Long-ago star Jack Holt, whose movie career started in 1914, portrayed the old chief, Bear Ghost. Other "redskins" (with help from Max Factor) included John Hodiak, sporting long pigtails, and J. Carroll Naish, taking time off from playing the Italian immigrant hero of radio's *Life with Luigi.* Gable found a role for his buddy Adolphe Menjou as one of the French trappers on the expedition.

William Wellman and cinematographer William Mellor selected an area of perpetually snow-capped mountains and lush green valleys near Durango, in the southwestern corner of Colorado, as the location site. The filming would take three months, but the shooting of Gable's scenes were arranged so that he wouldn't need to stick around for more than the first two.

His long experience as an outdoor sportsman told him to pack light and rough for the trip, but his wife ignored his advice and prepared as she would have for the royal horse-racing season at Ascot. She filled seventeen trunks and suitcases with clothing and personal accessories. Though the couple would be staying at a deluxe resort hotel, she also insisted on taking along bed, bath, and table linens, a Royal Doulton china service, and silverware, as well as eveything that she needed for her watercolor painting and needlepoint hobbies.

Gable ended up with four trunks of his own, though they contained more hunting and fishing gear than apparel. He also had several cases of guns and ammunition, so transporting everything the 750 miles to Durango became a major project. MGM sent one of its trucks to haul most of it, but Gable took the explosive remainder in his station wagon and drove to Durango, with Minnie the terrier as his only companion. Sylvia, who had a tendency to carsickness, flew to Durango on the twice-daily air shuttle that MGM operated to transport personnel and supplies and to pick up film for processing.

The Gables' temporary home was the largest guest cottage at El Rancho Encantado in the environs of Durango, a town of six thousand with three movie theaters and still untouched by TV for lack of any stations within receiving range. Sylvia immediately proceeded to beautify the cottage. She asked the management to add frilly curtains to the windows, which were covered only by venetian blinds, and to put plush carpeting over the tiled floors. Outside she had some of the lawn torn up so that she could have an instant garden with flower bushes and shrubs flown in from a nursery in Beverly Hills.

As one of only a few women in the Hollywood contingent of more than a hundred people, Sylvia's behavior attracted attention and comment. During the day she wore denim jumpsuits from Neiman Marcus or cowgirl dresses that looked designed for Dale Evans. When she accompanied Gable to the set, she usually brought along her needlepoint or paints and easel. She was just being herself, but it didn't match up with the surroundings. Gable's buddies cringed, and he along with them.

Everybody lunched together at long communal tables. Sylvia always had Minnie with her and plunked the dog in Gable's lap while she fed it morsels from her plate. Around her tiny neck Minnie wore a diamond-studded collar that Gable had bought for her during one of his rare spending sprees.

On his days off Gable took Sylvia hunting and fishing, or at least attempted to. She was a lousy shot and would have been a safety menace if permitted to continue. Her hands loaded down with rings and bracelets that she refused to remove, she had no dexterity for fly-casting either. When he tried to teach her to build a campfire and to cook simple meals, she didn't even know how to brew coffee or fry an egg.

After a month Sylvia grew bored and returned to Encino to do some more redecorating at the ranch and to prepare for the busy fall and winter social seasons ahead. Gable, meanwhile, had to cope with director William Wellman, who was attempting something "different" in westerns with a deliberately half-written script that left room for many scenes to be made up on the spot, requiring the actors to improvise. For realism, the Indian characters spoke only in their native language. In scenes when Indians and whites met, they always had interpreters among them. Their conversations and monologues were delivered in English and Blackfoot and consumed twice as much screen time.

By September, as the world held its breath over the escalating war in Korea, Gable was back home and trying to keep pace with the hectic social calendar devised by his wife. When they weren't hosting a cocktail party or a dinner at the ranch, they were attending the same at someone else's house or going to a premiere or society affair. Over the years they'd acquired some of the same friends, like the Gary Coopers, the Jack Bennys, and the Fred Astaires, but Sylvia's guest lists tended to favor visiting English and European aristocrats and piss-elegant types such as the Ronald Colmans, the Cole Porters, Noël Coward, and Clifton Webb.

When entertaining at the ranch, Sylvia usually ordered catering from the Brown Derby or Chasen's. For all her swankness, she adored the typically American serving utensil known as a lazy Susan, though hers were filled with caviar, foie gras, and other premium goodies. Cocktails were always vintage French champagne, which she ordered by the case and had shipped in from Harrod's in London.

With Gable free of film commitments for the moment, the couple had more time together and the marriage sputtered on. Neither he nor Sylvia seemed willing to admit that they had made a mistake. No doubt remaining together was preferable to becoming a public joke for one of the shortest celebrity marriages on record.

Sex was apparently not one of their problems. Gable once told his buddy Hal Rosson, "Sylvia's dynamite in bed and can French like a sailor's whore."

In October Gable's first film of the new decade, *To Please a Lady,* entered release and, despite good reviews, flopped at the box office. It was the fate of the majority of movies that year, as sales of home TV sets soared ever higher. The few blockbusters were Technicolor epics like *Samson and Delilah* and *King Solomon's Mines.* For lack of a hit, Gable fell from the 1950 list of the "Top Ten Box-Office Stars," his first absence since the years of his war service.

The choice of Gable's next vehicle was placed on hold until MGM finished editing *Across the Wide Missouri* and ran some test previews.

In mid-December the Gables traveled by train and ship to Nassau in the Bahamas to spend Christmas and New Year's at the estate of one of Sylvia's titled chums. On December 20 they celebrated their first wedding anniversary, which prompted Elsa Maxwell to gush in her syndicated newspaper column: "I've always been very fond of Clark and Sylvia, and I'm looking forward to their golden anniversary." Never mind that in 1999 Maxwell would have been 116 and the Gables both pushing 100.

Before returning to California, the Gables stopped over in New York to see Cole Porter's new stage musical *Out of This World* and to replenish their wardrobes. Gable had been ordering suits from Brooks Brothers' custom department since his stage acting days. John Garrity, the salesman who'd taken care of him since the end of the war, recalled that "Mr. Gable liked natural shoulders and trim, straight-cut trousers. He came to us to look like a well-turned-out gentleman."

On this visit Gable brought along his wife, the first time Garrity could remember a companion: "Mr. Gable was always good-natured when he came for fittings. But this time he was trying on a jacket, and his wife told him that he should have the shoulders widened. He told her to leave the fitting room, and she did. You could tell he was angry. He had very good taste in clothes and knew just what he wanted."

Once home again Gable distanced himself from some of Sylvia's socializing. If she had friends or relatives visiting whom he didn't like, he went golfing at the Bel-Air Country Club or saddled his horse and rode around the ranch.

He also started questioning Sylvia's expenditures. He couldn't understand why she needed a maid of her own just to take care of her boudoir, help her to get dressed, and prepare her baths. He finally told her, "We've got too much help. One of them has to go, and it's not going to be any of mine."

Another thorn was Sylvia's teenage nephew, Timothy Bleck, who had discovered the perks that went with having Clark Gable for an uncle. During a birthday tour of Europe paid for by his aunt, Timothy kept popping into MGM's offices to "borrow" cash, which eventually amounted to about a thousand dollars (a tidy sum for 1951) that Gable had to pay back.

His close friends attributed Gable's anger over his marriage to disappointment. His previous wives had always pampered him and made him feel like king of the roost. Sylvia tried to a certain degree, but she wasn't the type to subordinate herself or to give up people and activities that she loved. When Sylvia focused on others, he exploded, but like a child. Instead of talking about it, he pouted and kept to himself.

Their Waterloo may have been February 1, 1951, Gable's fiftieth birthday. By that time Sylvia had learned that her husband abhorred large formal gatherings with international society nabobs, so she arranged an intimate dinner party and invited only close friends of Gable's and a few of her own whom he liked. The group included the Al Menascos, the Howard Stricklings, the Z. Wayne Griffins, designer Gilbert Adrian and actress-wife Janet Gaynor, and Merle Oberon. The latter, newly divorced from cinematographer Lucien Ballard, had been Sylvia's best Hollywood chum since the Douglas Fairbanks era. Presumably Oberon's long-ago affair with Gable didn't bother either Sylvia or the birthday boy, or she wouldn't have been invited to the party.

To surprise him, Sylvia selected a menu of Gable's favorite fare, including chicken and dumplings. Unfortunately, the cook decided to save time by fricasseeing the chicken the day before and then neglected to put it in the refrigerator overnight. By dinnertime the next evening, the stew had spoiled, but the cook was too frightened to confess and just proceeded to make the dumplings and arrange everything on a silver serving platter.

Luckily, when the butler carried the platter into the dining room, the stench was enough to make even terrier Minnie whine. Everyone but Gable started laughing and cracking jokes about food poisoning and diarrhea. Gable's silent rage soon forced him to rise from his chair and storm out. He went upstairs to his bedroom suite, locked the door, and remained there for several hours. When he heard the guests leaving, he came down to say good-bye but offered no apologies for his behavior. His friends tried to pretend that it never happened.

Gable's marital turmoil, coupled with worries over his career, triggered a resumption of heavy boozing. Sylvia sensed that it was more than she could handle and took off on one of her banking trips to England, hoping that her husband would have mellowed by the time of her return.

In the interim Gable accepted MGM's proposal for an epic western entitled *Lone Star,* provided that his friend Z. Wayne Griffin again serve as the producer. Dore Schary picked Ava Gardner and recent Oscar winner Broderick Crawford for Gable's costars and also pulled Lionel Barrymore from semiretirement for a major supporting role.

While waiting for production to begin, Gable decided that he didn't want to be married any longer. When Sylvia returned from England, he wasted no time in telling her. One afternoon while she was in her bathroom soaking in the tub, he strolled in, said "I want a divorce," and left.

Stunned, Sylvia frantically phoned some of Gable's friends for help and advice, but none really wanted to get involved. "At first I couldn't believe that Clark was serious," Sylvia later recalled. "I stayed on at the house for several weeks, during which time he scarcely spoke to me. When he did, he was very sullen. I tried everything I knew how to get him to change his mind. Ultimately, I had to give in."

Sylvia moved in with her sister and family at the Santa Monica house that she had inherited from Douglas Fairbanks. Her pal Barbara Hutton persuaded her to retain Jerry Giesler, the foremost "celebrity lawyer," who had represented the Woolworth heiress in her divorces from Count Haugwitz-Reventlow and Cary Grant.

The fourth Mrs. Clark Gable filed for divorce in Santa Monica Superior Court on May 31, 1951. The marriage had lasted a total of one year, five months, and nine days.

The divorce proceedings would drag on for months. Meanwhile, as soon as Sylvia removed her personal possessions from the ranch, Gable changed all the locks and started to undo most of her renovations to the house. First on the list was his Early American gun room, which had been transformed into a reception area with a crystal chandelier and French Provincial furniture.

Given attorney Jerry Giesler's fame for winning huge divorce settlements for his clients, Gable's nerves were at the breaking point. He was drinking so heavily that it showed in his face and often caused the "shakes" when he was working under tense conditions at the studio. Observers who didn't know better gossiped that he was in the early stages of Parkinson's disease.

For *Lone Star,* Gable requested his longtime friend Hal Rosson for cinematographer. The western was shot in black and white because it was easier to control the lighting and mask some of Gable's problems.

Directed by Vincent Sherman, *Lone Star* found Gable as a Texas cattle baron involved in a complex fiction that dragged in such real characters as Sam Houston, Andrew Jackson, and Jim Bowie. Gable and senator Broderick Crawford slugged it out over politics and Ava Gardner, a vixen in the Scarlett O'Hara mold.

During the filming Gable served double duty by making a cameo guest appearance in *Callaway Went Thataway,* which MGM had in production at the same time. Gable played himself, supposedly out nightclubbing with a lady friend, when the movie's title character spots him and briefly stops at his table to chat. The spoof of TV western stars was the nearest Gable ever came to working with Esther Williams and Elizabeth Taylor, top MGM females, who also made guest appearances but in other scenes.

Through no fault of Gable's, the still-unreleased *Across the Wide Missouri* had become a major embarrassment for Dore Schary, who had selected the project, and L. B. Mayer, who approved the $5 million budget. In a series of test previews in big cities and small towns, audience reactions to the 135-minute epic were overwhelmingly negative; the confusing and rambling plot and the repetitive English/Blackfoot dialogue caused the most complaints.

To avert a probable financial disaster, Schary canceled the planned July 4 release and asked Sam Zimbalist, MGM's fair-haired boy since producing *King Solomon's Mines* and the recently completed *Quo Vadis?*, to try to fix the movie. Zimbalist proceeded to cut one hour, reducing the running time to seventy-six minutes and adding an unseen narrator to tie all the bits and pieces together into a comprehensible story. Scripter Talbot Jennings was recalled to write the narration, supposedly the words of the son of Gable and his Indian bride, now a grown man and telling the story of his parents. It got even crazier when Schary picked MGM's musical star Howard Keel to read the narration.

With the cuts in *Across the Wide Missouri,* about $2.5 million worth of Technicolor footage ended in the trash. Small wonder that Loew's-MGM's profits continued to plunge and president Nicholas Schenck decided to reorganize the studio again. This time L. B. Mayer got the boot, since he'd been there decades longer than Dore Schary and also had been fighting with Schenck for a salary hike and stock options.

Mayer's "resignation" on June 22, 1951, shocked the Hollywood industry. For twenty-seven years he'd been regarded as "mogul of the moguls" and the perfector, if not the inventor, of the star-driven studio factory system.

Gable's relationship with Mayer had always been cold and distant, so he wasn't bothered by his departure. But he saw difficulties ahead as Dore Schary became sole studio head. Gable's close friend Eddie Mannix, who'd long been Mayer's right hand, lost power by being assigned to an executive committee that served under Schary and had slight authority of its own.

Schary had a mandate from Schenck to cut operating costs while at the same time improving the quality of the product, a seeming contradiction. Schary believed that he could succeed by scrapping the contract roster system and hiring talent only on a picture-by-picture basis. MGM currently had hundreds of actors, writers, directors, producers, cinematographers, set designers, and the like under long-term contracts and had to pay them whether they were working or not. Years before, when the studio was turning out fifty or sixty features annually, that had made financial sense. But the yearly output had dropped to about twenty-five features, due to TV's decimation of theater attendance.

The major star actors were, by competitive necessity, the most highly paid of MGM's contract employees, so Schary's cuts had to start with them. Contracts were examined for expiration dates and "out" clauses. Greer Garson's was not renewed. Judy Garland's was canceled for undependable behavior.

Gable's contract had three more years to run, so he seemed safe for the moment. But with a divorce settlement looming, he wanted to protect himself and decided to change agents. Phil Berg had retired, but his partner, Bert Allenberg, had affiliated with the William Morris Agency and taken Gable with him. Allenberg had started agenting in the early days of vaudeville and silent movies and, in Gable's opinion, had failed to keep up with changes in the business. Though he had to pay $50,000 to end the Allenberg contract, he switched to George Chasin of MCA, which had been a leader in the postwar movement toward independent production and profit-sharing for talent.

When Gable finished *Lone Star,* Chasin showed him how he could keep more of the income from his present MGM contract by taking advantage of a loophole in the federal tax laws. If Gable worked and resided outside the United States for at least eighteen months, his earnings during that period would be exempt from income tax. Since Gable's income was in the highest tax bracket, that would be a huge saving.

It would also pay for some of Gable's divorce settlement, but Chasin first had to get MGM's cooperation. Dore Schary quickly saw the advantages because the studio was already heavily involved in foreign production. From the rentals of its films, MGM had millions in "frozen" funds that couldn't be exported from certain countries due to currency laws but could be spent locally to finance a film. Production costs were also about 50 percent less than in Hollywood due to nonunionized labor and the lower standards of living in economies still affected by the set-backs of World War II.

No single project could occupy Gable for eighteen months, so Schary would have to find two or three to make the plan feasible. While scripts and ideas were being considered, Gable and his lawyers prepared themselves for the invevitable showdown with Sylvia, who was already back to calling herself Lady Ashley in her social perambulations, and Jerry Giesler.

Giesler's aides were planting items in the gossip columns that hinted that Mrs. Gable's settlement would be equivalent to half the gold stored at Fort Knox. With nothing more traumatizing on his mind at the moment, Gable panicked and, on advice from his lawyers, decided to move to Nevada to establish residence so that *he* could divorce Sylvia before she got rid of him.

Before he left, he may have felt a compulsion to rectify some other past mistakes. In any case he paid a visit to Judy Lewis, who in November would turn sixteen but had yet to be told the identity of either of her real parents. When Judy returned home from school that day, she found Clark Gable standing alone in the foyer and assumed that he'd come to talk to her mother about some movie business.

"You must be Judy," he said with a smile. She wondered how he knew her, since she'd never met him in person before. "Yes, I am. And you're Mr. Gable, aren't you?" she politely replied.

Loretta Young suddenly appeared, and they all went into the living room to chat. Gable invited Judy to sit next to him on the sofa. He asked her about school and her personal interests.

"I was surprised," she later recalled. "Usually my mother's friends paid very little attention to me. Their questions were always polite, but they weren't interested in my answers, they just asked out of courtesy. But he was different. I could tell he really cared about what I was saying. I liked him, and I began to feel more at ease."

Her mother left the room, but the conversation continued. Judy told Gable of her current boyfriend, Jack Haley, Jr., son of the entertainer best known for the Tin Man in *The Wizard of Oz*. The time passed so quickly for Judy that she would later be unable to remember how long Gable stayed. When he finally left, he cupped her face in his huge hands, kissed her lightly on the forehead, and said, "Good-bye, Judy." She never saw him again.

To start the ball rolling on his Nevada divorce, Gable checked into the Glenbrook Lodge near Lake Tahoe and stayed the six weeks that were required to qualify as a resident of that state. He obtained a Nevada driver's license and paid the state's poll tax. On October 4 he drove to Reno and filed for the divorce.

At the same time he was also trying to transfer investments to Nevada to prevent them from being declared part of the marriage's community property. Free to visit California during his probationary period if he stayed less than twenty-four hours, he drove to Los Angeles, cashed in his several bank accounts, and took all the money back to Nevada in a suitcase.

When the Glenbrook Lodge shuttered for the winter, Gable moved to a dude ranch near Carson City. While staying there, he became romantically involved with a young Beverly Hills socialite, Natalie Thompson, who was also in the process of a divorce. Betty Chisholm, his wealthy pre-Sylvia friend in Arizona, frequently flew over from Phoenix to visit him as well, so he never lacked companionship.

Gable's advisers thought they'd outfoxed Jerry Giesler, but the latter filed for an injunction against the Nevada divorce and eventually won. The Nevada court conceded that Sylvia's California action was filed four months before her husband's and should take precedence.

Gable moved back to the Encino ranch to await the scheduling of the hearing in Santa Monica Superior Court. There would be an unexpected delay. While holidaying in the Bahamas, Sylvia broke her leg in a car crash. She was airlifted to New York for hospitalization.

Feeling lonely, Gable tried resuming his relationship with Virginia Grey, one of several consorts whom he dumped when he married Lady Ashley. Of all his flames, Grey had been on the perimeter the longest, going back to 1937 when she played a bit part in *Test Pilot*. Gossip columnists often pegged Grey as a potential Gable wife, but she could never pin him down. His wedding to the woman she called "Lady Ashcan" was the last straw. When Gable started calling her anew, she changed her phone number and never dated him again.

In February 1952 Gable's producer-friend Z. Wayne Griffin, also an activist in the Republican Party, persuaded him to attend a huge rally being held at Madison Square Garden in New York to "draft" General Dwight D. Eisenhower into running for president in the November election. Gable had never before endorsed any political candidate, but he revered Eisenhower and had met him several times during his air force service.

Currently the supreme allied commander, the general was head-quartered in Europe, which, in that era before intercontinental TV transmission, meant linking him to the rally by voice only on a direct telephone line. In front of a crowd of forty thousand rabid Republicans from all over the nation, Gable exchanged a few words with Eisenhower and then told him, "General, I'm sure that if you were here at this rally, there'd be no doubt in your mind that your fellow Americans want you as their next president. If you decide to run, that's the way it will be, because you *will* win."

When the applause and cheering subsided, Gable introduced "Mr. American Music himself," Irving Berlin. The pint-sized tunesmith proceeded to perform his latest work, "I Like Ike," which would become the Republican campaign anthem when Eisenhower accepted the candidacy.

Before returning to Los Angeles, Gable threw caution to the winds and visited Sylvia at New York Hospital. Wayne Griffin, who accompanied him, later recalled: "They got to laughing, joking, and talking. They were like two youngsters. I had to leave for a business appointment, but Clark stayed on for a couple of hours. He was in a great mood when I saw him later. I really thought there might be a reconciliation."

But during the train journey home, Gable had plenty of time to consider it. He either forgot about it or realized that it would never work. By April Sylvia was well enough to travel and to have her day in Santa Monica Superior Court. Walking with a cane and literally holding on to attorney Jerry Giesler for support, she survived fifteen minutes of tearful testimony before the judge.

Sylvia claimed that she'd made many attempts to save the marriage. "But when I asked my husband what was wrong, he couldn't specifically tell me," she said. "His only answer was 'There isn't anything that you have done wrong. You have been quite wonderful. I'm just not happy being a married man.' "

Gable's longtime valet, Rufus Martin, was called as a confirming witness. "At night, after dinner, Mr. Gable would go directly upstairs to his room. Mrs. Gable would sit alone by the television. He wouldn't talk to her. He was moody," Martin testified.

That was as raunchy as it got for newspaper reporters who'd arrived with hopes that some of the Gables' dirty linen would be exposed. On April 21 the divorce was granted in an eleven-page document that also awarded Sylvia a financial settlement that read like a movie contract. For the next five years she would receive a percentage of Gable's total earnings: 10 percent in the first year, and 7 percent in each of the following four years. Due to all the intangibles involved, it was impossible to put a cash value to the settlement, but if Gable was to earn a total of $2.5 million in those five years, Sylvia's share would be roughly $190,000.

In their less than eighteen months of married life, the Gables had acquired so little "community property" that Sylvia's half-share was appraised at a mere $6,002.47, which he was ordered to pay to her in cash. Apart from the settlement with Gable, Sylvia had her huge inheritance from Douglas Fairbanks, which continued to earn her a substantial annual income in interest alone. She eventually sold the three-thousand-acre Rancho Zorro to real estate developers for $7.5 million.

After it was all over, Gable's only public comment was to columnist Louella Parsons: "Sylvia's a fine woman. It's too bad that we couldn't get along." Privately he told his friend John Lee Mahin, "I must have been drunk when I proposed."

In May, after many complicated negotiations, agent George Chasin finally reached an agreement with MGM that cleared the way for Gable's eighteen-month "tax exile" abroad. By that time both *Across the Wide Missouri* and *Lone Star* had been released and taken box-office flops, so Dore Schary had the edge in the bargaining. Gable liked only one of the three projects offered—a remake of *Red Dust* with the locale changed to East Africa—but he realized that he couldn't be too fussy or the whole plan might fall through.

With MGM paying much of his expenses in addition to his salary, Gable had a sweet deal. The studio had to provide deluxe transportation and accommodation, as well as a thousand-dollar-per week living allowance. The only real "hardship" was that while working in England, where two of the three films were to be made, he would have to leave the country every Saturday and Sunday due to tax laws affecting MGM's U.K. operations. Since France was just across the Channel by boat train, he could easily spend the weekends there, but he would have to pay all expenses from his own pocket.

As he did when he left for military service, Gable entrusted the supervision of the Encino ranch to secretary Jean Garceau, this time with instructions to remove all traces of Sylvia's tenure by the time of his scheduled return in November 1953. Having sent ahead most of his luggage, including hunting, fishing, and golfing gear, by plane to London, he took the train to New York to connect with the S.S. *Liberte* to start his "exile" with a brief holiday in Paris.

Somewhere along the route Gable linked up with an exquisite twenty-seven-year-old fashion model, Suzanne Dadolle, who worked for Elsa Schiaparelli in the designer's Paris and New York salons. French but Turkish-born, the tall, willowy blonde accompanied Gable on the transatlantic crossing and became his favorite consort whenever he visited Paris or traveled around Europe during his breaks from moviemaking.

In June Gable arrived in London to start *Never Let Me Go,* which would be shot at MGM British Studios in suburban Boreham Wood and on various locations on the rugged coast of Cornwall in the West Country. Seven years after the end of the war, Britons were still subject to the rationing of food and consumer goods, but Gable would suffer few deprivations while residing in a luxury suite at the Dorchester Hotel on Park Lane. Soon after checking in, he somehow managed to jump a queue and get a confirmed order for a custom-made Jaguar sports car.

Clarence Brown, now semiretired and serving only as producer on *Never Let Me Go,* selected Gene Tierney to costar with Gable and Delmer Daves to direct. A longtime friend of Gable's dating back to his stage acting days, Daves also wrote scripts, but not this one, which was an adaptation by Ronald Millar and George Froeschel of Roger Bax's novel *Came the Dawn.*

The melodrama was reminiscent of *Comrade X,* with Gable again a Moscow-based news correspondent but now falling in love with and marrying a prima ballerina in place of a streetcar driver. In the twelve years between the two films, diplomatic relations between the United States and the Soviet Union had frozen over and gone from cautious cordiality to the brink of nuclear war, so Gable's attempts to help his wife escape from the "dirty commies" aren't played for laughs (or not intentionally anyway).

Needless to say, MGM had no chance of receiving cooperation from the Soviet government or any of its satellites, which meant that outdoor locations had to be faked within the limits of Britain's topography and the $1.5 million budget. With black-and-white photography, a preponderance of scenes taking place in the dark of night, and stock newsreel footage of Moscow and military maneuvers, the result was fairly convincing. Some of the story does take place in England, where Gable and a British friend who's also married to a ballerina buy a small fishing ship and sail to a resort town on the Baltic Sea, where their wives are dancing in a gala performance for a Russian general.

Gene Tierney, who at the time was in the throes of an affair with Prince Aly Khan, recently the ex-husband of Rita Hayworth, had slight chance to socialize with Gable. Borrowed for the film from 20th Century–Fox, she had never even met him before. "Working on a film, you expect to be taken to dinner by your leading man," Tierney later recalled. "Well, we had our 'date' in Cornwall. We went to a pub for dinner. I was depressed and not feeling well, and told him so. He talked about Carole. I also told him how hard it was on my feet to play at being a ballerina. That weekend, when he went to Paris, he came back with a gift for me: a tube of salve for my feet. He said they told him it was the best medicine in the world. It was so cute. A sweet gesture from a gentleman."

While working in Cornwall, Gable took delivery of his new Jaguar. "He kept talking about it from the day we arrived, but I didn't want to even know because stars aren't allowed to drive themselves to locations," Delmer Daves remembered. "Well, one day I'm directing him in a scene, and suddenly Clark says, 'Jesus Christ, here it comes.' And up the hill comes this Jaguar he designed. I said, 'Obviously this is the end of our shooting for the time being.' He said, 'Would you—could you—remember your lines with this beautiful monster standing here?' I turned to the crew and said, 'Lunch. Everybody eat.' And I got in that car and for the next hour Clark and I took every curve in Cornwall—vroooom, vroooom! He was a kid. That was the real joy of Clark, that he was a child, and a man. And slightly cornball."

In his working relationship with Gable, Daves never had conflicts. "He was more like my son than a friend. He needed a great deal of reassurance about his work. He would constantly refer to his stage background. It was his security blanket. He was always saying, 'Del, I'm really an actor,' and I would say, 'I know you are, Clark, you don't have to keep telling me.' Then he'd say again, 'You saw me in *The Last Mile*,' you know I'm an actor.' He wasn't, truly, he was a personality—an immense personality. I couldn't make him bend in a scene; he was not flexible. I'd try to get him to put a little more shading into a scene. I'd say, 'Clark, you know you're coming out—bang—with this,' and I'd show him what he should do instead. He'd say, 'How's this, boss?' or he'd call me 'governor,' like the British. 'How's that, governor?'—with a naughty grin on his face. . . . He was a smiling man. He always had a twinkle in his eye. We would laugh every day about something."

When production ended in late September, Gable drove the Jaguar to Paris to pick up Suzanne Dadolle for a leisurely trip across France, Switzerland, and Italy to Rome, where he was due to report for his next assignment on November 1. Due to cold and rainy weather, they virtually raced through until finding sunny skies over Lake Como, where Gable checked out the facilities at the famous Villa d'Este Hotel in Cernobbio and decided to stay. The eighteenth-century palazzo-estate had once been the residence of royalty, but Gable was most attracted by its modern championship golf course. He telephoned to London for his golf clubs and booked a suite until October 20, when the hotel closed down for the winter.

Meanwhile MGM had just about assembled all of the components for the remake of *Red Dust*, now titled *Mogambo* (a Swahili word denoting passion) and assigned to producer Sam Zimbalist, whose recent *Quo Vadis?* grossed more than any of the studio's releases since *GWTW*. *Mogambo* was intended as a follow-up, but not sequel, to another Zimbalist hit, *King Solomon's Mines*, filmed in Africa in 1950.

Gable's ex–air force buddy, John Lee Mahin, wrote the script, which followed Mahin's original one for *Red Dust* but changed or renamed characters and moved the setting from a rubber plantation in Indochina to a hunter's preserve in Kenya. Gable's primary occupation is capturing wild animals for zoos, but he also leads safaris, such as one for a British anthropologist studying the behavior of gorillas.

Mainly for the first-time experience of filming in the African jungle, freelance director John Ford, revered for westerns and other Americana, accepted the job held by Victor Fleming for the 1932 version. Cinematographer Robert Surtees, an Oscar winner for *King Solomon's Mines* and a nominee the following year for *Quo Vadis?*, would head the camera unit of the Technicolor production, which was Gable's first in color since *Across the Wide Missouri* and only his third to date. Although Hollywood was currently going through a technological revolution with stereoscopic 3-D viewing glasses and the wide-screen systems of Cinerama and CinemaScope, Dore Schary decided that they were too untested yet to use for *Mogambo,* which already had enough problems due to the distant locations amd unpredictable weather.

Lana Turner seemed MGM's most logical choice for the sexpot originated by Jean Harlow, but Turner's recent physical beating at the hands of her by-now ex-lover Fernando Lamas forced Dore Schary to replace her with Ava Gardner. Hopefully Turner would be well enough to take over the role that had been intended for Gardner in the third of Gable's foreign projects, which was still in development under the tentative title *Betrayed.*

For the part of the married "other woman" once played by Mary Astor, Dore Schary wanted Deborah Kerr, but John Ford considered her too ladylike. After screening film on a flock of younger candidates, they settled on Grace Kelly, whose only major screen credit so far was as sheriff Gary Cooper's Quaker wife in the black-and-white *High Noon.* Schary thought that she might be too bland, but Ford sensed dramatic depths and thought she'd photograph wonderfully in color. "I'll bet she'll knock us on our asses," Ford said.

At the end of their stay at Lake Como, Gable and Suzanne Dadolle drove to Rome for a week of sight-seeing and shopping before she returned to Paris. Paparazzi trailed them everywhere. When a reporter inquired about a rather large topaz ring on her finger, Dadolle said, "Mr. Gable gave it to me because it's my lucky stone. It was not exactly meant to be an engagement ring . . . but we'll see."

Gable apparently heard more than enough. He never liked women blabbing about him. When Dadolle returned to Paris, that was the end of the relationship.

MGM had selected Rome as the transit junction between its Boreham Wood Studio in London and the *Mogambo* production in Africa. All exterior scenes, amounting to about 75 percent of the movie, were to be shot on location, with the interiors to be done later in England.

To reach Kenya from Rome without resorting to a sea-and-land safari that could take weeks, Gable had to bite the bullet and fly on a dreaded airliner for the first time since Carole Lombard's death. As luck would have it, during the flight to Nairobi a terrible storm with hail the size of rocks forced the pilot to make an emergency landing on a clear patch in the middle of the jungle. No one was hurt, though the exterior of the Stratocruiser suffered some pockmarking by the heavy hailstones.

"I guess if the hail didn't get me, my time will come when it will come," Gable later told a friend. "I guess I can fly in anything from now on."

Gable arrived in Nairobi on November 1, followed the next day by Grace Kelly and on November 8 by Ava Gardner and Frank Sinatra, who celebrated their first wedding anniversary during the ten-thousand-mile trip from Los Angeles. Sinatra just came along for the ride and hoped to fly home as soon as his agent confirmed a pending screen test at Columbia Pictures for a plum role in *From Here to Eternity.*

John Ford and producer Sam Zimbalist had been in Africa for two months finishing preparations. Although it was kept secret at the time, a second camera unit was already working thousands of miles away in French Equatorial Africa, filming scenes with wild gorillas that John Ford considered too dangerous to do himself. Directing the unit was Yakima Canutt, a former stuntman who had doubled for Gable in the burning of Atlanta scenes in *GWTW.* Through rear projection and editing tricks, the gorilla tracking scenes would eventually create the illusion that Gable and some of the other actors were really there and risking their lives.

Gable and the rest of the main John Ford unit were based at hotels in Nairobi, where other dangers lurked due to recent and ongoing terrorism by black Mau Mau revolutionaries against Kenya's white settlers. Great Britain had dispatched ships and troops to the area. The British governor of Kenya assigned a squad of police to guard all the *Mogambo* visitors. MGM reportedly made a secret payment of fifty thousand dollars to Mau Mau leader Jomo Kenyatta for immunity from attack.

"Everyone in the cast was issued a weapon," Ava Gardner remembered. "Clark, an experienced hunter, got a high-powered hunting rifle, while they gave me a presumably more ladylike .38 police special revolver."

During the first week of production, everyone commuted daily by chartered plane to a location site at an animal preserve on Mount Kenya, about a hundred miles from Nairobi. After that the unit left Kenya for Tanganyika and a month of jungle locations. MGM built a temporary housing village next to the Kagera River, with individual tent-bungalows for the VIPs, dormitories for the crew members, a commissary, a hospital, a canteen with movie-projection facilities, and a landing strip for airplanes. After the shoot the tent village would be packed up and transported to Uganda for another two weeks of filming.

On November 12 everybody attended a surprise party in honor of Grace Kelly's twenty-third birthday. The next day Frank Sinatra received confirmation of his Columbia screen test and took off for Hollywood. During his stay Sinatra and Ava Gardner had been alternately battling and making up, often loudly enough for the whole *Mogambo* company to know. Gable and Grace Kelly tried to keep out of it, but in the process they were thrown together and fell passionately in love.

The green-eyed blonde was not only beautiful but a fine sportswoman and a crack shot, which Gable soon learned when he started taking her hunting and fishing. Gable ordered some of his old hunting clothes and Stetsons flown over from home, as well as his sixteen-millimeter movie camera and enough color film to make a miniepic of his own.

On their free days Gable and Kelly rose at four to beat the heat and went driving in a dilapidated old jeep. Kelly later told a friend that they once went "skinny-dipping" in Lake Victoria. On the set between takes, they always sat side by side in canvas folding chairs and talked or played cards.

After work Gable usually took Kelly and Ava Gardner to his tent for drinks. Gardner was a nonstop boozer like Gable, but Kelly could handle only one scotch and soda. "After that Gracie's little nose would get pink," Gardner recalled. "She'd get sick, and we'd have to rescue her. Or she'd get easily hurt by something that was said and run off into the darkness. Clark would catch on after a few seconds and say to me, 'Sugar, where's she gone? This is Africa. She can't just run off in Africa.' So I'd go and find her and bring her back before the lions ate her."

Kelly started calling Gable "Ba," the Swahili word for "father," which wasn't far from Lombard's "Pa." As filming of *Mogambo* progressed, they grew ever more intimate. Kelly discovered that, in contrast to his macho image, Gable was a sensitive and intelligent gentleman.

Despite her youth and the twenty-eight-year age gap between them, he found her a worldly wise woman with a sense of humor similar to his own.

"Clark's eyes were quite definitely on Gracie, and hers, for that matter, were on him," Ava Gardner recalled. "They were both single at the time, and it's very normal for any woman to be in love with Clark. But Gracie was a good Catholic girl, and she was having a hard time feeling the way she did about Clark. Not to mention that being in Africa, with exotic flora and fauna all over the place, and Clark, strong and smiling and completely at home, made her love him more."

"They were together most of the time," Donald Sinden, the debonair Briton who enacted Kelly's husband, later recalled. One night he stumbled into Gable's darkened tent and found Gable and Kelly in bed—"both of them starkers."

Frank Sinatra returned from Hollywood to await the results of his screen test and to check up on his wife. He was wildly jealous and thought that Gardner might be involved with Gable or Donald Sinden. When Sinatra learned that he'd won the role in *From Here to Eternity,* he departed again for Hollywood, this time leaving Ava Gardner in such a rage that she claimed to be seriously ill and demanded time off to fly to London for treatment.

Gardner was pregnant, according to *Mogambo* cinematographer Robert Surtees. "Ava hated Frank so intensely by this stage, she couldn't stand the idea of having his baby," Surtees recalled. "She went to London to have an abortion. I know, because my wife went to London to be at her side at all times through the operation and afterward, and to bring her back on the plane. She told my wife, 'I hated Frankie so much. I wanted that baby to go unborn.' "

Several weeks after Gardner's return, it was Gable's turn to get sick. He developed a gum infection involving his false teeth and wouldn't trust anyone but his own dentist back in Los Angeles to attend to it. Now that he'd gotten over his resistance to flying, that posed no problem. His eighteen-month "tax exile" was unaffected since U.S. law permitted a limited number of short visits for emergency reasons.

Gable's "shakes" were also causing problems. John Ford, a heavy drinker himself, tried to be understanding, but he also had a schedule to adhere to and wouldn't permit many retakes. Once after a complicated scene with Ava Gardner, Gable asked Ford if they could do it again, but the director just turned around and walked off the set.

Gable complained to producer Sam Zimbalist, who sympathized but advised him that "Ford's a tyrant. Do what John Wayne always does with him. When you get in there, you just say, 'Yes, coach,' and everything will be okay." Gable tried and gradually warmed up to Ford's ways, though not enough to want to work with him again.

In late January 1953 production shifted to the MGM studio near London for the remaining indoor scenes. Still very much involved with Grace Kelly, Gable moved from the Dorchester Hotel to the much smaller Connaught, which was in a more secluded part of Mayfair and better equipped to protect the privacy of its guests. Gable had a suite with a fireplace, but it's doubtful that he and Kelly spent much time roasting marshmallows.

Unfortunately for the lovers, Margaret "Ma" Kelly got upset by some items in the gossip columns and flew to London to stay with her daughter at the Savoy Hotel until *Mogambo* finished. "I was only too well aware of the emotions that our Gracie could arouse in men," Mrs. Kelly said later. She diagnosed her daughter's feelings for Gable as "nothing more than a schoolgirl crush" but decided that she should go along as chaperone whenever the couple went out in public.

A striking blonde in her early forties, Ma Kelly had long been a Clark Gable fan, so she relished the chance to share his company. But Gable balked and soon sensed that mother and daughter were in a plot to get him to the altar. He finally ended the fling by snubbing Kelly at the studio and not responding to the many messages that she left for him at the Connaught.

Kelly was desolate. But when she sought advice from Ava Gardner, her friend told her, "Don't be fooled by Clark's looks or his interest in you. He's been with so many women—you have no idea! I haven't had an affair with him myself, but I know what I'm talking about. Don't fall for it, because he'll cast you aside just as he has all the others. You'll be just another girl to him. He likes to conquer, and when he's done, he's through with them and he leaves them."

On their final day of working together, Gable surprised Kelly by gifting her with an expensive sixteen-millimeter movie camera. Kelly later told Ava Gardner, "He must have loved me very much to have given me that." Well aware of Gable's miserliness, Gardner replied, "Oh, of course, I agree."

For the sake of a photo opportunity, MGM publicist Morgan Hudgins persuaded Gable to escort Kelly to Heathrow Airport when she returned to Los Angeles. At the departure gate Gable pecked Kelly on the cheek and gave her a smiling good-bye, but she lost her composure. In front of a crowd of photographers and reporters, she broke into tears.

Gable would later have second thoughts about the affair. But in the meantime he had another six months to go on his "tax exile" and was also nearing the end of his long-term contract with MGM. Agent George Chasin had started negotiations for a new one that raised Gable's salary to ten thousand dollars per week and, for the first time, also gave him a percentage of his films' profits. Needless to say, Dore Schary was not too receptive.

In April Gable finally finished *Mogambo* and took a vacation trip to France and Italy with his California friends, the Al Menascos. While stopping over in Paris, he reconciled with Suzanne Dadolle, who stayed with the group until Rome and back. When the Menascos flew home, Gable stayed on in Paris at the Hotel Raphael. His public outings with Dadolle started new rumors of a pending marriage, but she again seemed to spoil any chance of that happening by telling a reporter that Gable had asked her to travel with him all over the world and to be his life's companion.

When the story broke, Gable returned to London and issued a press statement through MGM that he had no plans for an engagement, marriage, or anything else. He checked into the Connaught again to await the start of his next project, *Betrayed,* which would be filmed at the Boreham Wood Studio and at locations in Holland.

Meanwhile in the United States the first of Gable's overseas projects, *Never Let Me Go,* entered release, in many cases being shown at theaters with the new "giant wide screens" that were needed for CinemaScope and other processes. Though the black-and-white *Never Let Me Go* was shot at the long-standard squarish ratio of 1.33 feet in width to to 1 foot in height, MGM recommended that projectionists use a magnifying lens to blow it up to 1.85 to 1. The gain in width resulted in cropping off parts of heads and feet in many scenes.

New York Times critic Bosley Crowther, who viewed the movie on a fifty-foot-wide screen at the Capitol Theater on Broadway, felt it didn't make much difference to its quality. "It's reassuring to know that Clark Gable is one fellow, at least, who can still make the Soviet Union tough guys look like absolute monkeys," Crowther wrote. "This is the same Gable as *Comrade X,* but a little older, a little fatter, a little shrewder and more cynical."

John McCarten of *The New Yorker* noted, "On a screen as expansive as the celestial concave and with his dimples looking like the craters of the moon, Clark Gable in *Never Let Me Go* rips through the Iron Curtain with all the breeziness of a demonstrator showing off the latest can opener in Gimbel's basement. Mr. Gable, at this point in his career, is grizzled, not withered. And there can be little doubt that as long as he is able to get around, he will represent all that is wholesome, brave, kind and regular in the American male."

Never Let Me Go flopped miserably at the box office, which placed agent George Chasin at a distinct disadvantage in his negotiations with MGM for a new Gable contract. Since Gable was so identified with the studio, Dore Schary didn't want to lose him, but the most he would offer was a two-year extension of Gable's current contract, but with no profit participation as Chasin had been demanding. Schary had strict orders from Loew's president Nicholas Schenck that *no* stars should get participation deals, which threatened to destroy the studio-dominated system that had prevailed in Hollywood for decades.

Unless someone suddenly changed their mind, then, *Betrayed* would be Gable's last movie as an MGM contractee. Production finally started in September, with Gottfried Reinhardt, a son of the great Austrian stage director Max Reinhardt, serving as producer-director. Long a staff producer at MGM, the younger Reinhardt had worked with Gable before on *Comrade X* and *Homecoming.* His recent production of *The Red Badge of Courage,* with John Huston as director, had been the first major catastrophe of Dore Schary's regime, so *Betrayed* was his chance to redeem himself.

With a script by the same writing team that did *Never Let Me Go,* the project suddenly seemed risky, but too many commitments had been made to stop it. The World War II espionage thriller gave Gable his first non-American role since *Parnell,* as a Dutch Army intelligence officer involved in planning the Allied invasion of Nazi-occupied Holland.

For box-office insurance, *Betrayed* teamed Gable for the fourth time with Lana Turner, by now in a brunette phase of her career and portraying a Dutch spy. Victor Mature, whose popularity had soared since he flexed his muscles in *Samson and Delilah*, was hired to play a Dutch underground leader known as "the Scarf."

The filming had been delayed by Lana Turner's sudden decision to marry *Tarzan* star Lex Barker, who was the cause of her beating by Fernando Lamas, her previous lover. Lamas saw them dancing together at a party and vented his jealousy on Turner when they got home. After dumping Lamas, she started dating Barker and, when he quit the *Tarzan* series to work for European studios, moved with him to Paris.

To oblige Gable, who was nearing the end of his eighteen-month "tax exile" and didn't want to extend it, Gottfried Reinhardt rushed *Betrayed* through production in eight weeks. The expert British cinematographer Freddie Young used a new type of Eastman color film to achieve a dark Rembrandt effect that suited the Dutch background. Exteriors were shot in Arnhem and Amsterdam, marking the first time that major Hollywood stars had ever worked in Holland.

While Gable was finishing *Betrayed, Mogambo* opened to record-breaking business at New York's Radio City Music Hall and soon became the number-one box-office hit nationally. Many critics called Gable's performance his best in years and a possible Oscar winner.

Needless to say, Dore Schary tried to reopen contract negotiations. But by that time George Chasin had received several offers for independent production deals that stood to earn Gable much more in the long run.

As far as MGM was concerned, Gable instructed Chasin to "see how high you can get those sons-of-bitches to go. When you get their very best offer, tell them to take their money, their studio, their cameras and lighting equipment and shove it all up their ass!"

Gable returned to Los Angeles on December 13, 1953, wealthier by $500,000 in tax-exempt income and raring to break loose from twenty-three years of servitude to MGM.

21

THE FIFTH MRS. GABLE

I n March 1954 Clark Gable released the following statement to the press: "I am discontinuing my long-term association with Loew's, Inc., after being with the company for more than twenty years, in order to avail myself of the opportunity of entering the freelance field. I want to express my great appreciation to the many friends and associates at Loew's, Inc., whose help I have had and with whom I have had the pleasure of working.

"I wish also to pay tribute to my friends and associates who are no longer alive whose help and guidance over the years meant so much to me."

In that time Gable had worked in fifty-one MGM films, the vast majority of them produced within the confines of the Culver City plant. On his final day at the studio, he did some sound dubbing for *Betrayed* and posed for publicity portraits for staff photographer Clarence Bull. Afterward he returned to his dressing bungalow for the last time and removed the few things he'd left there when he took off on his eighteen-month sojourn.

Larry Barbier, one of his longtime publicists, walked Gable to his Jaguar in the parking lot. "Clark said, 'You know, those bastards in the front office didn't give me a farewell party or cake or anything. They didn't even bother to say good-bye.' It's not that Clark expected a party, but he felt bad that the studio whose reputation he helped build in the thirties treated him shabbily because of economic difficulties," Barbier recalled.

"When he drove off the lot that day, Clark vowed that he would never set foot on it again. He never did. And I guess in the years that followed he became more cynical about Metro. Whenever I ran into him, he'd ask me if I was 'still out at the goddamned factory'?"

Gable's only remaining link to MGM would be his stake in the studio's pension plan, which amounted to $400,000. He could take it in a lump sum or in annual payments for life of $31,000 if he started collecting now at age fifty-three or $49,000 if he waited another ten years until he was sixty-three. He opted for the latter but grumbled to his lawyer that with his luck, he probably wouldn't make it to sixty.

Since returning from abroad, Gable had resumed his affair with Grace Kelly, who was currently residing at the Bel-Air Hotel while filming Paramount's *The Country Girl*. Kelly was also keeping private company with her two costars, Bing Crosby and William Holden, but she somehow managed to juggle all three suitors.

As luck would have it, both Kelly and Ava Gardner were nominated for Oscars for their performances in *Mogambo*, though Kelly in the supporting actress category. Gable's work in *Mogambo* went unrecognized, but ironically, a frequent visitor to the African locations earned a nomination for his supporting performance in *From Here to Eternity*.

On March 25 Gable escorted Kelly to the Pantages Theater for the Oscar ceremonies, his first attendance since his *GWTW* disappointment in 1940. Since then the dinner banquet had been replaced by a stage spectacle with (after 1952) national TV coverage.

It proved an unlucky night for *Mogambo*. Kelly's best supporting actress rival Donna Reed won for *From Here to Eternity*. Ava Gardner, who'd separated from Sinatra and was not present, lost the best actress Oscar to Audrey Hepburn for *Roman Holiday*. Sinatra won best supporting actor for *From Here to Eternity*, which also received best picture and ended up with eight Oscars, equaling the all-time record of *GWTW*.

Gable and Kelly moved on to the after-party at Romanoff's, where William Holden, best actor winner for *Stalag 17*, was playfully awarding his Oscar to the film's director, Billy Wilder. Kelly threw her arms around Holden and hugged him as Gable and Mrs. Holden, actress Brenda Marshall, both looked a bit miffed.

Grace Kelly was on such a fast track in both her private life and her career that Gable eventually realized that he was too old for her and that a marriage would never work. He wanted, however, to continue the professional relationship by teaming with Kelly in his first independent project. But she was in such demand that she already had too many other deals on her slate.

In June, Gable's MCA agent George Chasin concluded a two-picture deal with 20th Century–Fox, whose studio head, Darryl F. Zanuck, had once refused to hire the young Clark Gable because of his floppy ears. For each of the two 20th–Fox movies, Gable would receive an advance of $400,000 against 10 percent of the gross film rentals. In other words, Gable was guaranteed $400,000 for making the movie and would later get 10 percent of rentals above $4 million. If the film brought in $10 million, which was ultrarare in those days, Gable would end up with $1 million. More likely, he would be lucky if he earned anything above his advance because even $4 million was a hard figure to reach in those depressed box-office times. In 1953 weekly movie theater attendance in the United States had dropped to 45.9 million, the lowest level since 1925, largely due to competition from home TV.

But 20th–Fox was currently riding high thanks to its CinemaScope process, introduced in September 1953 with the biblical spectacle *The Robe,* which quickly became the industry's biggest grosser since *GWTW.* Needless to say, all of 20th–Fox's major releases were now being shot in CinemaScope, which was also being licensed at hefty fees to other studios on a limited basis.

Gable's two films, *Soldier of Fortune,* an adventure drama set in Hong Kong, and *The Tall Men,* an epic western, suited the wide-screen format. He agreed to make them virtually back to back, but starting in November so that only one qualified as 1954 income, which would save him from a huge tax bill.

Meanwhile MGM released its last Gable film, *Betrayed,* which took a reverse direction from *Mogambo* and died at the box office. A review in *Newsweek* explained why: "It seems a little late in the day for so ingenuous a wartime adventure story to make much impact, and, in fact, *Betrayed,* directed, disappointingly, by Gottfried Reinhardt, proves a clumsy and overslow piece of melodrama. Lana Turner and Victor Mature go about their spying and resistance leading with no great conviction, and Clark Gable gives a rather tired, though solid, performance as the intelligence officer."

Fortunately for Gable's professional standing, the fiasco was quickly forgotten as MGM, in celebration of its thirtieth anniversary, rereleased *Gone With the Wind* with new Technicolor prints formatted for wide-screen projection with multichannel Perspecta sound. When the new edition premiered at the Egyptian Theater in Hollywood, Gable refused to attend. His bitterness toward David Selznick, who no longer had a financial stake in the movie, had ended, but he wanted nothing more to do with MGM.

The wide-screen release of *GWTW* was an enormous hit, grossing more than any *new* picture of 1954 and rubbing more salt into Gable's old wounds over not sharing in the profits. When the reissue brought MGM $9 million in rentals, he grouched that he would have pocketed $900,000 if he'd had the same deal that he now had with 20th–Fox.

But the 1954 revival gave Gable something that money can't buy. It transmogrified *Gone With the Wind* and everyone in it into a true heirloom that could be handed down from one generation to another and always be appreciated. By 1954 a whole new generation of moviegoers had seen it and accepted it on its own merits as a powerful drama and cinematic work of art.

That summer Gable found himself a new playmate, or rather a former one who'd since married, had two children, and been divorced. He first met Kay (Kathleen) Williams in 1944, when she was one of many $75-per-week starlets at MGM who enacted bit parts and did publicity modeling for the fan magazines. Fifteen years younger than Gable, she was born in Erie, Pennsylvania, which is only about fifty miles from Meadville, where both his parents were born and eventually married.

After a brief marriage to a college student, Kay moved to New York to become a professional model. She hit the jackpot with numerous magazine covers and marriage to Martin de Alzaga Unzue, a South American millionaire-playboy known in the gossip columns as "Macoco." The marriage lasted only ten days, but Kay won a bundle in the divorce settlement and moved on to sugar heir Adolph Spreckels II, whom she wed in 1945 after Gable dragged his feet. Spreckels had previously been married and divorced four times; each of his wives eventually accused him of physical abuse, alcoholism, and drug addiction.

As Kay Spreckels, she became a queen of West Coast high society with homes in Los Angeles and San Francisco, and she coproduced two heirs to the family's immense wealth, Adolph III, now aged five, and Joan, two. Kay also learned the hard way that her husband was all that his previous wives claimed. She finally divorced him in 1953, with Spreckels countercharging that she only married him for his money. In settlement Kay received about $500,000 in community property, including their mansion in Bel-Air, plus a million-dollar trust fund for each of the children. Not long after the divorce Spreckels got into a brawl with Kay over child custody and beat her unconscious, which landed him in jail for thirty days.

The headline-making incident caused Gable to phone Kay with condolences. As they started dating again, he found a mature woman instead of the flighty glamour girl he'd known before. Like Carole Lombard, she was fun to be with and a good sport who shared his interests in hunting, fishing, and golf. He also enjoyed taking Kay and her two kids on outings, which gave him a sense of belonging to a family.

In November Gable started his first freelance project, *Soldier of Fortune,* at 20th Century–Fox's studio near Beverly Hills in West Los Angeles. Producer Buddy Adler assigned the direction to Edward Dmytryk, a onetime target of the House Un-American Activities Committee who served time in federal prison for refusing to answer questions about alleged Communist ties but later cleared himself by giving evidence.

Soldier of Fortune was based on a novel by Ernest K. Gann, whose *The High and the Mighty* had recently been a blockbuster hit starring John Wayne. Gable's title character, Mike Lee, was a 1950s version of Rhett Butler, an exiled American con man who smuggles goods in and out of Red China from British-governed Hong Kong. When an American news photographer disappears while on assignment in Communist-controlled territory, the man's wife persuades Mike Lee to find out what happened to him and to rescue him if he's being held captive.

20th–Fox's top contract actress, Susan Hayward, who under her original name of Edythe Marrener was one of many starlets and models who tested unsuccessfully for Scarlett O'Hara in *GWTW,* finally got a chance to team with Gable. Unfortunately, a crisis developed when Hayward's ex-husband, Jess Barker, obtained a court order to prevent her from taking their nine-year-old twin sons out of U.S. jurisdiction to Hong Kong for the location work. Hayward refused to go without them, so Gable, who sympathized, suggested a solution that he had learned while finishing *Saratoga* after Jean Harlow died. Hayward's Hong Kong scenes were hurriedly rewritten so that they could be shot with a redheaded double or later faked in the studio through the use of rear projection.

En route to Hong Kong, Gable and Edward Dmytryk stopped over in Tokyo for a round of sight-seeing as guests of 20th–Fox's Japanese distribution company. "We went to a theater which had only women as performers," Dmytryk recalled. "After watching the show for a little while, we were taken backstage by the manager to meet the star of the production. She was in a Kabuki outfit, and her face was all made up with rice powder. She looked at Gable, who towered above her. He held out his hand, and she took it, and tears streamed out of her eyes down through her makeup on both cheeks, making little rivers right down to her chin. She didn't say a word. All she did was look at him and cry. Now obviously a man who has that kind of thing happen to him must know that he affects people, that he affects women. He also affected men, I must say, because he was a man's man, and I never knew a man's man like Gable."

Once work started in Hong Kong, Dmytryk had to learn to cope with a clause in Gable's contract. "He had the right to quit at five o'clock—I think so he could start drinking. Gable was quite a drinker. In fact, most of the veteran actors were; and Gable did as well as any of them. Never, of course, on the set. He always came to work ready and clear. But in the evening he was a very heavy drinker. As a matter of fact, he told me once that if he couldn't drink he'd just as soon die," the director remembered.

Gable had trouble doing long scenes. "Under tension—not normally, strangely enough, just under tension—he used to shake," Dmytryk said. "For instance, he wouldn't do it during a rehearsal, but as soon as we started shooting, almost as soon as you said action, he would start a slight tremor, and then if the scene went for any length of time, it would get to be a decided shake. So I used to have to cut the scenes down to three or four lines, no more than that. In the long shots it didn't matter, of course, because it wasn't noticeable, but in the close shots it was. I imagine the tension was due to nerves. Part of it may have been physical. I don't know. It may have been due to his having been such a good solid drinker most of his life. It could have been just nerves, but God knows he'd made pictures for an awful long time. I think he felt fairly secure as an actor. He believed in himself as an actor."

After a month in Hong Kong, Gable returned home in time to celebrate Christmas with Kay Spreckels and her children. Kay, in fact, met

Gable at the airport, which started rumors in the gossip columns about an imminent wedding. Gable blew his stack and accused Kay of trying to rush him into making a proposal. By New Year's 1955 the romance had resumed, but Gable was still reluctant to commit himself.

Upon finishing *Soldier of Fortune*, Gable went on a crash diet to lose twenty-five pounds before starting his next 20th–Fox project. When he saw some of the rushes of his first work in wide-screen CinemaScope, he was horrified by the close-ups, which in their rectangular shape tended to make his face and jowls balloon up in size. He persuaded Edward Dmytryk to cut the worst bits and vowed to take better care of his appearance in the future.

For *The Tall Men* Darryl Zanuck hired Gable's old friend Raoul Walsh to be the director. Walsh was not only a master of the western genre but also accustomed to working at the fast, "one-take" speed in which Gable had been trained at MGM. He was also a one-eyed wonder, with a black patch covering a right socket that had been empty since a 1928 car crash.

The Tall Men seemed an inappropriate title for an epic shot in wide CinemaScope, teaming Clark Gable with Jane Russell and her celebrated mammaries. Based on a pulp novel by Clay Fisher, the Sydney Boehm–Frank Nugent screenplay told of a long cattle drive between Texas and Montana via hostile Indian territory. Along the way Gable and villain Robert Ryan tussle over Russell, whom Gable jokingly nicknames "Grandma" after they sleep together while taking shelter from a blizzard.

Because Texas and Montana no longer looked as they did in the 1860s and also were short on herds of longhorn cattle, Raoul Walsh looked elsewhere and found what he needed near Durango, Mexico, about six hundred miles below the U.S. border. For Gable, the two-month location trip meant a long separation from Kay Spreckels, but he invited her to make some weekend visits with her children, to take them horseback riding and to meet the cowboys.

Gable agreed to share a rented hacienda with Raoul Walsh, the original owner and builder of his ranch in Encino. One day Walsh decided to play a prank on Gable and placed a tame deodorized skunk in his bedroom. When Gable discovered it, he shouted for help, assuming that it was wild and capable of ejecting a stink that would make the whole house unlivable. Walsh rushed in and told him that skunks were terrified of music. If Gable whistled to it, it would be too stunned to react, and Walsh would be able to grab it and remove it. While Gable stood in the corner whistling "Old Man River" and "If I Loved You," Walsh moved in and played the hero.

In front of the whole company on the set the next day, Gable praised Walsh's courage. "I wouldn't have touched that little bastard for a million dollars," he said. Walsh kept a straight face and thanked him.

During the filming Gable became friendly with Jane Russell and her husband, ex-football star Bob Waterfield. The couple were in the process of forming their own independent production company and urged Gable to do the same. Besides many tax advantages, Gable would be able to package his own vehicles and to receive a larger share of revenues than he did as an actor for hire. Gable instructed his agent, George Chasin, to get on it.

By the time he finished *The Tall Men,* Gable had decided that he wanted to marry Kay Spreckels. One day while she was visiting at the Encino ranch, he took her into the rose garden and proposed. Needless to say, Kay accepted, but with the understanding that her two children, "Bunker" and Joanie, would come to live with them.

By a bizarre coincidence, while wedding arrangements were being made, Gable became the latest Hollywood victim of the notorious muckraking magazine *Confidential,* which published an exposé entitled "The Wife Clark Gable Forgot" in its July 1955 issue. The front cover featured a handsome photo of Gable superimposed against one of Josephine Dillon, who looked old enough to be his great-grandmother.

Started in 1952 as a snarling alternative to the sappy fan magazines that covered the celebrity world, *Confidential* by this time had a national circulation of 4 million copies, exceeding that of the revered *Saturday Evening Post* and *Look.* Professing to be "telling the facts and naming the names," its research was conducted by an army of private detectives, wiretap experts, and hidden-microphone specialists who relied on tips from disgruntled spouses, prostitutes, hotel clerks, nightclub waiters, office cleaners, and anyone else who might have some "dirt" to sell.

Josephine Dillon reportedly received $2,500 for helping with the article, which included several photographs of her in the dilapidated, two-room converted barn where she lived in North Hollywood. Now seventy-one, she told writer Alfred Garvey about several decades of hard luck and serious illnesses, during which time Gable never offered help. "He is the King and I'm nothing," she said.

Like the majority of *Confidential*'s targets, Gable chose to ignore the article rather than file a libel suit that could only result in even more scandalous publicity. But he was incensed by some of Dillon's claims, which failed to mention that he owned the building where she resided and that he permitted her to stay there rent-free. In his will he had also provided for her to inherit the place if she happened to survive him.

The article also caused permanent distress for Gable because it revealed the exact location of his own home at 4525 Pettit Street in Encino to the millions of *Confidential* readers. It immediately started a flood of sight-seers and tour buses, as well as a mountain of letters from fans who were angered and disillusioned by his alleged maltreatment of Dillon. He increased security and, with a ready-made family on the way, thought it might be best to sell the ranch and move.

Thirty-one years and three more marriages had passed since Gable wed Dillon in 1924. On July 11, 1955, Kay Spreckels became wife number five in a civil ceremony before a justice of the peace in Minden, Nevada, near Lake Tahoe. Gable's close friends, the Al Menascos, and Kay's married sister, Elizabeth Nesser, were the only witnesses.

Out of habit Gable asked his former MGM colleague Howard Strickling to handle the press announcement. By that time the Gables were already honeymooning at the Menascos' estate in St. Helena in the wine-producing Napa Valley in northern California.

Five days later the newlyweds drove down to Encino to prepare for the arrival of Kay's children, who had been staying temporarily with relatives. Alterations had just been completed on the guest cottage, which provided a bedroom suite for each child and quarters for a live-in governess.

Kay had taken to calling Gable "Pa" or "Mr. G.," which Bunker and Joan picked up and started using as well. Gable discouraged Kay's efforts to teach them "Dearest Stepfather," which he thought too formal and pompous. He tagged Kay with "Ma" but more often used her full name, Kathleen, an old Irish favorite of poets and songwriters.

Unlike Lady Sylvia, Kay tried to adapt to Gable's accustomed lifestyle rather than change it. When he suggested buying a new home in Beverly Hills or Bel-Air if it would make her happier, she said, "Oh no,

Pa, you love the ranch, and I love it too. It's an ideal place to bring up children. Let's not even think of moving."

The house's interior was still in the Early American decor selected by Carole Lombard. Lady Sylvia's modifications had by now been erased. The one major change was dictated by Gable himself after he discovered six-year-old Bunker playing with one of his antique pistols. Gable moved his entire artillery collection to a steel vault in his bedroom and converted the gun room into a family den, complete with a console TV-radio-phonograph and a stack of nesting snack tables.

Within three months the thirty-nine-year-old bride tested pregnant, with an expected delivery date of May 1956. Gable was ecstatic and became convinced that it would be a boy. He boasted to friends about "my son" and how he intended to teach him to hunt and fish and to educate him at Harvard or Yale. It was an entirely different reaction from that of twenty-one years ago when Loretta Young gave him similar news.

Unfortunately, in early November Kay contracted influenza and took a new "wonder drug" that had yet to be fully tested for safety during pregnancy. She went into a coma and had to be rushed by ambulance to Hollywood Presbyterian Hospital, where she suffered a miscarriage while doctors struggled to save her own life.

When the news got out, Gable dismissed condolences, telling columnist Louella Parsons that "Kay's a strong woman. I've never known her to be frail—and I'm sure she'll be able to have another baby. She wants to so much—and so do I. We had such plans."

But privately Gable confided to his friend, Al Menasco, "The combined ages of Kay and myself amount to almost a hundred years. I don't know. It might be too late." He postponed plans to add a nursery to the house, guessing that it might be tempting fate.

Gable spent the first part of 1956 helping Kay to regain her health. Right after his two back-to-back projects for 20th–Fox, he had decided to take a year off to await the results, so he had no urgent business to take him away from home.

Kay Gable once described a typical day, which usually started with her husband serving her breakfast in bed. "He reads the newspapers and then checks with his two gardeners and spends the rest of the morning with them, plowing, pruning, watering, and painting fences. Around two o'clock we lunch on trays by the pool, or on the lazy rocking-chair porch. The afternoons, while I am arranging flowers or working on my scrapbooks, he spends in his study making phone calls, discussing films with writers and directors, or reading scripts," she said.

At five-thirty they gathered with the two children in the den. "While they have their dinner, we have our cocktails and nibble on cheese and crackers," Kay said. "Then I work on my needlepoint while Clark and the kids watch television. Sometimes we all have a game of bingo before they go off to bed. . . . After dinner we look at television. Sometimes, but not often, I can persuade Mr. G. to run one of his old pictures on his projection machine."

Gable owned sixteen-millimeter prints of many of his movies, but not of *GWTW,* for which MGM once wanted to charge him $3,500 to prepare. Several decades later the 222-minute epic would be sold on videotape cassettes and laser disks for $39.99!

By the time of Gable's fifty-fifth birthday in February, Kay was well enough for him to start planning for his next freelance project. Returns were also coming in on his two 20th–Fox movies, *Soldier of Fortune,* which had been released in June 1955, and *The Tall Men,* which came out in October. In another bad year for the Hollywood industry generally, neither film did blockbuster business, but both did well enough to be profitable and to earn Gable royalties beyond his advances. *The Tall Men* was the more successful, with world rentals of $8.3 million, which gave Gable another $430,000 to add to his original $400,000. *Soldier of Fortune* had world rentals of $5 million, adding only another $100,000 to his $400,000 advance.

Now that he'd experienced the benefits of percentage deals, Gable decided to go all the way by forming his own independent production company, which agent George Chasin suggested be called Gabco. For his first venture, his friends Jane Russell and Bob Waterfield persuaded Gable to join forces with their own Russ-Field Productions for a western script that the couple owned entitled *The Last Man in Wagon Mound.* None of the costarring roles really suited Jane Russell, so she would not be in the film, but her husband would be executive producer. Due to their good experience with Raoul Walsh on *The Tall Men,* they hired him to direct and to help with the preparations.

United Artists agreed to arrange the financing and to distribute the film, which quickly underwent a title change to *The King and Four*

Queens. Gable, who'd been spoiled by the studio factory system where everything was done for him, soon regretted becoming a producer. For two months before filming began, he had to get involved in selecting the cast and technical crew, choosing the locations, and so on. Since United Artists wasn't a studio in the literal sense of the word, it had no production facilities or staffs of craftsmen, all of which had to be rented. Costs were charged to Gabco and Russ-Field. The two companies stood to make no money until the movie got released and UA earned its investment back.

In *The King and Four Queens* Gable played a fugitive outlaw seeking refuge in a near–ghost town where the only residents are four young married women and their domineering mother-in-law, all related to a quartet of brother bandits who stashed their gold loot somewhere in the area. All the brothers are believed dead, but one of the wives knows the location of the stolen treasure. Gable is only interested in the gold, but he has to romance the four sex-starved women in order to find the one who can lead him to it. Eleanor Parker portrayed the wife whom Gable eventually rides off with into the sunset, with Barbara Nichols, Jean Willes, and Sara Shane as the other three.

Jo Van Fleet, a recent Oscar winner for her supporting role as James Dean's mother in *East of Eden,* got the part of the sharpshooting mother-in-law. Van Fleet gave such a riveting performance that she stole the movie from Gable and everyone else in the cast. Later, during the editing, Gable, in his capacity as coproducer, tried trimming some of Van Fleet's scenes, but it only resulted in making sections of the story confusing or incoherent.

Gable went on another diet before starting the CinemaScope production, for which he and Raoul Walsh selected desert country around St. George in southwestern Utah as the location site. Kay was now strong enough to accompany her husband on the six-week trip, but the two young children promised to be too much of a distraction and stayed home with their governess.

Gable rented a furnished bungalow in St. George for the duration. Unlike Lady Sylvia during *Across the Wide Missouri,* Kay Gable stayed away from the set and played homemaker, even joining the local needlework and quilting groups.

When his actor's job ended in June, producer Gable still had two more months of work ahead in Hollywood, making sure that the editing and the musical scoring were finished in time for UA's planned Christmas release of the film. Gable was under such tension at the time that while driving to the studio one morning, freeway police stopped him and gave him a ticket for going *too slow* and impeding traffic!

Moviemaking soon had to take a backseat when Kay Gable started suffering occasional chest pains, and she finally landed in Cedars of Lebanon Hospital with a diagnosis of severe angina pectoris. After an attack that lasted twenty-five minutes, she underwent three weeks of drug therapy. Gable was so worried that he booked the hospital room next to hers so that he could stay over every night.

By the couple's first wedding anniversary on July 11, Kay had improved enough to be taken home by ambulance, but she had strict orders to remain in bed and to continue on the medication. On August 7, her fortieth birthday, she was permitted to go downstairs to the dining room for a party with Gable, the children, and a few close relatives and friends.

As Kay's health continued to improve, Gable returned to winding up *The King and Four Queens,* which proved his first and last effort as the producer of one of his own films. When released in December 1956, it flopped at the box office and received unfavorable reviews, including a scathing one from Bosley Crowther of *The New York Times:* "Clark Gable may still be regarded as the 'king' of Hollywood, but he won't be for long if he continues to appear in pictures such as *The King and Four Queens.* It certainly represents a dreary comedown for Hollywood royalty."

For Gable's next project, agent George Chasin reverted to the usual star-for-hire deal of $400,000 against 10 percent of gross film rentals, this time with Warner Bros. for a Civil War epic based on Robert Penn Warren's best-selling novel *Band of Angels,* which production chief Jack L. Warner envisioned as another *Gone With the Wind.* Warner's first brainstorm was to hire Max Steiner to again compose the musical score.

Gable's character, Hamish Bond, a rich plantation owner and former slave trader, bore slight traces of Rhett Butler, but his romance with Amantha Starr, a half-black heiress whom he rescues from the slave auction block, had no parallel in *GWTW.* Taking place in and around New Orleans in the midst of the Civil War, the story includes a mysterious young black rebel named Rau-Ru, very possibly the son of Hamish Bond and an African woman who was killed during one of Bond's expeditions to capture natives to sell as slaves.

For *Band of Angels* Gable again insisted on his buddy, Raoul Walsh, for director. Although the Hollywood industry was finally trying to employ more black talent to keep up with the changing social attitudes toward race, Walsh and Jack Warner resisted the chance to contribute and gave the role of half-black Amantha Starr to all-white Yvonne De Carlo. It could just as easily have been played by a fair-skinned black such as Dorothy Dandridge, who was the same age as De Carlo and equally beautiful and charismatic.

Sidney Poitier, whose star had been rising rapidly since recent successes in *The Blackboard Jungle* and *Edge of the City,* got the role of Rau-Ru, along with the dubious distinction of portraying the celluloid Clark Gable's first and only black child. Shades of Bonnie Blue Butler!

Gable, who never had to travel beyond the Selznick studio in Culver City while making *GWTW,* was required to spend six weeks in Baton Rouge, Louisiana, for the outdoor location scenes for *Band of Angels.* Happily, by the time that rolled around in January 1957, Mrs. Gable was pronounced well enough to make the trip with him, provided that she didn't exert herself or spend too much time away from their luxury hotel suite.

"Kay was constantly forgetting to take her heart medication," Yvonne De Carlo remembered. "Clark would say to her, 'You take that medicine, Ma. If you don't do what I tell you, I'll give you a kick in the ass.' She retorted, 'You kick me in the ass, and you know where I'll kick you.' Then they'd both laugh together and were very pleased with themselves."

On Gable's fifty-sixth birthday on February 1, Kay threw a big surprise party at the Baton Rouge Country Club. "Throughout the Louisiana location, it rained a lot," Yvonne De Carlo recalled. "Many dreary afternoons were brightened by cocktails in the Gables' hotel suite. Clark was one to pour king-size drinks, which endeared him to all the boozers amongst us."

De Carlo eventually alienated Gable when she woke up feeling sick one morning and phoned the production manager for permission to report for work later in the day. "I was told it would be perfectly all right," she recalled. "However, at precisely nine-ten A.M. I got another call to get to the set—fast! Clark did not like to be kept waiting. I didn't realize what a no-no it was to be late for a Gable shoot. I wanted to explain the reason, but all I got from Clark was ice."

Thirty-three-year-old Sidney Poitier, who had sparse film acting experience up to then, received "a lesson in professionalism" from working with Gable. "He came to the set each day knowing every word of his dialogue—every word," Poitier remembered. "When director Raoul Walsh called for a rehearsal, Gable would play the scene exactly the way he ended up playing it in front of the camera. Exactly. Impressed with his ability to commit to memory ten or more pages of dialogue, and on a moment's notice execute them without a single fluff, I set about picking his brain, trying to ferret out how he did it. That he studied his scripts aggressively and that he sometimes recorded his lines on tape to be played back while he slept was about all he would allow me to unearth.

"But there had to be more, and I wondered what the missing elements would be," Poitier continued. "If I hadn't been so young and flip, I would have recognized them easily. I would have seen an old, tough professional who had been pounded into shape by the grueling regimen of the proving ground that was the American film business in the vibrant Thirties, where one could learn only by doing—doing—and doing."

Poitier diagnosed the "shakes" that plagued Gable late in his career as "a kind of palsy." The actor remembered that Gable's "head and hands would shake involuntarily almost all the time, but when the cameras turned they would stop. He managed to control the shaking throughout a scene, and then he would release whatever mechanism he had been calling on and go back to shaking. It was not too noticeable— you had to be close to him to pick it up—but he was definitely afflicted with a malfunction in the nervous system."

Jack Warner rushed *Band of Angels* through postproduction so that it could be released that summer, three months ahead of another Civil War epic made by MGM entitled *Raintree County,* which boasted Elizabeth Taylor, Montgomery Clift, a $6 million budget, and a new giant screen process known as Camera 65. The $3 million *Band of Angels* was a comparative cheapie shot only in WarnerColor, an Eastman Kodak facsimile of Technicolor.

With inevitable comparisons to *Gone With the Wind, Band of Angels* proved the biggest disaster of Gable's entire career. The review in

Newsweek said, "Here is a movie so bad that it must be seen to be disbelieved. Performances, including Gable's, make summer TV's replacement programs seem as dramatically powerful as the Old Vic." Bosley Crowther of *The New York Times* called it "melodramatic and absurd." *The New Yorker* noted that "Mr. Gable's dimples look tired."

The industry bible *Variety,* which usually tried to find something to commend in every Hollywood product, observed that Gable "contributes a warm, decisive portrayal that carries tremendous authority. It is too bad, however, that he is allowed to look so unusually and unfairly worn. It makes his romance with Miss De Carlo, convincingly presented as a young woman in her early twenties, seem somewhat incredible. Most of the other actors are allowed to play their roles as if they were giving their first readings, but it is unfair to blame them for what is the director's responsibility."

Not surprisingly, Gable decided to part company with Raoul Walsh on future projects. He read the reviews seriously and vowed to reject any scripts that tried to capitalize on his past glories and that might cause him more ridicule and embarrassment. "If it doesn't suit an old geezer with false teeth, forget about it," he told agent George Chasin.

Taking Gable at his word, Chasin sold him to Perlberg-Seaton Productions, one of several independent companies affiliated with Paramount Pictures, for *Teacher's Pet,* a contemporary comedy written by the married team of Michael and Fay Kanin, best known for writing Spencer Tracy and Katharine Hepburn's first film together, *Woman of the Year.* Gable would portray a crusty old self-taught newspaper editor who despises college journalism courses and the people who "teach" them. After he rejects an invitation to give a guest lecture at a local university, he winds up becoming romantically involved with the beautiful professor who sent it.

Producer William Perlberg and director George Seaton offered the costarring role to Doris Day, who jumped at the chance to work with someone she'd worshiped since her early moviegoing days in Cincinnati, Ohio. In the interim, Day had developed into a popular recording artist and Hollywood musical star, but she had only recently branched out into straight acting roles with Alfred Hitchcock's *The Man Who Knew Too Much* and her own self-produced (in partnership with husband Martin Melcher) suspenser, *Julie.*

After a string of color films, Gable decided that he preferred black-and-white photography, which went faster and also made it easier for the cinematographer and lighting crew to conceal some of his weathered looks and overweight. *Teacher's Pet*'s only concession to the latest fads in moviemaking would be the inclusion of a title song by Roy Webb and Joe Lubin, performed (unseen) by Doris Day behind the opening credits and later issued as a 45-rpm Columbia Records single to promote the movie's release.

Director George Seaton, who had guided Grace Kelly to an Oscar-winning performance in *The Country Girl*, encouraged Gable to loosen up and to emulate the low comedy style of Wallace Beery, with lots of exaggerated facial expressions and eyebrow-raising. With Doris Day enacting a crisp, no-nonsense virgin, the opposite approaches somehow worked. The twenty-three-year age difference between the two stars didn't matter.

"When Clark came on the set in the mornings, I could actually feel the magnetic force of his personality," Doris Day remembered. "He dressed in marvelous tweeds, which obviously had belonged to him for a long time, or in leather, and he wore heavy, thick-soled ox-blood brogues that were always shined. He had very big hands and a thick, large-boned physique that gave him great dimension. There was something very affirmative about him, and a directness that suggested great inner strength."

Day believed that Gable truly deserved the appellation "the King." "No actor I ever performed with had such public appeal," she said. "He was as masculine as any man I've ever known, and as much a little boy as a grown man could be—it was this combination that had such a devastating effect on women. But there was nothing of the King about his personality. Just the opposite. Utter simplicity. Uncomplicated. A man who lived on a simple, down-to-earth scale."

Day found Gable different from most of the "legends" whom she had worked with. "He was totally unaware of the impact that he had on people. He steered clear of the Hollywood social whirl. At the end of a day's filming, Clark would go to his dressing room and have a drink of Scotch with his make-up man and his stand-in. They'd shoot the breeze for a while, then Clark would head home to Encino. That was the only staff he had—those two men. Quite a contrast to Frank Sinatra, who also had a kind of royal status in the entertainment world but only moved behind a phalanx of bodyguards."

Paramount studio chief Y. Frank Freeman was so pleased by the daily rushes for *Teacher's Pet* that he offered Gable a deal for two more films. Quite luckily for Gable, George Chasin had also received an offer from Hecht-Hill-Lancaster Productions for its next United Artists venture. Virtually overnight Chasin found himself in the driver's seat and was able to raise Gable's asking price to $500,000 per picture against the usual 10 percent of gross rentals. Before 1957 was over Gable found himself with contracts for three jobs that would earn him at least $1.5 million for no more than about six months of actual labor.

22

Right after the completion of *Teacher's Pet*, Clark and Kay Gable took off to Hawaii for a brief vacation before he started location work for *Run Silent, Run Deep*. Much of the wartime psychological thriller took place in the interiors of submarines and would be filmed at rented studio facilities in Hollywood, but the outdoor scenes of sea and aerial combat were scheduled for shooting first at the U.S. Navy base near San Diego. Ironically, Gable had worked there twenty-six years ago for part of *Hell Divers*, his MGM collaboration with Wallace Beery.

Run Silent, Run Deep was a new experience for Gable, the first time that a costar—in this case, Burt Lancaster—also happened to be his employer. The actor's Hecht-Hill-Lancaster (a partnership with producers Harold Hecht and James Hill) had become one of the leading independent companies, making some films with Lancaster in the cast and others without him, such as the multi-Oscar-winning *Marty* with Ernest Borgnine. It was a path that Gable might have followed if he hadn't been discouraged by his first and only attempt with the unsuccessful *The King and Four Queens*.

Nearly thirteen years younger than Gable, Burt Lancaster was a product of postwar Hollywood. Since becoming a major star in the late 1940s, he'd never been a big box-office draw except when teamed with other rugged males like Gary Cooper or Kirk Douglas, which explains why, as a producer, he was so eager to hire Clark Gable for half a million dollars plus a percentage and to give him top billing in the credits and advertising.

Based on a best-selling novel by Navy veteran Edward L. Beach, *Run*

Silent, Run Deep had a *Moby-Dick* quality, with submarine commander Gable almost insanely obssessed with finding and sinking a Japanese destroyer that once sank him. Executive officer Lancaster is at first doubting and mutinous, but he gets sucked into the frenzy of the pursuit and ends up in command after Gable sinks his quarry but dies heroically in the process.

Gable's on-screen death was a rarity, his first since expiring in the arms of Myrna Loy in *Parnell* back in 1937. All but missing was romance, although a short onshore scene gave commander Gable a wife, portrayed by television actress Mary LaRoche.

Burt Lancaster took his producer's position seriously and hired Robert Wise, a onetime film cutter for Orson Welles who had a flair for gritty realism, to direct. The navy loaned the U.S.S. *Redfish* to double for commander Gable's submarine, the *Nerka*. To stay within the $4 million budget, photography was in black and white, which also made it easier to fake some of the combat scenes by using miniature submarines and ships in a studio tank.

Gable's working relationship with Burt Lancaster got off to a rocky start when Hecht-Hill-Lancaster held an evening get-acquainted meeting at its headquarters in one of the office buildings on Canon Drive in Beverly Hills. Scriptwriter John Gay arrived about ten minutes early and found Gable and his wife sitting on the front steps. "What are you doing out here?" Gay asked.

"The fucking place is locked up," Gable snarled. "You can't get in. What kind of cheesy, crummy outfit is this?"

Without a key, Gay raced to a drugstore on the corner and phoned Lancaster's partner, Harold Hecht, who, it turned out, had put the meeting back an hour but forgot to inform Gable or Gay. "Harold apologized and said 'Oh, my God, I'll get over there immediately,'" John Gay recalled, "but by the time he arrived, the damage had been done. I think that kind of colored Gable's relationship with Hecht-Hill-Lancaster. He really was furious about that."

According to John Gay, "Gable had this suspicion that Burt, because he was the producer, was going to get the best moments in the script, but that didn't happen. It turned out to be far more Gable's movie than Burt's. Furthermore, Burt looked upon Gable as anybody would—

a huge star deserving of respect. Behind his back, Burt and his partner James Hill, who were best buddies, made good-natured jokes about Gable's dentures and so forth, but they made fun of everyone."

By now fifty-six and past his prime, Gable may have been jealous of Lancaster, who was still very much the hero type and in excellent physical shape, but they usually got along and had only one major argument. About three weeks into the filming, Gable suddenly objected to a scene where the commander makes a serious error in judgment during a battle with a Japanese ship and Lancaster takes charge of the submarine.

"I'm not going to do it. He's not going to take over the boat," Gable announced. Since the rest of the story depended on that plot development, Lancaster, Robert Wise, and John Gay reminded Gable that he'd already approved the script with that scene in it. But nothing they said could sway Gable, and production ground to a halt for two days while scripter John Gay consulted original author Edward Beach for a solution that would satisfy Gable and also still cause the commander's removal from duty.

What apparently bugged Gable was that the scene contradicted the infallible superhero image of his MGM era, which would make him seem weak and turn the audience's sympathy against him.

"Finally, we found something that we thought would work," John Gay recalled, "so we went to Gable and his agent and said, 'Look, Clark, suppose that instead of screwing up, you're severely injured and you're suddenly physically incapable of commanding the ship.' And he said, 'You mean I conk out,' and I said, 'That's it, that's it.' So the next morning, Clark was back on the set, working again."

Gable used some of his $500,000 advance from *Run Silent, Run Deep* to purchase an ultramodern second home in Palm Springs, overlooking the Bermuda Dunes Golf Club. With a backlog of two unreleased movies, he could loaf to his heart's content until Paramount Pictures came up with the two projects he'd contracted for. One was under development by Perlberg-Seaton Productions and the other by a similar unit run by the writer-producer-director team of Melville Shavelson and Jack Rose.

By this time Kay Gable was about as healthy as anyone with a history of cardiac problems can be, so the couple divided their time between Encino and Palm Springs, with some occasional hunting and/or fishing trips thrown in. Kay's two children were usually part of the package. Gable had taught them horseback riding and fishing, but their mother drew the line at guns, knives, and axes.

Amusingly, Bunker and Joanie had never realized their stepfather's fame until MGM recently started to lease some of its backlog to television for the very first time. Under pressure from exhibitors, all the major Hollywood studios had pledged to televise no features that were less than ten years old, but Gable hits like *San Francisco* and *Mutiny on the Bounty* were being beamed into millions of homes and winning him kid fans. Bunker's schoolmates were always bugging him to bring them Gable autographs or signed photos.

Needless to say, Gable and his agent were also being deluged by TV producers with offers of series and dramatic specials, but he hated the medium and refused to even consider them. "The movie business made me, and I'll stick by it," he once said. "People will not go out to a movie theater if they can see me in their living room for free."

His ex-flame Loretta Young was now a bigger star on television than she'd ever been in movies. Her NBC dramatic anthology series had become an instant legend with its opening shots of her twirling through a doorway to show off her latest designer frock. Much against her mother's wishes, Judy Lewis had also become a TV actress, but she'd yet to make it past supporting roles in daytime series such as *The Verdict Is Yours* and the short-lived soap opera version of *Kitty Foyle*.

Gable wouldn't appear on TV even to promote his movies, but in March 1958 he finally did for the first and only time, as a favor to his *Teacher's Pet* director, George Seaton, who also happened to be the current president of the Academy of Motion Picture Arts and Sciences. During the NBC telecast of the 1957 awards ceremony at the Pantages Theater in Hollywood, Gable partnered with Doris Day in presenting the Oscars for screenwriting. With Gable in white tie and tails and Day in an Edith Head evening gown, the duo marched onstage to the music from the title song for *Teacher's Pet* and zipped through the two writing prizes, which went to *The Bridge on the River Kwai* for best adaptation from another medium, and *Designing Woman* for best original screenplay.

A week later Paramount released *Teacher's Pet*, which proved a box-office hit and survived a collision with *Run Silent, Run Deep*, which

United Artists rushed out at the same time to take advantage of the crowds that usually flocked to movies during the Easter holiday season. While hardly a flop, *Run Silent, Run Deep* came in second, suggesting that Gable's fans still preferred to see him in romantic parts, even though he was turning gray, wrinkled, and jowly.

Gable received favorable reviews for both films, with *Variety* citing his work in *Teacher's Pet* as "one of his best performances in years." Bosley Crowther of *The New York Times* called *Run Silent, Run Deep* one of the best submarine dramas ever made: "It has the hard, cold ring of truth, with superior acting on the part of Mr. Gable."

In May the Gables received an invitation to the June 21 wedding in Beverly Hills of Judith Lewis, now twenty-two, to Joseph Tinney, a young television director originally from Philadelphia. Not surprisingly, the Gables sent regrets that they would be unable to attend. They also neglected to send a gift.

The ceremony at the Roman Catholic Church of the Good Shepherd nearly got canceled when Judy became queasy about listing Tom Lewis as her father on the license application. Since he'd never legally adopted her, Judy thought that lying about it might invalidate the license. While trying to coax her into it, her fiancé let it drop that Clark Gable was really her father.

Judy, one of the few who didn't know, went into shock when he told her. Her trauma was so great that she refused to get married until she could learn her father's identity. Deciding that her mother would never tell her, she tried the Catholic church where she was baptized but got nowhere. Finally, when priests assured her that she had the legal right to call herself Judy Lewis due to living in Lewis's household for much of her life, she felt better. But for the wedding ceremony she insisted that the officiating priest should use only first names when speaking of the bride and groom.

While dressing for the church, Judy was so agitated that her mother sent for a doctor to give her a tranquilizing injection. Judy went through the proceedings like a zombie and was still zonked by the time the newlyweds left for their honeymoon trip to Hawaii.

During that summer of 1958 Clark Gable popped in and out of Paramount's Hollywood studio for conferences on his two commitments. He accepted Perlberg-Seaton's proposal for another romantic comedy, this one based on the 1934 Broadway play *Accent on Youth,* but custom-revamped for Gable by one of the hottest of the current crop of scriptwriters, John Michael Hayes, whose hits included *Rear Window, To Catch a Thief,* and *Peyton Place.* George Seaton, who directed *Teacher's Pet,* had other commitments, so he agreed to Gable's suggestion of Walter Lang, a longtime 20th–Fox contractee turned freelance. Since buying his house in Palm Springs, Gable had renewed his friendship with Lang, who resided there year-round and was married to Carole Lombard's bosom buddy, Fieldsie.

Gable had a more difficult time coming to terms with Melville Shavelson and Jack Rose, who proposed teaming him with Paramount contractee Sophia Loren in an original script by Shavelson entitled *Bay of Naples.* Gable, who was thirty-three years older than Loren, had vowed to avoid such potentially embarrassing May-December combinations. But Shavelson and Rose persuaded him by screening their previous work with Loren, *Houseboat,* where she costarred with Cary Grant, who was Gable's junior by only three years. Gable admired the film, as well as its box-office success, which earned Cary Grant nearly $1 million in an advance-against-percentage deal like the one that Gable also had with Paramount.

Kay Gable also encouraged him to accept. She was now healthy enough for foreign travel, and a three-month location assignment in picturesque southern Italy, with all expenses paid by Paramount, seemed too good to resist. Due to all the preproduction work required, Shavelson and Rose gave Gable a tentative starting date in July or August 1959. That pleased agent George Chasin, who thought he might be able to squeeze in another independent deal for Gable after he finished the Perlberg-Seaton film for Paramount.

Unfortunately, the first offer that Chasin fielded was from director Vincente Minnelli, who wanted Gable for *Home from the Hill,* based on William Humphrey's critically acclaimed novel about the troubled relationship between a supermacho southern patriarch and his wife and two sons. Gable liked the semi–King Lear character, but he also still detested MGM, the film's producer. Minnelli finally had to settle for Robert Mitchum, who gave a performance that many critics considered the best of his career.

In November, Gable started Perlberg-Seaton's black-and-white *But*

Not for Me, the new title for *Accent on Youth,* which seemed inappropriate for the sixty-fifth movie of its fifty-seven-year-old star. Director Walter Lang suggested the new handle, which made a wry comment on Gable's romantic predicament in the film and also provided a theme song in the George and Ira Gershwin standard originally written for the 1930 Broadway musical *Girl Crazy.* Jazz diva Ella Fitzgerald would perform the song behind the movie's opening credits and also feature it in her forthcoming five LP-record "songbook" of Gershwin evergreens.

Paramount had already filmed *Accent on Youth* twice, first under that title in 1935 with debonair Herbert Marshall, then in 1950 as the considerably altered and song-filled *Mr. Music,* starring Bing Crosby. Ironically, the three romantic idols all had secrets that were unknown to most of their fans: Marshall a wooden leg due to an amputation during World War I for battle wounds, Crosby a toupee for premature baldness, and Gable full dentures. Like the original 1934 play written by Samson Raphaelson, the first two film versions of *Accent on Youth* told of a successful middle-aged man who falls for his much-younger secretary and eventually wins her after she initially rejects him for a lover her own age.

For Bing Crosby, the man had been turned into a Broadway songwriter, but in the other versions he was a playwright. For Clark Gable, who'd rarely played intellectual types, the character was transformed into a theatrical producer having problems putting on his next play. When his young secretary, who also happens to be an aspiring actress, suggests some solutions, a romance erupts and she winds up starring in the play, which becomes a smash hit.

Due to Gable's sensitivity about dirty old men leching after young women, scriptwriter John Michael Hayes changed the plot and especially the ending of *Accent on Youth,* in which the May-December lovers reconciled after her affair with a younger man proved too boring. Whatever romantic feelings Gable has for his secretary are explained away as midlife crisis. He finally wakes up to his craziness and reconciles with his ex-wife, a maturing but still glamorous stage star, while the girl finds that she prefers one of her fellow young actors.

Twenty-seven-year-old Carroll Baker, who had become an overnight Hollywood sex symbol in 1956 as the wanton child-bride in the Tennessee Williams–Elia Kazan sizzler *Baby Doll,* got the role of the secretary. Lilli

Palmer, the alluring German-British star who recently ended her marriage and acting partnership with Rex Harrison, was hired to play Gable's ex-wife. John Michael Hayes added a comic sidekick for Gable, a washed-up, booze-addicted playwright portrayed by character star Lee J. Cobb, best known for acting the role of Willy Loman in the original Broadway stage production of Arthur Miller's *Death of a Salesman*.

In the character of producer Russell Ward, Gable did a reverse turn on his long-established image and became the love object rather than the aggressor. He made jokes about his age, and when Carroll Baker's sexy nymph cornered him, he told her, "I'm getting too old for this kind of thing." For some scenes director Walter Lang encouraged him to wear bifocal eyeglasses and even less makeup than he usually did.

In a press interview at the time, Gable said, "My days of playing the dashing lover are over. I'm no longer believable in those parts. There has been considerable talk about older guys wooing and winning leading ladies half their age. I don't think the public likes it, and I don't care for it myself. It's not realistic. Actresses that I started out with like Joan Crawford and Barbara Stanwyck have long since quit playing glamour girls and sweet young things. Now it's time I acted my age.

"Let's be honest," he continued. "It's a character role, and I'll be playing more of them. There's a risk involved, of course. I have no idea if I can attain the success as a character actor as I did playing the dashing young lover, but it's a chance I have to take. Not everybody is able to do it."

At the wrap-up of *But Not for Me,* Gable gifted his coworkers with potted potato plants and bags of deep-fried chips that his wife had made from their own crop at the ranch. It reminded Walter Lang of Gable and Carole Lombard's efforts to be part-time farmers. The director, who had lost touch with Gable in the years after Lombard's death, was startled by the fifth Mrs. Gable's resemblance to the third. Kay cursed like Lombard, dressed like her, and catered to Gable in the same way.

"Sometimes I could close my eyes and listen to Clark and Kay calling each other Ma and Pa and exchanging quips and insults and think that I was listening to a road company of Clark and Carole," Lang recalled.

Due to her history of cardiac problems and her postforty age, it seemed increasingly unlikely that Kay would ever produce a Gable heir, but her own two children seemed all the family that he needed. Life for the Gables was marvelous, and friends had never seen him happier.

The couple often took the kids to a public park in Encino and became involved in neighborhood life. When the local government tried to sell the park to a land developer, Gable led a successful campaign to preserve it. On Halloween he always dressed up in costume and took Bunker and Joanie trick-or-treating. One year he was a scarecrow, the next a circus clown.

Now pushing sixty, Gable continued to smoke cigarettes and to drink liquor as heavily as always. Except for the occasional shakes, which may not have been related to either of those habits, he seemed in reasonably good health and made no efforts to stop, despite warnings from doctors and friends.

By the spring of 1959, Gable had given his final approval to the script for *Bay of Naples,* which henceforth would be known as *It Started in Naples* to suggest romantic high jinks in the vein of his Oscar-winning *It Happened One Night.* All but forgotten for twenty-five years, the latter had recently achieved "classic" status through its first broadcasts on television.

The Italy-based production was due to start in August, but Gable decided to take his family on a tour of Europe beforehand. With the children's governess added, they flew to New York on June 21, the first experience for any of them with jet-propelled airliners, which had just been introduced and that reduced the coast-to-coast trip to a mere five hours. Though it was possible to fly to Europe the same way in another seven, the Gable group made a more relaxed transatlantic crossing on the Dutch luxury liner *Nieuw Amsterdam.* After some sight-seeing in Holland, England, and France, they rented a chalet near Salzburg, Austria, for the balance of their holiday, which coincided with the Gables' fourth wedding anniversary.

On August 10 they arrived in Rome to take up residence at a villa that Paramount had leased for them near Anzio, an Allied beachhead in some of the bloodiest wartime combat but by now fully restored to a picturesque seaside resort. Gable could drive the fifteen miles to the Cinecittà Studios in Rome in about the same time that it took him to reach any of the Hollywood plants from Encino.

Most of the interior scenes for *It Started in Naples,* amounting to about a third of the script, would be shot at Cinecittà, with all of the exteriors scheduled for Naples and the island of Capri, about 150 miles south of Rome. Gable's stepchildren and their governess would remain the whole time in Anzio to avoid problems on the locations, where he and Kay would stay in hotels with the rest of the company.

Gable, writer-director Mel Shavelson, producer Jack Rose, and cinematographer Robert Surtees (who had worked with Gable on *Mogambo* and had just finished the Rome-based *Ben-Hur*) were among the few non-Italians on the project. As the seventh in a multipicture deal that Sophia Loren had made with Paramount in 1957, it was also the first to be produced on her native turf and consequently used many actors and others whom she'd known since her first Italian films in 1950.

Foremost among them were actor-director Vittorio De Sica and scriptwriter Suso Cecchi d'Amico, who had collaborated on the neorealistic classic, *The Bicycle Thief,* and agreed to help Jewish-American Mel Shavelson to add some typically Neapolitan touches and characters to the screenplay. De Sica also ended up with a costarring role, which was big news in Italy, where he held a regal position comparable to Gable's in Hollywood.

Gable played a prudish Philadelphia lawyer, Michael Hamilton, visiting Naples to settle the estate of his wastrel younger brother, who was killed in a car crash together with his common-law Italian wife. To his shock, Mike discovers that he has an eight-year-old nephew, already a cigarette-smoking, wine-guzzling street thug who is being raised by his twentyish maternal aunt, Lucia Curcio, a honky-tonk nightclub performer with movie star aspirations. Some of Loren's character was based on her original self, Sofia Scicolone, illegitimate daughter of a Roman playboy and a starstruck Neapolitan peasant.

Loren and Carlo Ponti, her longtime lover and impresario, were currently being prosecuted in Italy over an allegedly illegal proxy marriage in Mexico, so she sort of sneaked into her homeland just long enough to make the movie. It seemed unlikely that the Italian government would take any action against her since the Paramount production was pumping four million much-needed American dollars into the economy and also promised to boost tourism when moviegoers saw the gorgeous Technicolor vistas of southern Italy.

Loren would soon turn twenty-five, which made her Gable's youngest leading lady since Lana Turner, who was only twenty-one when she first worked with Gable. The thirty-three-year age gap between Gable and Loren promised to alienate anyone unsympathetic to May-December romance. When Gable accepted the assignment, he must have suffered memory lapse over his vow to avoid such teamings. But, unlike *But Not for Me,* the comedy was not about Gable being too old for Loren but about the differences between the American and Italian ways of life.

With Gable occupied with his wife and stepchildren and Loren living in hiding to avoid the paparazzi, the costars never socialized beyond the set. But Loren loved to cook and often prepared lunch for Gable in her dressing trailer. As a result he got hooked on pasta, and by the time that production ended, his weight soared to a lifetime high of 230 pounds. Since the scenes were filmed randomly and rarely in the order that they would eventually appear on screen, Gable's jowls and overall heft ballooned and deflated noticeably throughout the finished product.

After her first week of working with Gable, Loren became upset by his tendency to grab the most flattering camera angles for himself. "I know he's considered 'the King' and a very great star, but I don't think he's being fair with me," she complained to director Mel Shavelson. "Somehow he manages to position himself so that my worst side is always turned toward the camera. He doesn't have to worry about his career anymore, but I have to worry about mine."

When Shavelson spoke to him, Gable responded with a growl and a few expletives. "What the hell's she talking about? She's lucky. *Both* sides of my face are lousy, and my backside isn't that good-looking either. You just tell me what side she wants to show, and I'll get out of her way!"

Before the unit moved south to Naples, Loren gave in to pestering from actor-friend Marcello Mastroianni, who idolized Gable and wanted an introduction. Unlike Loren, Mastroianni had no interest in working in Hollywood, so it seemed that this might be his only chance to meet "The King."

"Sophia finally fixed it, but it was only for a few minutes," Mastroianni recalled. "In cases like that, you have too much to say, so you end up saying practically nothing. I found Gable to be the only exception, at least in my mind, to the theory of the actor as an amorphous entity waiting to be shaped by a director. He had so much personality that he had no need to do characters in the way that we normally say an actor does a character."

Though Sophia Loren grew up near Naples in the fishing village of Pozzuoli, she and her family were too poor to be able to afford the ferry fare to Capri, so Clark Gable's very first visit to the mountainous island paradise was hers as well. Needless to say, the movie's script included a romantic interlude in the legendary Blue Grotto, where the light reflecting off the surface of the water creates effects of breathtaking beauty. While riding in a rowboat, the lovers decide to take a swim and strip naked. Gable had never done a nude scene and was hardly willing to start exposing himself at age fifty-eight, so a considerably younger and svelter body double took over. Loren also insisted on a double since her huge breasts might be mistaken for a life preserver. The camera angles were carefully arranged so that the body doubles were seen only in silhouette and could pass for the stars.

On September 20 Gable helped to smuggle Carlo Ponti on to Capri to attend a surprise party for Loren's twenty-fifth birthday. Her fugitive middle-aged "husband," who in the view of the Italian judiciary was a bigamist still married to a previous wife, chartered a plane to fly from exile on the French Riviera to Naples. Gable and his wife, who had a motorized yacht at their disposal during the location, spent the day sight-seeing in Naples and brought Ponti back with them. Ponti departed the next morning, leaving behind Loren's birthday gift, a $75,000 diamond-and-ruby necklace.

Mel Shavelson rushed Gable through his final scenes so that he could take his family home to Encino. Bunker and Joan had already missed the start of their school terms. Gable had no work on the immediate horizon, but George Chasin had a pile of scripts waiting for him to read.

In October Paramount released *But Not for Me,* which flopped at the box office despite more favorable reviews than the hit *Teacher's Pet.* Exhibitors blamed the failure on Gable's costar, Carroll Baker, who had yet to win a huge fan following like Doris Day's and who also became a favorite target of Catholic pressure groups like the Legion of Decency due to her connection with *Baby Doll,* considered by some to be the most obscene Hollywood movie ever made.

Although *But Not for Me* failed to gross enough to earn Gable anything beyond the $500,000 advance guarantee that he'd already collected in his percentage deal, it endeared him to film critics, some of whom had treated him harshly in recent years. *Life* magazine, in those days America's most-read weekly, said, "For more than a quarter of a century, Clark Gable's persuasive charm has drawn movie-lovers by the millions. Radiating good-humored masculine appeal, he had something for everybody. For ladies he was the great lover; for men he was the hard-fighting man's man; for both he was the fun-loving comedian. Now in his sixty-fifth film, he proves that despite his fifty-seven years he is still the indestructible all-around charmer."

Life's sister newsweekly, *Time,* noted, "No director has ever been presumptuous enough to ask 'The King' to act, but his presence alone gives any film the atmosphere of Hollywood's glorious pre-Method past. Gable's voice may croak a little, but he still has the confidence of a man who knows that so long as he goes on playing the King, no one will dare play the Ace."

Bosley Crowther of *The New York Times* congratulated Gable on his willingness to act his age: "What's more, he is willing to make jokes about it and let his script writers make jokes about it, too. . . . With a delightful pretense of uncertainty about the age of the character he plays, which ranges in the course of conversation from forty-four to fifty-six, he runs away with this glib little trifle."

Paramount, so far batting .500 at the box office with its Gable projects, decided to await the results of *It Started in Naples* before making any more commitments with him. Meanwhile, Gable went on a strict low-starch diet to lose the excess poundage he gained in Pastaland. At 230 pounds he was about forty pounds above the "acceptable" weight for a male of his six-foot-one height.

Besides the need to look trim, Gable had to be reasonably healthy and able to pass a physical examination for production insurance. In the old factory days, the studios themselves carried enough insurance to cover any catastrophe, but independent producers working with strict budgets and/or hard-raised financing had to take out individual short-term policies on their stars and directors in the event of a serious accident or death. In 1958 forty-five-year-old Tyrone Power had died of a heart attack while filming a strenuous scene for *Solomon and Sheba.*

Without insurance on Power, producer Edward Small would have had to cancel the project and lose the $4 million he'd spent so far, but with the settlement he was soon able to start over with Yul Brynner as Power's replacement.

On November 16 Gable and Loretta Young became grandparents with the birth of Maria Tinney. Needless to say, the complete truth went unreported at the time, but gossip queen Louella Parsons rushed into print with congratulations to Young, who, at age forty-eight, deserved the crown of "Hollywood's Most Glamorous Granny."

While catching up with scripts that had been submitted during his months abroad, Gable became intrigued by *The Misfits,* written by revered stage dramatist Arthur Miller as an original screen vehicle for his wife, Marilyn Monroe. Not easily categorized, it was a blend of contemporary western, psychological character study, and moral parable.

Gable was more curious than eager to sign on. Although his longtime friend John Huston had already agreed to direct *The Misfits,* he sensed problems with Marilyn Monroe, a notorious neurotic who'd caused major crises on nearly every film she'd made. Though her screen persona reminded him of Carole Lombard and Jean Harlow, he considered Monroe "a self-indulgent twat" who would never have been tolerated by the strict-disciplinarian moguls of old.

But George Chasin finally persuaded Gable to at least meet with Arthur Miller to discuss the project. During a long lunch at the Beverly Hills Hotel, the actor and author both realized that they needed each other. "I've never been able to connect stars with parts I write," Arthur Miller recalled, "but after meeting Gable I could see him as Gay Langland. He had the same sort of lyricism underneath, something one didn't usually think of, watching him. It was his secret charm—tough but responsive to feeling and ideals."

Miller surmised that "Gable didn't understand *The Misfits* because it was a western yet somehow not a western, and he didn't think he understood what I was driving at. After a couple of hours' talk he understood perfectly—Gay was just like *him.*"

Gay (an abbreviation of Gaylord) was an aging, no-longer-in-demand Nevada desert cowboy involved with three other misfits, including a burlesque stripper who came to Reno for a quickie divorce, a washed-up rodeo bronco buster, and a World War II fighter pilot reduced to fixing cars. The four of them team up to capture wild horses that will be sold for slaughtering as meat for canned dog food. The script's title had a double meaning; *misfit* is also a cowboy term for the breed of mustangs being caught, which are too small for riding or pulling wagons.

Before accepting the role, Gable asked his writer-friend and one-time air force buddy John Lee Mahin to read the script and to give him an opinion. Mahin's advice was, "You're dead if you shoot this script, Clark. You're a good competent actor, but you're no Spencer Tracy, and people don't come to see you because you're a great actor, you know that. You can hold your own, old boy, you and I both know that. But how about that scene with a mare and a hungry little colt nudging her tit? You guess that they must weigh about eight hundred pounds combined and will net you ninety dollars when you sell them. You'll be dead! You're dead from the moment you *start* to harass the horses. Just for dog food? I understand what Arthur's getting at, and I like a lot of it, but it's a misfit for Clark Gable."

But Arthur Miller and producer Frank Taylor were now so eager to hire Gable that George Chasin persuaded him to sign if they could wrench big bucks from Seven Arts Productions, which was financing the project with help from its distributor, United Artists. Chasin promised Gable that he'd get him more money than he'd ever earned before, as well as protection against Marilyn Monroe's famed delinquencies.

Contract negotiations dragged on for two months but were finally concluded by Gable's fifty-ninth birthday in February 1960. Chasin kept his word with the highest one-picture fee that Gable or any other Holly-wood star had ever received—$750,000 against 10 percent of gross rentals. The advance guarantee was a quarter-of-a-million jump from his previous high of $500,000. Besides Gable's usual nine-to-five working hours, Chasin locked him into a sixteen-week shooting schedule. If the production wasn't completed by then, Gable would receive additional pay of $48,000 per week for as long as his services were required. The overtime would be treated like a bonus and would not be charged against his advance in the reckoning of his 10 percent share of film rentals.

With most of the filming to be done on location in Reno and the surrounding desert region, John Huston set an April starting date to avoid Nevada's scorching and windswept summer. Gable, who was still dieting, rushed down to his retreat in Palm Springs with Kay to study the script and to get some much-needed exercise playing golf and tennis.

Unfortunately, Gable failed his physical exam for production insurance, which put the whole deal in jeopardy. His personal physician sent him to bed for two weeks, on medication for hypertension, forbidden to smoke or booze. Gable passed the next examination and went straight home to celebrate with a cigar and brandy.

By April Marilyn Monroe was still before the cameras in 20th–Fox's *Let's Make Love,* which had started the previous November but was delayed by a two-week industry-wide strike by the Screen Actors Guild over residuals for TV reruns and, more drastically, by fallout from Monroe's blatant affair with her imported costar, Yves Montand. The romance threatened to break up her marriage to Arthur Miller, as well as Montand's to actress Simone Signoret, who had accompanied him from France for the filming. The psychological strain on Monroe had her popping tranquilizers and amphetamines; if she came to work at all, it was usually for a couple of hours or less.

John Huston optimistically set a new starting date of June 1 for *The Misfits,* which gave Gable two more months to rest and build himself up. With rumors flying that Monroe and Arthur Miller were on the verge of getting divorced, he wondered if the movie would ever be made.

Monroe finally finished *Let's Make Love* in May but was too exhausted to go straight on to *The Misfits.* When John Huston announced a new date of July 18, Gable insisted that it must be or they'd have to find themselves a new star actor.

By this time Paramount Pictures was near to releasing *It Started in Naples,* which had already received highly favorable audience reactions in a series of test previews around the country and promised to be a hit. The studio had just signed a multipicture deal with producer-director Howard Hawks, who was interested in hiring Gable, an old friend and hunting buddy, for at least one of them.

Gable agreed to meet with Hawks, and to make a long story short, they eventually shook hands on an African adventure entitled *Hatari,* the Swahili word for "danger." Gable would costar with another of Hawks's buddies, John Wayne, provided that they both approved a script that had yet to be written but would focus on two rogues who trap wild animals for zoos and circuses. Gable warned Hawks that he would expect top billing and a $1 million guarantee against his usual 10 percent.

Seemingly miraculously, John Huston was able to keep to the July 18 "go" signal for *The Misfits*. The Gables left for Nevada a few days early to celebrate their fifth wedding anniversary in Minden, the little resort town where they were married. For the duration of *The Misfits*, their home was a rented house with a swimming pool in the outskirts of Reno. Joining them were the two Spreckels children and their governess, as well as one of the maids from the ranch.

Ironically, with *The Misfits* Gable's movie career came full circle with another desert western. It was excactly thirty years before that he had made his talkie feature debut in *The Painted Desert*, part of it filmed in neighboring Arizona.

Except for his old friend John Huston, Gable literally felt like a misfit as he became acquainted with his principal coworkers. In addition to Marilyn Monroe Miller, there was another potential troublemaker in thirty-nine-year-old Montgomery Clift, who had been addicted to drugs since a nearly fatal face-disfiguring car crash in 1956. Eli Wallach was a wiseacre New Yorker. Both actors, as well as Monroe, practiced Lee Strasberg's "Method," which Gable shunned like an alien religion.

Gable had met Marilyn Monroe only once before, in 1954 while working at 20th Century–Fox in *Soldier of Fortune,* when all the stars on the lot were invited to a wrap party celebrating the conclusion of her *The Seven Year Itch.* Gable ended up dancing with Monroe and listening to a confession that she grew up believing that he was the runaway father whom she'd never known. When her mother once showed her a photo of the man, the then-very-young movie fan Norma Jean Mortenson had mistaken him for Clark Gable. Her mother, a certified loony who spent most of her life in and out of institutions, did nothing to discourage her.

Not surprisingly, Monroe arrived two hours late for her very first scene with Gable. The night before, high anxiety drove her to take an extra dose of Nembutal, so she overslept and had to be revitalized with Benzedrine and black coffee. By the time her entourage of thirteen, including Arthur Miller, acting coach Paula Strasberg, and assorted body attendants, delivered her to the set, she was feeling sick and had to run to the portable lavatory wagon to vomit. When she returned, it took another hour for her assistants to help her dress and to fix her hair and makeup.

When Monroe finally tottered out in stiletto heels and a low-cut white dress, she marched straight over to Gable and apologized for the delay. Gable put his arms around her and said, "You're not late, honey," then took her by the hand and led her to a quiet corner for a private chat. Whatever Gable told her made her giggle and then laugh out loud. From then on they had a cordial working relationship, or at least on those rare days when Monroe managed to make it to the job on time.

Gable was fascinated and yet appalled by Montgomery Clift. He admired his blunt, naturalistic style, which reminded him of Spencer Tracy. But he had no patience with Clift's drug habit, which caused him to bungle his lines and often required umpteen retakes of their scenes together. During an especially bad day, Gable snarled at him, "If you weren't such a little runt, I'd smash my fist into your face."

Eli Wallach liked to play the court jester and was always needling Gable with jokes such as "Hey, King, can you lower my taxes?" Gable tried to even the score with cracks about Wallach's training at the Actors Studio. One day while they were waiting for the chow wagon to arrive and Wallach wondered, "What's for lunch?" Gable told him, "Boiled ham."

Surprisingly, Gable had a rough time with old friend John Huston, an addicted gambler who was losing pots of money gambling all night at Reno's casinos and then taking it out on everybody the next day by behaving like a tyrant. Huston seemed to take special delight in a morning-after bedroom scene where Gable, already up and dressed, had to wake Monroe, still naked beneath a sheet. Huston made them do the five-minute dialogue scene seven times while he decided whether Monroe should drop the sheet and expose a breast or maybe two to the camera. He finally opted to keep them covered but insisted on another six retakes before he was content with Gable's and Monroe's performances.

As expected, Nevada's summer heat was oppressive; temperatures under the desert sun bubbled around the 130-degree mark, which made it even harder for Monroe and almost everyone except Gable to put in a full day's work. Though he had a chauffeured limousine at his disposal, he drove himself back and forth to work in his silver Mercedes-Benz SC.

He always arrived punctually at eight-forty-five A.M., bringing along gallon Thermoses of booze-spiked lemonade and iced tea to fortify himself. For the better part of the morning, he would sit around studying that day's script pages or gabbing with the crew while waiting for the other principals to arrive.

Though the delays were driving him mad, he tried not to show it. But one day while his writer-friend John Lee Mahin was visiting from Los Angeles, Gable told him, "It's not professional, John, it's stealing. It's stealing the bank's money and United Artists' money. I don't see how they're going to get a picture out of this, but I'm stuck with it now, and I'm trying to do the best I can. It's been hard on me."

In mid-August, a week after her forty-fourth birthday, Kay Gable tested pregnant. The couple were overjoyed but decided to keep it secret until Kay got through those early weeks when miscarriages are most likely to happen. Gable watched her like a hawk. One evening while the Gables were hosting a dinner party for visiting United Artists executives, one of the wives collapsed from too many cocktails, and Kay half-lifted the woman while helping her get back on her feet. "Mr. Gable went right through the roof," their maid Louisa recalled. "He was afraid she was going to lose the baby. They fought and fought all night. And Mrs. Gable cried and cried."

On August 27 Marilyn Monroe broke down and was flown to Los Angeles for treatment at a private clinic that specialized in quick "cures" for drug abuse. While she recuperated from what was reported to the press as "acute exhaustion," production of *The Misfits* halted because her absenteeism had already caused John Huston to run out of scenes that could be shot without her. Gable suggested a betting pool on how long it would take for her to return. But she surprised everybody and was absent for just one week, arriving back in time for the company's Labor Day barbecue.

By the end of September, the pregnant Kay Gable was doing so well that her doctor considered it safe to make her condition public. Columnist Louella Parsons, who long before had been denied an exclusive on the Gable-Lombard elopement, was the first to be told.

"Clark sort of flourished when the news got out," according to Harry Mines, the location publicist for *The Misfits,* who did all the contact work. "He kept saying to everybody, 'Imagine, I'm going to be a father.' His big joke, once everyone knew, was to tell people that his and Kay's combined ages were over one hundred. He kept grinning and crediting it to the altitude in Nevada. The area where we were shooting was about four thousand feet above sea level."

Gable was convinced that he and Kay would have a son. He told friends that he would make one more movie and then retire to play full-time father at the ranch. He planned to build a new addition to the house so that his boy and two stepchildren could all be together.

In October, as *The Misfits* dragged on, Gable's compensation spurted into $48,000 per week overtime. Marilyn Monroe, by now back on barbiturates and living separately from Arthur Miller, whom she still had to confront during working hours, became even more delinquent, threw tantrums on the set, and had trouble remembering the simplest lines.

From the start of production, Miller and John Huston had tried to help Monroe by shooting the script straight through, as a play is performed on the stage. Monroe's coach, Paula Strasberg, believed that it would make it easier for her to resume her character each day. As a result, Gable had been sitting nervously for three months without getting to his most physically demanding moments, which came in the harrowing climax of the film, where the four misfits try to capture a small herd of wild mustangs.

John Huston hired expert stuntpeople to double for the stars, but for medium shots and close-ups that could not be faked with imposters, he succeeded in goading the three males and even Monroe into dangerously exerting themselves. Gable had moments that no man of his age or out-of-shape physical condition should have risked. While pretending to be drunk and standing on the engine hood of a car, he had to lose his balance and tumble to the pavement, hitting a fender along the way. In the desert he had to run a hundred yards trying to catch up with a speeding truck. After he lassoed a mustang, the scene required him to be knocked off his feet and dragged on his stomach through alkali desert as the horse tried to break loose of the rope.

To satisfy Huston and/or cinematographer Russell Metty, who was shooting in black and white with natural light only, Gable had to do each take not once but several times. Despite whatever protective padding could be concealed beneath his shirts and jeans, he went home sore, bruised, and bleeding every night. His suffering was evident in the footage, much of which was never used in the final cut of *The Misfits* because of its gruesomeness.

Location work concluded on October 18, but production of a few remaining interior scenes continued for two more weeks at rented facilities at the Paramount lot in Hollywood. On Friday, November 4, Gable and Monroe shot the movie's concluding moment, which showed them sitting in the cab of a truck, driving away from the desert to start some kind of a life together. As they looked out at the night sky, Gable's final line of dialogue was, "Just head for that big star. It will take us home."

That weekend Gable planned to go duck hunting, but he woke up Saturday morning feeling as if he might be coming down with the flu, so he decided to stay home and rest. By afternoon he was feeling better and went to the garage to change a damaged tire on his jeep. While jacking up the car, he felt a stabbing pain in his chest and dropped to his knees in a cold sweat. When the pain quickly passed, he returned to the house. Kay thought he looked ghastly, but he wouldn't let her call a doctor. He ate a light supper and went to bed early to read *Diamond Head,* a new novel that Columbia Pictures had pitched to his agent as a likely vehicle.

In the middle of the night, Gable awoke with a severe headache and took some aspirin. He fell back to sleep, but when his interior clock went off as usual around seven-thirty in the morning, he got up and started to dress. He suddenly felt a recurrence of the previous day's chest pain, only worse. He woke his wife and told her, "It feels like a huge hand has crawled inside me and is tearing my rib cage apart."

His face was ashen and beaded with sweat. Kay phoned his doctor, Fred Cerini, who promised to come immediately and also called the Encino Fire Department to send its rescue squad with oxygen support. By the time Dr. Cerini arrived at the ranch, Gable was already attached to a respirator and seemed in need of hospitalization, so he summoned an ambulance. Gable didn't want to leave for fear that all the excitement might cause Kay to suffer a miscarriage. But she agreed with Dr. Cerini and insisted on riding with Gable in the ambulance to Presbyterian Hospital in Hollywood.

Hospital tests quickly confirmed Dr. Cerini's diagnosis of a severe coronary thrombosis. If Gable survived the next few days, he had a fair chance of recovering, but would likely live no more than about five years, according to the current statistics for such cases.

Right after Clark Gable's hospitalization hit the news wires, President Dwight D. Eisenhower sent him a telegram: "Be a good boy, Clark, and do as the doctors tell you to do. With my best wishes, Ike." Himself a heart attack survivor, Eisenhower also recommended one of his caretakers, Dr. George Griffiths, whom Kay Gable immediately retained.

As her husband had done during her own serious illness three years before, Kay stayed with him around the clock, sleeping on a cot at the foot of his bed. When the room became too crowded with doctors, nurses, technicians, and monitoring equipment, she booked the room across the hall. Gable was being treated with anticoagulants and sedatives. He had oxygen tubes in his nostrils to ease his breathing.

By Tuesday, November 8, which just happened to be the national Election Day, Gable felt well enough to cast an absentee ballot. Presumably he supported his Republican pal "Ike" by voting for Richard M. Nixon for president, though Democrat John F. Kennedy turned out the winner.

After only forty-eight hours in the hospital, Gable had received more than five thousand telegrams, greeting cards, and letters from well-wishers all over the world. Dozens of reporters and photographers were camped outside, but Gable's longtime friend Howard Strickling, still head of MGM publicity, kept them at bay and the news bulletins optimistic.

Ironically, Gable's stroke occurred on the morning of the twenty-fifth birthday of Judy Lewis Tinney, who still had no actual proof that he was her father. When she heard on the radio that he was recovering, she considered visiting him in the hospital because it might be her last chance ever to confront him on the matter. But she also realized the repercussions if Loretta Young's "adopted" daughter suddenly turned up there, so she decided to stay away.

Gable seemed to be getting progressively better. He could sit up and read or watch television. One day Kay arranged a surprise that delighted him. While her obstetrician was visiting, he let Gable listen to the baby's heartbeat through a stethoscope. The delivery, which would be by cesarean section, was tentatively scheduled for four months later, on March 20, 1961.

After a week Gable had improved enough that Kay felt it safe to go home for a few hours to pick up some things for both of them. When she returned, Gable bawled her out and told her not to leave him alone again.

On November 16, the tenth day of his confinement, Gable's doctors predicted that he would soon be off the danger list. That night, about forty minutes after Kay retired to her room across the hall, Gable suffered another heart attack while reading a magazine. His nurse summoned help, but it was too late. He died instantly. He would have turned sixty on his next birthday in February.

In her room across the hall, Kay Gable was fast asleep, so the head doctor sent for her obstetrician to wake her up and break the news. She reacted as expected and ran to her husband's bedside. "I held him in my arms for two hours, until they made me leave," she recalled. Friends came to take her home, sneaking her out through a back door of the hospital to avoid the press mob in the lobby.

The Associated Press's annual poll of newspaper editors later listed Clark Gable's death as the top entertainment news story of 1960 because it marked the end of the golden, glamorous era of Hollywood moviemaking that he dominated.

In an editorial headlined "The King Is Dead," *The New York Times* noted, "Even among the hierarchy of great motion-picture stars, of whom there were many in the happy years of his ascendance, he was acknowledged supreme. Perhaps he was not the most skillful and subtle in the way of technique. Perhaps he did not possess the polish of some of the latterly imported British stars. But what Gable had in a measure that no other star quite matched—or projected as ferociously as he did—was a true masculine personality. Whatever the role, Gable was as certain as the sunrise. He was consistently and stubbornly all Man. . . . People everywhere—men, women and small boys—admired Clark Gable. He was a conspicuous symbol of the rugged American throughout the world."

An editorial in *The Los Angeles Times* praised Gable's "rare human qualities: virility graced by humor, good nature adorned by comprehension, an easy manner unspoiled by pretensions. To these engaging traits he added professional integrity and personal sincerity, not easily found in the competitive atmosphere of the screen."

Adela Rogers St. Johns, always the journalist closest to Gable, wrote that "The King is dead. Long live the King. There has been no successor, nor will be. The title died with him." She recalled that Gable once told her, "I don't believe I'm king of anything, but I know why they like to think I am. I'm not much of an actor, but I'm not bad unless it's one of those things outside my comprehension. I work hard. I'm no Adonis, and I'm as American as the telephone poles I used to climb to make a living. So men don't get sore if their women folks like me on the screen. I'm one of them, they know it, so it's a compliment to them. They see me broke, in trouble, scared of things that go bump in the night, but I come out fighting. They see me making love to Jean Harlow or Claudette Colbert, and they say, 'If he can do it, I can do it,' and figure it'll be fun to go home and to make love to their wives."

Many reporters asked Presbyterian Hospital authorities whether Gable's death might have been prevented if he'd been connected to a heart-monitoring machine. He had been when admitted, but it was later removed from his room when he showed substantial improvement. A doctor described that as routine procedure because it was of great psychological benefit to the patient as proof that he was getting better.

Over the years Gable had often told Howard Strickling, "When I die, don't let them make a circus out of it." Kay and his friends tried to keep that wish, but the U.S. Air Force got into the act and produced a full-dress military funeral in respect of Major Gable's wartime service.

On the day of the rites on November 19, all the Hollywood studios, including MGM, flew their flags at half-mast to honor the departed King. The funeral seemed a partial rerun of Carole Lombard Gable's in 1942, which had been held in the same chapel, the Church of the Recessional, at Forest Lawn Memorial Park, and with many of the same mourners, now eighteen years older. Three of Gable's MGM contemporaries—Spencer Tracy, Robert Taylor, and James Stewart—served as pallbearers, along with Howard Strickling, Eddie Mannix, and family friends Ray Hommes and Ernie Dunliner.

The long-retired Norma Shearer was the only one of Gable's many leading ladies to attend the service, though most were still living. Conspicuously absent were his former flames Joan Crawford and Loretta Young, as well as his most recent costar, Marilyn Monroe, who *was* represented by her soon-to-be-ex-husband, Arthur Miller.

At Gable's request the casket was closed from viewing. He once told Kay, "I don't want a lot of strangers looking down at my wrinkles and my big fat belly when I'm dead."

In his will he left instructions for no eulogies, so Episcopalian air force chaplain Johnson West conducted only a brief service of Bible readings from the Book of Psalms, numbers 46 and 121. The only music played was a medley of waltzes by Gable's favorite composers, the Strausses.

The pregnant Mrs. Gable sat in the front pew with her Spreckels children, Bunker and Joan. Gable's casket was covered with a blanket of red roses, atop which sat a regent's crown made from miniature roses of a much darker red. At the conclusion of the service, air force guardsmen sounded taps.

Due to construction work going on in Forest Lawn's Great Mausoleum, Gable's entombment in the section known as the Sanctuary of Trust had to be delayed four days, until November 23. Only Kay, her two children, and a few close friends were present as the air force contingent returned for another round of psalm readings and taps.

Per arrangements made at the time of Carole Lombard's death, Gable's casket was placed in the wall vault next to hers. All three vaults that Gable had purchased in 1942 were now filled, with Lombard's remains in the center vault and her mother's in the one to her right. Kay Gable was given assurances that when her own time came, a fourth vault could be cut into the wall so that Gable ended up centered between his two wives.

After a week of private mourning, the widow blurted some of her pent-up feelings to columnist Louella Parsons and blamed Gable's death on his experiences during the making of *The Misfits.* Though she didn't mention Marilyn Monroe's name, Kay Gable practically accused her of contributing to the tragedy.

"It wasn't the physical exertion that killed him," she said. "It was the horrible tension, that eternal waiting, waiting, waiting. He waited around forever, for everybody. He'd get so angry that he'd just go ahead and do anything to keep occupied. That's why he did those awful horse scenes where they dragged him on his stomach. He had a stand-in and a stuntman, but he did most of it himself. I told him, 'You're crazy,' but he wouldn't listen."

By this time Monroe had split from Arthur Miller and was staying in New York while making daily visits to a psychoanalyst. When reporters tracked her down and asked her if she felt guilty about Gable's death, she refused to answer. But as the possibility that she'd harmed Gable dawned on her, she became deeply disturbed, wondering if she'd done it subconsciously to punish the absentee father whom she had once confused with Gable. *The Misfits* turned out to be her own last film as well as Gable's. After several frustrated attempts at suicide, she finally succeeded in the summer of 1962.

Gable's death threw United Artists and the producers of *The Misfits* into a dither. Exhibitors were clamoring for an instant release of the movie to cash in on all the publicity and notoriety. There was also a temptation to get it out in time to qualify for the 1960 Academy Awards. Gable seemed a certainty to get a sympathy nomination and to go on to win the first posthumous Oscar for a starring role.

But editor George Tomasini and background music composer Alex North couldn't meet UA's tight deadlines. The release was finally set for February 1, 1961, which would have been Gable's sixtieth birthday and would still make him eligible for an Oscar nomination when that year's awards came around.

Unfortunately, *The Misfits* turned out to be one of the worst disappointments of Gable's entire sixty-six-feature career. Released at a time when the movie industry was still geared to single-screen theaters and a staggered distribution system that started with a small number of theaters and gradually swelled to never more than several hundred at a time, *The Misfits* became a victim of mixed critical reviews and overwhelmingly negative word of mouth. Launched with a massive advertising campaign that stressed its "adults only" content (in that era there were no audience ratings), it did record-breaking business for several days. But as soon as disappointed Gable and Monroe fans started streaming out and spreading their opinions, it was dead in the water.

Throughout the 124-minute drama, Gable looked old and haggard, while Monroe matched him with her zombielike performance. Combined with the symbolism and parable of Arthur Miller's dialogue-heavy script, it was hardly the riveting experience that moviegoers had been led to expect.

Not surprisingly, neither Gable's performance nor anything else in *The Misfits* lingered in memory long enough to win nominations in the 1961 Oscar handicap. And due to Gable's high advance guarantee of $750,000, his estate would receive nothing further from *The Misfits*. World film rentals were only $6 million, or $1.5 million short of activating his 10 percent share.

In a will executed in September 1955, two months after he married Kay Spreckels, Gable left everything to his wife except for a house in North Hollywood that he bequeathed to Josephine Dillon. The probate revealed only that his estate was valued "in excess of $10,000" and that, at the time of signing the will, he claimed to have no children.

Friends guessed Gable's wealth to be modest by Hollywood's megastandards, probably in the four-to-six-million-dollar range. For most of his twenty-nine years as a film star, he was a high-salaried employee of MGM but spent most of it as he went along. For the nine freelance films that he made after leaving MGM, he earned a total of $4.25 million in advances and probably no more than another $1 million in royalties, since none were box-office blockbusters. His homes in Encino and Palm Springs were estimated to be worth about $1 million total. His investment portfolio consisted of 37,783 shares of common stock in twenty companies, but only 2,783 were in blue chips such as Standard Oil (514), Caterpillar Tractor (400), and Goodyear Tire (312).

On March 20, 1961, one hundred and twenty-four days after Gable's death, his wish for a son was fulfilled with the cesarean delivery of eight-pound John Clark. The name had been agreed on before Gable's stroke. His posthumous fatherhood was Hollywood's second in recent years, preceded in 1959 by the arrival of Tyrone Power III sixty-eight days after his daddy's death.

John Clark Gable turned out to be blond, blue-eyed, and strikingly reminiscent of his mother and his half-siblings, Bunker and Joan Spreckels. Unlike his father's illegitimate daughter with Loretta Young, he did not inherit the jumbo Gable ears. Throughout his life he would have to contend with rumors that he was not really Gable's child.

Years before, while still shattered by Carole Lombard's death, Gable gave his 1934 Oscar for *It Happened One Night* to their godchild, Richard Lang, the son of Fieldsie and director Walter Lang. Now twenty-two and an apprentice film director, Richard Lang decided that the statuette really belonged to the newborn baby. He returned it to Kay, along with a note to John Clark that said, "It is only in your possession. The real Oscar is your father's alone forever from all those people who gave it to him with supreme thanks for giving us a part of himself."

By the time he was six months old, Clark Gable's heir had been pictured on the front covers of magazines and tabloids all over the world. His mother became paranoid about a possible kidnapping attempt and decided to retreat from public view as much as possible.

In 1966 Judy Lewis, by then thirty-one and acting a major role in the ultrapopular daytime TV serial *The Secret Storm,* finally worked up the courage to confront her mother about her parentage. As always, Loretta Young's answers were evasive, but under pressure she confessed that Clark Gable was the father. Inadvertently, Young also let slip that she was Judy's real mother, something that her daughter had long believed but had never actually been told.

Much against her mother's wishes, Judy Lewis later wrote about her experiences as the illegitimate child of Clark Gable and Loretta Young in the memoir *Uncommon Knowledge,* published in 1994. By that time Lewis was a divorced mother with a grown daughter and two grandsons. After a discouraging acting career, at age fifty she had enrolled at Antioch University and eventually earned a master's degree in clinical psychology, which enabled her to become a practicing family therapist.

Kay Gable never married again. Friends claim that she devoted herself to her three children and to using her clout as Mrs. Clark Gable to help charitable and community causes. She was involved in more than forty organizations and moved in the highest levels of the Los Angeles social register.

In 1973 Kay sold the Encino ranch, originally purchased by Carole

Lombard from Raoul Walsh in 1938 for $50,000, for a total of $1 million. A property developer paid $800,000 for nineteen acres, while the house and its surrounding two acres fetched another $200,000 from a buyer who intended to live there. The open land was subdivided into thirty-seven plots for luxury homes under the name "Clark Gable Ranch Estates."

Kay bought a mansion in Beverly Hills while John Clark, now twelve, continued his private education. He attended the Buckley School in Los Angeles, followed by Brooks in Andover, Massachusetts. Kay sent him abroad to college at Aiglon in Villars, Switzerland, but he eventually became homesick and finished his studies at Santa Monica College.

Gable had often said that he'd turn over in his grave if any child of his became an actor, so Kay tried to keep John Clark shielded from the showbiz world. No doubt she also realized that as an actor he would have to contend with his father's royal status and would always be judged severely.

In 1983, after many years of cardiac problems, Kay Gable underwent triple bypass surgery at Methodist Hospital in Houston. Following the operation she never regained consciousness. She died two weeks later on May 25, three months prior to what would have been her sixty-seventh birthday.

John Clark, by then a handsome six-footer of twenty-two, was devastated, but he had already started a life of his own in automotives, an interest that he may have inherited from his father. An expert mechanic and welder, he ran a repair business and also built racing cars and pickup trucks that he drove himself in dirt track competitions. In 1983 he was named "Rookie of the Year" after racing at 140 miles per hour in the grueling Baja 1000, ironically over some of the same rugged terrain where his father used to go hunting.

Competing in about ten major dirt track races per season, John Clark inevitably received offers from movie producers who were eager to capitalize on the Gable name. He turned them all down, but after marrying Tracey Yarro in 1985 and the births of Kayley Gable in 1986 and Clark James Gable in 1988, he couldn't afford to reject a lucrative offer from independent producer Al Ruddy for a lead role in *Bad Jim,* a western centering on a horse once owned by Billy the Kid. Teamed with James Brolin and Richard Roundtree, John Clark played the youngest of a trio of kindhearted bank robbers. Through no fault of John Clark, who gave an adequate performance, the Clyde Ware–directed movie proved too mediocre for theatrical release and went straight onto video-cassette and near oblivion.

John Clark continued racing and made a name for himself in the dirt track field, but he was a private person like his father and led a low-key life. His divorce and second marriage to a longtime sweetheart went unreported. Though he inherited a fortune from his mother, most of it was in trust funds and annuities, so he experienced financial problems. In December 1996 he shocked the Hollywood establishment by putting his father's 1934 Oscar up for sale in an auction at Christie's. Such trans-actions are frowned on by the Academy of Motion Picture Arts and Sci-ences because they tarnish the Oscar's image, making it seem like a prize that can be bought instead of earned by merit.

Despite some denunciations in the Hollywood trade papers, John Clark couldn't be dissuaded from selling the Oscar, which promised to fetch a high price due to his father's popularity as well as to *It Happened One Night,* which ranks high in the pantheon of all-time movie classics. Happily, both John Clark and the Academy got what they wanted when producer-director Steven Spielberg made the winning bid of $607,500. Spielberg then donated the Oscar to the Academy for permanent display in the museum at its library-archives in Beverly Hills.

In recent years John Clark has been actively involved with the Clark Gable Foundation, a nonprofit group in Cadiz, Ohio, that has restored his father's birthplace and turned it into a mecca for fans and tourists. The two-story house on Charleston Street had to be completely rebuilt and moved ten feet to conform to current building codes. The eleven-year project was finally completed in the spring of 1999 with the opening of the Clark Gable Birthplace Museum, which occupies the five-room apartment on the top floor where he spent his first months of life.

Decorated with period furniture, wallpaper, and window coverings that were recommended by the Ohio Historical Society, the museum has displays of photographs, movie posters, and personal artifacts such as Gable's boyhood sled and (parked outside) his baby blue 1954 Cadillac Coup DeVille convertible. Every year on the weekend nearest to Gable's February 1 birthday, the Foundation stages two days of fund-raising fes-tivities, including a dinner dance, appearances by guest Hollywood celebrities, and an auction of movie memorabilia donated by the membership.

"I never met anyone who didn't like Clark Gable," director Mervyn LeRoy once said. "He was a great individual, a great citizen, and was admired by all who knew him. He will be remembered when most other stars are 'gone with the wind.' "

He is, ultimately, the standard against which all other screen actors are measured. In the seventy years since his first starring roles, he has never been surpassed.

ACKNOWLEDGMENTS

The work on this biography really started with my first book, *Gable & Lombard,* in 1972. Although the main story spanned less than a decade, I had to thoroughly research Clark Gable's entire life and career. Fortunately, many of the people closest to him were still living at the time, and much of the information I obtained came "straight from the horse's mouth" rather than from secondary sources. In the intervening decades, some people have died or are unaccounted for and others are still going strong; I will list their names as if they're all still with us, which in a sense they are: Pandro Berman, Adela Rogers St. John, Myrna Loy, Joan Crawford, William Wellman, Phil Berg, Una Merkel, Howard Strickling, Jill Winkler Rath, Garson Kanin, Ann Sothern, Radie Harris, Eli Wallach, Jerome Zerbe, Rosalind Russell, Ann Miller, Jean Garceau, Frederick Peters, Doris Day, Deborah Kerr, Walter Plunkett, David Niven, George Cukor, Marcella Rabwin, Cesar Romero, Lana Turner, Robert Stack, Irene Mayer Selznick, Arthur Hornblow, Jr., George Bagnall, Jack Benny, Clarence Bull, Stanley Campbell, Howard Dietz, King Vidor, Joseph Szigeti, Claudette Colbert, Frank Capra, John Lee Mahin, Al Menasco, Cornwell Jackson, Edith Head, John Engstead, Lloyd Pantages, Dr. Franklyn Thorpe, Ruth Waterbury. In my nearly thirty years of interviewing people about Clark Gable, there were also some who requested anonymity.

My thanks also go to the staffs of the following research centers for their splendid assistance: the Margaret Herrick Library of the Motion Picture Academy of Arts & Sciences, Los Angeles; the American Film Institute Library, Los Angeles; the Performing Arts Library at Lincoln Center, New York City; and the British Film Institute Library, London. Background information was also generously provided by the Clark

Gable Foundation of Cadiz, Ohio, which operates a birthplace museum in his honor.

A further note of gratitude to my agents, Dan Strone and Owen Laster, as well as to editor Shaye Areheart and her assistant, Teryn Johnson. For their encouragement and good cheer, heartfelt thanks to my relatives and friends, especially Stella and Russell Harris, Lisa & Brian & Kyle & Jack Wrage, Ruth and Steve Spratt, Marilyn and Phil Isby, Carlton and Lillian Friedman, Dave and Edith Martorana, Jodie Wrage and Jerry Rappaport, Jerrold and the late Yaffa Weitzman, Rodger Robinson, Georgina Hale, Nen Roeterdink, James Kirkup, Jack Robinson, Fred Beall, Dan Harter, Barry and Joan Goodkin, Jerry Alexander, George Bester, June Spickett, Stevie and Spike Heatley, Ron Samuels, Nick Cunningham, and the late Barry Conley.

Agee, James. *Agee on Film: Reviews and Comments.* New York: McDowell, Obolensky, 1958.

Behlmer, Rudy, ed. *Memo from David O. Selznick.* New York: Viking Press, 1972.

Bull, Clarence, with Raymond Lee. *The Faces of Hollywood.* South Brunswick, N.J., and New York: A. S. Barnes & Co., 1968.

Capra, Frank. *The Name Above the Title.* New York: Macmillan, 1971.

Crawford, Joan, with Jane Kesner Ardmore. *A Portrait of Joan.* New York: Doubleday & Co., 1962.

Crowther, Bosley. *The Lion's Share: The Story of an Entertainment Empire.* New York: E. P. Dutton, 1957.

De Carlo, Yvonne, with Doug Warren. *Yvonne: An Autobiography.* New York: St. Martin's Press, 1987.

Dietz, Howard. *Dancing in the Dark.* New York: Quadrangle, 1974.

Dmytryk, Edward. *It's a Hell of a Life but Not a Bad Living.* New York: Times Books, 1978.

Dooley, Roger. *From Scarface to Scarlett: American Films in the 1930s.* New York: Harcourt Brace Jovanovich, 1981.

Eames, John Douglas. *The MGM Story: The Complete History of Over Fifty Roaring Years.* New York: Crown, 1975.

Eells, George. *Hedda and Louella.* New York: G. P. Putnam's Sons, 1972.

Engstead, John. *Star Shots.* New York: E. P. Dutton, 1978.

Essoe, Gabe. *The Films of Clark Gable.* Secaucus, N.J.: Citadel Press, 1972.

Fairbanks, Douglas, Jr. *The Salad Days.* New York: Doubleday, 1988.

Finch, Christopher, and Linda Rosenkrantz. *Gone Hollywood: The Movie Colony in the Golden Age.* Garden City, N.Y.: Doubleday & Co., 1979.

Finler, Joel W. *The Hollywood Story*. New York: Crown, 1988.

Flamini, Roland. *Thalberg*. New York: Crown, 1994.

Gardner, Ava. *Ava: My Story*. New York: Bantam Books, 1990.

Grady, Billy. *The Irish Peacock: The Confessions of a Legendary Talent Agent*. New Rochelle, N.Y.: Arlington House, 1972.

Guilaroff, Sidney. *Crowning Glory*. Santa Monica, Calif.: General Publishing Group, 1996.

Guiles, Fred Lawrence. *Marion Davies*. New York: McGraw-Hill, 1972.

Haver, Ronald. *David O. Selznick's Hollywood*. New York: Alfred A. Knopf, 1980.

Hay, Peter. *MGM: When the Lion Roars*. Atlanta, Ga.: Turner, 1991.

Huston, John. *An Open Book*. New York: Alfred A. Knopf, 1980.

Jackson, Carlton. *Hattie: The Life of Hattie McDaniel*. Lanham, Md.: Madison Books, 1990.

Kanin, Garson. *Hollywood*. New York: Viking Press, 1974.

Keith, Slim, with Annette Tapert. *Slim: Memories of a Rich and Imperfect Life*. New York: Simon & Schuster, 1990.

Lamarr, Hedy. *Ecstasy and Me: My Life As a Woman*. New York: Macfadden-Bartell, 1966.

Lambert, Gavin. *Norma Shearer*. New York: Alfred A. Knopf, 1990.

LeRoy, Mervyn, with Dick Kleiner. *Take One*. New York: Hawthorn Books, 1974.

Lewis, Judy. *Uncommon Knowledge*. New York: Pocket Books, 1994.

Loos, Anita. *Cast of Thousands*. New York: Grosset & Dunlap, 1977.

Loy, Myrna, with James Kotsibilas-Davis. *Myrna Loy: Being and Becoming*. New York: Alfred A. Knopf, 1987.

Marion, Frances. *Off with Their Heads*. New York: Macmillan, 1972.

Marx, Samuel. *Mayer and Thalberg: The Make-Believe Saints*. New York: Random House, 1975.

McGilligan, Pat, ed. *Backstory: Interviews with Screenwriters of Hollywood's Golden Age*. Berkeley and Los Angeles: University of California Press, 1986.

Niven, David. *Bring On the Empty Horses*. New York: G. P. Putnam's Sons, 1975.

Paris, Barry. *Garbo*. New York: Alfred A. Knopf, 1994.

Peters, Margot. *The House of Barrymore*. New York: Alfred A. Knopf, 1990.

Poitier, Sidney. *This Life/Sidney Poitier*. New York: Alfred A. Knopf, 1980.

Roeburt, John. *Get Me Giesler*. New York: Belmont Books, 1962.

Russell, Rosalind, with Chris Chase. *Life Is a Banquet*. New York: Random House, 1977.

St. Johns, Adela Rogers. *Love, Laughter and Tears: My Hollywood Story*. Garden City, N.Y.: Doubleday & Co., 1978.

Schary, Dore. *Heyday*. Boston, Toronto: Little, Brown, 1979.

Selznick, Irene Mayer. *A Private View*. New York: Alfred A. Knopf, 1983.

Stenn, David. *Bombshell: The Life and Death of Jean Harlow*. New York: Doubleday & Co., 1993.

Stine, Whitney. *Stars and Star Handlers: The Business of Show*. Santa Monica, Calif.: Roundtable, 1985.

Thomas, Bob. *Thalberg: Life and Legend*. Garden City, N.Y.: Doubleday & Co., 1969.

Turner, Lana. *Lana: The Lady, the Legend, the Truth*. New York: E. P. Dutton, 1982.

Vidor, King. *King Vidor on Film Making*. New York: David McKay, 1972.

Wallace, Charles B. *The Young Mr. Gable*. Cadiz, Oh.: Harrison County Historical Society, 1983.

Walsh, Raoul. *Each Man in His Time: The Life Story of a Director*. New York: Farrar, Straus & Giroux, 1974.

Warner, Jack L., with Dean Jennings. *My First Hundred Years in Hollywood*. New York: Random House, 1964.

Wellman, William A. *A Short Time for Insanity*. New York: Hawthorn Books, 1974.

Wiley, Mason, and Damien Bona. *Inside Oscar: The Unofficial History of the Academy Awards*. New York: Ballantine Books, 1986.

Wilkerson, Tichi, with Marcia Borie. *The Hollywood Reporter: The Golden Years*. New York: Coward-McCann, 1984.

Williams, Esther, with Digby Diehl. *The Million Dollar Mermaid*. New York: Simon & Schuster, 1999.

Years are dates of first theatrical release. Except where noted, cinematography was in black and white.

The Painted Desert (RKO Pathé, 1931). Cast: William Boyd, Helen Twelvetrees, William Farnum, J. Farrell MacDonald, CG, Charles Sellon, Will Walling. Producer: E. B. Derr. Director: Howard Higgin. Screenplay: Howard Higgin, Tom Buckingham. 80 minutes.

The Easiest Way (Metro-Goldwyn-Mayer, 1931). Cast: Constance Bennett, Adolphe Menjou, Robert Montgomery, Anita Page, Marjorie Rambeau, J. Farrell MacDonald, Clara Blandick, CG. Producer: Hunt Stromberg. Director: Jack Conway. Screenplay: Edith Ellis, based on the stage play by Eugene Walter. 86 minutes.

Dance, Fools, Dance (MGM, 1931). Cast: Joan Crawford, Lester Vail, Cliff Edwards, William Bakewell, William Holden, CG, Earle Foxe, Hale Hamilton, Natalie Moorhead. Director: Harry Beaumont. Screenplay: Richard Schayer, Aurania Rouverol. 82 minutes.

The Secret Six (MGM, 1931). Cast: Wallace Beery, Lewis Stone, John Mack Brown, Jean Harlow, Marjorie Rambeau, Paul Hurst, CG, Ralph Bellamy, John Miljan. Producer: Harry Rapf. Director: George Hill. Screenplay: Frances Marion. 83 minutes.

The Finger Points (First National–Warner Bros., 1931). Cast: Richard Barthelmess, Fay Wray, Regis Toomey, Robert Elliott, CG, Oscar Apfel, Noel Madison. Director: John Francis Dillon. Screenplay: Robert Lord, based on a story by John Monk Saunders and W. R. Burnett. 90 minutes.

Laughing Sinners (MGM, 1931). Cast: Joan Crawford, Neil Hamilton, CG, Marjorie Rambeau, Guy Kibbee, Cliff Edwards, Roscoe Karns, George F. Marion. Director: Harry Beaumont. Screenplay: Bess Meredyth, based on the stage play *Torch Song* by Kenyon Nicholson. 71 minutes.

A Free Soul (MGM, 1931). Cast: Norma Shearer, Leslie Howard, Lionel Barrymore, CG, James Gleason, Lucy Beaumont. Producer: Bernard Hyman. Director: Clarence Brown. Screenplay: John Meehan, based on the novel by Adela Rogers St. Johns. 91 minutes.

Night Nurse (Warner Bros., 1931). Cast: Barbara Stanwyck, Ben Lyon, Joan Blondell, CG, Charles Winninger, Vera Lewis, Blanche Frederici. Director: William Wellman.

Screenplay: Oliver H. P. Garrett and Charles Kenyon, based on the novel by Dora Macy. 72 minutes.

Sporting Blood (MGM, 1931). Cast: CG, Ernest Torrence, Madge Evans, Lew Cody, Marie Prevost, Harry Holman, J. Farrell MacDonald. Director: Charles Brabin. Screenplay: Willard Mack and Wanda Tuchock, based on the novel *Horseflesh* by Frederick Hazlitt Brennan. 82 minutes.

Susan Lenox—Her Fall and Rise (MGM, 1931). Cast: Greta Garbo, CG, Jean Hersholt, John Miljan, Alan Hale, Hilda Vaughn, Russell Simpson, Cecil Cunningham, Ian Keith. Producer: Paul Bern. Director: Robert Z. Leonard. Screenplay: Wanda Tuchock, Zelda Sears, and Edith Fitzgerald, based on the novel by David Graham Phillips. 84 minutes.

Possessed (MGM, 1931). Cast: Joan Crawford, CG, Wallace Ford, Skeets Gallagher, Frank Conroy, Marjorie White, John Miljan, Clara Blandick. Producer: Harry Rapf. Director: Clarence Brown. Screenplay: Lenore Coffee, based on the stage play *The Mirage* by Edgar Selwyn. 76 minutes.

Hell Divers (MGM, 1931). Cast: Wallace Beery, CG, Conrad Nagel, Dorothy Jordan, Marjorie Rambeau, Marie Prevost, Cliff Edwards, John Miljan. Director: George Hill. Screenplay: Harvey Gates and Malcolm Stuart Boylan, based on a story by Lieutenant Commander Frank Wead. 100 minutes.

Polly of the Circus (MGM, 1932). Cast: Marion Davies, CG, C. Aubrey Smith, Raymond Hatton, David Landau, Ruth Selwyn, Maude Eburne, Ray Milland. Producer: Cosmopolitan Pictures (W. R. Hearst). Director: Alfred Santell. Screenplay: Carey Wilson and Laurence Johnson, based on the stage play by Margaret Mayo. 72 minutes.

Red Dust (MGM, 1932). Cast: CG, Jean Harlow, Gene Raymond, Mary Astor, Donald Crisp, Tully Marshall, Forrester Harvey, Willie Fung. Producer: Hunt Stromberg. Director: Victor Fleming. Screenplay: John Lee Mahin, based on the stage play by Wilson Collison. 83 minutes.

Strange Interlude (MGM, 1932). Cast: Norma Shearer, CG, Alexander Kirkland, Ralph Morgan, Robert Young, May Robson, Maureen O'Sullivan, Henry B. Walthall, Mary Alden, Tad Alexander. Producer: Irving Thalberg. Director: Robert Z. Leonard. Screenplay: Bess Meredyth and C. Gardner Sullivan, based on the stage play by Eugene O'Neill. 110 minutes.

No Man of Her Own (Paramount, 1932). Cast: CG, Carole Lombard, Dorothy Mackaill, Grant Mitchell, George Barbier, Elizabeth Patterson, J. Farrell MacDonald, Tommy Conlon. Director: Wesley Ruggles. Screenplay: Maurine Watkins and Milton H. Gropper, based on a story by Edmund Goulding and Benjamin Glazer. 85 minutes.

The White Sister (MGM, 1933). Cast: Helen Hayes, CG, Lewis Stone, Louise Closser Hale, May Robson, Edward Arnold, Alan Edwards. Producer: Hunt Stromberg. Director: Victor Fleming. Screenplay: Donald Ogden Stewart, based on the novel by F. Marion Crawford and a stage adaptation by Walter Hackett. 110 minutes.

Hold Your Man (MGM, 1933). Cast: Jean Harlow, CG, Stuart Erwin, Dorothy Burgess, Muriel Kirkland, Garry Owen, Barbara Barondess, Paul Hurst, Elizabeth

Patterson, Inez Courtney, Blanche Frederici, Helen Freeman. Producer: Bernard Hyman. Director: Sam Wood. Screenplay: Anita Loos and Howard Emmett Rogers, from an original story by Loos. 89 minutes.

Night Flight (MGM, 1933). Cast: John Barrymore, Helen Hayes, CG, Lionel Barrymore, Robert Montgomery, Myrna Loy, William Gargan, C. Henry Gordon, Leslie Fenton, Harry Beresford, Frank Conroy. Producer: David O. Selznick. Director: Clarence Brown. Screenplay: Oliver H. P. Garrett, based on the novel by Antoine de Saint-Exupéry. 84 minutes.

Dancing Lady (MGM, 1933). Cast: Joan Crawford, CG, Franchot Tone, May Robson, Winnie Lightner, Fred Astaire, Robert Benchley, Nelson Eddy, Ted Healy, the Three Stooges (Moe Howard, Jerry Howard, Larry Fine). Producer: David O. Selznick. Director: Robert Z. Leonard. Screenplay: Allen Rivkin and P. J. Wolfson, based on the novel by James Warner Bellah. 94 minutes.

It Happened One Night (Columbia, 1934). Cast: CG, Claudette Colbert, Walter Connolly, Roscoe Karns, Jameson Thomas, Alan Hale, Ward Bond, Eddie Chandler. Producer-Director: Frank Capra. Screenplay: Robert Riskin, based on the short story "Night Bus" by Samuel Hopkins Adams. 105 minutes.

Men in White (MGM, 1934). Cast: CG, Myrna Loy, Jean Hersholt, Elizabeth Allan, Otto Kruger, C. Henry Gordon, Russell Hardie, Wallace Ford, Henry B. Walthall, Samuel S. Hinds, Frank Puglia. Producer: Monta Bell. Director: Richard Boleslawski. Screenplay: Waldemar Young, based on the stage play by Sidney Kingsley. 80 minutes.

Manhattan Melodrama (MGM, 1934). Cast: CG, William Powell, Myrna Loy, Leo Carrillo, Nat Pendleton, George Sidney, Isabel Jewell, Muriel Evans, Frank Conroy, Noel Madison, Mickey Rooney, Jimmy Butler. Producer: David O. Selznick, for Cosmopolitan Pictures. Director: W. S. Van Dyke. Screenplay: Oliver H. P. Garrett and Joseph L. Mankiewicz, from an an original story by Arthur Caesar. 93 minutes.

Chained (MGM, 1934). Cast: Joan Crawford, CG, Otto Kruger, Stuart Erwin, Una O'Connor, Marjorie Gateson, Akim Tamiroff. Producer: Hunt Stromberg. Director: Clarence Brown. Screenplay: John Lee Mahin, from an original story by Edgar Selwyn. 74 minutes.

Forsaking All Others (MGM, 1934). Cast: Joan Crawford, CG, Robert Montgomery, Charles Butterworth, Billie Burke, Frances Drake, Rosalind Russell, Tom Ricketts, Arthur Treacher, Ted Healy. Producer: Bernard Hyman. Director: W. S. Van Dyke. Screenplay: Joseph L. Mankiewicz, based on the stage play by Edward Roberts and Frank Cavett. 82 minutes.

After Office Hours (MGM, 1935). Cast: Constance Bennett, CG, Stuart Erwin, Billie Burke, Harvey Stephens, Katherine Alexander, Hale Hamilton, Henry Travers, Henry Armetta. Producer: Bernard Hyman. Director: Robert Z. Leonard. Screenplay: Herman J. Mankiewicz, from an original story by Laurence Stallings and Dale Van Every. 75 minutes.

The Call of the Wild (20th Century Pictures–United Artists, 1935). Cast: CG, Loretta Young, Jack Oakie, Reginald Owen, Frank Conroy, Katherine DeMille, Sidney

Toler, James Burke, Charles Stevens, Herman Bing. Producer: Darryl F. Zanuck. Director: William Wellman. Screenplay: Gene Fowler and Leonard Praskins, based on the novel by Jack London. 95 minutes.

China Seas (MGM, 1935). Cast: CG, Jean Harlow, Wallace Beery, Lewis Stone, Rosalind Russell, Dudley Digges, C. Aubrey Smith, Robert Benchley, William Henry, Lillian Bond, Edward Brophy, Donald Meek, Hattie McDaniel, Akim Tamiroff, Ivan Lebedeff. Producer: Albert Lewin. Director: Tay Garnett. Screenplay: Jules Furthman and James K. McGuinness, based on the novel by Crosbie Garstin. 90 minutes.

Mutiny on the Bounty (MGM, 1935). Cast: CG, Charles Laughton, Franchot Tone, Herbert Mundin, Eddie Quillan, Dudley Digges, Donald Crisp, Henry Stephenson, Spring Byington, Francis Lister, Movita Castenada, Mamo Clark, Ian Wolfe. Producer: Irving Thalberg. Director: Frank Lloyd. Screenplay: Talbot Jennings, Jules Furthman, and Carey Wilson, based on the trilogy of novels by Charles Nordhoff and James Norman Hall. 132 minutes.

Wife vs. Secretary (MGM, 1936). Cast: CG, Jean Harlow, Myrna Loy, May Robson, George Barbier, James Stewart, Hobart Cavanaugh, Gilbert Emery, Margaret Irving, William Newell, Marjorie Gateson, Gloria Holden, Tom Dugan. Producer: Hunt Stromberg. Director: Clarence Brown. Screenplay: Norman Krasna, Alice Duer Miller, and John Lee Mahin, based on the novel by Faith Baldwin. 88 minutes.

San Francisco (MGM, 1936). Cast: CG, Jeanette MacDonald, Spencer Tracy, Jack Holt, Jessie Ralph, Ted Healy, Shirley Ross, Margaret Irving, Harold Huber, Al Shean, William Ricciardi, Kenneth Harlan, Roger Imhof, Bert Roach, Warren Hymer, Edgar Kennedy. Producers: Bernard Hyman and John Emerson. Director: W. S. Van Dyke. Screenplay: Anita Loos, from an original story by Robert Hopkins. 115 minutes.

Cain and Mabel (Warner Bros., 1936). Cast: Marion Davies, CG, Allen Jenkins, Roscoe Karns, Walter Catlett, David Carlyle, Hobart Cavanaugh, Ruth Donnelly, Pert Kelton, William Collier, Sr., Sammy White, E. E. Clive, Allen Pomeroy. Producer: Sam Bischoff, for Cosmopolitan Pictures. Director: Lloyd Bacon. Screenplay: Laird Doyle, based on a story by H. C. Witwer. 90 minutes.

Love on the Run (MGM, 1936). Cast: Joan Crawford, CG, Franchot Tone, Reginald Owen, Mona Barrie, Ivan Lebedeff, Charles Judels, William Demarest. Producer: Joseph L. Mankiewicz. Director: W. S. Van Dyke. Screenplay: John Lee Mahin, Manuel Seff, and Gladys Hurlbut, based on a story by Alan Green and Julian Brodie. 81 minutes.

Parnell (MGM, 1937). Cast: CG, Myrna Loy, Edna May Oliver, Edmund Gwenn, Alan Marshal, Donald Crisp, Billie Burke, Berton Churchill, Donald Meek, Montagu Love, Neil Fitzgerald, George Zucco. Producer-Director: John M. Stahl. Screenplay: John Van Druten and S. N. Behrman, based on the stage play by Elsie Schauffler. 96 minutes.

Saratoga (MGM, 1937). Cast: CG, Jean Harlow, Lionel Barrymore, Frank Morgan, Walter Pidgeon, Una Merkel, Cliff Edwards, George Zucco, Jonathan Hale, Hattie McDaniel, Frankie Darro. Producer: Bernard Hyman. Director: Jack Conway. Screenplay: Anita Loos and Robert Hopkins. 102 minutes.

Test Pilot (MGM, 1938). Cast: CG, Myrna Loy, Spencer Tracy, Lionel Barrymore, Samuel S. Hinds, Marjorie Main, Ted Pearson, Gloria Holden, Louis Jean Heydt, Virginia Grey, Priscilla Lawson. Producer: Louis Lighton. Director: Victor Fleming. Screenplay: Vincent Lawrence and Waldemar Young, based on a story by Lieutenant Commander Frank Wead. 118 minutes.

Too Hot to Handle (MGM, 1938). Cast: CG, Myrna Loy, Walter Connolly, Walter Pidgeon, Leo Carrillo, Johnny Hines, Virginia Weidler, Marjorie Main, Al Shean, Willie Fung, Lillie Mui, Patsy O'Connor. Producer: Lawrence Weingarten. Director: Jack Conway. Screenplay: Laurence Stallings and John Lee Mahin, based on a story by Len Hammond. 105 minutes.

Idiot's Delight (MGM, 1939). Cast: Norma Shearer, CG, Edward Arnold, Charles Coburn, Joseph Schildkraut, Burgess Meredith, Laura Hope Crews, Skeets Gallagher, Peter Willes, Pat Paterson, Fritz Feld, Virginia Grey. Producer: Hunt Stromberg. Director: Clarence Brown. Screenplay: Robert E. Sherwood, based on his stage play. 105 minutes.

Gone With the Wind (Selznick International–MGM, 1939). Cast: CG, Vivien Leigh, Leslie Howard, Olivia de Havilland, Hattie McDaniel, Thomas Mitchell, Oscar Polk, Barbara O'Neill, Butterfly McQueen, Ann Rutherford, Evelyn Keyes, Victor Jory, Laura Hope Crews, Harry Davenport, Jane Darwell, Ona Munson, Isabel Jewell, Ward Bond, Cammie King, George Reeves, Rand Brooks, and others too numerous to mention. Producer: David O. Selznick. Director: Victor Fleming. Screenplay: Sidney Howard, based on the novel by Margaret Mitchell. Technicolor, 222 minutes.

Strange Cargo (MGM, 1940). Cast: CG, Joan Crawford, Ian Hunter, Peter Lorre, Paul Lukas, Albert Dekker, J. Edward Bromberg, Eduardo Ciannelli, John Arledge, Victor Varconi. Producer: Joseph L. Mankiewicz. Director: Frank Borzage. Screenplay: Lawrence Hazard, based on the novel *Not Too Narrow, Not Too Deep* by Richard Sale. 105 minutes.

Boom Town (MGM, 1940). Cast: CG, Claudette Colbert, Spencer Tracy, Hedy Lamarr, Frank Morgan, Lionel Atwill, Chill Wills, Marion Martin, Minna Gombell, Joe Yule, Richard Lane, Sara Haden, Curt Bois. Producer: Sam Zimbalist. Director: Jack Conway. Screenplay: John Lee Mahin, based on a story by James Edward Grant. 116 minutes.

Comrade X (MGM, 1940). Cast: CG, Hedy Lamarr, Oscar Homolka, Felix Bressart, Eve Arden, Sig Ruman, Natasha Lytess, Vladimir Sokoloff, Edgar Barrier, Mikhail Rasumny. Producer: Gottfried Reinhardt. Director: King Vidor. Screenplay: Ben Hecht and Charles Lederer, based on a story by Walter Reisch. 90 minutes.

They Met in Bombay (MGM, 1941). Cast: CG, Rosalind Russell, Peter Lorre, Jessie Ralph, Reginald Owen, Matthew Boulton, Eduardo Ciannelli, Luis Alberni, Rosina Galli, Jay Novello. Producer: Hunt Stromberg. Director: Clarence Brown. Screenplay: Edwin Justus Mayer, Anita Loos, and Leon Gordon, based on a story by John Kafka. 86 minutes.

Honky Tonk (MGM, 1941). Cast: CG, Lana Turner, Frank Morgan, Claire Trevor, Marjorie Main, Albert Dekker, Henry O'Neill, Chill Wills, Veda Ann Borg. Producer: Pandro S. Berman. Director: Jack Conway. Screenplay: Marguerite Roberts and John Sanford. 105 minutes.

Somewhere I'll Find You (MGM, 1942). Cast: CG, Lana Turner, Robert Sterling, Patricia Dane, Reginald Owen, Lee Patrick, Charles Dingle, "Rags" Ragland, William Henry, Van Johnson. Producer: Pandro S. Berman. Director: Wesley Ruggles. Screenplay: Marguerite Roberts, based on a story by Charles Hoffman, adapted by Walter Reisch. 108 minutes.

Adventure (MGM, 1945). Cast: CG, Greer Garson, Joan Blondell, Thomas Mitchell, Tom Tully, John Qualen, Richard Haydn, Lina Romay, Philip Merivale, Harry Davenport. Producer: Sam Zimbalist. Director: Victor Fleming. Screenplay: Frederick Hazlitt Brennan and Vincent Lawrence, based on the novel *This Strange Adventure* by Clyde Brion Davis, adaptation by Anthony Veiller and William H. Wright. 125 minutes.

The Hucksters (MGM, 1947). Cast: CG, Deborah Kerr, Sydney Greenstreet, Adolphe Menjou, Ava Gardner, Keenan Wynn, Edward Arnold, Aubrey Mather, Richard Gaines, Frank Albertson, Douglas Fowley, Clinton Sundberg, Gloria Holden, Connie Gilchrist, Lillian Bronson. Producer: Arthur Hornblow, Jr. Director: Jack Conway. Screenplay: Luther Davis, based on the novel by Frederic Wakeman. 115 minutes.

Homecoming (MGM, 1948). Cast: CG, Lana Turner, Anne Baxter, John Hodiak, Ray Collins, Gladys Cooper, Cameron Mitchell, Marshall Thompson, Lurene Tuttle, Jessica Grayson. Producer: Sidney Franklin. Director: Mervyn LeRoy. Screenplay: Paul Osborn, based on the story "The Homecoming of Ulysses" by Sidney Kingsley, adapted by Jan Lustig. 113 minutes.

Command Decision (MGM, 1948). Cast: CG, Walter Pidgeon, Van Johnson, Brian Donlevy, Charles Bickford, John Hodiak, Edward Arnold, Marshall Thompson, Richard Quine, Cameron Mitchell, Clinton Sundberg, Ray Collins, Warner Anderson, John McIntire, Moroni Olsen. Producer: Sidney Franklin. Director: Sam Wood. Screenplay: William R. Laidlaw and George Froeschel, based on the stage play by William Wister Haines.

Any Number Can Play (MGM, 1949). Cast: CG, Alexis Smith, Wendell Corey, Audrey Totter, Frank Morgan, Mary Astor, Lewis Stone, Barry Sullivan, Marjorie Rambeau, Edgar Buchanan, Leon Ames, Mickey Knox, Richard Rober, William Conrad, Darryl Hickman, Dorothy Comingore, Art Baker. Producer: Arthur Freed. Director: Mervyn LeRoy. Screenplay: Richard Brooks, based on the novel by Edward Harris Heth. 112 minutes.

Key to the City (MGM, 1950). Cast: CG, Loretta Young, Frank Morgan, James Gleason, Marilyn Maxwell, Raymond Burr, Lewis Stone, Raymond Walburn, Pamela Britton, Zamah Cunningham, Clinton Sundberg, Marion Martin, Clara Blandick. Producer: Z. Wayne Griffin. Director: George Sidney. Screenplay: Robert Riley Crutcher, based on a story by Albert Beich. 99 minutes.

To Please a Lady (MGM, 1950). Cast: CG, Barbara Stanwyck, Adolphe Menjou, Will Geer, Roland Winters, William C. McGaw, Lela Bliss, Emory Parnell, Frank Jenks, Lew Smith, Hal K. Dawson, Ted Husing. Producer-Director: Clarence Brown. Screenplay: Barré Lyndon and Marge Decker. 91 minutes.

Across the Wide Missouri (MGM, 1951). Cast: CG, Ricardo Montalban, John Hodiak, Adolphe Menjou, María Elena Marqués, J. Carroll Naish, Jack Holt, Alan Napier, George Chandler, Richard Anderson. Producer: Robert Sisk. Director: William Wellman. Screenplay: Talbot Jennings, based on a story by Jennings and Frank Cavett. Technicolor, 78 minutes.

Lone Star (MGM, 1952). Cast: CG, Ava Gardner, Broderick Crawford, Lionel Barrymore, Beulah Bondi, Ed Begley, James Burke, William Farnum, Lowell Gilmore, Moroni Olsen, Russell Simpson, William Conrad, Victor Sutherland. Producer: Z. Wayne Griffin. Director: Vincent Sherman. Screenplay: Borden Chase and Howard Estabrook, based on Chase's short story. 94 minutes.

Never Let Me Go (MGM, 1953). Cast: CG, Gene Tierney, Richard Haydn, Bernard Miles, Belita, Kenneth More, Karel Stepanek, Theodore Bikel, Anna Valentina, Frederick Valk, Peter Illing. Producer: Clarence Brown. Director: Delmer Daves. Screenplay: Ronald Millar and George Froeschel, based on the novel *Came the Dawn* by Roger Bax. 69 minutes.

Mogambo (MGM, 1953). Cast: CG, Ava Gardner, Grace Kelly, Donald Sinden, Philip Stainton, Eric Pohlmann, Laurence Naismith, Dennis O'Dea. Producer: Sam Zimbalist. Director: John Ford. Screenplay: John Lee Mahin, based on the stage play *Red Dust* by Wilson Collison. Technicolor, 115 minutes.

Betrayed (MGM, 1954). Cast: CG, Lana Turner, Victor Mature, Louis Calhern, O. E. Hasse, Wilfrid Hyde-White, Ian Carmichael, Niall MacGinnis, Nora Swinburne, Roland Culver, Leslie Weston. Producer-Director: Gottfried Reinhardt. Screenplay: Ronald Millar and George Froeschel. Eastman Color, 108 minutes.

Soldier of Fortune (20th Century–Fox, 1955). Cast: CG, Susan Hayward, Michael Rennie, Gene Barry, Alexander D'Arcy, Tom Tully, Anna Sten, Russell Collins, Leo Gordon, Richard Loo, Soo Yong, Frank Tang, Jack Kruschen. Producer: Buddy Adler. Director: Edward Dmytryk. Screenplay: Ernest K. Gann, based on his novel. CinemaScope and DeLuxe Color, 96 minutes.

The Tall Men (20th–Fox, 1955). Cast: CG, Jane Russell, Robert Ryan, Cameron Mitchell, Juan García, Harry Shannon, Emile Meyer, Steve Darrell, Will Wright, Russell Simpson, Mae Marsh, Argentina Brunetti, Tom Fadden, Doris Kemper. Producers: William A. Bacher and William B. Hawks. Director: Raoul Walsh. Screenplay: Sydney Boehm and Frank Nugent, based on the novel by Clay Fisher. CinemaScope and DeLuxe Color, 122 minutes.

The King and Four Queens (United Artists, 1956). Cast: CG, Eleanor Parker, Jo Van Fleet, Jean Willes, Barbara Nichols, Sara Shane, Roy Roberts, Jay C. Flippen, Arthur Shields. Producer: David Hempstead. Director: Raoul Walsh. Screenplay: Margaret Fitts and Richard Alan Simmons, based on an original story by Fitts. CinemaScope and DeLuxe Color, 86 minutes.

Band of Angels (Warner Bros., 1957). Cast: CG, Yvonne De Carlo, Sidney Poitier, Efrem Zimbalist, Jr., Patric Knowles, Rex Reason, Torin Thatcher, Andrea King, Ray Teal, Russell Evans, Noreen Corcoran. Director: Raoul Walsh. Screenplay: John Twist, Ivan Goff and Ben Roberts, based on the novel by Robert Penn Warren. WarnerColor, 127 minutes.

Run Silent, Run Deep (UA, 1958). Cast: CG, Burt Lancaster, Jack Warden, Brad Dexter, Nick Cravat, Joe Maross, Mary LaRoche, Eddie Foy III, Rudy Bond, Don Rickles, John Bryant, Ken Lynch. Producer: Harold Hecht. Director: Robert Wise. Screenplay: John Gay, based on a novel by Commander Edward L. Beach. 93 minutes.

Teacher's Pet (Paramount, 1958). Cast: CG, Doris Day, Gig Young, Mamie Van Doren, Nick Adams, Peter Baldwin, Marion Ross, Charles Lane, Jack Albertson, Vivian Nathan. Producer: William Perlberg. Director: George Seaton. Screenplay: Fay and Michael Kanin. 120 minutes.

But Not for Me (Paramount, 1959). Cast: CG, Carroll Baker, Lilli Palmer, Lee J. Cobb, Barry Coe, Thomas Gomez, Tommy Duggan, Charles Lane, Wendell Holmes. Producers: William Perlberg and George Seaton. Director: Walter Lang. Screenplay: John Michael Hayes, based on the stage play *Accent on Youth* by Samson Raphaelson. 105 minutes.

It Started in Naples (Paramount, 1960). Cast: CG, Sophia Loren, Vittorio De Sica, Marietto, Paolo Carlini, Claudio Ermelli, Giovanni Filidoro. Producer: Jack Rose. Director: Melville Shavelson. Screenplay: Melville Shavelson, Jack Rose, and Suso Cecchi d'Amico, based on a story idea by Michael Pertwee and Jack Davies. VistaVision and Technicolor, 100 minutes.

The Misfits (UA, 1961). Cast: CG, Marilyn Monroe, Montgomery Clift, Thelma Ritter, Eli Wallach, James Barton, Estelle Winwood, Kevin McCarthy, Dennis Shaw, Philip Mitchell, Walter Ramage, Peggy Barton, Lew Smith, Marietta Tree. Producer: Frank E. Taylor. Director: John Huston. Screenplay: Arthur Miller. 124 minutes.